Continuum Studies in
Research in Education

Teaching and Learning a Second Language

Teaching and Learning a Second Language

A review of recent research

Ernesto Macaro

continuum
LONDON • NEW YORK

For my mother

Continuum

The Tower Building   15 East 26th Street
11 York Road   New York
London SE1 7NX   NY 10010

www.continuumbooks.com

© Ernesto Macaro 2003

First published 2003. Reprinted 2005.

British Library Cataloguing-in-Publication Data
A catalogue record for this book is available from the British Library.

ISBN   0–8264–6720–2 (hardback)
        0–8264–7737–2 (paperback)

Typeset by YHT Ltd, London
Printed and bound in Great Britain by The Bath Press, Bath

Book 4

Contents

Figures

Tables

Series Editor's Introduction

The need for the series

Internationally, the gap between research, policy and practice in public life has become a matter of concern. When professional practice – in nursing, education, local governance and other fields – is uninformed by research, it tends to reinvent itself in the light of a range of (often conflicting) principles. Research uninformed by practical considerations tends to be ignored by practitioners, however good it is academically. Similarly, the axis between policy and research needs to be a working one if each is to inform the other. Research is important to the professions, just as it is in industry and the economy: we have seen in the last 15 years especially that companies which do not invest in research tend to become service agents for those companies that are the cutting edge of practice.

Part of the function of the present series is to provide ready access to the evidence base for busy teachers, teacher-researchers, parents and governors in order to help them improve teaching which, in turn, will improve learning and raise standards. But it is worth discussing here what the evidence base is for teaching a school subject, and how it might be applied to the acts of teaching of learning.

Evidence is inert. It needs not so much application as *transformation* in order to make learning happen in the classroom. That transformation requires the teacher to weigh up the available evidence, devise pedagogical approaches to be included in an overall teaching programme for a year, term, week or unit of work and then to put those approaches into action. Evidence can inform both the planning and the actual delivery. Imagine yourself in the middle of teaching a class about differences between spoken standard English and a number of dialects. You can draw on the evidence to help you plan and teach the lesson, but you will also need to depend on the evidence in order to improvise, adapt and meet particular learning needs *during* the course of the lesson.

The focus on subjects, at early years, primary/elementary and secondary/high school levels

The series is built around subjects. At the time of going to press, there are titles on English, Mathematics, Science, Design and Technology, Modern Foreign Languages and Economics and Business Studies either published or in the pipeline. Further titles will be added in due course. All but one of these subjects applies to primary/elementary and secondary/high school levels; one of the aims of the series is to ensure that research in the teaching and learning of school subjects is not confined by phase, but is applicable from the early years through to the end of compulsory education.

The focus on subjects is a pragmatic one. Although there is considerable pressure to move away from an essentially nineteenth-century conception of the curriculum as divided into disciplines and subjects, the current National Curriculum in England and Wales, and curricula elsewhere in the world, are still largely designed on the basis of subjects. The research we have drawn on in the making of the present series therefore derives from the core discipline, the school subject and the teaching of the school subject in each case. Where other research is contributory to practice, we have not stopped at including it (for example the work of the social psychologist Vygotsky in relation to the teaching of English) so that each book is an interpretation by the author(s) of the significance of research to teaching and learning within the subject. With some subjects, the research literature is vast and the authors have made what they take to be appropriate selections for the busy teacher or parent; with other subjects, there is less material to draw on and the tendency has been to use what research there is, often carried out by the author or authors themselves.

We take it that research into the development of learning in a subject at primary school level will be of interest to secondary school teachers, and vice-versa. The books will also provide a bridge between phases of education, seeing the development of learning as a continuous activity.

The international range

The series is international in scope. It aims not only to draw on research undertaken in a range of countries across the world in order to get at the best evidence possible; it will also apply to different systems across the world because of its attempt to get at the bedrock of good teaching and learning. References to particular education systems are kept to a minimum, and are only used when it is necessary to illuminate the context of the research. Where possible, comparative research is referred to.

Such an international perspective is important for a number of reasons: first, because research is sometimes carried out internationally; second, because globalization in learning is raising questions about the basis of new approaches to learning; third, because different perspectives can enhance the overall sense of what works best in different contexts. The series is committed to such diversity, both in drawing on research across the world and in serving the needs of learners and teachers across the world.

The time frame for the research

In general, the series looks at research from the 1960s to the present. Some of the most significant research in some subjects was undertaken in the 60s. In the 1990s, the advent of the internet and the World Wide Web has meant that the research toolkit has been increased. It is now possible to undertake literature reviews online and via resources in formats such as CDRom, as well as via the conventional print formats of journals and books. The books cannot claim to be comprehensive; at the same time each is an attempt to represent the best of research in particular fields for the illumination of teaching and learning.

Research is not the same as evaluation

It is helpful to distinguish between research and evaluation for the purposes of the present series. Research is the critical pursuit of truth or new knowledge through enquiry; or, to use a now obsolete but nevertheless telling definition from the eighteenth century, research in music is the seeking out of patterns of harmony which, once discovered, can be applied in the piece to be played afterwards. In other words, research is about discovery of new patterns, new explanations for data – or the testing of existing theories against new data – which can inform practice.

Evaluation is different. One can evaluate something without researching it or using research techniques. But formal evaluation of education initiatives often requires the use of research approaches to determine the exact nature of the developments that have taken place or the value and worth of those developments. Evaluation almost always assumes critical detachment and the disinterested weighing up of strengths and weaknesses. It should always be sensitive to the particular aims of a project and should try to weigh the aims against the methods and results, judging the appropriateness of the methods and the validity and effect (or likely effect) of the results. It can be formative or summative: formative when it works alongside the project it is evaluating, contributing to its development in a critical, dispassionate way; and summative when it is asked to identify at the end of a project the particular strengths and weaknesses of the approach.

Evaluation can use any of the techniques and methods that research uses in order to gather and analyse data. For example, an evaluation of the strengths and weaknesses of the Teacher Training Agency's School-Based Research Consortia (England) could use formal questionnaires, semi-structured interviews and case studies of individual teachers' development to assess the impact of the consortia. Research methods that provide quantitative data (largely numerical) or qualitative data (largely verbal) could be used.

Essentially, the difference between research and evaluation comes down to a difference in function: the function of research is to discover new knowledge via a testing of hypothesis, the answering of a research question or the solving of a problem – or indeed the creation of a hypothesis, the asking of a question or the formulating or exploring of a problem. The function of evaluation is simply to evaluate an existing phenomenon.

How to access, read and interpret research

The series provides a digest of the best and most relevant research in the teaching and learning of school subjects. Each of the authors aims to mediate between the plethora of research in the field and the needs of the busy teacher, headteacher, adviser, parent or governor who wants to know how best to improve practice in teaching in order to improve standards in learning. In other words, much of the work of seeking out research and interpreting it is done for you by the authors of the individual books in the series.

At the same time, the series is intended to help you to access and interpret research more generally. Research is continuing all the time; it is impossible for a book series, however comprehensive, to cover all research or to present the very latest research in a particular field. The publisher and authors of individual titles will be happy to hear from readers who feel that a particular piece of research is missing from the account, or about new research that extends our understanding of the field.

In order to help you access, read and interpret research the following guidelines might help:

- how clear is the research question or problem or hypothesis?
- if there is more than one question or problem, can you identify a main question or problem as opposed to subsidiary ones? Does the researcher make the distinction clear?
- is any review of the literature included? How comprehensive is it? How critical is it of past research? Does it, for instance, merely cite previous literature to make a new space for itself? Or does it build on existing research?
- determine the size of the sample used in the research. Is this a case study of a particular child or a series of interviews with, say, ten pupils, or a survey of tens or hundreds of pupils? The generalizability of the research will depend on its scale and range.
- is the sample a fair reflection of the population that is being researched? For example, if all the 12 to 13-year-old pupils in a particular town are being researched (there might be 600 of them) what is the size of the sample?
- are the methods used appropriate for the study?
- is the data gathered appropriate for an answering of the question, testing of the hypothesis or solving of the problem?
- what conclusions, if any, are drawn? Are they reasonable?
- is the researcher making recommendations based on sound results, or are implications for practice drawn out? Is the researcher aware of the limitations of the study?
- is there a clear sense of what further research needs to be undertaken?

Equipped with questions like these, and guided by the authors of the books in the series, you will be better prepared to make sense of research findings and apply them to the improvement of your practice for the benefit of the students you teach. The bibliographies at the end of each book will provide you with the means of exploring the field more extensively, according to your own particular interests and needs.

Richard Andrews
York 2003

Outline of the Book

This book is divided into two parts. Part 1 is a short account of the teaching and research context, both the generic research context in England and the foreign-language or second-language (L2) acquisition research context internationally. Part 2 provides an extensive review of studies in L2 acquisition and L2 or foreign language pedagogy.

Chapter 1 is a brief insight into what language teachers might want from research. Based on a survey of a small sample of secondary teachers in England it explores the broad themes of language teaching as well as the more individual skill-oriented questions. What do teachers want the research to illuminate? How do language teachers perceive L2 research? How accessible is L2 research? It asks what languages research and development teachers had been involved in and to what extent they had found this useful.

Chapter 2 examines the research response by providing an overview of what the broad lines of research endeavour have been. What have some of the research journals been able to offer in recent years? In other words we match the teachers' needs and aspirations in wanting to improve practice through research with what the research effort of the last 12 years or so has tried to illuminate. Although it appears at first glance that the research community is not responding to the teachers' needs, a more sustained analysis suggests that the answers may be out there but that they are sometimes camouflaged by complex terminology, cultural gaps between professional communities, and an inability for teachers and researchers to work together on a common agenda. In addition, this chapter explores the problem of the constant interaction between trying to get at the big picture of language learning and trying to fathom its small constituent parts.

Chapter 3 asks what research says generally about the ways second-language learners learn. It looks at three interconnected themes: how the brain acquires language, developments in teaching methods and insights into the rules systems of languages. From these interconnected themes springs a number of questions. Can second languages be learnt simply by repeating and imitating native speakers or more proficient speakers? Are we born with an innate ability to learn a language and, if so, is this the same for first- and second-language learning? Is linguistic knowledge different from other types of knowledge? What do the latest theories in cognitive development have to offer? For example, what are the functions and limitations of working memory and how does it interact with long-term memory? What do we mean by connectionism, by interlanguage and by progression and how does this help us to understand or undermine the concept of ability? What in general does research say about the effectiveness of teaching methods? Should we be focusing on the language as the object of study or focusing on communicating through the language? In sum, Chapter 3 touches on general issues in research on L2 acquisition which are picked up in later chapters in much finer detail.

Chapters 4 and 5 investigate two fundamental variables which affect language learning. They ask whether it is variables in the learner's brain which matter the most or whether it is the society and culture the individual lives in that have the greatest impact. Thus Chapter 4 looks in greater detail at cognition, particularly the processes of storing, processing and retrieving the second-language vocabulary. It investigates research into what it means to 'know a word'; how learners deploy semantic clustering; whether vocabulary is best stored in a syntactic context, through a keyword technique or by semantic association; what is the relative importance of acquiring nouns and verbs; what is the role of first language in processing the second language; what affects the speed of retrieval? Chapter 5, on the other hand, explores research into overcoming social barriers to language learning. How is motivation affected by a culturally linked reluctance to learn, by a sense of failure, by attribution of success and by peer pressure? To what extent are gender, socioeconomic factors, teaching styles, learner strategies and information technology important considerations in getting learners in the right frame of mind for language learning?

The next four chapters of the book look at research into the four language skills. However, the themes in these chapters do not lend themselves to being presented as completely separate entities. Thus Chapter 6 looks at the findings of research into reading, but in doing so cannot disentangle the process of reading from earlier discussions on vocabulary. Chapter 7 looks at research on listening but sees parallels both with access to the written word and to the discussion on oral interaction in the ensuing chapter. Chapter 8 therefore looks not only at issues such as fluency and speaking strategies, but also makes a more in-depth assessment of the research evidence provided by the topic of classroom-based oral interaction. Chapter 9 investigates findings in the field of writing but draws from a theme visited earlier in Chapter 3, namely the development of the rule system. Another strand binding these four chapters is that the research reviewed focuses to a great extent on the processes involved in the skill rather than the end products. These processes include the very learning strategies that students deploy in order to improve their proficiency. For this reason there is no isolated chapter on learner strategies and learner autonomy as these themes are picked up again and again in the book. I have not given comprehensive lists of learner strategies for each skill. Rather, I have tried to let the research do the talking, suggesting clusters of strategies that have particularly been detected in individual or groups of studies.

The concluding chapter attempts to stand back and provide an overview of what the research is telling us and identifies those areas where research is lacking. It also evaluates whether the direction we are going in and the methods we are using are the most appropriate. Some recommendations for language teaching, based on the research evidence, are made.

How the selection of studies was made

This book tries to achieve a number of overarching aims. Firstly, in order to arrive at what I have called in Chapter 1 'a convergence of research agendas', it tries to address directly all the interests in research that teachers indicated that they had in the small-scale survey described in Chapter 1. At the same time it gives an account of research findings in the areas most recently covered by research where there was clearly a pool of interest by researchers. The convergence is thus attempted through the selection of the studies examined. Secondly, the book tries to demonstrate that virtually all second-language-acquisition research, whether it be carried out in a laboratory or in a class-room, has *some* application and relevance in the modern-languages classroom. Thus, in order to fulfil this second aim, there was no deliberate selection process which favoured classroom-based research. The reader will judge for himself or herself whether the claims made for relevance to classroom practice are valid. Thirdly, the book tries to demonstrate that, whatever the educational or linguistic context of the studies examined, the findings are indeed transferable to other contexts. Thus if we are teachers of 13-year-olds in Birmingham, England, we should not automatically ignore a study of university students in Birmingham, Alabama. To do so would be to over-emphasize social, cultural and institutional differences and ignore the similarities of linguistic processes in the brain. Again, therefore, educational or linguistic context was not a selection criteria. The only other selection process has been on the basis of accessibility of material. Some themes have only been covered in a superficial way simply because there is not much research out there; at least, not a lot was captured in the trawl that I carried out. I am convinced that there is a lot of important research out there which is not published. Some of this, for example PhD theses, are eventually obtainable after considerable effort and cost and I have reviewed some of these. However, to have done a comprehensive review of all the themes, including unpublished materials, would have been a mammoth undertaking and far too expensive a task.

The book's approach is one where in-depth reviews of a smaller quantity of studies is preferred to a superficial scanning of a more comprehensive list. Having said that, some studies are described in greater detail than others. There are a number of reasons for this. Firstly, whilst not claiming that the longer descriptions are of seminal studies on each of the themes addressed, I am nevertheless foregrounding certain research evidence which seems to me to have particular relevance to the classroom or whose implications are, in my opinion, important. Secondly, in reporting some studies in greater detail I hope to provide the reader with a more in-depth under-standing of the research questions asked, the sample of subjects selected and the research methods used. This should not only contextualize the findings better for the reader but provide beginner researchers and teacher-researchers with some examples of how to go about their own research.

Wherever possible I have tried to go to the original reporting of the study rather than someone else's review. On the few occasions where this has not been possible, I have acknowledged the previous reviewer in the references section. In this respect, I am particularly indebted to the reviews by Melinda Reichelt (2001) by Alderson and Banerjee (2002) and by Zoltán Dörnyei (1998). The responsibility for the accuracy of what is written in this book is, however, entirely mine.

A further aim of this book is to attempt to demystify some of the jargon used in second-language-acquisition research whilst at the same time recognizing that teachers and researchers do need to build up a common language with which to talk to one another. In order to do this I have retained, for the most part, the technical terms used in the original studies but have, wherever seemed appropriate, given an immediate explanation or illustration of what the term means.

Acknowledgements

I am extremely grateful to the following people for having taken the time to comment on various chapters of this book: Suzanne Graham, Brian Richards, Gianfranco Conti, Yasuo Nakatani, Lynn Erler, Ros Mitchell, Kim Brown, Mike Grenfell, Bob Vanderplank, Jonathan Flint. Thanks also go to Richard Andrews for struggling through the whole lot. I would also like to thank Ursula Wingate and Vee Harris for letting me have some of their material at short notice. I am very grateful to everyone at Continuum for believing that I could actually finish what has, at times, seemed an impossible task. I am very much indebted to Judy Reading and Nick Watts in OUDES library for all their help in obtaining material from far-flung libraries and to my family for, once again, putting up with my late nights.

Ernesto Macaro
Oxford, September 2002

Part 1

Second-Language Research, Teachers and Researchers

Chapter 1

What do Second-language Teachers want from Research?

'Do we need another book on second language research?'

If we enter any large academic bookshop we rarely have difficulty in locating shelves of volumes dedicated to the learning and teaching of second languages, particularly to the teaching of English as a foreign language. Many of these contain accounts or reviews of second-language-acquisition research. A glance through the abstracting journal *Language Teaching* reveals an astonishing number of different journals from which it draws its articles, over one hundred and fifty, in fact! The difficulty for the teacher, teacher educator and beginner researcher is that it is easy to be overwhelmed by the sheer quantity of research being carried out internationally. This sense of being overwhelmed often increases when they begin to read an article in a journal or a chapter in a book. Sometimes the context in which the research is being carried out seems alien to the reader. At other times there is an assumption that the reader already knows a great deal about the subject and is just looking to top up their knowledge via the latest developments.

There is another aspect, too, that gives rise to frustration. This is that researchers may not necessarily be delving into the area that the teacher needs at a particular point in time in order to inform his or her practice. The research agenda is being set almost entirely by the research community.

This book begins by trying to address this aspect of the problem and to redress the balance. It does so by asking teachers themselves what they would like to know more about and by trying to identify their attitudes and perceptions of second-language research in general. Although the sample of teachers consulted for this chapter is relatively small and localized to England, it nevertheless allows us to take the first step in placing the interests of teachers squarely in the picture of what we want second-language research to do.

Specifically for this book, then, I carried out a small survey of what language teachers in England wanted from research. 250 questionnaires were sent out, at random, to heads of modern languages in a full range of local education authorities in England. The questionnaires contained both closed and open questions. 80 questionnaires were returned by the deadline, giving us a 32% return. This is quite a low return and therefore the findings need to be treated with a little caution as, for example, only those teachers well disposed to research may have bothered to return the questionnaire. On the other hand, we could always claim that if there were teachers out there who were thoroughly disgruntled with the whole business of research they might have taken the time to put pen to paper and tell me!

Biographical data from the sample

As the questionnaire was sent out to departments of modern languages in schools I can only report on the 11-18 sector here, that is, not early foreign-language learning nor language learning in higher education. Moreover, as the teachers who received the questionnaire were heads of modern languages it is not too surprising that they were all very experienced teachers. In fact 23% said they had taught for between five and eight years and 76% had taught for over nine years. Only one teacher in fact had taught for less than five years. Of the 80 returns 71% were female and 28% were male, reflecting very much the gender bias in England when it comes to foreign-language teachers. It was also not surprising that 21% of the sample said they taught only one language but 79% said they taught two or more languages. In England there is both an implicit government policy and explicit policies at the school level to encourage entrants to the profession who can offer more than one foreign language. In other countries such as France and Italy this is not the case. Generally, you either teach one foreign language or another and consider yourself a specialist in that language. In England this feature probably results in a tendency to regard language teaching and learning as very much a generic activity. The research evidence, however, is that different languages do require some differences in pedagogies. An obvious one is that some languages pose fairly major grapheme-phoneme problems whereas others do not. For example, English and, to a certain extent, French are not written as they are pronounced.

The questionnaire returns also reflected a difference in the geographical and therefore socioeconomic make up of the country as 40% of teachers taught in a rural environment or small town, 37% of teachers in a suburban environment and 24% in an inner city.

The questionnaire asked a number of general questions about research before asking teachers to focus on a number of specific skills, processes and areas in language teaching and then requiring them to comment on how useful research in that field would be to them in the classroom. We will start with the specific skills, processes and areas first. Table 1.1 provides the full list of 17 items they had to respond to. This was not meant to be a comprehensive list but one which I felt they would most relate to in their teaching context. So, you see, already there is some 'filtering' going on by the researcher. But that's always a problem with research.

As we can see from Table 1.1, most of the areas of research were thought to be very useful or fairly useful to language teachers. In fact overall, more than 80% of responses were positive towards the usefulness of these areas of research. This positive attitude towards research is supported by the earlier (in the questionnaire) question about the usefulness *in general* of languages research. 29% of language teachers thought research was very useful and 55% thought it was fairly useful. This finding not only helps to give the questionnaire what is sometimes called *internal validity* but it also has encouraged me to embark on the writing of some 100,000 words on

Table 1.1 Teachers' interest in research in order of 'most useful'

	Means (1 = very useful; 4 = not at all useful)	Very useful %	Fairly useful %
Vocabulary acquisition	1.27	74	25
How the rules of the language are best learnt	1.30	73	25
Motivation	1.38	68	25
How learners make progress with language learning	1.43	58	40
Differences among learners (e.g. boys/girls; younger/older)	1.56	53	38
Speaking	1.60	51	41
How the brain stores and retrieves language	1.62	58	28
KS4 (Lower intermediate) research	1.76	37	51
Writing	1.82	39	45
KS3 (beginner) research	1.84	29	57
Role of English (LI) in FL learning	1.88	35	45
Assessment	1.98	22	50
Comprehension of spoken texts	2.02	25	53
Aptitude	2.03	21	41
Comprehension of written texts	2.04	27	49
Post-16 research	2.12	35	32
Differences between languages	2.20	30	37
		43.2%	40%

languages research with a little more enthusiasm than would otherwise have been the case!

However there was less unanimity with regard to *how accessible* research was with an almost even split between positive and negative responses. Worryingly only 3% of respondents thought that research was *very accessible*. The implications that this has for research-based practice are enormous. The prime activity for teachers is to teach, not to study research, and they quite rightly prioritize their time accordingly. If what little time they can devote to reading about research is undermined by its inaccessibility, then aspirations about development towards research informed practice are going to be quite unrealistic. The qualitative data gives a clearer picture of in what ways they found the research inaccessible and we will return to this a little later. For the moment, though, it looks as if teachers want their practice to be informed by research but don't want necessarily to have to spend three years poring over second-language-acquisition journals in order to understand it. So that's why we need another book on second-language research, *voilà*!

Let us now return to Table 1.1. Three of the four most popular areas of research were, surprisingly, more about mental processes in the learners than observable language skills. In a way this is very welcome since skills such as speaking and writing are more easily observable than *progress with internalizing the rules of the language* or *how the brain stores language*. If these are less observable, then it's up to researchers to try to identify them. They are, after all, the underlying processes that give rise to improvements in the skills. Missing from the list in the questionnaire was any reference to learning strategies (sometimes called learner strategies). If you haven't come across this term, they are all the 'actions' (both immediate and more long term), with which learners engage, in order to help themselves learn. Later in this book I will try to show how processes are made up of lots and lots of strategies. Because there are so many strategies and because they permeate so much of language learning, *research into learning strategies* was an item left out of the questionnaire.

The fact that teachers placed near the top of the list 'how the rules of the language are best learnt' reflects a preoccupation with the current shift back towards grammar teaching both internationally, as expressed in the frequent critiques of Communicative Language Teaching (CLT), and in England, as expressed by the very recent insertion in the National Curriculum for MFL of the requirement: 'pupils should be taught the grammar of the target language and how to apply it' (DfEE 1999). Clearly, everyone would wish their learners to demonstrate in their speaking and writing that they had noticed and internalized the patterns or rules of the target language. However, the debate has, for many years, been how best to achieve this in the context of language learning in general.

Of the four language skills, the one that our teachers felt there was most need for research to illuminate was *speaking*. This is a little surprising given the emphasis in the past two decades on Communicative Language Teaching. Certainly, secondary classrooms are filled to the brim with oral interaction, especially in lower secondary. Perhaps the concern then is that learners don't make much progress with their speaking or rarely develop the confidence to initiate a discussion. Why should there be so much effort devoted to speaking with such minimal returns? Perhaps research can help to illuminate the factors surrounding this problem.

'Aptitude' in language learning comes fairly low in Table 1.1. Is this because it is still regarded as 'incorrect' to think of aptitude as a discriminating factor in individuals, perhaps leading to setting, or is it just that teachers are not familiar with the body of research in this area?

'Motivation' and 'gender differences' come high on the list. Clearly these are areas that need to be unpicked and explored. Motivation, as a construct, I have always found difficult to grasp. My feeling is that teachers also find it difficult to define. Are we referring to some inner drive that propels us along the road to learning in a general holistic way, a kind of inner force that is fuelled by a desire to learn. Or is it to do with the minutiae of learning, the day to day decision making of whether to focus at length on a problem or whether to let it go unresolved?

Finally we notice that the perception seems to be that the unresolved problems revolving around language learning are those in the compulsory-education phase rather than later, for example, between the ages of 16 and 19. Why should this be? Is it the case that problems occurring with younger pupils manifest themselves more clearly in demotivation and disengagement from language learning? Are A level students more 'passive' and just expected to cope? Or is it that, quite simply, A level students are those who have reached the higher levels of language proficiency and/or have chosen to study a language because they are highly motivated?

Interestingly no statistically significant[1] variables ($p > .05$) were found in the data in terms of teachers' attitudes to research nor their interest in particular areas of research. For example there were no significant differences among male and female teachers, nor between those teachers that had qualified more recently or less recently.

There were no significant differences between those teachers who taught more than one language, not even, as one might have expected, with regard to the question on whether research into the differences between languages would be useful. Finally, the catchment area of the school made no difference as to how the teachers viewed the value, accessibility or the prioritization of research. This lack of significant variation may have been due to the general unanimity with which teachers viewed the usefulness of research (i.e. fairly positively) coupled to the fact that gender, number of languages taught and teacher experience were fairly skewed. In other words, a larger sample might have produced more significant differences. Moreover, if the sample had included more recently qualified teachers (for example less than three years) the results may have been different.

In the questionnaire, 45% of teachers said that they had been involved in some aspect of research. One very interesting finding was that there were no significant differences between those teachers who had been involved in research and those who had not. One might have hypothesized that the former would have had different attitudes to the usefulness or accessibility of research than the latter.

So far, we have been looking at the quantitative data from the survey of teachers. By 'quantitative' I mean all the data that can be used in statistics. This is a useful way of looking at research but it does have its drawbacks. We can't really say that the typical language teacher is 80% in favour of research and 20% against. That sort of 'reality' just doesn't exist. So we balance this with qualitative data which essentially is accessed through words rather than numbers. The problem with qualitative data, of course, is that it's much more difficult to get the 'big picture' from it.

The qualitative data is based on:

1 The open-ended questions in the questionnaire
2 A series of six interviews carried out with a convenience[2] sample of teachers.

In the open-ended question on 'what kind of research would be useful to illuminate practice', by far the greatest concern was the theme of *motivation* and this supports its high position in the table above. Motivation was mentioned at least 23 times by the 80 teachers. However, with the aid of the qualitative data we can now sub-categorize this concept into:

i   motivating boys and the gender issue in general
ii motivating slow learners
iii motivating reluctant learners who perhaps have poor attitudes to MFL learning and xenophobic attitudes in general
iv the value of short-term goals in order to motivate reluctant learners.

Research may be able to offer insights into these various aspects of motivation and teachers are clearly aware of this.

As we have said, vocabulary was high on the list of areas for research to turn its attention to and, with respect to vocabulary, teachers particularly wanted to know what memorization techniques worked.

Learner autonomy featured high as a theme even though it wasn't on the subsequent list of themes for teachers to react to. However, none of the teachers ventured into an explanation of what they meant by learner autonomy. This concept, in the research literature, is notoriously difficult to define. I hope to demonstrate in later chapters that the concept of autonomy can best be grasped through an exploration of learner-strategies research.

Speaking, as we have seen, was the skill that many teachers wanted to know more about in terms of research. Here particularly it was how to develop 'advanced or more sophisticated speaking and communication skills'. Writing and the comprehension of written texts (reading), by contrast, were rarely mentioned. This is despite inspection evidence, in England, that both these skills are underdeveloped in both lower and upper secondary. On the other hand it could be argued that the heavy emphasis placed on grammar in the open questions (at least 11 mentions) reflects a concern with a lack of written accuracy as well as:

'How to deliver it'
'How to teach grammar communicatively'
'Teaching the deep structures of the language'
'(does) explicit grammar teaching work'

Some interesting comments were given by teachers on the inaccessibility of research:

Lack of Time
'Lack of time to read it is a problem'
'No time to search it out'
'INSET is usually taken up with whole school issues – little time given to development in language teaching'

Lack of expertise
'I don't always know where to look'
'Too technical'
'Findings too detailed – tends to be skimmed rather than read thoroughly'

Lack of appropriateness for context
'Yes, but it's too adult oriented or HE-relevant'
'Some is *too academic* to be useful'

This last aspect is an interesting one and it is one of the main objectives for this book. I hope to demonstrate that virtually all research findings are relevant and useful. The problem is that their applicability to practice is rarely sufficiently explored and that their applicability to different contexts is not sufficiently examined.

Some teachers offered descriptions of the types of research they had been involved in. However, much of what was cited would not normally come under the category of 'being involved in research' but rather on the receiving end of 'experts' advice'. This is general in-service training usually as a result of development work in response to government initiatives. The comments gave the impression that most of their research involvement was with research ideas brought in from outside rather than generated by the interests and concerns of the teacher. However, a few did mention research as being part of a certificated course such as a Masters degree. Of the themes they had researched or had been involved in developing, by far the most cited was the gender issue as these short quotes illustrate:

> 'Gender-based learning'
> 'Boys learning languages'
> 'Boys' performance'
> 'Boy/girl perception of teacher method'
> 'Gender issue in languages'
> 'Gender differences'
> 'Gender preferences (skills/topics and approaches)'
> '(The effectiveness of) boys only groups in yr 11'

We have gone from the impersonal (statistical) data to the more personal (qualitative data) where we begin to hear the actual voices of the teachers but still very much as a 'group without a body'. I will now attempt to present a case study of one teacher from the interviews that were conducted. This profile is intended to give a real life example of a teacher who, by and large, is committed to the value of research in her practice.

Profile of one teacher from the interviews: Barbara

Barbara accesses research essentially through her head of department because of lack of time to do her own investigations. She says it would be useful to have a whole day of INSET on research. The aspect of research that would be most of interest to her is the effectiveness of communicative teaching because she learned languages in 'a very dry way which alienated 95% of the students'. In other words, she would like to know more about which general approach is most effective. She would also like to know more about strategies for learning a word and to 'be able to tell the kids' about this process so that they take on board that there is a reasoning behind her pedagogy. Research isn't just for her own information but for the students to understand as well. She would like to know why there is 'such a difference between listening and reading' and then be able to tell her students about techniques for effective listening. She would like to know of research which would help her students 'make the jump' from simple phrases to more complex sentences because 'our expectations about writing are probably not high enough'. She's also interested in 'spelling rules'. She knows that 'in France they use little patterns of sentences to remember spellings' but that in England we never teach strategies like these. She would like to know more fundamental issues about the learners: what are their obstacles to learning? For example, would a double spaced text help them to read more easily? Would the brain process it more easily? She's 'interested in the psychology of it all' – are boys more extrovert than girls? Do the introvert ones actually learn more 'by taking it all in but never giving anything back or do the ones who shout more get more language'? She thinks that it's much more important to find out about how learners learn than about how teachers teach: 'at the end of the day you're left as yourself as a teacher, so you need to know how learners learn to adapt to your own teaching'.

The above account is a wonderful example of a teacher constantly asking herself questions, constantly attemping to understand her learners. She touches on many vital areas of research and shows an acute awareness of the limitations of teaching methods.

So, will the research out there be able to offer any answers to Barbara's questions? In the next chapter we will see to what extent there is a convergence of 'research agendas', to what extent the teachers' needs are matched by the researchers' interests.

Notes

1. By this we mean that the results were so pronounced that we can say with some certainty that they are generalizable to all teachers in England.
2. This means that they were not randomly selected.

Chapter 2

The Research Response to Teachers' Needs

In Chapter 1 we examined what aspects of practice teachers, in a small scale survey, said they wanted research to illuminate. We saw that motivation came high on the list, although this had a number of different definitions in the minds of the teachers and a number of sub-topics. Speaking skills also appeared to be causing the sample of teachers some concern. Generally, we noted that teachers were favourable to research as a vehicle for providing answers but as yet were not clear in what way it was providing those answers. It was also evident that teachers had not had the time nor the remaining energy to find out what research was actually available.

So, what do researchers have to offer our sample of teachers? What second language research do the researchers appear to be interested in? Is there a consensus of learning concerns? Are both communities converging towards the same research agenda?

In order to answer this question we would have to be able to decide what the best indicators would be. On the international stage, for example, we can look back over the last 10 or so years and examine the journal *Language Teaching*.

In this journal there is a *state of the art* article at the beginning of each issue providing a review of research on a theme of 'current importance' as defined by the editor. Table 2.1 shows the themes reviewed in the last 10 years. In the third column is my interpretation, if this is necessary, of what the title means and a thumbnail description of the content. Column 4 provides a comparison with the interest in research shown by the sample of teachers in Chapter 1.

We can see why our sample of teachers might feel a little despondent. Their questions, at first glance, are only rarely addressed by these 'leading articles' on research. However, a liberal interpretation (see column 3) does suggest that some of these research reviews can be made applicable to all sorts of classrooms. Moreover, if we were to peruse the Index of the abstracts which follow the lead article in *Language Teaching*, we would discover that virtually all of the themes which interest our sample of teachers are, indeed, covered.

Another international indicator would be the reviews of recent research interest that are published from time to time in *The Modern Language Journal,* a journal that, incidentally, has provided quite a number of studies reviewed later in this book. *The Modern Language Journal* is an American journal of the National Federation of Modern Language Teachers Associations, with a circulation of about 5,000. One reason that a

Table 2.1   Compendium of 'lead articles' in *Language Teaching*

Date of issue	'State of the art' topic/theme	Some interpretations of the topic/theme	Teachers in sample's interest (whether mentioned at least twice)
April 1990	Computer-assisted language learning	Do computers help learners to learn?	Yes
January 1990	Pedagogical grammar	Approaches to the acquisition of the rule system	Yes
October 1990	Learner language (interlanguage/error)	How learners make progress with the rule system of the L2	Yes
January 1991	Educational technology and language learning	Radio, video, computers: how do teachers use them?	Yes
April 1991	Writing L1-L2	Evaluation of students' written output	No
October 1991	Language and gender	Do males and females *use* language differently?	No
April 1992	English and other languages for younger children	International perspective of the English learnt by 6-11 year olds	No
July 1993	Intercultural communication	The study of cultural differences and similarities	No
October 1993	Business English		No
January 1994	Needs analysis in language teaching	Basing syllabi or course content on specific group needs	No
April 1994	Evaluation and ELT	The evaluation of the effectiveness of language programmes	No
July 1994	Narrative analysis	The purposes, functions and structure of stories	No
October 1994	Self-managed learning	Independent learning and autonomy	Yes
July 1995	Language planning in Europe	The policies and practice of L2 learning in Europe	No
January 1995	Contrastive studies	How does the grammar of different languages differ?	No
April 1995	Pragmatics	A theoretical look at communication skills	No
October 1996	Literature in a FL	Attitudes to the teaching of L2 literature and communicative approaches	No
October 1996	European perspectives on language learning	How is language learning in Europe changing?	No
January 1996	Pragmatics	A theoretical look at communication skills	No
April 1996(a)	ELT in China		No

Table 2.1 Contd

Date of issue	'State of the art' topic/theme	Some interpretations of the topic/theme	Teachers in sample's interest (whether mentioned at least twice)
April 1996 (b)	MFL for European Citizenship	Language learning's interaction with accepting foreign cultures	Yes
April 1997	Form focused instruction	Awareness of language patterns in communicative classrooms	Yes
January 1998	ELT in Central Europe		No
April 1998	Computers and language learning	History, current practices and the future	Yes
July 1998	Motivation	Attitudes and motivation in language learning	Yes
October 1998 (a)	Primary FL teaching in Europe		No
October 1998 (b)	European perspectives on MFL		No
January 1999	Learner strategies	Learning styles; how learners learn	Yes
April 1999	Metaphor	How does metaphor work in language?	No
October 1999	Formulaic language	How do learners use set phrases in the L2 and why?	Yes
January 2000	Bilingual classroom interaction	Speaking in classrooms where two languages are present	Yes
April 2000	L2 learning as a mediated process	How teachers act as intermediaries between the L2 and the learner; socio-cultural theory	No
October 2000	Language and gender	How do males and females experience L2 learning differently?	Yes
January 2001	World English and World Englishes	Different variations of English and the tensions this cause	No
April 2001	Learning difficulties	What learning difficulties do *some* learners experience?	No

considerable number of studies from this journal have found their way into this book is that many of the problems of language learning experienced by teachers in the UK are also experienced in the USA. Another reason is that they are generally very well written and well edited, thus accessible. Anyway, back to the reviews of research interest. Heidi Byrnes (2000) looking back over 50 years of contributions in the journal sees some major trends. Whereas in the 50s and 60s researchers were primarily interested in language and how it worked (linguistics), the 70s, 80s and 90s saw a 'dramatic rise in the prominence of psycholinguistic models' (how the human brain deals with language). As a result of that shift, research has focused on error analysis, on performance, proficiency and testing, on models of information processing or connectionism and the acquisition of vocabulary.

How does all the research activity internationally square up with what the teachers in Chapter 1 were currently interested in? At first glance the match-up is not obvious. However, I believe that part of the problem is the different metalanguage and terminology being used, especially if one considers that much of the research comes from North America. On the other hand, in many schools and universities the monolingual learning context is very similar between the UK and the US.

In the UK an indicator of research interest would be *Language Learning Journal*, the journal of the Association for Language Learning. Table 2.2 gives an overview of the topics and themes covered by the journal since 1994. Note that only the left-hand column catalogues articles based on empirical research. *Language Learning Journal* has, in the past, tended to publish a lot of articles of a general discursive nature.

Language Learning Journal appears to have a closer rapport with the research aspirations of the teachers in the English sample. This is reassuring as it is written primarily for teachers and teacher educators in the UK! However, there is a worry-

Table 2.2 Summary of articles in *Language Learning Journal* since 1994

LLJ issue	Empirically oriented articles	Theoretical/discursive/ general pedagogy articles
24	Computer-mediated communication, translation, National Literacy Strategy and MFL, communication strategies, dictionary skills	Content teaching, CALL, policy, language learning-uptake
23	Language policy and multilingualism, MFL take-up post-16, gender and learning styles, language-learning interests and university, ELT in Japan	Initial teacher education (ITE), ITE and language competence, grammar teaching
22	Exchange visits, year abroad, teachers and voice projection, learner strategies and dictionaries	Primary languages, role-play and drama, language policy, visual images and lexical phrases
21	Gender, ICT, vocabulary, motivation, lectors, affective issues, dictionary use, needs analysis, exchange visits	Learning styles
20	*Ab initio* versus A level eventual competence, primary languages, motivation and attitudes, motivation, motivation, learner strategies, policy	Interpreting, community languages, policy
19	Target language use, dictionary use, teaching grammar, primary languages, study practices in higher education	Teaching grammar, videoconferencing, tandem learning, culture, review of communicative methods
18	Bilingual dictionaries, GCSE and diversification, learning strategies, internet use (higher), www use (higher), videoconferencing, language laboratory (higher), vocabulary (comparative), mentoring skills, in-service needs	Teaching grammar, bilingual (content) teaching, gender, exam results/ statistics

Table 2.2 Contd

LLJ issue	Empirically oriented articles	Theoretical/discursive/ general pedagogy articles
17	Verb development, learner strategies, supportive classroom environments, comparative curricula and materials	Boys' underachievement, reading strategies and the NC, cloze tests, culture, policy (Austria), self access and autonomy (higher), open and self access (higher) policy
16	Gender, cultural, cultural	Differentiation, teaching grammar, review of CLT, autonomy, video, CDRom, methods review
15	ICT (provision of), bilingual teaching (content)	Dictionary skills, differentiation, autonomy and less able, computer conferencing, role-play and suggestopedia, language curriculum, European dimension, culture, European policy
14	TL testing, oral testing, attitudes to (German), gender, A level curriculum	GCSE testing, NC design, curriculum planning, listening, corpora, ITE, software evaluation, professional development
13	Primary languages, FL and visually impaired, German (attitudes to), reading (strategies), testing speaking (GCSE), negative affect (attitudes) (higher), listening skills, ITE and ICT, CALL, year abroad (higher), learning strategies (mnemonic)	Learning styles, video and literature, curriculum materials, evaluation of methods, German vocabulary, use of CDRom, self-access
12	Cultural awareness, advanced language learner (characteristics), learning strategies, advanced (weak) student, decline of verbs, use of video	ITE, cultural awareness, differentiation, policy (higher), course design (higher), primary languages, grammar (German), language and society, use of cloze, Greek, writing (higher)
11	Testing speaking, language curriculum, TL use (comparative), FL for legal practitioners, business FL, business German, autonomy and video camera, grammar rules	Cross curricular themes, ITE, MFL and EBD, gender, motivation and group context, cultural awareness, self-access (higher), drama, drama (Russian), transferable skills, Business Studies, Arabic, concordances, ITE, review of methods
10	NC survey, ineffective lessons, TL use, year abroad (higher), special needs, accelerated learning adult), Community Studies, Portuguese, Romany, community languages (Australia), CALL	ITE Policy, TL testing, TL use, European policy, creative writing, autonomy
9	Culture, learner strategies, attitudes to MFL, motivation, diversification, needs analysis, competence and policy (higher), accelerated learning (adult)	Policy (NC), FL and technology, teaching grammar, reading and writing (review), position of literature, literature, dictionary use, policy, Turkish, lesser taught langs, Arabic

ingly low number of research-based articles and most of these are small-scale or exploratory such that generalizable conclusions are rarely possible.

So we are left with a situation where there is an enormous amount of research literature out there but much of it is confined to the English language-teaching context. In addition, it has been carried out predominantly in higher education and, for the most part, in North America.

The book's response

In the rest of this book I will endeavour to achieve my aim, stated in the outline of the book, of arriving at a convergence of research agendas between teachers and researchers. Will this be possible and will 'the answers be out there'? I don't know yet. My initial gut feeling is that they probably are but they are not as crystal clear as we would like them. The trick will be to demonstrate that all learning contexts can get at least something out of internationally published research.

Some of the narrower and more focused questions that teachers asked fit into a bigger picture of how learners learn and how, therefore, we should teach. How learners learn could be answered by going down two separate roads of exploration. We could explore what are the processes of learning a second language over which a learner has no control and the processes over which the learner has some control. In asking the question how learners learn we might be envisaging social and institutional factors such as what schools and universities are like; how learning is arranged; how decisions about what learning is to take place are made; how where you are born and live influences the way you regard a second language. All these factors are important and could be examined in terms of the measure of control over learning that the learner has. But the impression I get from language teachers is that they are really asking a question about how learning takes place in the brain. So the question would be something like: what aspects of 'brain-oriented language learning' (what we might call *psycholinguistics*) do the learners have no control over? The second question would then be, what aspects of psycholinguistics do they have at least some measure of control over? Only when some of these questions are answered can we go back to the question of how teachers should teach.

Recently I ran a whole-day workshop in a large secondary school on *learner strategies*. At the end of a day of looking at various pieces of research evidence a teacher asked 'but what method works best?' I suddenly realised I would not be able to give a confident answer. And yet I felt I had to. Could all this research effort really not produce a simple answer to a simple question? Surprisingly, my answer came not from the research evidence but from my own intuition and experience of language teaching. I said I felt that, generally, on the whole, and all things considered, and when all said and done, a flexible version of communicative language teaching was still, after more than 20 years, the best method for the majority of learners. I was pleased to see that the teacher felt reassured by this answer. Being reassured of the value of a flexible CLT approach is almost like the feeling of being reassured of the value of centre-left politics – you know that you should believe in it, it feels right to believe in it, but you want proof.

So is intuition and experience, in the end, as powerful a determinant of how one should teach as the amassed research evidence? Have all those years of research effort been to no avail? Perhaps the answer lies in the very fact that there *is* indeed plenty of literature out there. Let us ask why there should be so much. Surely it can't be that bilinguals and multilinguals have got too much to say for themselves. Or, perhaps, this answer is not so mischievous. Firstly, taking a global perspective, bilinguals and multilinguals by far outnumber monolinguals. There is, therefore, a thriving market for research into learning a second language. Secondly, there are at least three fundamental differences in learning a modern language to, say, learning history, geography, physics or even the classics. There is the 'subject as medium' reason. The subject that we are learning is the very medium through which it is being taught and learnt. We cannot detach ourselves from it. Unlike the learning of Latin or Ancient Greek where we can compartmentalize it and see it is as a *body* of knowledge to be learnt, the interrelationship between language acquisition and language use, in L2 classrooms, is irrefutable. The second reason (and not disconnected from the first) is that learning a second language affects integral parts of an individual's identity. In becoming bilinguals we become different people, not only linguistically but emotionally and culturally. I'm not convinced that we have to change our identity in order to become physicists. The third reason is that, unlike most other subjects, we have another 'subject' constantly knocking on our pedagogical door: the learners' (and in many situations the teacher's) first language. In every activity that as learners we engage in, whether it be conscious or subconscious, oral or written, there is this parrot sitting on our shoulder either interfering with or facilitating our reception, production and progress with the second language we are attempting to learn. So perhaps, the very fact that bilinguals and multilinguals are what they are, enables them to generate double or treble the number of ideas, hypotheses and theories that monolinguals can generate and to test them and compare them in a multitude of educational settings. Thus the fact that I could not immediately provide the teacher colleague with an answer to what method works best according to research is not that the research effort has been a waste of time but that the answer is elusive and difficult to distil into a few words because of the ubiquitous and complex nature of second-language learning. To arrive at a single overarching theory of second-language acquisition, and therefore a method for teaching it is, and will be, a long haul. So we'd better keep doing the blood circulation exercises, ensure that we have embarked on the right flight path and not allow the winds of factionalism or unwarranted orthodoxy to send us in the wrong direction.

I will end this brief chapter by returning to teachers and researchers. Why has there been in the past such a gulf between them, indeed a gulf which has sometimes engendered mistrust? The answer may lie in what appears to teachers as unequal power relations and the fact that research in the past has not always been independent of the influence of policy makers rather than influencing policy. We therefore need to redraw the relationship between research, practitioners and researchers. As Heidi Byrnes (2000) says:

> no longer is it necessary for practitioners to suppress their misgivings about those forces who put pressure on them . . . no longer need they be consumers of research . . . they are increasingly challenged to influence that research if not in its actual conduct at the very least in the topics it should address and how it should address them.

Part 2

Language Learning, the Brain and the Social Context

Chapter 3

Theories, Grammar and Methods

The two most fundamental questions in second-language-acquisition research are:

1. through what processes do learners learn a second language?
2. how can teachers best enable and support those processes?

In order to begin to answer the first question we will look at work which has contributed to the generation of *theories* of how learners acquire a second language. A theory is an attempt to arrive at a logical and coherent set of propositions, based on empirical evidence, which best explain a recognizable phenomenon. In other words a theory attempts to make sense of some aspect of the world. In order to answer the second question we will look at the research evidence on which approaches to language teaching appear to be the most promising in delivering learning in the classroom. Ironically, this second exploration is made difficult by two trends in the field. Firstly, research-based theories of L2 acquisition have paid insufficient attention to classroom-based learning, preferring to scan a broader horizon of acquisition in general and often in experimental laboratory-type settings. Secondly, about 30 years ago, researchers decided to stop researching 'clear-cut methods' in order to see what worked best. Although certain aspects of methods have begun to surface, for example input processing approaches (see below), they have eschewed comprehensive and coherent methods which related directly to a theory of language acquisition. They stopped this line of research because they considered it a fruitless expenditure of effort, providing simplistic and often contradictory answers. Instead, they began to focus much more on the processes of learning and on specific sub-components of the interaction between teaching and learning rather than the overt pedagogical behaviour of the teacher. Whilst this has resulted in greater depth of understanding, it has not facilitated the 'standing back' and seeing the whole picture. I hope that by the end of this chapter that picture will begin to re-emerge and that by the end of the book much of the detail will have been filled in.

In this chapter, therefore, we will look at some overarching theories of second-language acquisition and see their relationships with teaching approaches or methods. Particularly, and in response to the survey in Chapter 1, we will consider the spectrum of positions and approaches to the learning of grammar, the rules and patterns of the target language.

The four-way stretch of second-language acquisition

Broadly speaking, theories of second-language acquisition (SLA) can be viewed as operating on two axes as represented in Figure 3.1. The horizontal axis represents the polarization between implicit and explicit language input, conscious and sub-conscious mental activity, acquisition and learning, natural versus artificial teaching methods.

The vertical axis represents beliefs about how the human brain has developed and how language input is processed; whether language acquisition is something quite special in humans, something we are born with, or whether it is merely a highly specialized form of knowledge just like any other knowledge; whether the language-learning environment can have much of an effect on the rate and final achievement of the learning, and how the environment interacts with innate faculties.

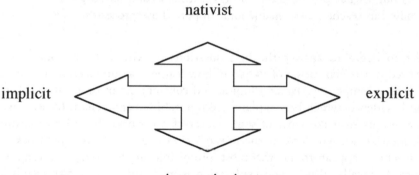

Figure 3.1 The four-way stretch of SLA

Of course polarizations are never absolute and theories as well as individuals place themselves on various stages along the continuum of each of these axes. Indeed a number of theories could be plotted along both axes thus enabling a theoretical position to be 'somewhat more nativist-implicit than interactionist-explicit'. We will now explore these ideas in greater detail and try to present research evidence to back them up.

Behaviourism

Between the 1940s and 1960s, language acquisition was dominated by the psycho-logical theory of behaviourism (Skinner 1957). This posited that language learning was very much like other forms of learning. We learn through two processes: imi-tation and repetitive action, and these lead to habit formation or conditioning. Based on evidence that animals can be trained to perform certain actions through repetitive exposure to certain stimuli-response-reward mechanisms (for example, with dogs: ring bell – sit up and beg – obtain food), it was believed that language was learnt through a series of such mechanisms. Every time a stimulus was associated with a particular response, the mental connection became strengthened. Behaviourist theories attempted to explain how learners can learn the more difficult aspects of the L2, that is, the elements which are least like their first language (L1). For example, *I will buy/j'achèterai* are reasonably similar and stable structures in English and French. By contrast *I gave it to him/je le lui ai donné* are diverging structures in the two languages. Similar structures needed relatively little stimulus-response practice. Dissimilar structures needed a lot. By repeatedly stimulating the right response in a situation where the 'L1-L2 match-up' was not obvious, the learner was gradually weaned off 'thinking in the L1'. Contrastive Analysis is the name given to the study of the similarities and differences in the morphology and syntax between two languages.

Behaviourist theories are lucidly illustrated by a book *Talk French* (Upton 1969) in which learners are asked to listen to a tape and look at, for example, three pictures: the moon, the sun, the stars. They first have to listen. They then repeat after each one: *je vois la lune*; *je vois le soleil*; *je vois les étoiles* (imitation). They then hear only the first picture: *je vois la lune* followed by two beeps (the stimuli) to which they are expected to provide the respective answers to the next two pictures (the response) in the timed gap provided. After each response the tape provides the correct answer again in confirmation (reward). The exercise then goes on to the next set: *je fais la vaisselle*; *je fais le lit*; *je fais les courses*. And so on. The contrastive analysis here determines the need for a lot of practice. 'I can see', is a relatively different structure to '*je vois*' and poses the learner who wants to mentally translate from English into French a number of problems. The contrast between the use of '*faire*' in French and its different equivalents in English (do the washing up; make the beds; do the shopping) poses similar transfer problems. The learner is being encouraged to by-pass reference to his or her L1.

Talk French was supposed to be used in conjunction with the language laboratory, a complementary novelty of the 'white heat of technology' of the post-war period. The idea was that learners could learn on their own, that technology could, in part, replace the teacher. I used *Talk French* with secondary students in the late 1970s. I don't know whether it helped them learn. I think it probably did. It certainly kept them 'quiet'. Some of them even liked using it. Some of them hated it. The fact that the tape kept coming off the spools might have had an impact on the reaction of the latter. I don't know. There are so many variables in language teaching and learning!

Universal Grammar

Chomsky (1965) argued that to conceptualize language as a conditioned response did not take into account just how complex language structure was, nor how young children manage to acquire such mastery of the language without having access either to enough quantity nor to sufficient quality. Put simply, young children can say things they have never heard, so clearly they cannot just be imitating. Children do not listen to 'perfect sentences' from their parents and caregivers but, rather, short, disconnected utterances. Yet children can build their own utterances and even produce (generate) perfect sentences if the situation requires it. Sometimes they make mistakes (e.g. he broked the stick) but this is because they are *generalizing* (extending from a rule or pattern previously learnt or noticed) the lexical input they have received using astonishingly complex but systematic processes. The answer, for Chomsky, therefore, must be that humans are born with a structure in the brain which allows them to 'sort out' any input they receive. This structure was first called by Chomsky, the *Language Acquisition Device* (LAD). This device, it was claimed, was present in all humans, and moreover must be universal because a young child can 'sort out' input whether the input is in Chinese, Spanish or Punjabi. Unfortunately, although there appeared to be theoretical evidence for the LAD's existence, it wasn't very clear what this device actually looked like in the brain. One could describe it by analogy or metaphor but not biologically. For example we could say that it looks like a set of different shapes and sizes of boxes. As an utterance arrives from 'outside' it is sifted for its different morphological or syntactic bits so that each bit can only fit into each individual box. The boxes are then linked in such a way that some utterances or sentences are impossible in any language (e.g. *pen the black*). The problem is that we have found no biological evidence of boxes in the brain. Nevertheless this nativist theory (the belief that humans are born with a special language asset) persisted, despite some challenges, right up to the end of the late 1980s as the theoretical model on which both L1 and L2 learning was built. The model of language acquisition was elaborated and strengthened by researchers (including Chomsky 1980) who investigated the following related areas:

1. Principles and parameters
2. Natural order of acquisition
3. Teachability hypothesis
4. Comprehensible input.

All these related areas had one common denominator: language is rule-governed and it is therefore more or less fruitless to try to intervene; what you are born with is more important than the environment you are interacting with. Let us look at these areas in a little detail.

Principles and parameters

We have noted above that children are able to make very quick progress in learning their first language. This is only possible if language is constrained or governed by some sort of organizing *principle* which cannot be violated. For example, nativist researchers have noted that the structure of an utterance or phrase is dominated by the noun (or subject pronoun) which forms part of a noun-phrase such as 'the tired, overworked and underpaid language teacher' where the 'language teacher' (or 'he/she') is the *head* of the phrase – it governs the structure of the rest of the phrase and any possible additions to that phrase, for example: *the tired, overworked and underpaid language teacher, who was not due for retirement, went to see his boss.* We can move some words around in this sentence but only in a limited number of ways. Sentences are structure-dependent in all languages. This is a universal principle, it is claimed, which actually helps young children acquire the language at this astonishingly fast rate.

Parameters on the other hand are the ways in which, whilst adhering to the principles, languages differ from one another. Nevertheless, they are a finite set of options in a language and they also help the young child to make sense of the input and then use it much more quickly. A parameter which is often cited by authors is the *pro-drop parameter* whereby some languages insist that the pronoun be present in the *head* in declarative sentences (e.g. French: *il arrive en retard*), whereas in other languages the pronoun drops out although its 'trace' can be perceived elsewhere (e.g. in Italian, *arriva in ritardo* is permitted but can only be third person singular). Another parameter difference in French and Italian is the *clitic object pronoun*. In French the following sentence is correct: *le voyant devant le cinéma je* . . . (seeing *him* in front of the cinema I . . .) whereas in Italian the phrase can be expressed as: *vedendolo davanti al cinema ho* . . .   That is, the object pronoun can be stuck on the end of the verb. The fact that these parameters are 'set' either in one way or the other, makes the child's task of learning the first language so much easier. They will need relatively little input in order to 'set' the parameter according to the language they are learning. This helps to give universal grammar theory its explanatory power. The question for second-language theorists is whether adolescent or adult second-language learners still have the same language faculty for 'setting' new parameters. That is, parameters which differ in the L2 from their L1. The question is an important one because if this faculty for 'setting' is still there, then the learner will need very little language input in order to learn rules which are different from the L1.

Natural order of acquisition

The nativist perspective of second-language acquisition includes the notion that certain important language elements are acquired in a particular order and that they cannot be acquired in a different order very easily. This belief, in part, stems from research in first-language acquisition where some fairly invariable sequences of acquisition have been discovered. Moreover, in L2 acquisition, whilst not being rigidly the same, the sequences are similar regardless of the learner's first language. One of the earliest studies which claimed to identify a natural order of L2 acquisition was by Dulay and Burt (1974) who found that Chinese and Spanish children acquired a cluster of English morphemes in the same order. This study was replicated with adults by Bailey, Madden and Krashen (1974) and by Larsen-Freeman (1976) with a greater number of L1s. Thus by 1977, Krashen (1977) felt able to assert that, in the acquisition of L2 English, the *ing* verb ending, the *plural* and the *copula* were acquired before the *auxiliary* or the *irregular past tense*. In his later writings, as we shall see, he was able to argue that there is no point trying to teach these grammatical elements in a different order because the learner's brain will not be ready for them. Like children learning a first language, L2 learners also had their 'in-built syllabus'. Krashen, in fact argued that it was pointless trying 'to teach' them at all. But that's another issue.

Researchers have followed up these studies in other languages. For example Bautier Castaing (1977) found that the difference between 4-year-old French (L1) children's acquired and not acquired structures was not dissimilar from that of 4-5-year-old children with mixed L1s (including Portuguese and Vietnamese) learning French as a

L2, tested after about nine months of living in France. For example, for both groups, the gender differences in the definite and indefinite articles were acquired early whereas direct and indirect object pronouns had not yet been acquired. Building on this study, Harris (1988) found some similarities between French L1 acquisition orders and French L2 acquisition orders in classrooms in England. For example, the present tense of 1st conjugation verbs were acquired early by both groups whereas preceding direct and indirect objects were also acquired late by the English students studying French.

   One problem that these researchers had difficultly resolving was what do we mean when we say that a language element has been acquired? Do we mean we hear it spoken correctly? Written correctly? How often? And so on. One way that researchers tried to solve this problem was to use a system called 'Obligatory Occasion Analysis' whereby if an element was used correctly in those language situations when it *had* to be used and in a sufficiently high percentage of occasions, then it was *acquired*. This partly answered the problem of accuracy and frequency, but not the problem of what acquisition actually is. There were further criticisms of the morpheme studies:

1. What should we make of elements which are misused in situations when they are *not* 'obligatory'?
2. Ranking the order of acquisition was a very coarse way of demonstrating the acquisition sequence, given the number of individual variables found in the studies
3. The research was restricted to a very small set of morphemes
4. The 'sum' of the morphemes came nowhere near constituting the grammar of the target language
5. It suggested that SLA is merely a process of acquiring grammatical items one at a time rather than a number of language elements being encountered and consolidated at any one time and interacting with one another.

The teachability hypothesis

Despite the criticisms of the morphemes studies, a number of researchers accepted that there were some restrictions in the order that we can acquire certain features of the target language. To date, very few studies have demonstrated that explicit instruction of syntax and morphology have a clear effect on the order of acquisition, or at least that the effect is maintained over a long period of time. As a compromise, Pienemann (1984) proposed a hypothesis which posited that the most beneficial type of teaching is one which targets the next development stage of the learner. His research showed that if one attempts to teach far beyond the current stage of the learner, he or she will fail to move to a higher stage, a finding that was supported in a study by Mackey and Philp (1998) which looked at the acquisition of question forms in English. The participants were adult ESL learners with mixed L1s. These were divided into a 'ready group'. These were said to be at a stage where they were hypothetically able to acquire relatively advanced stages of question forms such as 'What do you have?' and 'Doesn't your cat look black?' There was also an 'unready group'. These were at or below a stage where they were still producing questions in a canonical word order which was turned into a question simply by the intonation

('Your car is black?'). They were therefore not ready, it was hypthesized, to acquire the structure at the higher stage. Both groups received corrective feedback in the form of recasts (see below). The researchers found that the 'ready' group were much more likely to move up one stage than the 'unready' group.

Spada and Lightbown (1999) also looked at this very important issue of the acquisition of question patterns in English (L2) among 11-12-year-old learners who had French as their L1. Previous research, such as that of Mackey and Philp (1998), suggested that there were five stages in the acquisition of English (L2) questions:

Stage 1. single words or fragments (without verb): 'Spot on the dog?'

Stage 2. *Subject-Verb-Object with rising intonation*: 'A boy throw ball?'

Stage 3. *Fronting*: 'Do the boy is beside the bus?' (i.e. where all questions start with 'do' – perhaps interference from French *est-ce que*)

Stage 4. *Wh- with copula*; *yes/no questions with inversion*: 'Where is the space ship?'; 'Is there a dog on the bus?'

Stage 5. *Wh- with auxiliary second*: 'What is the boy throwing?'

Spada and Lightbown used a sample of 144 students in Quebec in non-immersion classes – that is, in classes where school work was normally done in L1. However, they had spent five months in intensive ESL classes using broadly communicative methods where the focus was overwhelmingly on meaning rather than correct linguistic form. Pre-tests showed the students to be either at stage 2 or stage 3 with their acquisition of English L2 questions. The classes were subjected to a two-week intervention of an hour a day during which the students were provided with high exposure to English questions at stages 4 and 5. In other words, the teaching was essentially implicit. They found at post-test that:

1. Only 29% of students moved from stage 2 to stage 3
2. Only 18% of students moved from stage 3 to stage 4
3. Only 3 of 144 students moved up by more than one stage
4. Students were not able to cope with inversion and non-inversion with noun and with subject pronouns. That is, they accepted wrong phrases resulting from L1 influence. They found it difficult to acquire the 'Can John come to the party?' inversion.

Clearly their results do not lend much support for the teachability hypothesis which would have predicted that *many more* students would have moved up one stage given the 'input flood' they were exposed to. On the other hand, the learners that *did progress* did so through the acquisition sequence without skipping stages. In that sense Pienemann's hypothesis *was* supported. The researchers tentatively concluded that it could be the *type of instruction* that did not lead to more students moving up a stage and even skipping stages. We will return to this study later when we look at types of teaching methods and grammar.

A number of other researchers have put Pienemann's hypothesis to the test. Whilst accepting that there was strong evidence of patterns in the order in which learners acquire features of the L2, and similarly among different first-language groups learning the same L2, they nevertheless felt that there was also evidence of the influence of the L1 in developmental sequences.

Zobl (1985) for example investigated the acquisition of *possessive adjectives* between French and English. The problem with this feature of the two languages is that French uses the same pronoun for both *his* and *her*. In fact it could be said that the words 'his' and 'her' do not exist in French. Zobl proposed that the most advanced stage in the acquisition of this feature was when French (L1) learners could correctly use *his* and *her* (English L2) where the object had 'natural gender' – that is when it most countered what we might call 'L1 intuition and interference': *her father; his mother*. If the French (L1) learner could acquire these more difficult features, they wouldn't have any problem with, for example, *his car* and *her pen* which are comparatively neutral. Zobl's hypothesis was confirmed. Learning the most difficult features of possessive adjectives did automatically trigger implicit learning of easier features of the same syntactic element. Of course this countered Pienemann's hypothesis only in part. That is, it demonstrated that within syntactic or morphemic stages a rate of learning could be projected successfully to a higher level, not that stages could be skipped altogether.

The teachability hypothesis remains controversial. Yet it is very important to teachers and curriculum planners. As Rod Ellis (1994: 627) puts it:

> It is of both theoretical interest to SLA researchers and of practical importance for language pedagogy, to ask whether formal instruction can 'subvert' the natural order and also whether it can enable the learner to acquire target language constructions immediately and so to avoid transitional constructions.

Comprehensible input

We will have noted that Spada and Lightbown (1999) used implicit teaching methods for trying to put across the difficult (and in terms of contrastive analysis different) concept of questioning in English. This approach stems, to a large extent, from the writings of Stephen Krashen and his associates (Krashen 1981, 1987, Krashen and Terrell 1988). Taking into account the earlier nativist notions of *principles and parameters* and of *natural order of acquisition,* Krashen formulated the now famous Comprehensible Input hypothesis (CIH) which together with his Monitor Theory provided the constituents of his model of L2 acquisition. I will only restate the CIH part of Krashen's work as this is most pertinent to the present discussion.

Input that can be understood by the learner is the primary vehicle of second-language acquisition and development. Input is made comprehensible by the teacher (or the native speaker interlocutor) adapting the language roughly to the comprehension level (N.B. not the production level) of the learner. The learner's knowledge of the context will fill in the missing bits and understand any new language items. The marriage of context and language will ensure that any new language in the input is acquired. Elements in comprehensible input, following our 'boxes' analogy earlier, will flow into the brain and lodge themselves in the right boxes. As a natural order of acquisition obtains, the teacher need not target the input at the next stage (what Krashen calls *information + 1*) in any formal way. The teacher can go beyond the next stage as long as the input is comprehensible. The only other condition that is needed is for the learner to be open to the acquisition process. Learners need to have a low 'affective filter' in order to be emotionally well disposed to the input. According to

Krashen, 'speaking is a result of acquisition and not its cause' (Krashen 1985: 2). Speaking emerges as a result of a system of language competence having been established in the brain through exposure to comprehensible input over time.

One of the biggest challenges to CIH came from studies of immersion classes in Canada where young students were exposed to enormous amounts of comprehensible input and where relatively little talking in the L2 was required of them. Harley and Swain (1984) found from their research that these children continued to make a large number of errors when they spoke. The issue here is not whether immersion is a good or bad teaching method, nor whether accuracy is important. Immersion may well deliver the objectives of fluency, range of vocabulary and idiom, and generate self-confidence. The issue was that, at a theoretical level, comprehensible input alone was not delivering the acquisition of all language patterns. If students were converting input into competence, why was that competence faulty?

The other objections to CIH were that, as a theory, it was simply too vague:

- What exactly is the difference between *acquisition* and *learning*?
- What does *comprehensible* actually mean?
- What does *information + 1* actually mean?
- Does the *affective filter* exist in biological terms?

A number of researchers, therefore, set about modifying CIH. We will be looking in detail at some of this research in the chapters on listening, on oral interaction and also later in this chapter in the discussion with regard to the teaching of grammar. However, I briefly summarize here the historical flow of the research and debate following Krashen's CIH. It should be noted at this stage that these are all still claims to theory with different levels of support.

1. In order for the learner to comprehend, it is not sufficient for the teacher simply to modify his or her input. The listener must also be involved in modifying the input through clarification requests and confirmation signals. Teachers need to carry out comprehension checks by asking the learners if they have understood. Listening is an *interactive* process. Meaning has to be *negotiated*.
2. In order to acquire new language it is not sufficient simply to understand it. The learner must bring about some kind of *selective attention* to the new language item, spotlighting it long enough in order to process it and store it. The best time to do this is during a breakdown in interaction and when, as a consequence, meaning is being negotiated.
3. In order to acquire new language it is not sufficient just to spotlight it and keep silent. In order for acquisition of language to occur the learner must also *use* the language in oral production. This does three things: it increases the intensity of the spotlight on the new item as *input*; it forces the learner to attend to the construction of the new language just before and during *output*; it encourages confirmation from the teacher/interlocutor that the production is correct providing additional evidence for the learner's hypotheses about the target language. This has come to be known as the Comprehensible Output Hypothesis. (Swain 1985)

We will return to these interaction-related themes several times later on this book.

Cognitive processing

Although the above challenges to Krashen's acquisition hypotheses were significant, they remained, by and large, within the nativist paradigm. According to this paradigm, we should remind ourselves, there is something different about language learning from the learning, say, of a date in history or how to drive a car. This paradigm was not really challenged until the late 1980s. When the challenge came, in the form of cognitive processing, it came once again from psychology rather than linguistics and it marked half a pendulum's swing worth of return to behaviourist models of language acquisition. Interestingly, this swing coincided with another major advancement, the development of the microchip and of extremely powerful and efficient computers. One of the major criticisms of the nativist position was that their explanation of second-language acquisition did not provide a *process*, a rational and detailed explanation of the way the L2 was acquired. The nativists, to put it crudely, made it sound a bit like magic. Computers, with their mathematically generated systems of learning, and with their reliance on electronically conducted impulses, provided psycholinguists not only with an analogy for the brain, but an actual (although basic) prototype for the human mind.

The quest for cognitive psychologists is to find scientific means for studying the processes in the brain involved in the acquisition and application of knowledge. As McLaughlin argues, the focus is *not* stimulus-response (as in behaviourism) but *mental events*. The cognitive approach also emphasises *mental structure* or *organization*. The cognitive approach stresses the notion that the individual is *active, constructive* and *planful* (McLaughlin 1990).

We will consider two aspects of the broad term *cognitive processing*:

1. The role of working memory and its relationship with long-term memory
2. Connectionism

As always, these aspects are not discrete nor their boundaries impermeable. We will then look at other aspects of cognition both in later chapters and in the section on progression and development in this chapter.

Working memory and long-term memory

An enormous interest has been displayed by psychologists, in the past three decades, in the different components of memory and this has been a very fruitful effort in terms of being able to explain language-acquisition processes. Although views differ as to what the components of memory actually are and how they function in relation to one another (see for example an excellent book edited by Miyake and Shah 1999), there is general consensus as to how their performance affects cognition. By cognition we mean how information from the world outside our brains is perceived, decoded, processed, stored, retrieved and re-encoded. Much of this information, of course, is in the form of aural and visual language. The consensus among psychologists lies principally in the notions of *capacity* and *duration*. In order to explain this we will need to look at one model of memory, that of Baddeley and his associates, and one which after nearly 30 years of being posited (Baddeley and Hitch 1974) still has the power of credibility (Baddeley and Logie 1999). Figure 3.2 illustrates the components of working memory (WM). These components interact in order to operate as the 'go-betweens' of the outside world and long-term memory (LTM).

A model of memory

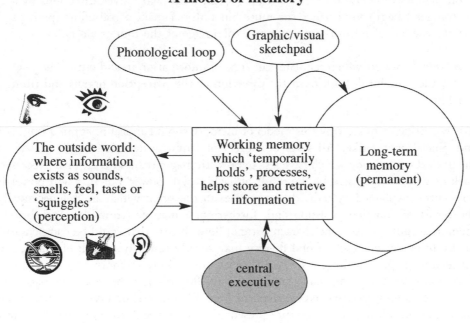

Figure 3.2   A model of memory. Adapted from Baddeley and Logie 1999

LTM, as far as we know, is permanent. Once information is 'properly' stored in LTM it cannot be deleted unless by disease or physical intervention such as a blow to the head or a surgical operation. We do not forget because the information in LTM decays but because the components in working memory are not able to access the information because the strength of the pathways to LTM have not been activated for some time. The phone number of the house I lived in ten years ago was 'properly stored' in LTM but I can't, just this minute, retrieve it. I may be able to if I work hard enough at the task. Of course, what one means by 'properly stored' is not absolutely clear but this is one of the reasons why researchers in applied linguistics in experiments give participants a 'delayed post-test'. It is an attempt to ensure that the information has had the opportunity to be properly stored before they can make any claims that it has been learnt. As we can see from Figure 3.2, WM has three main components. In very simplified form these are:

A *phonological loop* which temporarily stores linguistic information and allows us to keep circulating the information so that it does not decay. For example when making an arithmetic calculation we keep the information activated by repeating certain bits of it under our breath. The loop has limited *capacity* (for example the number of digits that it can deal with at any one time) and limited *duration* (how long it can hold that set of digits in the loop).

A *visuo-spatial sketchpad* which projects internal images for us. Again the visuo-spatial sketchpad is temporary. The graphic image of a word or phrase will be wiped off if we do not constantly attempt to re-activate it. It will also be wiped off if something else interferes with it. When I am being given directions by a stranger I begin to visualize the route but unless I make a real effort (perhaps with the aid of auditory information), the image of the route soon fades.

A *central executive* which regulates the flow of information in and out of the loop and the sketchpad, both from the direction of the perception organs and from LTM.

It is not difficult to see why this model of memory should appeal to applied linguists and practitioners alike. All sorts of aspects of language learning begin to have a theoretical explanation which have less to do with magic than with rational processes. Lack of *attention* may still be the result of 'lack of will power' but that will power is now better explained by individual processes in the brain which are not necessarily the result of conscious volition and, furthermore, may be 'treatable'. Inability to memorize could be just one characteristic of 'low ability' that could be compensated for by intervention. Lack of oral fluency may simply result from lack of practice in processing longer and longer strings of words in working memory.

A cognitive processing model of SLA is a reaffirmation of the repetitive nature of human learning. Practice makes perfect. As Nick Ellis (2001) observes, we should not allow the complexity of the picture presented to us by SLA to camouflage the fact that underlying it are some remarkably simple development processes. Language is cognitive information just like other information. It's just that adult humans, because of their complex interactions, have turned it into extremely complex information. Ellis argues, alluding to Darwin who also made the complex simple, 'we are enlightened when we substitute a process description for a state description, when we describe the development rather than the final state, when we focus on the language acquisition process rather than the language acquisition device' (2001: 38).

Connectionism

In the previous section we focused more on the working memory half of the WM-LTM partnership. We will now look briefly at how, according to cognitive-processing models, LTM stores language.

Connectionist explanations of language acquisition (McClelland and Rumelhart 1986) perceive language storage as an infinitely complex set of connections between *nodes* (or cells) in the brain. This reinforces the analogy with the computer. Connectionism is sometimes known as *parallel distributed processing* because of the *non-linear*, *multiple-source* and *contemporaneous* conceptualization of how language is processed.

The individual nodes are able to contain fragments of information and it is in their interconnections that language is stored and retrieved. These interconnections form pools of information and they are the structures within which regularities, rules and patterns begin to be formed. There are then connections between these pools of nodes allowing ever-increasing strengthening and weakening of connections. Moreover, the model allows for different processes to occur simultaneously, or in parallel.

How is language stored and retrieved in the connectionist model? Picture a pin-ball machine with its series of mushroom-like posts that light up (or 'fire') as the ball rebounds and ricochets between them. Think of the ball as the input stimulus, for example a new (L2) English word such as 'the ash' which has been noticed and worked on in the WM of a French (L1) adolescent. The word hits a post with which it *associates* but also rebounds and makes a number of connections with other posts: *hâche* (L1 phonological connection), hash (other L2 phonological connection), *le frêne* (L1 semantic connection), tree (L2 semantic connection), *arbre* (L1 semantic connection), *the* tree (syntactic L2 connection) *l'arbre* (syntactic L1 connection) *le/un frêne* (L1 syntactic connection), the ash *is* big (syntactic connection), *les frênes* (morphological connection), *le frêne dans le jardin de ma grand-mère* (emotional connection).

The storage of the word 'the ash' will have been secured by these connections and many more. Retrieval will be via the *activation* of these connections. The pin-ball input is fired in, cannons around firing up a number of posts/nodes. But which post/nodes does it activate (psychologists might say *excite*)? What will stop any given stimulus from, say, producing 'the ash are tree'? In other words where are the rules that avoid the chaos? Connectionist principles are founded on the absence of pre-determined rules (the boxes in the brain), but there has to be a substitute system. According to the model, chaos is avoided by the building up of *probabilities*. Because of the sheer number of repeated interconnections there is a *very high probability* that our French L1 speaker will not say 'the ash are tree'. Probabilities, according to connectionist theorists, explain better than do innate rule systems, how we can learn exceptions to rules such as irregular verb inflections. The rule-governed regularities in language are gradually built into a kind of *L1 architecture* (to which there is a predisposition in humans) where the position of language elements in different types of sentences (declarative, interrogative, passive) are constantly reinforced. Once developed, the architecture stays constant and can be accessed when operating in L2.

This part of the model explains *where* linguistic information is stored and *from where* it is retrieved but not precisely *how* it is stored and retrieved. We have no secure *biological* definition of this process. In other words, we do not know if each node (as a living organism) contains ideational information (information which does not have linguistic form) or language-encoded information. It is more likely that the information is not language encoded. This would account for the fact that, in the model, linguistic knowledge is not seen as distinct from other types of knowledge (e.g. the fact that fire hurts if you touch it) and for the belief that there is no separation between the L1 and L2 lexicon (see vocabulary chapter for a fuller account of this). However, for the purposes of the explanation above I have taken the nodes to contain language-specific information as if they were somehow *tagged* as L1 or L2.

For some theorists, the *regularities* in the connectionist model are not the same as Universal Grammar (UG). Connectionism according to some (e.g. Pinker and Prince 1988; N. Ellis 2001) is irreconcilable with nativist models. The hidden mechanisms, 'the architectures' within connectionist models, are incompatible with UG which is governed by universal principles and limited sets of parameters. Others, for example Ney and Pearson (1990), argue that connectionism and UG are not totally incompatible precisely because connectionism does not totally exclude innate neurological mechanisms which determine *to some extent* the structure of language and how it is used (1990: 477).

Ney and Pearson demonstrate the practical application of the two dimensions of connectionism, that is, the rule-governed dimension (the architecture) and the rote learning of exceptions to rules via associative patterns. They do this, interestingly enough, through a return to more behaviourist approaches to teaching (Paulston 1970), that is, through an exploration of the pedagogical micro-objectives of the types of drills found in L2 classrooms:

1. mechanical drills – controlled response; no need to understand the content.
   Example:
   Pattern: *I'm holding a book*
   Cue: *magazine*
   Response: *I'm holding a magazine*
   Cue: *Banana*
   Response: *I'm holding a banana*
   Cue: *Wug*
   Response: *I'm holding a wug*

2. meaningful drills – controlled response; learner needs to understand both the structure and the semantics of the message. Example:
   Question: *When did you arrive this morning?*
   Answer: *I arrived at 9 o'clock.*
   Question: *When will you leave this evening?*
   Answer: *I'll leave at six o'clock.*

3. communicative drills – no control of the response; the student has a free choice of answer; both speaker and interlocutor need to attend to meaning; learner needs to make form-meaning connections and use rule-based utterances.
   Example:
   Question: *What did you have for breakfast?*
   Orthodox response: *I had toast and coffee for breakfast.*
   (alternatively)
   Possible unorthodox response: *I overslept and skipped breakfast so I wouldn't miss the bus.*
   (Examples cited in Rivers 1983: 45-6)

Connectionism, therefore takes a big leap forwards from pure behaviourism in that language learning results from the growing strength of interconnections between nodes through individual volition, filtering and restructuring of input. The associative patterns become so strong that the speaker acts *as if* he/she has an unlimited capacity to generate new utterances. The implication for the teacher is that while L2 teaching need not exclude non-communicative activities, it must include a strong communicative component in order to move the learner towards freedom of expression.

Connectionism is given further 'order' by research into the processes of *competition* in the brain. MacWhinney's competition model (1987a, 1987b, 2001) is designed to quantify the ways in which input is distributed around the nodes in order to control language processing and hence language learning. The basic claims of the model are that:

1. Language comprehension is based on the detection of a series of *cues* (present in any given language) in the input.
2. In infancy, areas involved in auditory processing and motor control are under intense pressure towards neural 'commitment' to these cues and to the refinement of these cues (*pre-disposition*).
3. Examples of these cues to which a language learner's nodes *commit* themselves are: Pre-verbal positioning of nouns; verb agreement; nominative case markings for pronouns.
4. Lexical items are activated *before* full syntactic frames. Lexical items dominate the processing of the input.
5. Cues are in constant *competition* with one another both in comprehension and production. For example, words compete for lexical activation, phrases compete for syntax order, and sounds compete for insertion into syllabic slots.
6. The *reliability* of these cues – how constant they are in the language – and the *availability* of these cues how often they occur in the language determines the strength of the cues when we try to understand an utterance/sentence and hence the *probability* that we will understand (or in reverse order produce) it correctly.
7. Cues are different in different languages and much more varied than the system of *principles and parameters* we met in the nativist model. L2 learners will attempt to transfer L1 cues to L2 comprehension and production.
8. In post-infancy L2 learning, the competition is increased by the presence of the L1 but it is kept within bounds (i.e. there are fewer errors than we would expect) by the fact that a great deal of transfer occurs smoothly and directly and some types of transfer errors are quickly corrected by the L2 learner. Transfer errors lead to transfer cues being weakened. That is, the L2 learners will progressively rely less on L1 cues which do not transfer unproblematically.

To illustrate this section on connectionism, let us look at a study by Watanabe (1997) in which he investigated whether glosses in reading texts help with vocabulary retention and why. We will look at further studies on vocabulary acquisition in Chapter 4 but this one provides a good example of what we mean by *in-depth processing* within a connectionist model. We should note, however, that this contributes to an explanation of vocabulary acquisition rather than to the acquisition of the rule system. Watanabe noted that previous research had concluded that *incidental* vocabulary learning through context (i.e. without selective attention focusing on it) is possible but it is not always efficient. L1 research suggested that vocabulary acquisition through reading can be improved by:

1. illuminating the context around the unknown word;
2. clarifying the connection between the context and the unknown word;
3. making the contextual information explicit;
4. the completeness of the contextual information being provided.

Watanabe therefore sampled 231 Japanese (L1) learners of English at Japanese universities. They were assigned to different experimental groups plus a control group. The text consisted of 500 words of which 16 *new* target words were to be recalled by the students (i.e. evidence of learning) after reading it. Watanabe made a number of modifications of the reading text by adding L1 glosses:

1. in the text (immediately after a new word, in between two commas). In other words, the gloss was non-explicit.
2. in the margins. The gloss was explicit.
3. in the margins but as multiple choice (in order to see whether the decision involved in selection helped to strengthen the memory trace).

Watanabe found that:

1. marginal glosses and multiple-choice glosses produced significantly better recall than 'in the text' glosses;
2. there were no differences between marginal and multiple-choice glosses in terms of recall;
3. all experimental groups recalled the words better than the control group who just read the text.

He speculated on the reasons for these results:

1. 'In the text' glosses lacked clarity of connection between the explanations and words to be explained.
2. The reader may have thought the 'in the text' glosses were additional information not an explanation.
3. The reader may have skipped over the new word since the gloss was immediately provided.
4. Glosses in the margin, on the other hand, forced the reader into three input processes:
   (a) Input 1 – first encounter with unknown word (hold in visual memory; possibly sound out in phonological loop for connections)
   (b) Input 2 – understand its meaning from the gloss (further connections made)
   (c) Input 3 – attention returns to the word in text and checks that meaning fits in the context (further connections made with context).

Watanabe wondered if the multiple-choice glosses failed to be more successful in producing recall because the students chose the wrong alternative or whether they were confusing. There is another possible explanation and that is that one connection trace competed with another thus cancelling out each other's strength. Whatever the reason, this study illustrates how acquisition is greatly enhanced by selective attention to form-meaning relationship by increasing the depth of processing.

Initial implications

At this point we will have an initial round-up of the SLA theories described so far and their implications for language-teaching approaches and methods. Nativist models argue that since we are born with a special language facility and that facility is still available when we learn a second language as adults, the amount of influence that targeted input can have is minimal. The crucial factor is that there should be plenty of realistic input for the innate rule system to work on. Interactionist models explain acquisition much more via the brain's interaction with the complexity that is language in the outside world. The type of language the brain comes into contact with and the type of input and interaction will establish the associations which affect acquisition. Nativists would not require learners to employ much attention and effort. Interactionists and cognitivists claim that learning a language requires just as much attention and effort as the learning of other knowledge.

Both these models of language acquisition, therefore, depend on the primacy of input. Where they differ is on the type of input. Nevertheless they differ on input within certain boundaries and this should lead us to draw some tentative first conclusions with regard to teaching methods. I am making the assumption that our goal in second-language teaching is still to lead students towards the kind of communicative competence originally defined by Canale and Swain (1980). That is, an L2 speaker should demonstrate *grammatical competence* by showing strong evidence, through performance, of having internalized the rules and patterns of the target language; s/he should demonstrate *strategic and discourse competence* by using the kinds of communication strategies in and awareness of the conventions of discourse transferable from first language; that s/he demonstrate *sociolinguistic competence* through an awareness of how the target language is used in the different speech communities where that language is used. With this premise in mind, it is unlikely that the 'traditional' grammar-translation method would provide the kind of input that would lead to communicative competence. There is, as we shall see, compelling evidence that learners can learn *some* language implicitly, it is also unlikely that the nineteenth century's Direct Method will lead to the language autonomy and language-learning autonomy that underpin communicative competence because of its refusal to look upon interaction as being a complex set of un-sentence-like exchanges.

Certain aspects of audiolingualism can be, and indeed are, incorporated into approaches that may lead to communicative competence. However, they are *not sufficient* to lead to it. The input is not sufficiently realistic and the interaction is not of sufficient quality to lead to communicative competence.

Some explicit focus on form would, however, appear to be necessary. If we take as evidence the Spada and Lightbown study above (1999) on the acquisition of questions, negative evidence in the input would appear to be essential. Without explicit instruction of this kind it may be that learners will continue to assume that English, like French, permits un-inverted questions. Students may need to be told that questions with noun subjects and no inversion are not grammatical in English.

What we are left with, therefore, is a process of constant exploration within a broad and eclectic approach called communicative language teaching. The theoretical evidence so far does not underscore the efficacy of a strong version of CLT where learners in the classroom learn entirely from teachers and students producing communicative utterances in the L2, ones which the listener did not already know the content of. We have to set forth on a path of deciding what we mean by a weak version of communicative language teaching. It is the purpose of the rest of this chapter to explore what that weak version of CLT might look like and how this helps learners to progress towards communicative competence. However, not all learning environments are the same. In fact second-language learning is characterized by an astonishing array of different learning contexts. It is the strength of CLT to adapt to different learning contexts which gives it its durability.

The COLT observation schedule

I have alluded above to the few recent research studies focusing on specific teaching methodologies and, as we have noted, the number of different learning contexts introduces a huge number of variables when one tries to test the efficacy of a teaching method. One path we could therefore explore in our search for what CLT looks like for our particular classroom is by returning to the work of Fröhlich, Spada and Allen (1985) in the mid 1980s. They devised a schedule which was aimed at differentiating between different types of classroom by examining the Communicative Orientation of the Language Teaching in different types of young student classrooms in Canada: Core French (closest to the FL learning environment in monolingual contexts such as that of England); Extended French; French Immersion; English as a Second Language. The schedule was divided into two parts:

Part A looked at Learning activity; Participant organization; Lesson content; Student modality; Materials

Part B looked at opportunities to produce language; engage in sustained speech; initiate discourse; react to meaning; exchange unknown or relatively unpredictable information. Analysis included *rating the communicative orientation* of different classrooms via:

1. How much group work was offered;
2. How much focus on meaning there was as opposed to focus on form;
3. How much use of extended texts there was;
4. How often semi-authentic and authentic materials were used.

They found that Core French had the least communicative orientation; students gave fewer unpredictable responses; students had the shortest speaking turns; had the most restricted utterances (i.e. the topic and structure of the discourse was imposed by the teachers).

The question we have to ask ourselves with this study in mind is does the learning context determine the communicative orientation of the teaching? Is it unavoidable, given the circumstances? If we are teaching in the 'core French' type of classroom, is that as far along the communicative continuum that we can go? One way of attempting to answer this question is to look at teaching approaches which do not have an input-leading-to-output direction of progression.

An input processing model of L2 teaching

The notion of selective attention (the spotlight on the new word or form) is taken a stage further by VanPatten who has proposed that the explicit exposure to grammar rules *prior to* input processing by the learner raises the learner's sensitivity to features in the input and an awareness of the ineffective processing strategies that should be avoided (VanPatten and Cadierno 1993; VanPatten 1996). Perhaps more importantly, a further four principles are proposed by VanPatten in his model of input processing. I have adapted these to create the conditions for what might be described as *quality input processing*.

1. Learners should not be asked to go against their natural inclination to process input for meaning before they process it for form.
2. If learners *are* to attend to form-meaning connections in input this should be in situations which do not produce cognitive overload.
3. Learners' natural inclination is to focus attention on lexical items (see MacWhinney above), nouns in particular, and especially first nouns in an utterance (the *first-noun strategy*).
4. Because of WM capacity limitations, learners process the initial parts of an utterance best. If we want them to focus on the latter parts of an utterance, the input would have to be of a special kind in order to change the way the input is processed by learners.
5. There should be *no focus on output* (as in traditional grammar teaching).
6. The intake must continually provide the developing system with examples of correct form-meaning connections that are the results of input processing.

This issue of whether selective attention is best focused on quality input processing or on output-based instruction was put to the test in a study by Benati (2001). He took a sample of 39 university students of Italian (English L1) in England on an institution-wide language programme (i.e. not language specialists). The instructional focus was the acquisition of the future tense which, it has to be said, is not very difficult. The sample was divided into two experimental groups and one control group (randomly assigned). Benati provided the experimental groups with an intervention of 6 hours duration.

- *Group 1* the teaching was entirely comprehension-based; non-paradigmatic explanation of rules; lexical tense markers (temporal adverbs such as 'tomorrow') were removed in order to force students to focus only on inflected endings in order to get the meaning
- *Group 2* output-based practice; explanation of rules by paradigm; less focus on meaning
- *Group 3* (control) received no instruction in target features but was subject to a comparable amount of exposure to the target feature (but not systematic like group 1).

He then gave all groups a series of tests based on the standard pre-test; post-test; delayed-test (three weeks later) design.

- *Test 1* measurement of knowledge – interpretation tasks; subjects established whether sentences were in the present or the future.
- *Test 2* written grammar test – future derived from the infinitive.
- *Test 3* oral test based on pictures.

Benati found that:

1. On test 1, both experimental groups outperformed the control group.
2. Group 1 outperformed group 2.
3. On tests 2 and 3, both experimental groups outperformed the control group but no difference was found between group 1 and group 2.
4. The delayed post-test showed that the instruction effect was maintained.

This study suggests that students can learn certain features of the target language, such as the future tense without having had output-based instruction. Quality input-processing can be sufficient. There is no need, therefore, to subject learners to mechanical output drills. However, this type of form-focused instruction does lead to greater acquisition of grammatical features than instruction that does not attend to form in any way. Three caveats should be borne in mind with this study. The sample size was rather small. The future tense in Italian is relatively straightforward. The control group's form of instruction is not sufficiently well explained for us to be clear how it differed from the other two groups.

Task-based approaches to teaching

One challenge to the inertia built into secondary foreign language classrooms (see above) comes from the notion of task-based learning (di Pietro 1987; Prabhu 1987; Skehan 1998). This approach starts with the notion that the problem-solving properties in a task are the driving force behind the learning of new language rather than new language learnt being exemplified or assessed via an eventual task such as a role play, simulation or information-gap activity. Task-based approaches to language learning are in direct opposition to Presentation, Practice and Production (PPP) approaches. For Skehan (1998: 95) the following are the concepts and definitions of this approach.

A task is an activity in which

1. meaning is primary;
2. there is some communication problem to resolve;
3. there is some sort of relationship to comparable real-world activities;
4. task completion has some priority;
5. the assessment of the task is in terms of outcome.

Tasks:

1. do not give learners other people's language to regurgitate;
2. are not concerned with language display;
3. are not conformity orientated;

4. are not practice orientated;
5. do not embed language into materials so that specific structures can be focused upon.

The types of tasks that Skehan proposes are not that different from tasks that appear in some of the more imaginative PPP classrooms. The difference is one of emphasis and procedure. That is, the objectives that learners are given to undertake and the way they are given to achieve the task, and the fact that they start with the task. Whilst one is intuitively attracted to the notion of task-based learning because of its forcing of highly demanding cognitive effort and because of its avoidance of the drudgery of language input, there remain in the literature a number of unanswered questions.

1. How do tasks operate for beginners or near beginners? Where does the language that *they* will need come from? For example most tasks proposed by Skehan are of the type and level: 'explain to your partner how to get to your house so that an oven which has been left on can be turned off' (1998: 110). Task-based approaches therefore appear to pre-suppose a certain threshold of proficiency.
2. The role of the first language in the classroom is unclear. Is the task to be resourced by monolingual resources (i.e. materials and teacher operating only in L2) or by bilingual resources?
3. Where is the direct evidence that task-based learning leads to better proficiency than, say, PPP approaches?

Particularly teachers who are operating in the secondary foreign-language classroom would need answers to these three questions. We will now look at one of them. The role of the first language.

Codeswitching in the L2 classroom

The use of the first language has been of great interest to me both as a teacher and as a researcher. Perhaps it is as a result of going through a personal period of changing bilingualism during which the second language gradually became the first language. Anecdotally, *balanced bilingual*[1] teachers seem to be able to perceive a greater role for the learners' first language in the L2 classroom than do less-balanced bilingual teachers.

From a theoretical perspective, the use of the first language as part of the input is more justified in the cognitive-processing models of language than in the Universal Grammar model. Particularly in a connectionist model which incorporates a non-language-specific lexicon, where all connections have, as it were, equal value, the first language can have at least as substantial a facilitating acquisitional role as it can have an inhibitory role.

Empirical evidence, as we have begun to see from the Watanabe study, exists that L1 explanations can assist with the acquisition of vocabulary during reading. We will explore further evidence of this in later chapters.

Evidence from surveys of teachers and learners, regarding their opinion as to whether the L1 should be excluded from the L2 classroom, is quite clear that it should not (Macaro 2000b). The way that L1 is regarded and how much of it should be present in the input and interaction, however, is still highly contested (Macaro 1997, 2001b).

Internationally, there has been a recognition that the native-speaker-teacher model is no longer necessarily the most productive one (Cook 1999). In part this is a reaction to the destabilising effects on first language and home culture of the creeping internationalization of the English language – some would say its linguistic imperialism (Phillipson 1992; Skutnabb-Kangas and Phillipson 1995). Another reason for this transformation is the increasing view that the non-native-speaker-teacher is actually more in tune with the L2 learner by sharing his or her mental characteristics and history of learning (Medgyes 1999).

For the above reasons, a number of researchers including myself have stopped using what might be considered pejorative terms for the use of the L1 in the classroom (for example, 'recourse to L1', as in Macaro 1997) and opted for the more positive term, *codeswitching* (switching between two or more languages). French researchers now use an equally positive term: *alternance* (Castellotti 1998; Coste 1998; Garabédian and Lerasle 1998; Simon 1998). I would want to argue that we should see codeswitching as positive because:

1. Codeswitching in *naturalistic* discourse (i.e. outside the classroom) occurs when a speaker and an interlocutor share more than one language or dialect. It occurs because the speaker finds it easier or more appropriate, in the linguistic and/or cultural context, to communicate by switching than by keeping the utterance totally in the same language.
2. Codeswitching occurs frequently and is widespread throughout the world's bilingual and multilingual communities. The fact that bilinguals can codeswitch is an asset and a valuable addition to their array of communication strategies.
3. In an increasingly global economy speakers from different countries will need to be able to codeswitch effectively for the purposes of communication rather than relying on operating in a single language.
4. Codeswitching in the L2 classroom should therefore be considered as a valuable communication strategy, perhaps of equal value as input modification by the teacher and even, possibly, approaching the value of interactional modification between teachers and learners. Forbidding learners to codeswitch will result in them not being able to learn how to use it sparingly and in a principled way.
5. Teacher codeswitching (following on from points 2 and 3) may be a way of modelling some essential learning strategies for learners to consider deploying themselves – for example, strategies which lighten the cognitive load whilst reading.
6. There is as yet no evidence that teacher codeswitching correlates with increased learner use of the L1 in oral interaction (Macaro 2001b; Macaro and Mutton 2002). Conversely, there is no evidence that banning the L1 from the classroom produces better L2 learning.
7. Banning codeswitching from classrooms, particularly beginner and lower-intermediate classrooms, may lead to a number of undesirable pedagogical

practices, for example teacher domination of discourse or obstacles to learner-centred oral interaction. There is some evidence of this in my study of novice teachers (Macaro 2001b) and those of experienced teachers (Macaro 1997; Macaro and Mutton 2002).

Further research evidence is needed on the positive and negative effects of, particularly, teacher codeswitching. For example, studies need to explore whether (and in what circumstances) input modification (such as paraphrase; L2 exemplification; stress and intonation) or negotiation of meaning (clarification requests, comprehension checks) are more likely to result in acquisition of new vocabulary, and in what circumstances, than a brief teacher codeswitch. This research evidence would contribute to an eventual pedagogical set of principles of codeswitching in the L2 classroom.

Progression and development

We have taken time-out from theories of SLA to look at some initial implications for language teaching. It is time to return now to a consideration of theories regarding how learners progress in general in their language learning and how they develop from one stage to another. We have already touched on this in our consideration of the *developmental stages* of learners and the *teachability hypothesis* for which, we concluded, there was some evidence, with *some* morphemes and *some* syntactic patterns, for a sequence of acquisition which was fairly constant across learners and which was difficult to change or subvert through highly targeted teaching. Let us now look at other ways L2 learners progress and develop.

A basic principle: the interlanguage hypothesis

The *interlanguage hypothesis* (a term first coined by Selinker 1972) has grown out of the same fertile research soil as the discovery of developmental stages. The hypothesis considers the distance that the L2 learner has to travel from his/her L1 monolingual state to L2 native speaker like competence and makes a number of assertions.

1. The errors that learners make at every stage of their development demonstrate strong features of *systematicity*.
2. The errors that learners make at every stage are not the result of laziness, stupidity or lack of care, but are a consequence of them trying to generate hypotheses about what the target language must be like.
3. Their *interlanguage* however is *unstable* and during certain stages a learner can produce two or more variations of an error. It is this state of instability, together with further evidence from input, which stops errors from becoming *fossilized*.
4. That L2 learners' hypotheses are erroneous is in part due to transfer from rules in their L1 but by no means overwhelmingly so. They are just as likely to over-generalize (some researchers call it over-extend) rules from what they already know of the L2.

5. Learners create unique rules in their heads which are neither L1 rules nor L2 rules. In a sense, they are creating a series of 'mini-grammars'.

The interlanguage hypothesis, as the underlying principle of L2 progression, has stood the test of time and can now can be considered as a stable theory underpinning much of the SLA research enterprise. The implication for teachers is that learner errors should be treated as part of the process of learning and not discouraged. Moreover, the interlanguage hypothesis paved the way for pair and group work because 'their mistakes were minor irritants rather than major hazards' (Cook 2001: 16) and bad habits and/or immediate fossilization were not likely to occur from listening to a peer's uncorrected mistakes.

From declarative knowledge to procedural knowledge

The transition in LTM from *declarative knowledge* (knowledge that is known and understood as a fact – the 'what' and the 'that') to *declarative knowledge* combining with *procedural knowledge* (knowledge of 'how to do') owes much to the work of Anderson (1983) and his Adaptive Control of Thought (ACT) model. In this model, all knowledge is initially declarative. Declarative knowledge is retrieved from LTM by 'interpretive' mechanisms in working memory via a process of selection, evaluation, rejection/acceptance. Procedural knowledge is retrieved by a process of 'match and execute' – if Y then X; if red traffic light, stop car. This transition from declarative to procedural knowledge, for some aspects of cognitive behaviour, *has* to happen. We would not, otherwise be able to explain the complexity of our actions in, for example, playing the piano. In the case of language production, this transition explains the fact that we don't have to select, evaluate and accept/reject every word. Procedural knowledge takes up less space in the limited confines of working memory than does declarative knowledge. Proceduralized retrieval allows complete productions to be accessed at the same time (Towell *et al.* 1996). Proceduralization does have its drawbacks, however. Once knowledge has become 'automatized' it no longer has the same flexibility for change within itself, nor can it be modified by selective attention and consequent action. In order to modify procedural knowledge, the acquirer of that knowledge has to make a considerable effort to focus on the proceduralized action for sufficient time in order to 'bring it back under conscious control'.

The transition from declarative knowledge to procedural knowledge is an important theory underpinning research on learning strategies. The actions that learners engage in order to learn a language, because of their repetitive and often fleeting nature, are considered to go through a transition from declarative knowledge to procedural knowledge. For a comprehensive account of declarative and procedural knowledge linked to strategy research see O'Malley and Chamot (1990). Some implications of declarative and procedural knowledge for teaching are given throughout the 'skills chapters' in this book.

Restructuring

Restructuring is a term usually attributed to the work of McLaughlin and his associates. In Anderson's ACT model we may be able to see the initial state and the end result but not the stages or processes that learners go through. Like Anderson, McLaughlin's work demonstrates that second languages are learnt via the progressive integration of subskills which start as controlled processes but which then become automatic (McLaughlin 1987). The *Restructuring* can be viewed as 'a process in which the components of a task are coordinated, integrated or reorganized into new units thereby allowing the procedure involving old components to be replaced with a more efficient procedure' (McLaughlin 1990: 118).

This restructuring, in second-language acquisition, often results in a U-shaped curve of learning. The progression may be from an exemplar-based representation in the brain to more rule-based representations. Let us take a number of examples. In the case of morphological development (Figure 3.3) *Cheval-chevaux* may first be learnt as set equivalents for horse and for horses. The learning then appears to dip as the learner experiments with *chevals* as a hypothesis for the plural before rising again to a rule-based automatized *cheval-chevaux*. In Figure 3.3 we can see a similar U-shaped curve in *syntactic* development where the lack of equivalence in French-Italian gender for 'flower' temporarily causes the learner problems before a restructuring occurs. Figure 3.3 gives an example of a *semantic/collocational* dip (English L1, French L2) whereby the initial stage is context specific (take = *prendre*), the second stage results in an unacceptable L1 transfer before a gradual restructuring returning finally to an automatized *sort*. Finally, Figure 3.3 shows a U-shaped *strategic* progression from recourse to a formulaic phrase, to an unpacked or generated (possibly short and possibly incorrect) phase, to a final phase which involves re-chunking but this time in more flexible form. This last figure demonstrating restructuring is complex and will be further explained in the next section.

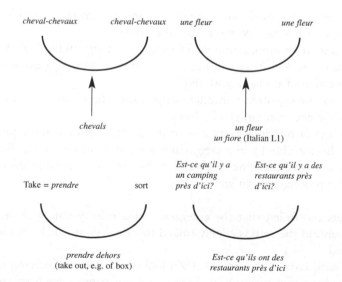

Figure 3.3 Four U-shaped curves

From formula to generated phrase and back again

A formulaic phrase is basically a cluster of words which are used by a learner automatically, without thought to the different bits which constitute it. As I have
suggested in Figure 3.3 this may be because the learner does not have the grammatical knowledge to analyse what is inside the phrase or because he/she has
restructured and moved beyond the need to *control* (to bring selective attention to) the
bits inside the phrase. That is, they are used as a production strategy in order to
increase fluency. In the research we are about to review in this chapter, however, we
will be focusing on the first type, that is to say the learner who has not yet learnt to
unpack the formulas. Formulaic phrases are also known as *unanalysed chunks* or *set
phrases*. Weinert (1995) proposes that the criteria for recognizing a chunk should be:

1. fluent, non-hesitant production
2. frequently used
3. longer and complex (i.e. recognizably above level of learner)
4. situationally dependent (e.g. *'j'ai fini'* in class at the end of a task)
5. community-wide use (i.e. in L1 or classroom community)
6. inappropriate/incorrect use in certain contexts.

Myles *et al.* (1998) add that chunks should be at least two morphemes in length (i.e.
j'ai can be a chunk) and that they may be used wrongly or inappropriately. Myles *et
al.* (1998) studied the gradual unpacking of chunks of a group of 16 pupils in years 7
and 8 in England, learning French. The data was collected over the two years. Using
pair tasks both with peers and with the researcher involving information gap, they
focused on *j'aime, j'adore, j'habite* as unanalysed chunks to see how these developed
over the research period. They also observed how these interacted with other phrases
such as questions (*Où habites-tu?*) and negatives. They found that:

1. Pupils frequently used *j'aime* in over-generalizations (for example, *la garçon
   j'aime le cricket* – for 'Does the boy like cricket?').
2. There was an enormous amount of variation among individuals both in
   amount of use and in rate of progression from chunk to analysis (i.e. in the
   segmentation of pronoun and verb).
3. There was a recognizable interlanguage stage where there was a mixture of
   target-like and non-target-like forms.
4. The subset of pupils who used *je* creatively included the same pupils who
   could also use chunks in a target-like way, without over-extending them.
5. Pupils who were breaking down the chunk did not stop using the chunk when
   it was appropriate to do so.

The researchers concluded that the emergence of a rule system with regard to the
subject pronoun and the verb is closely linked to a process in which the chunk begins
to get analysed.

Using the same data, Myles *et al.* (1999) looked at chunks involving questions in
French. As we have seen earlier with English L2, questions have been considered of
major importance in terms of observing the interlanguage development in L2 learners. The researchers ensured that the oral tasks from which the data were collected

could not be completed successfully merely by the recitation of complete, memorized dialogues. They focused on 'naming questions' (*Comment t'appelles-tu?*). They wanted to see when the students started to use third person reference (i.e. *il/elle*) with increased frequency – having been exposed to these on a number of occasions by the teacher. They found that:

1. Only one student had completely internalized the third person form of questions by the end of the research period.
2. Subjects resorted to a variety of different strategies: extending questions (over-generalizing) without internal alteration: *Comment t'appelles-tu . . . un garçon?* (for 'What's his name?').
3. It was difficult to trace any clear collective developmental patterns in the group data. However, inversion did provide a pattern. Inversion is commonly hypothesized as complex and it is predicted that subjects shift as a developmental stage, to the canonical form when generating or translating. By round 5 of the data collection, more than half the interrogatives had shifted to a declarative order.
4. There was a school effect – emphasis in the teaching led to more use of *il* and *elle* as components of their naming questions.

Table 3.1 provides an example of the development of three of the students from the Myles *et al.* (1999) study.

Table 3.1   Progression from formulaic phrase to generated phrase in interrogatives

Student 2	Student 1	Student 3
Comment t'appelles-tu? (formulaic)	*Comment t'appelles-tu?* (formulaic)	*Comment t'appelles-tu?* (formulaic)
	Comment s'appelles-tu?	
	Comment t'appelle-euh s-s-comment s'appelle-tu?	
To:	To:	To:
Comment s'appelle la fille? *Comment s'appelle qu'elle?* (which suggests phonology issues)	*Comment s'appelle-tu?*	*Comment il t'appelles-tu?* *Comment elle t'appelles-tu?*
Clear progression towards TL production	Some analysis taking place	Awareness of need to unpack but no resources with which to do it

Adapted from Myles *et al.* (1999)

Myles *et al.* invite us to note that the *Comment t'appelles-tu* and the *il/elle s'appelle* chunks seem to be interacting in order to help the learners sort out the subject pronoun system. Again, the researchers concluded that interrogatives provide evidence that analysis of chunks form the basis of a fledgling creativity in language production.

It is interesting to see evidence of the interlanguage principle in this progression. It is clear that the fact that the more generated phrases are wrong doesn't mean that they (and the learners) are not developing.

Once these phrases have been 'unpacked', there is a return to more automatized uses of them in order to promote fluency. Although they appear to be more automatized, we should be aware that, at this final stage the phrases are available for further unpacking and restructuring by the learner should this be necessary. We will return to this under the topic of fluency in the chapter on speaking.

Initial implications of progression research

We have seen that, in a variety of developmental features, things may seem to get worse before they can get better. As teachers we need to encourage the dip in the U-shaped curve, recognizing and feeding back to the students that they are making progress. But there are questions still to be answered at the pedagogical level. At what point in the stages might some kind of teacher intervention most profitably be employed? Should it be at the middle stage when the students seem ready to start unpacking the formulas? And just how is a teacher to differentiate between students who are further along the stage of formula analysis? Why do some learners start unpacking and others do not? Is the reason psycholinguistic or is it sociolinguistic? Is it the result of teacher behaviour, for example, of the learner not being encouraged to look for meaning in a chunk beyond the function it serves?

We should not necessarily draw the conclusion that the mistakes are the result of lack of grammar teaching. For example, a study by Kuhlmeier *et al.* (1996) found that students using a communicative course achieved higher scores than those using a grammar-translation course in writing, grammar, spelling, vocabulary knowledge and listening. This brings us neatly to the topic of how to teach grammar. Perhaps it is better to put this in a way that doesn't focus on the teacher. We should ask, how are the rules and patterns of the target language best learnt?

Ways of learning grammar

The backlash against Krashen's pure implicit approach to language acquisition has been international. We have seen some evidence of this in studies above. In the USA Tracey Terrell (1991), co-author with Krashen of 'the natural approach' (Krashen and Terrell 1988), provides a powerful rearguard action against explicit grammar instruction (EGI) by concluding from the evidence available that EGI does not increase fluency, rate of learning, order of learning or ultimate attainment and that even with regard to accuracy the improvement does not show immediately although it may show long term. Nevertheless she concedes that EGI can affect the acquisition process by

1. acting as an advanced organizer of input (see VanPatten earlier)
2. acting as a meaning-form focuser or developer

3. by providing forms of monitoring which, in turn, will be available to assist with acquisition during the moment of output.

In England too there has been a backlash against 'communicative methods'. Wright (1999) alludes to a critique of CLT provided in *Language Learning Journal* by Hurman (1992), by Metcalfe *et al.* (1998) and by Klapper (1997). The problem is that these are inadequate critiques of CLT. Hurman's study provides evidence of reduced accuracy but greater fluency and range of vocabulary as a result of the introduction of 'communicative-based' GCSEs (exams at 16 in England and Wales). Metcalfe *et al.* identify a teaching problem, the lack of verb awareness, but this is related more to poor quality teacher-pupil interaction rather than the failure of implicit or semi-implicit methods. Klapper (1997), as I read him, far from advocating a return to formal grammar teaching (i.e. explicit and adopting syllabuses which are structurally led), provides a very balanced account of the respective requirements of secondary and higher education. He points to the fact that higher education in fact misses out on opportunities for 'varied and effective language teaching' (1997:23) and seems to identify at least two institutional problems: university tutors don't like having to teach grammar and, more and more, language in higher education is being taught by inexperienced teachers. Critiques of CLT can quite rightly be made of its 'pure form', as Klapper goes on to argue. But the pure form of CLT certainly is not what has been the majority of practice in English secondary schools. The problem of slow progress towards communicative competence is much more complex and I try to unpick this throughout the course of this book. The whole 'grammar debate' in England has been conducted at a very superficial level. While this book will (I predict!) end up basically agreeing with Wright on the need to improve *competence* in the secondary phase (1999: 38), this is to be done as an eventual product of a much more informed debate about how learners learn the rules of the target language. The debate, in my view, cannot be conducted on the basis of vague terms such as Wright employs (italicized below by me with page numbers in brackets) without a much clearer definition being provided:

> Grammar was somehow *out* (33)
> *Formal* instruction (34)
> *Explicit* positive evidence (34)
> A *grasp* of underlying grammar (35)
> Grammar *control* (35)
> *Accuracy* (35)
> Full *ability* range (35)
> The *less able* (35)
> *Teaching* at least the *key grammatical concepts* such as gender, tense, negatives, number, questions, imperatives (35)

Some research evidence

Frantzen (1995) investigated whether explicit grammar teaching plus corrective feedback improved (a) grammar knowledge (b) writing accuracy. She used a sample of 44 intermediate level (Spanish L2, English L1) second-year university students studying a 'content' course. She assigned them to experimental and control groups.

The treatment lasted over one semester and consisted of 15 minutes of explicit grammar teaching/review, and corrective feedback consisting of correct models of errors, some notes in margins, correction of errors by students in class and resubmission to the teacher. The control group's errors were circled only by the teacher. She used pre- and post-tests: a discrete-point grammar test; an essay of 200-250 words. She analysed the essays for both fluency and accuracy. She found that

1. both the experimental and control groups made significant progress in both types of tests over the semester in terms of accuracy;
2. the experimental group improved more than the control group on the grammar test;
3. there were no significant differences on the essay for fluency and accuracy. In fact the control group outperformed the experimental group on one measure of accuracy, the Indicative.

Frantzen concluded that grammar accuracy can be improved by message-oriented interaction. Explicit grammar teaching improves explicit grammar knowledge but not accuracy in performance. That is, it is not carried over to performance of language such as writing an essay. Discrete-point tests and essays, in fact, give evidence of different types of grammar abilities. We should also note that no other holistic measures of proficiency are given. For example, it would be interesting to know if the experimental group's 'content knowledge' suffered as a result of losing 15 minutes to grammar instruction.

Manley and Calk (1997) also investigated whether explicit grammar teaching led to reduced errors and improved writing performance. They found that although *some* error reduction resulted with *some* aspects of the French rule system, this did not lead to holistic improvement in writing. This study is reviewed in greater detail in Chapter 9.

Spada (1997) provides an excellent overview of the research on how the rules and patterns of the target language can be learnt. The review, however, is framed within the confines of form-focused instruction (FFI) which she defines as 'any pedagogical effort which is used to draw the learner's attention to language form either implicitly or explicitly'. She adds that FFI research has been primarily in contexts where L2 instruction is essentially meaning based, that is, not in a context in which grammatical rules are presented first, in explicit fashion and then practised, let alone in a grammar-translation methodology. It is only within these tighter parameters that she asks the question, does the type of instruction make a difference?

Spada's conclusions are that there is no definitive answer to this question. Some studies suggested that a mixture of corrective feedback *and* metalinguistic teaching were most beneficial. Some studies suggested that only *some* features of language benefited from this mixture. Some studies showed that *simultaneous* focus on meaning and form can overload the learners' cognitive system. Some showed that *learner-learner* interaction allows learners to focus on both form and meaning. Some showed that learners can focus on form better in *receptive tasks* than in productive tasks. In other words, even within the parameters of essentially meaning-based classrooms, the results are mixed and in any case relate only to the acquisition of targeted language features rather than the whole picture of proficiency. The research literature does not yet allow us to stand back, try to look at the bigger picture and say anything more precise than this: In most contexts it is more beneficial to focus on communicating meaning rather than on explicit grammar teaching. However, in that communication of meaning, the spotlight must be directed, by the teacher, at certain aspects of the form of the target language.

But how does the teacher direct the spotlight? One way that has been investigated almost exhaustively is in the area of *recasts*.

Recasts and teacher echo

Considerable attention has been given to recasts and teacher echo as one of the simplest ways for teachers to encourage the learner to focus on form. A typical recast is the third part of an Initiation-Response-Feedback exchange, although it can occur in less structured discourse:

> T: *Paul, tu as un animal à la maison?*
> Paul: *Oui, j'ai une chat.*
> T: *Oui, j'ai un chat.*

Thus recasts are utterances by the teacher that repeat the student's incorrect utterance but make the minimal changes needed to reproduce a correct utterance, not change the meaning in any way. A recast can, in addition, have varying degrees of emphasis: stress on the corrected language element; pause immediately before it; louder voice during it; body language, and so on. Teacher echo is simply a teacher's repetition of correct responses.

Why should we be interested in this?

Recasts are, as we shall see from the research, a highly prevalent feature of all communicatively oriented language classrooms. But what function do they serve? Do they result in *uptake* by the learner? That is, do the learners notice the recast as feedback and stop and reflect on it? Do learners attempt a self-repair as a result? Do recasts, in effect, provide effective negative evidence for the learner responding? What is the effect on the other learners? If recasts do draw the learner's attention to the error do they also risk upsetting the sensitive student in front of his/her peers?

Recasts have a pedigree stretching back to L1 research of the 1970s where *interactionists* demonstrated that simple recasts were effective in helping the child make more rapid progress in L1 development (Richards 1990a and 1990b). In other words the 'language environment' could make a difference to the rate of acquisition. However, in the L2 classrooms the recast has an additional function and that is to acknowledge the content of the preceding turn, thereby allowing the teacher to retain a high measure of discourse control. Does this run the risk of the recast being ineffective because it becomes so routinized that the student who has responded (nor the others in the class who are listening) does not notice the corrected feature? *Noticing* (that is bringing one's selective attention to a feature of the target language) is for many researchers a necessary requirement of language development (see Schmidt 1990 for an account of the noticing hypothesis as part of the role of consciousness) although its effectiveness has been critiqued (Truscott 1998).

Routinization of recasts is exacerbated by *teacher echo*. Teacher echo, as we have noted, is simply repeating in the feedback, what the student has said in the response even though the response was correct. I consider the implications of teacher echo more thoroughly in Chapter 8. For the moment we will conceive the practice as being detrimental to *noticing* because it does not help the learner make a distinction between correct and incorrect target language forms.

The research evidence

Nicholas *et al*. (2001) provide a comprehensive overview of L2 recasts as negative feedback to learners and the arguments as to their effectiveness. The reader wishing to explore this theme in depth would do well to start with this review.

Recasts, as I have suggested, are extensively used in classrooms. According to a study by Doughty (1994), they represented nearly 60% of teacher feedback. In her study recasts were more likely to follow a single, minor error in a student's response rather than 'big problems'. There was no indication either way in her data of whether learners noticed the corrective feedback. Further evidence of lack of *uptake* as a result of recasts is provided elsewhere. For example in Lochtman's (2000) German foreign language classes in Belgium, uptake was low. However, of course, we do not know whether the students were repeating the corrected form in their heads or sub-vocalizing.

Havranek (1999) investigated to what extent learners recall corrective feedback from the teacher of their own or their peers' mistakes, and whether these recasts led to improved performance in tests. She also wondered whether there was a connection between recall of corrective feedback and test results. She therefore recorded 1,700 instances of recasts, provided the students with questionnaires to see what they could recall of their teacher's corrections and adminstered a number of tests. She found:

1. There was only about a 50% success rate. Half the errors were committed again either in the same way or in a different form.
2. Less than a third of the learners who were corrected remembered having been corrected.
3. Peers paid little attention to the correction of others.
4. Whether the corrections were recalled or not recalled made little difference to whether the errors were or were not committed later.

Calvé (1992) after a discussion of the relative types of errors that the teacher is confronted with (in oral discourse) observes that teachers on the whole apply a fairly haphazard approach to recasts. For him coherence and systematicity of recast is of prime importance, followed closely by the necessity not to demotivate or embarrass the student responding. Furthermore he proposes that students should be informed of the purpose of recasts and be given supporting materials during interaction which help them to notice and process errors.

Doughty and Varela (1998) carried out a study in middle-school ESL (science) lessons taught by one teacher (Elizabeth Varela). The authors had noted that although a theoretical construct of 'focus on form' had been posited, there were few clear procedures for how a teacher might go about *focusing on form* without undermining the overarching communicative orientation of the lesson. The authors chose a narrow focus, past time reference, as a treatment for the experimental class. They observed inaccurate use of past tenses over a series of science report tasks which had past tense as a prevalent and natural feature. Varela therefore used recasts over the treatment period in order to see if this improved the students' interlanguage. An example given is:

Student: *I think that the worm would go under the soil.*
Teacher: *I think that the worm will go under the soil?*
Student: *no response.*
Teacher: *I thought that the worm would go under the soil.*
Student: *I thought that the worm would go under the soil (continues with experiment report).*
(from Doughty and Varela 1998: 124)

Using pre- and post-tests, they found that the experimental class made significant gains over the control class both in oral and written measures of the past and conditional tense. Indeed the experimental class maintained their advantage even in a delayed test. They noted, moreover, that the students were beginning to self-correct before the teacher had the opportunity to recast. The authors conclude that this type of focus on form is unobtrusive, and is effective particularly if it is carefully planned, frequently applied but has a narrow focus, that is, it should not be indiscriminate recasting.

Thus one feature of recasting that seems to be important is that they should be fairly salient in the discourse. Nicholas *et al.* (2001) observe that when teachers are familiar with the types of errors students make they are able to understand the students' meaning in spite of the errors and will offer a recast as a natural, almost conversational type of feedback (2001: 741). In other words the recast lacks salience and fades into the background of the discourse.

A coherent and in-depth collection of studies has been carried out by Lyster and his associates. Lyster and Ranta (1997) identified six main feedback-to-error moves in L2 classroom interaction:

1. *Explicit correction* teacher clearly indicates that the student utterance is incorrect and supplies the correct form.
2. *Recasts* teacher implicitly reformulates all or part of the student's utterance.
3. *Elicitation* teacher directly elicits a reformulation by asking questions (*Comment ça s'appelle?*) or by pausing to allow students to complete teacher's utterance (*parce que c'est . . .* (student) *un éléphant*).
4. *Metalinguistic clues* teacher provides comments, information or questions related to the well-formedness of the student's utterance (e.g. *C'est masculin?*).
5. *Clarification requests* teacher uses phrases such as 'Pardon?'; and 'I don't understand.'
6. *Repetition* teacher repeats the student's ill-formed utterance, adjusting intonation to highlight the error (but taking the problem no further unless there is uptake from the student).

The results of their analysis showed that recasts were by far the most widely used feedback-to-error technique. However recasts resulted in the *lowest rate of repair* by the students. In contrast elicitation, metalinguistic clues, clarification requests and repetition of error not only led to higher rates of uptake (i.e. noticing the feedback) but also highest rates of self or peer repair. Thus Lyster and Ranta considered Moves 3-6 to be a kind of *negotiation of form.*

Lyster (1998a) wondered to what extent feedback from teachers actually constituted Form-Focused Instruction. He noted that some have argued (e.g Van Lier 1988) that teachers should delay corrective feedback so as not to deny the learner the opportunity to self-repair. Lyster therefore analysed 27 lessons (18 hours) taught by four French immersion teachers in grades 4 and 5 (primary – English L1). The recasts were catagorized by *type* and coded as

1. isolated declarative (corrected model provided, with falling intonation, no additional meaning)
2. isolated interrogative (repeat in isolation learner's mistake with rising tone)
3. incorporated declarative (corrected item embedded in further information)
4. incorporated interrogative (corrected item embedded in further developed question – rising tone).

Lyster found that Type 1 was used in 67% of recasts; Type 2 in 12%; type 3 in 17%; type 4 in 4%. Thus the vast majority were recasts which neither provided nor sought additional information (i.e. one might speculate that the learner's focus is on form). However, once again, almost two-thirds of recasts did not result in uptake by the students. He concluded that the majority of recasts, in communicatively oriented L2 classrooms, are unlikely to be either negotiated or noticed by young L2 learners as negative evidence. Moreover, it is difficult for learners to distinguish the purpose of recasts from L2 teacher echoes.

Using the same data, Lyster (1998b) analysed to what extent different forms of teacher feedback were used as reactions to different errors and also what was the resulting repair by the students. Errors were coded as grammatical errors; lexical errors; phonological errors; unsolicited uses of L1. His analysis of the 921 'error sequences' showed that

1. 61% were followed by corrective feedback of some sort
2. 33% of corrective feedback led to learner repair
3. 46% of all feedback followed grammatical errors; 24% lexical errors; 19% phonological errors; 11% uses of L1
4. 60% of feedback moves were recasts; 34% negotiation of form; 6% explicit corrections
5. Recasts were used mostly for grammatical and phonological errors (probably for social and expediency reasons)
6. *Negotiation of form* was used mostly for lexical errors
7. Interaction between error type and feedback type was significant
8. Phonological errors had the highest rate of repair followed by lexical errors
9. Only 22% of the grammatical errors were repaired
10. Only 17% of L1 use was repaired
11. Where grammatical errors *were* followed by negotiation of form, this produced most repairs (significantly more than recasts)

12. Grammatical errors tended to recur within the same lesson in spite of corrective feedback.

In contrast to other studies (for example Calvé's above), Lyster did detect some degree of systematicity in teacher feedback:

1. Teachers gave most feedback to error types which occurred most frequently.
2. Corrective feedback on phonological and lexical errors was quite consistent.
3. Teachers did tend to select feedback types in accordance with error types.

Lyster concluded that recasts of grammatical errors probably do not provide young learners with the negative evidence that they require to know what is acceptable in the L2 and that perhaps teachers need to draw more frequently on *negotiation of form* in response to grammatical errors.

In the Mackey and Philp (1998) study already looked at in the section 'The teachability hypothesis', the participants were also divided into those that received recasts and those that did not. They found that the 'ready' group who received recasts were more successful than the 'ready' group that did not. The 'unready' group did not do significantly better as the result of receiving recasts. These researchers also looked at the response that the learners gave to the recast (sometimes known as 'uptake'). Most learner responses were 'continues' (they did not repeat correctly or modify their initial wrong response). However, given that recasts appeared to be beneficial in delayed post-tests, Mackey and Philp concluded that the fact that most learners do not respond (uptake) to the recast does not mean that they are not learning from it. The recasts may function as part of a 'database' for the language learner.

Ellis *et al.* (2001) were also concerned with learner uptake (what we might also call 'evidence of noticing the focus on form by the teacher'). They wanted to research whether learner uptake was taking place and if so where, how and why. The reasons for being interested in uptake were:

1. It is a student *move* (a contribution in the discourse).
2. The move is optional (i.e. Focus on Form does not obligate the student to provide an uptake move).
3. An uptake move occurs in episodes where there has been an observable gap in knowledge.

Ellis *et al.* researched three adult classes in New Zealand studying English with mixed L1s. The lessons were divided into neat halves. The first half consisted of explicit grammar teaching followed by a break. The second half was 'broadly communicative'. The researchers analysed 12 hours of CLT. They identified FFEs (Focus on Form Episodes) and identified an FFE in every 1.6 minutes of the second half of the lessons. They divided them into three categories:

1. responding FFEs (when the teacher spots a problem and provides a recast)
2. student initiated FFEs (when the learner identifies a problem they are having)
3. teacher initiated FFE (when teacher thinks there might be a problem and preempts the problem via a Focus on Form).

The researchers discovered the following aspects of uptake:

1. There were high levels of uptake overall even in response to recasts (contradicting earlier studies).
2. Uptake was most frequent in student-initiated FFEs.
3. Uptake was most likely to occur in episodes involving negotiation of meaning.
4. *Successful* uptake (i.e. correct form produced) occurred most frequently in responding FFEs.

Ellis *et al.* report no negative effects on the communicative orientation of the lesson. Teachers and students appeared to be able to navigate in and out of FFEs without problems and while keeping the overall orientation to message intact. They concluded that encouraging the students to ask their own questions about form (in addition to teacher feedback) was very effective. However, they observed that recasts are not a problem in motivated adult classes but may be a problem with younger children, presumably because of greater socializing effects.

Initial implications of recasts and teacher echoes

The evidence as to the beneficial effects of recasting is mixed. Some studies suggest that the classroom context may not always make it easy for learners to notice recasts and therefore they may not result in learning the targeted form. Modified output occurs most often when teachers signal an explicit need for clarification rather than simply providing a recast. There is some evidence of effectiveness in narrowly focused, highly salient recasts, perhaps with particular aspects of the target language rule system. However, a teaching approach that emphasises self-repair is more likely to improve the learners' ability to monitor their own L2 speech. It is the saliency of the correct form that leads to acquisition not merely the provision of implicit negative evidence. This may be because in speaking rather than writing the student has less time to focus attention simultaneously and autonomously on both meaning and form. However, there are two problems with over-emphasizing negotiation of form. Firstly it may gradually lead the focus of the lesson towards a single or series of grammatical points. Secondly it may throw the spotlight too much on individual students, particularly beginners and younger students, who are struggling with form and who may be embarrassed in front of their peers. Ways round this latter problem are proposed by Calvé (see above) and I have suggested (in Macaro 2001a) a number of scaffolding materials which can help (at least) the students not immediately engaged in the interactive exchange to note down what they have 'noticed'. Teacher explanation of the purpose of these materials would be essential. This could have the additional benefit of keeping large classes attentive during teacher-whole-class interaction. Unfortunately there is not enough space to pursue this here.

We have seen that FFI is conceptualized in the literature as being meaning-centred but observable behaviour in the interaction between teacher and students. Further research is needed to establish whether (as Ellis *et al.* 2001 define it) it should be incidental (as the problem arises), transitory (teachers do not dwell on the problem) and broadly focused (many different forms can be focused on in the same lesson).

Horses for courses

Some very interesting research has gone into investigating whether some aspects of the L2 rule system can be taught more explicitly than others. As Mitchell (2000) observes, we are not yet in a position to know how to select which grammar items might effectively be taught. Some teachers, of course, may feel with a degree of justification, that their experience is enough to tell them which grammar *can* be taught explicitly, which grammar *must* be taught explicitly and which grammar is best just *forgotten about* with certain groups of learners. An interesting account of 'good rules' and 'bad rules' is given in Forth and Naismith (1995) with practical suggestions for how to approach them. Nevertheless, some empirical basis for intuition and experience is always useful.

In a fascinating study, Green and Hecht (1992) investigated 300 German learners of English with between 3 and 12 years of exposure to English. Most were from secondary schools: Gymnasium, Realschule and Hauptschule, an indication of the achievement levels of the students. They were asked to correct 12 errors in context and offer explanations of the rule. A comparison group of native speakers of English was used to ensure validity. They found that:

1. Most students had not learnt the rules they had been taught (only 46% produced an acceptable rule).
2. Higher achieving students did better at providing rules. (However, given the different schools, this may have been due to teaching approaches.)
3. Learners were able to correct the errors without knowing the rules.
4. If they had produced a correct rule, however, they almost always were able to correct the mistake.
5. Some rules had obviously been easier 'to learn explicitly' than others.

That learners were able to correct errors without knowing rules, for Green and Hecht these results suggested that there is no simple relationship between knowledge of explicit rules and being able to correct. For them, 'the solution may lie in distinguishing between rules that are easy and rules which are hard to learn. The pay-off for the time investment may be much greater for the former' (1992: 179).

The difficulty of learning a rule may have to be counterbalanced by how important in the target language it is to have a mastery of a particular rule or set of rules. I have always had an interest in the 'teachability' of *aspect* in Italian and French, the difference between the *perfect* (PR) and *imperfect* (IMP). For students with English L1, aspect in these two languages is important because

1. PR and IMP are the most common past-tense verbs used both orally and in written form;
2. in many messages, the speaker/writer is forced into making a decision between these two past tenses whereas in English s/he is not (for example, by using the past simple as in 'I went to the beach every day');
3. the IMP often lacks direct correspondence with the English lexical equivalent 'was/were'. For example: 'I was scared' is by no means automatically *J'avais peur/Avevo paura*;

4. in French IMP endings sound the same, both in their paradigm and when compared to PR endings.

Moreover, and perhaps because of the above difficulty, textbooks (and some grammar books) provide inadequate explanations of aspect. In Macaro (2002a) I provide evidence of the contortions that some grammar-book writers get into in order to provide a rule for *aspect*. Those that try to be 'student friendly' end up giving helpful but ultimately insufficient explanations of the rules. In my experience native speakers of French or Italian are just as incapable of giving explanations of rules for aspect as non-natives. So are the rules of aspect un-teachable?

Blyth (1997) proposes a *constructivist* approach to the teaching of aspect. He dismisses non-learner-centred approaches to the learning of grammar because they conceal 'the dynamic relationship between grammar and the mind' (53) and perpetuate the myth that

1. a grammatical syllabus can be derived without problems from a language;
2. grammar consists of isolated facts called grammar points;
3. acquisition of the rule system is simply a matter of the accumulation of these grammar points;
4. learning of grammar can be done by explanation of rules followed by mechanical drills and the occasional communicative exercise.

A constructivist approach bases itself on the notion that there is *no actual reality out there*. Each person constructs his or her view of reality. A constructivist acquisition of the high-level rules of aspect is through the learner slowly accumulating evidence from input. Both Blyth (1997) and Macaro (2002a) demonstrate the futility of drawing horizontal lines on the board in order to show that the perfect aspect ends the action. Indeed I posit that, if anything, it is the beginning of the action that will provide clues as to PR and IMP.

Ayoun (2001) neatly tied up our interest in recasts with the problems of aspect in French in her study of the role of positive and negative feedback. Citing Harley's (1989) study of aspect, she noted that past research suggests that whilst focused input showed *some* signs of enabling learners to use the distinction better in production, the evidence was not conclusive as the effect did not last over time. Ayoun used a sample of 145 US university students (English L1) at three different proficiency levels to investigate the effects of recasts in the written form. The groups were divided into *three conditions*: recasts provided (i.e. negative evidence); model provided (pre-emptive, positive evidence); grammar provided (explicit grammar teaching with rules). The *recasts* group had to respond to computerized stimuli of sentences in a story which were either the *imparfait* or the *passé composé*. They were exposed to it for three seconds then provided with a gapped version which they had to fill in. The correct version then came up on the screen. The *model* group were shown a sentence for three seconds. They were then required to answer a related question with the infinitive part of the verb only being given. Ayoun found that

1. all three groups improved significantly between pre- and post-test;
2. *recast* students improved the most followed by *model* students and then *grammar* students;

3. differences between *recast* students and *grammar* students were significant.

Ayoun concluded that negative feedback is more effective than traditional grammar instruction and may also be more effective than simple positive evidence. Students (at least adults as in this study) need an environment which promotes the processes of attention and memory, while stimulating their interests (i.e. through communication). One problem with Ayoun's study was that the recast was in written form. One wonders whether the same results would obtain in the oral medium whole-class interaction situation.

Implications for the teaching of aspect

The way forward is to approach aspect (and other complex/opaque rules) from a number of directions.

1. Massive exposure to target-language input containing contextualized examples of PR and IMP. This allows a gradual restructuring in the brain with regard to the problems of transfer from L1. Particularly it develops in the learner an awareness of the *backgrounding* and *foregrounding* effect of aspect in a text (Blyth 1997). Rather than a clear cut distinction between description (imperfect aspect) and action (perfect aspect) it is a question of perceiving which, in the context, is more in the foreground.
2. Form-focused instruction. In essence all narratives depend on perfect aspect to advance the plot. The imperfect does not advance the plot. Get students to put an arrow on every verb in a narrative text that advances the plot (Blyth 1997). Ensure that students are considering aspect from the perspective of the speaker/writer as it is actually occurring, not from some imagined reality.
3. If students still require further help (or demand a rule), try the following from Macaro (2002a):
   (a) If it's describing age, time, size and colour in the past – it's *likely* to be imperfect.
   (b) If it's not (a), then isolate the verb that's causing you the problem. Can you put *e poi* ('and then') in front of the verb so that it feels OK to you – in other words is the verb bringing the story on a bit? – *e poi, e poi, e poi?*
   (c) Think about the text and context around what you are trying to say. Is there evidence 'in *your* mind's eye' that there was a time *before* the action when the action definitely was not happening?
   (d) Is the action pretty much in the foreground?
   (e) If the answer to (b), (c) and (d) is 'yes' then it's *very likely* to be the perfect.

For the 5% of sentences that these rules of thumb don't work, well it just doesn't matter!

Conclusions

This chapter has charted the development of theories in second-language acquisition and attempted to draw broad implications for the teaching and learning of L2 in the classroom. We have seen an initial pendulum swing away from behaviourist, audio-lingual approaches, through Chomskyan inspired theories of how all languages are acquired and a partial return swing in the shape of cognitive-processing models of SLA. This return was, in part, because nativist accounts were not able to provide a comprehensive pedagogical approach (whether input driven or rule-governed) for teaching in the huge variety of educational contexts in the world of the late twentieth and early twenty-first centuries. Moreover, aspects of language, such as formulaic language sequences, could not easily be accounted for in terms of an economical system of generative rules (Weinert 1995).

We have observed that a pure version of CLT, where the focus was on the meaning of the utterance at all costs and at all times, was also too inflexible to provide the basis for the ubiquitous nature of language teaching. A weaker version of CLT, including varying degrees of implicit-explicit focus on form, but with the underlying thrust being the communication of meaning, is still now the most enduring form of instruction supported by the research evidence. Where a form-focused component was added to meaning-based instruction (i.e. weak form of CLT), *in general* it was found to be the most beneficial overall teaching approach. However, results are still 'coming in mixed'. The advantages of FFI do not always remain on delayed tests; they sometimes remain for writing but not for speaking.

There is convincing evidence that learners can learn *some* aspects of the target rule system implicitly. Some aspects need a spotlight shone on them in order to help the learner. We still have some way to go in defining which is the most appropriate model of form-focused instruction. My hunch is that a definitive model for every teaching and learning situation is an illusion. However, what we must do is provide practitioners and policy makers with a reasonably narrow spectrum in which to make informed decisions. Recasts are often the result of automatic response to learner error rather than informed decision making. It looks as if skilled use of recasts does not negatively affect the discourse, nor learner sensibilities, especially adult learners. We have still to determine conclusively, however, that recasts are effective in eliminating error and progressing interlanguage. Indeed, as Nicholas *et al.* (2001) point out we are not even in a position to identify *what constitutes evidence* that recasts work. For example, does the learner have to have begun using the particular linguistic feature for the recast to be judged effective or is recognition of error sufficient? Should evidence of correct use be searched for immediately after the recast? If not how do we know whether the correct form will surface later? Fewer doubts regarding uptake apply to *negotiation of form* but concerns still remain about how much negotiation of form can be engaged in by teachers and learners in a communicatively oriented lesson.

We have begun to detect a paradox in second-language acquisition. Grammatical competence must be an integral part of communicative competence but learning grammar does not seem to help either with communication nor with grammatical competence (Terrell 1991). The answer would seem to lie in *not* equating accuracy with competence. We must learn to de-couple these two aspects of teaching and learning. The fundamental misconception is that we teach grammar (either implicitly or explicitly) in order to improve accuracy. This may be a very long-term competence-related goal, but the fundamental objective of focus on form is to enable the learner to make progress with internalizing the rules of the language. That is, to act upon the instability of his/her interlanguage in order to shift the learner along to new hypotheses about models of the target language. In that sense, and to be deliberately controversial, I would argue that we should focus on forms in order to generate *more* learner errors, more *inaccuracy*.

We have seen that ready-made chunks of productive language are as important as productive rules in interlanguage (Weinert 1995). Formulaic language in learning needs to be investigated more closely. Practitioners need more information about how to deal with the gradual unpacking of beginners' formulaic phrases. This unpacking is one of the central mechanisms in progression. But there are other developments and transitions that are equally important. Some developmental sequences can be affected by direct teaching, some cannot, just as some patterns can be taught explicitly and some cannot. However, we still need to resolve whether the learners' analyses resulted from formulas becoming inadequate or whether some learners simply start translating individual words in the chunk.

L2 curricula should take into account how learners progress by considering with much greater degrees of seriousness the research evidence. All these developments, as I have argued elsewhere (Macaro 1997), must lead to autonomy of language (the ability to say what you want to say, not regurgitate other people's language) and autonomy of language learning (the ability to take responsibility for your own learning generally and on those occasions when the teacher is not available to support you). These two 'autonomies' in conjunction with autonomy of choice (the control over the why and what of language learning), are three dimensions that ultimately encapsulate all our research efforts.

Note

1. By this is meant that the second language is as proficient or nearly as proficient as the first language.

Chapter 4

Research on Vocabulary

In this chapter we will focus on an area of language learning that has received a lot of attention from researchers: the learner's vocabulary or lexicon. We will also remember from Chapter 1 that secondary language teachers in my survey put vocabulary at the very top of their list of topics which they wanted research to illuminate in order to improve the teaching and learning in their classrooms. To cap it all, students of foreign languages cite vocabulary as their number one priority (Knight 1994). So perhaps we should start by asking ourselves why it should be that researchers, practitioners and learners seem to have reached a high degree of consensus as to the importance of vocabulary in second-language learning. Why should it be that the word is so dominant in both our investigations and our pedagogy? After all, language is not just made up of individual words but has units smaller than words: phonemes and morphemes. It also has units bigger than words: clauses, utterances, sentences, paragraphs, monologues, dialogues, whole books! Is it simply that words are an easy unit to work with?

It is interesting that the most often used resource in language learning and language use is probably the dictionary and a dictionary is organized alphabetically according to words in order to give us their meaning. And it is the dictionary that begins to give us clues as to the importance of individual words. A dictionary gives us a lot more information than just the meaning of words. A monolingual dictionary tells us how the word is pronounced (phonetic spelling), the class of word that a particular item is (verb, noun, etc.), the definition of the word, collocations of the word, whether the word can be used in polite company and where the word originates. Some words have many definitions and collocations. Thus a word is a highly complex linguistic phenomenon and a dictionary alerts us to problems regarding spoken-written forms, problems regarding grammatical functions and effects, difficulties with meaning, how the word is used with particular other words, how it is used in society and so on. And that's just a monolingual dictionary. With a bilingual dictionary you can easily extend that list of problems!

So the first reason that vocabulary is important in language learning is that words are complex things in relation to other words and to us humans that use them. Words imply and entail other words. Words may even trigger our thought processes and therefore the utterances and sentences we produce. We saw in Chapter 3 that the competition model was based on 'cues' which are triggered by certain lexical items in an utterance or sentence. Sociolinguists see words as a central element in the social system of communication (Harley 1995). Researchers into oral interaction see the word as 'driving' speech production. Moreover, as we know from educational studies in L1, the expansion of the lexicon is a key to educational success. So, the second reason why L2 vocabulary learning is important is that it helps you achieve things. For example, the more words in a spoken or written text that you can recognize the more that you can use tricks (strategies) to help you understand the bits that you don't recognize. This is regardless of whether you know the grammatical rules of the target language. People who read more know more vocabulary which in turn makes reading easier. There appears therefore to be a two-way causal link between the printed word and vocabulary knowledge. A large L2 vocabulary also helps you to overcome problems in speaking because, if there is a word you don't know, you have access to other words which you can use in order to approximate your meaning. Words help us to understand the world and to communicate with it. We must therefore learn the conceptual underpinnings that determine the place of the word in our entire conceptual system (Ellis, N. 1995).

Yet vocabulary learning as a separate and structured activity is remarkably lacking from foreign-language courses whereas courses on the four language skills, on grammar and on the culture of the target country appear frequently in L2 courses (Oxford and Crookall 1990). Vocabulary learning has been subjected to the usual pendulum swings in language learning. Early research on vocabulary learning implied that the lexical store could be enlarged through exposure to authentic texts and interaction. That is, that vocabulary could be learnt entirely through implicit processes. Moreover it was claimed that it was impractical to learn so much vocabulary in a structured and explicit way given the time constraints of the L2 classroom. Since then it has been recognized that learners have to develop large vocabularies in order to become proficient in the skills of the target language. The dichotomy seems to have been solved by giving learners strategy training, making them more responsible for their own learning, thus freeing up the time in the classroom to focus on other language processes and skills.

Categorizing vocabulary

If we want to research vocabulary acquisition, indeed if we even want to read about it, we have to have a system of word categorization. In this way it is then possible to have a standardized way of counting words and exploring what words do. So the following are a few essential word categories.

Tokens
Tokens are sometimes called running words (e.g. Nation 2001). These are literally the total number of words in a text. For example in my last sentence there were eleven tokens.

Types
Types are the different words in a text. So if we wanted to measure the range of vocabulary used in the essay of an advanced learner of a second language we would measure the number of types that he/she used. In the previous two

sentences I used 40 tokens (total number of words) but the word 'of' occurred four times. If we were counting types, therefore, we would only count 'of' once.

Word families
A word family is made up of a 'headword' (e.g. 'sustain') and all the words that are derived from it: sustainable, unsustainable, sustenance, sustainment.

Lemmas
Lemmas are a bit like word families but more syntactically oriented. A lemma consists of a headword (e.g. 'to jump') and its inflected forms: jumps, jumped, jumping. Lemmas can also include contracted forms (e.g. 'are not, aren't')

The reason for us to be interested in Types and Tokens is that we can measure the lexical diversity of texts (Richards and Malvern 1997). The reason for us to be interested in Word Families and Lemmas is that they are both connected with the notion of the 'learning burden' of a word (Nation 2001) and with the burden of retrieval. By this we mean that if you learn the L2 word 'sustain', then it is actually easier to learn all its derivatives. If you learn the L2 word 'to jump' and you know how the grammar works, it saves you learning by heart all the other inflected endings. You can, instead, make informed guesses. Clearly the number of mental connections made within word families and within lemmas will also assist the process of retrieval from long-term memory. The issue of making learning easier is also linked to the next category of words.

High-frequency words
There are various lists of high-frequency words, such as the one compiled by West (1953) which identifies 2,000 word families of which many are function words. Function words are words such as *of, and, yet, the, an, he, which*. They do not have clear and discrete semantic meaning. Rather, they carry 'grammatical meaning'. These are to be distinguished from *content* words such as nouns, verbs, adjectives and adverbs. A very important feature of function words is that they cannot be added to in the lexicon of a language. Whereas we are constantly coining new content words ('google-search', 'Blairite'), we could not coin a new pronoun or a new preposition without changing the English language dramatically. The fact that virtually all function words are in the 2,000 most frequently used words (at least in English) would lead us to determine that they should be taught in L2 classrooms and taught early. Without them our learners cannot function in the foreign language. They contribute to the autonomy of language and to the progression that we discussed in Chapter 3. There is another reason that teaching function words is important. This is that they are not necessarily the same between languages. For example, the preposition *'dans'* in French is a function word. In English the word 'in' is both a preposition and an adverb. That is why we can say 'he is in' but not *'il est dans'*.

Other categories of words are *low-frequency words*, *academic words* and *technical words* (Nation 2001). For the L2 learner academic words (e.g. *proportional, context*) become very important once he/she has gone beyond the intermediate language-learning phase and is beginning to learn about academic content (e.g. area studies, psychology, economics) through the medium of the second language. Academic words are, by and large, used in all academic disciplines whereas technical words are context- and discipline-specific. There are many thousands of low-frequency words in all major languages but, by definition, they are not used a lot. Some of these are precisely the kinds of words which dominate our beginner to lower-intermediate syllabuses: *timetable, baguette, prescription, horse-riding*. Of course, these low-frequency words might make it into the high-frequency list in certain contexts (if you were a baker, for example). Nevertheless it would make sense for us to ensure that our learners quickly learn the high-frequency words at least at the same time as a selection of transactional, low-frequency vocabulary. Although function words might not be very exciting, these should be learnt early before moving on too quickly to other categories so that learners are able to operate reasonably autonomously (see Chapter 3) in the foreign language.

Breadth and size of vocabulary

An average native speaker of English possesses a vocabulary of about 50,000 words (Aitchison 1994). How much vocabulary do you need in order to operate autonomously in the second language? This is not an easy question to answer as users of an L2 use the language for different purposes and therefore require different vocabulary breadth. Moreover, a distinction that we will be making often in this chapter is the one between receptive and productive skills. In terms of identifying some sort of threshold in listening and reading it has been estimated that the L2 user will need to be able to know at least 95% of the tokens in a text in order to go beyond gist comprehension (Laufer 1989). I shall be arguing in later chapters that to expect language learners to be satisfied with mere gist comprehension may be a demotivating pedagogical goal. Nation's (2001) research indicates that in order to read for pleasure the L2 user should be able to understand about 98% of the tokens in a text. My interpretation of reading for pleasure is that it is the opposite of reading for the specific purpose of increasing language competence, although of course this may happen indirectly. Thus, reading for pleasure does not include exploitation exercises nor anything more than the occasional use of the dictionary. That 98% of the tokens in a text should be known in order to read for pleasure has serious pedagogical implications for the types of texts we encourage our learners to read.

The amount of vocabulary that we will need for speaking and writing will be less than for the receptive skills. We can, after all, put across a message by using a reduced code. Nevertheless, it would be difficult to communicate without a strong (semantic) knowledge of pronouns and prepositions, particularly in the written form where the writer does not have mime, gesture and facial expression to help him/her put the message across. We should also note that high-frequency words are more a feature of spoken text; low-frequency words are more often found in written discourse. Thus over-emphasis on oral interaction in the classroom may result in low vocabulary gains although it may lead to expert use of communication strategies.

In sum, in order to read comfortably a fully authentic academic text, the L2 user will need to know at least 15,000 words (Nation 2001: 20). Clearly these sorts of levels of word knowledge are well beyond the scope of most students in most secondary foreign-language-learning contexts. In any case teachers and syllabus designers will need to take into account factors other than vocabulary breadth. It is much more likely, therefore, that a threshold level of high-frequency word families, somewhere around the 1,500 mark, will be achievable in say, seven years of language study. That is words that are 'fully known'. A further 1,500 words may be needed to engage fully with academic tasks. But what do we mean by 'knowing a word'?

Depth of vocabulary knowledge

Again, we can make the distinction between receptive and productive knowledge. It is much easier for the learner to recognize a word than to produce it. But why should this be? In order to answer this question we need to make a short return to how, it is believed, vocabulary is stored in the brain.

Most researchers now agree that the brain of a bilingual is different from the brain of a monolingual (Cummins 1976; Harley 1995; Libben 2000; Cook 2001). In a sense this is obvious as soon as we accept the cognitive and connectionist paradigm proposed in Chapter 3. By storing L2 words, the brain is storing additional information that a monolingual does not have. However, it is believed that the brain is also 'tagging' the information in some way in order to distinguish between the bilingual's L1 knowledge and his/her L2 knowledge (Libben 2000).

One of the questions that still needs to be answered is what do we mean by 'bilingual'. Does knowing 100 L2 words make you bilingual? 1,000? 2,000? We have certainly moved away from the concept of a bilingual being someone who can use both the L1 and L2 with roughly equal proficiency, but it would be counter-intuitive to suggest that an L2 learner was bilingual after a couple of months of a foreign-language course. Research cannot yet provide an answer to this question although some would argue that you become bilingual when you can use the L2 in order to be able to survive comfortably in an L2 environment.

The second question is how is L1 and L2 vocabulary stored and retrieved in the bilingual's brain? Previous models suggested clear separations between the L1 and L2 lexical store (Figure 4.1), with different representations for lexical items in each language. The current view is that the bilingual has a common storage system of word representations accessed by both L1 and L2 word forms (sometimes known as the *interdependence model*). De Groot and Hoeks (1995) maintain that L2 proficiency determines the bilinguals' memory organization – the better you know a language the more direct the links between the L2 lexical form and its meaning representation. Moreover, research by other psychologists suggests that there is no progression in *the way* the brain stores and retrieves L2 vocabulary at different levels of language competence (Libben 2000). All connections have, as it were, *equal status*. What makes it easier to retrieve an L1 word is the sheer number of connections and repeated activations compared to L2 words. Figure 4.2 gives an idea of what we mean by equal status but unequal number of connections. Consequently, the L1 word 'church' activates a whole host of other connected words: synonyms, antonyms, homonyms, homophones, collocations, as well as previously recorded feelings and reactions to this word family.

So, we can now begin to see why recognition of an L2 word should be easier than production of most L2 words. In the receptive condition, the Italian L2 word *'vestito'* will make a straight connection with its English L1 equivalent 'dress' because this will be how the word will probably have been stored in the first place. In the productive condition 'dress' will have a number of (L1) neural paths to choose from and working memory will have its work cut out to choose the right one and stop

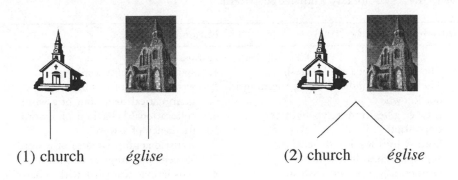

(1) church   *église*   (2) church   *église*

Figure 4.1   Previous models of the mental lexicon. Adapted from Libben (2000)

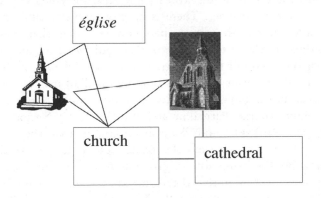

Figure 4.2   More recent model of the mental lexicon

competition from other 'blind alley' L1 paths. What psycholinguistic theory doesn't explain, however, is how and why, as the learner's mental L2 lexicon increases and makes more L2 connections, production speeds up. It may simply be that the sheer number of L2 to L2 activations overrides any wrong selection of pathways. Nevertheless, there is some evidence to suggest that even with advanced learners it is difficult to suppress activation of the L1 form. Hermans *et. al.* (1998) gave Dutch advanced learners of English picture cues and found that even they found it difficult to go straight to the (well-known) L2 word without first activating the Dutch word.

There is a further reason why retrieving and then producing an L2 word will be more difficult. As the complex process of retrieval is being carried out, fluency requirements will dictate that working memory will already be bracing itself for the mechanical problems associated with its actual production: phonetic unfamiliarity in the case of speaking and graphic unfamiliarity in the case of writing. This overload may well contribute to the delay or failure to produce a word. As we all know, we do have to be highly motivated to contend with working memory overload.

Table 4.1 Vocabulary knowledge criteria

Paribakht and Wesche (1993)	Nation (1990)
	Learner knows
1. The word is not familiar at all	1. spoken form of a word
2. The word is familiar but the meaning is not known	2. written form of a word
3. Learner gives correct synonym or translation	3. grammatical behaviour of a word
4. Learner uses word with semantic appropriateness in a sentence	4. collocational behaviour of a word
5. Learner uses word with semantic appropriateness and grammatical accuracy in a sentence	5. frequency of a word
	6. stylistic appropriateness of a word
	7. concept meanings of a word
	8. associations word has with other related words

So, let us return to what it is to know a word. As well as the receptive-productive distinction, there are other criteria related to depth of knowledge. Moreover, as Schmitt (1998) and others argue, words are learned incrementally and not in a *not-acquired* versus *acquired* manner. There is no clear and definable moment when we 'suddenly' know a word. Most researchers now recognize that these increments in word knowledge are related to the *form* of the word (what it looks and sounds like); the *meaning* of the word (all its semantic associations); the *use* of the word (how the word is used by the relevant language community). Full mastery of a word requires much more than just a knowledge of its meaning. Table 4.1 provides two different lexical knowledge criteria (Paribakht and Wesche 1993; Nation 1990). What we notice about the Paribakht and Wesche criteria is that they are proposing an incremental scale where, for example, being able to use a word with semantic appropriateness implies being able to give a correct synonym. Does using the word appropriately in context mean that the learner knows all synonyms of that word? This problem with scaling knowledge recalls the problem associated with language progression in general that we touched on in Chapter 3. Nation's criteria are not scaled and suggest that one has to have a particular kind of knowledge to understand and use a word appropriately according to the particular moment or situation.

Schmitt (1998) claims that we don't really know what the acquisition stages are that a word might move through. He recognizes that intuition would suggest some hierarchy but that as yet we don't know what that hierarchy is. Schmitt therefore gave three adult and highly proficient L2 English speakers tests of depth of word knowledge over the course of a year to track how their knowledge of 11 words developed. He judged their knowledge according to *spelling, association* with other words, *word class* (syntax) and *meaning*. He found:

1. they had little trouble with spelling, being able to spell some even unknown words;
2. none of the words were known 'completely'. None achieved top marks on the rating scale;
3. meaning sense appeared to have a certain amount of inertia. The depth of meaning attached to a word did not change easily over the course of a year although it improved more than it deteriorated;

4. association and grammar knowledge seemed to increase in line with meaning knowledge. However, not all four word classes were known for many of the words, questioning the assumption that a learner who knows one member of a word family need not be taught the others;
5. increases in association knowledge were mainly due to knowing certain collocations or idioms (e.g. spur = 'spur of the moment'). This is probably a good reason for teaching collocations;
6. verb and noun forms seemed to have been *noticed* more than adjectives and adverbs, suggesting that (at least at this level of proficiency) teaching should give greater attention to adjectives and adverbs.

Rate of vocabulary development

Laufer (1998) was interested in how the quantity of L2 vocabulary knowledge *develops over time*, as well as depth of knowledge. She claimed that few quantitative studies had measured vocabulary at different stages of language learning and over a long period of time. Or, studies have usually investigated the acquisition of words which have been specifically chosen for an experiment rather than changes in the global vocabulary size. She therefore based her research on measuring the gain in a real classroom rather than in an artificial experiment. Taking a class of 17-year-olds (secondary school in Israel, Hebrew L1) she measured their gain in English L2 vocabulary as compared to a class of 16-year-olds. Both classes were carefully matched for teaching environment and conditions. Nevertheless, the limitation of it not being a true longitudinal study remained and should be borne in mind when considering the findings below. She measured the gains according to:

1. Passive vocabulary: understanding of the basic meaning of a word;
2. Controlled-active: producing a word when prompted by a specific task (cloze exercise);
3. Free-active: with no specific prompt (a free essay with short task rubrics).

She found that:

1. passive vocabulary increased significantly by 84%;
2. controlled-active vocabulary increased significantly by 50%;
3. free-active vocabulary did not increase significantly. Students were using the same proportion of productive vocabulary a year later when not prompted to do so by teacher or task;
4. the gap between passive and controlled-active had increased over the course of the year;
5. the average vocabulary gain per lesson was about 8-9 word families.

Laufer felt that this raised both a number of theoretical questions and pedagogical implications. Why did it take six years to learn 1,900 (passive) words when 1,600 were actually learnt in one year with no intervention? Why did it take six years to learn 1,700 (controlled-active) productive words when 850 were actually learnt in one year? Why did free-active vocabulary reach such an obvious plateau? Was it due to lack of emphasis on vocabulary learning? Was it to do with emphasis on accuracy (perhaps by exams and tests), thereby not encouraging the learner to take risks and use more difficult vocabulary?

In these findings and implications we return again to the thorny issue of progression that we examined in Chapter 3. We need to take care to remind ourselves once more that progression is a multi-faceted phenomenon and that progression, as Nation (2001) reminds us, needs to be over a range of language-learning aspects, not just vocabulary. On the other hand it does raise the question of the extent to which depth and breadth of vocabulary are related. In recent years some evidence has been discovered that depth and breadth are associated (Schmitt and Meara 1997) and that therefore we should not make too strict a distinction between the breadth and the depth of vocabulary knowledge. Laufer's findings would seem to contradict this trend somewhat.

Daniels (2000) attempted an intervention study into vocabulary gain by involving lower-secondary-school students in intensive language work outside the classroom, speculating that the central problem of vocabulary acquisition may be to do with the nature of the learning environment (e.g. a single teacher interacting with many learners). He therefore set up, for the experimental group, an intensive and active-learning programme in a residential area in the English Lake District which 'contrasted strongly with the generally passive and receptive nature' of much classroom work (2000: 14). As well as measuring gains after the treatment, Daniels measured the shift in the continuum from receptive vocabulary knowledge to productive knowledge using the Meara and Buxton (1987) test which includes some nonsense words to check reliability on subjects' claims of receptive vocabulary knowledge. He also measured retention four months later. He found:

1. There were significant increases in experimental scores in post-test and virtually no attrition in the delayed test four months later. These increased scores were not matched by their peers in the control group.
2. The majority of words which were acquired by the experimental students were new words to them.
3. Students commented that 'in normal French lessons you don't always say sentences' – in other words the communicative requirement of the treatment condition produced the effect of moving the vocabulary along the continuum. Students also said that, after the treatment, the words came much more quickly indicating both a shift along the receptive-to-active continuum and an increase in speed of retrieval.

Daniels concludes that there may well be such a construct as *vocabulary dormancy* where a number of words become fixed in a classroom learning situation, at an intermediate stage on the vocabulary knowledge continuum. A study by Fisher and Evans (2000) also found that a period of intensive interaction (exchange visit with France) resulted in vocabulary and use of idiom gains. However, this is not reported by the authors in great detail.

How do we best learn vocabulary?

Probably the issue that has most divided theorists and teachers is how vocabulary should be taught. The issue stems from the natural learning versus artificial learning debate that we raised in Chapter 3. This, in turn, is linked to beliefs about explicit and implicit learning processes and whether language can consciously be taught. These disagreements at a theoretical level are then transferred to disagreement at the classroom level. Do teachers want to force learners to learn, by rote, lists of vocabulary? Will learners be demotivated by this? Should vocabulary be 'embedded' in a series of motivating real-life activities? Is it not better to interact with the students thereby hoping (expecting?) them to 'pick up' the vocabulary, a bit like dandelion seeds on a windy day sticking to a woolly jumper.

Studies of L1 vocabulary acquisition, of course, are able to look to evidence of significant increases in incidental learning during normal reading activities (Nagy *et al.* 1985). Nevertheless, even in L1 acquisition, researchers whilst acknowledging the potential value of inferring meaning from context, are aware that this is a complex strategy and advocate training in it. Fukkink and de Glopper (1998) carried out a meta-analysis of 21 different L1 studies investigating teaching approaches aimed at enhancing the skill of deriving meaning from context during reading. They found that, in many of these studies, experimental groups outperformed control groups. Whilst pointing to a series of studies that show that direct instruction of word meanings is beneficial for poor and average readers they nevertheless conclude that 'it makes sense to teach students how to derive word meaning from context'(461).

One of the problems is that there is just so much vocabulary to learn for a student who is in a formal foreign-language-learning situation with little or no possibility of spending time in the target-language community – in other words 'an input-poor' environment. The questions for researchers and teachers are:

(a) what are the cost-benefits of learners acquiring vocabulary by deriving meaning from context and

(b) what are the cost-benefits of spending valuable classroom time training the students to derive meaning from context? Note that I will deal with the other side of the coin in the chapter on reading. In other words we are not concerned here with the benefits to reading (of doing extended reading) but with the benefits of extended reading to vocabulary acquisition and retention.

Learning vocabulary from context

Ellis, N. (1995) proposes four hypotheses.

1. The strong implicit hypothesis. This claims that the meaning of a new word is 'acquired totally unconsciously as a result of abstraction from repeated exposures in a range of activated contexts'.
2. The weak implicit hypothesis. Vocabulary is mostly learnt subconsciously but at least some conscious 'noticing' of a new word has to take place.
3. The weak explicit hypothesis. We cannot be taught all the L2 words we know

but we can teach ourselves by selectively attending to lexis and using a variety of strategies to infer its meaning from context.
4. The strong explicit hypothesis. The application of a range of strategies is a necessary condition of acquisition: noting the new word; attempting to infer the meaning from context; consolidating via repetition and association.

Ellis reminds us that in the early stages of any skill we use conscious declarative knowledge on the way to automatization. Strategies for learning vocabulary follow the same process towards automatization. Thus learners with high levels of effective strategy deployment are able to infer meaning quickly, to 'enmesh them in meaning networks and map the surface forms to rich meaning representations' (1995: 5). He concludes that, in this sense, vocabulary acquisition is an explicit learning process.

So what do a selection of studies say that can add to these speculations regarding the implicit-explicit continuum?

The research evidence

As we have already seen above, Daniels found that with lower-secondary students there were clear benefits to vocabulary growth in intensive exposure and active involvement in L2 interaction. Clearly some 'weak implicit' processes were present in the acquisition of this vocabulary.

A number of studies have demonstrated that students, especially students with higher verbal ability, can correctly guess at the meaning of unknown words (Sternberg 1987). The ability to guess correctly also depended on the text itself: the number of occurrences of a word in the text; the helpfulness of the surrounding text. Other studies have found that readers are often unable to get to the meaning of an unknown word (Bensoussan and Laufer 1984). As Knight (1994) points out, part of the difficulty is that the texts used to test this hypothesis have all been different. Some have used artificial words, some haven't. Still others have included different amounts of contextual support in order to help learners derive the meaning of vocabulary. Another problem is that research on deriving meaning using *natural texts* is lacking.

Of course, the above discussion pertains to readability of texts. The question that it is asking is can one understand a word from context? This of course is important. The purpose of this chapter, however, is to examine vocabulary acquisition. So the question we are asking is: are new words learnt from context while reading 'learnt better' than from more explicit and de-contextualized methods? By 'learnt better' we mean that the right depth of meaning is achieved; they are remembered better.

Knight (1994) carried out a study in order to ascertain whether vocabulary was best learnt by deriving meaning from context and what the variables were. Using a sample of 105 second-year university students (English L1, Spanish L2) she first of all divided the students into two groups based on L1 verbal scores: a high-verbal group and low-verbal group using a median split. She then gave the students an authentic Spanish text which contained about 12 words which she knew were unknown to them. Immediately after reading, the students were given a test on their knowledge of the meaning of the 12 words and these measures were compared to a test of vocabulary out of context. In order to measure different levels of depth of word learning, she provided two different tests: (a) students were asked to supply a definition (L1 equivalent or L2 definition), (b) students were asked to select a definition from a multiple choice. She also gave them a test two weeks later on the same words. She found:

1. All subjects learnt more new words when exposed to them in context than when they were not exposed to the context. This difference remained when tested two weeks later.
2. High-verbal-ability students learnt more words from context than low-verbal-ability students.
3. High-verbal-ability students, in the test where they had to supply their own definition (or L1 equivalent), learnt more vocabulary than did low-verbal-ability students.

A similar study was carried out by Prince (1996) who used 48 French university students with English as their L2. Half the group had to learn 44 L2 words from sentences (i.e. in a 'context condition'), half the group had to learn them with their L1 equivalents ('translation condition'). Additionally, they were divided into 'more advanced' and 'weaker' learners, although they had all had roughly the same learning histories. They were asked to recall the words 40 minutes later. Half the words were in a 'context condition' and half were in a 'translation condition'. Hence for all students half were matched to the way they had learnt them and half were not. Prince found:

1. Both groups recalled words better in the translation condition than with the context condition.
2. The weaker group performed less well in the context condition than did the advanced group.
3. The more advanced group were more able to *use* a word in an appropriate L2 context. More advanced learners were better at transferring what they had learnt to a new context.

Prince argues that 'the inability of the weaker group to transfer knowledge represents a clear limit to the usefulness of their otherwise impressive ability to learn words with their translations' (1996: 486). They may have been over-dependent on translation links and may have failed to develop certain processing strategies crucial to the effective use of context. Their persistent reliance on L1, stemming from a desire to understand quickly, is one factor that may lead to ineffective learning. This is quite a strong claim to make from the available research evidence. The implications of this cluster of results are that students can, indeed, learn vocabulary from context and that some students are better at this than others. However, to claim that recourse to mental translation is a poor learning strategy would have to be substantiated by further research.

The question we might ask is can students learn vocabulary better if they *combine* both contextualized and de-contextualized processes? One way we can explore this question is to look at studies which have investigated dictionary use.

The role of a dictionary in vocabulary acquisition

Using the same data as in the earlier study (Knight 1994), Knight set up the reading of the texts on a computer such that some of the participants were able to access a computerized dictionary and others were not. The computer was also able to track the number of times participants accessed the electronic dictionary. She found:

1. Those who had dictionaries *as well as* the context learned most vocabulary.
2. Those participants with dictionary access scored better at supplying a definition of the word than those without access to the dictionary. This was highly predictable as the dictionary would give accurate L1 equivalents.
3. High-verbal-ability students used the dictionary more than low-verbal-ability students. However low-verbal-ability students benefited more from dictionary access. This suggests that the high-verbal-ability students need not have looked up some of the words as they had already managed to infer the words from context. They were just checking – probably unnecessarily.

The implications of these results is that students should not be barred from using dictionaries and not told to 'just try and guess from context'. Rather, a combination of inferring and dictionary use strategies will achieve the greatest vocabulary acquisition. However, an additional metacognitive strategy will have to be used: students will have to evaluate to what extent it is worth looking up words, despite the time this takes, in order to acquire a richer vocabulary. Clearly, teachers should be prepared to offer different strategy training to different types/levels of learners, or to help them make evaluative decisions about which strategies to use at which times.

A study by Paribakht and Wesche (1996) would seem to confirm the above results and implications for pedagogy. In their study, ESL university students made vocabulary gains when, in addition to reading the text, they engaged in various vocabulary exercises. However, doing vocabulary exercises based on a text undermines the objective of reading for pleasure. So, is the dictionary the best way to enable selective attention to be focused on a new word without resorting to mechanical exercises?

There is one other way. The teacher can give an L1 or L2 gloss in the margins or somewhere else on the page. Most studies have found that glosses have a positive effect on vocabulary learning (Nation 2001), presumably by focusing selective attention on new words for just long enough but without stopping the flow of the reading. As we saw in Chapter 3, Watanabe (1997) found that glosses provided in the margins were more effective than glosses in the text, thus supporting the evidence so far. In what language should the glosses be? Myong (1995) found that L1 glosses resulted in better vocabulary learning. Jacobs *et al.* (1994) found no difference between L1 and L2 glosses but found that learners declared themselves to have a preference for glosses in the margins rather than elsewhere in the text or the page. The important criteria would seem to be the level of proficiency of the learner in terms of L1 or L2 glosses. The gloss has to convey the meaning of the new word effectively and efficiently. Clearly, a beginner or lower-intermediate-level student faced with a complex L2 gloss will be discouraged and turn his/her selective attention elsewhere. However, the literature is surprisingly silent with regard to studies with beginners and lower-intermediate students.

Vocabulary acquisition and negotiation

Not all vocabulary acquisition occurs in receptive learning tasks. We can notice a new word that another speaker has said whilst we are having a conversation with them. Of course the amount of time we have in order to process the new incoming word, infer its meaning from context and store it in long-term memory is much reduced compared to the time we have when reading. It is true, there is a growing body of evidence (as usual at a more advanced level) that learners can pick up new vocabulary as they are being read to or are listening to a text. Nevertheless, in order to bring selective attention to bear on a problem new word, the learner will need processing time. The only way that he/she can gain that processing time is if he/she attempts to negotiate the meaning.

Ellis, R. (1995) and Ellis and He (1999) were two studies that sought to identify the effect on vocabulary learning, during an oral task, of different types of input. In the Ellis, R. (1995) study they received either

unmodified input. This input from the teacher was just as a native speaker would speak.

premodified input. The difficult vocabulary in the input was pre-empted and simplified.

interactionally modified input. The learners 'negotiated' (see Chapter 3) with the teacher as the task was being done – they could ask: what is X? what do you mean by Y? Can you say Z again please?

Ellis, R. (1995) found that, although more word meanings were learnt from the interactionally modified input than from premodified input, the rate of acquisition was faster with the latter group.

In the Ellis and He (1999) study, 50 students (mixed L1s and mixed ages) learning English (L2) were used. They were divided into

A *pre-modified input group*
An *interactionally modified input group*
A *modified output group*.

In the last group, the interaction was between two students on an information-gap task where items of furniture had to be placed in a house. The subject whose vocabulary acquisition was subsequently being tested was sometimes forced to modify his or her output by the other student's lack of comprehension. The authors give the following example:

Student 1: *Please put the comforter on the bed*
Student 2: *Comfortable?*
Student 1: *No comforter. Comforter is like a blanket. Do you know meaning?*
Student 2: *Yes put comforter on the bed?*

The post-tests measured receptive vocabulary acquisition and productive vocabulary acquisition. Unlike other studies, all groups received the same amount of time for the processing of the new vocabulary to occur. Ellis and He found that the modified output group outperformed the other two groups on comprehension (they eventually got the meaning of their interlocutor better); vocabulary recognition (receptive vocabulary acquisition); vocabulary production. The researchers concluded that producing new words helps learners to process words more deeply, whether for comprehension or for acquisition than simply hearing them, no matter how much they have been modifed.

These are interesting results and we shall return to the impact of interaction in Chapter 8. For the moment however, as Nation (2001) points out, all these conditions are only as good as the quality of input in the first place. A teacher who knows his/her class will be able to pre-modify his/her input better than a teacher who does not but who allows meaning negotiation. Ellis and Heimback (1997) found that very young children (six years approximately) varied in their ability to negotiate L2 meaning and that this resulted in fairly low levels of vocabulary acquisition.

Learning vocabulary through explicit learning strategies

As we have seen above, explicit learning is possible. It is also possible to learn more words than those which one is expressly taught by a teacher. I have argued elsewhere (Macaro 2001a) that this can only be achieved by the learner taking an active part in the learning process both inside and outside the classroom. Taking an active part can be at a cognitive-strategy level (the direct interface between the brain and the foreign language) and at the metacognitive-strategy level. With metacognitive strategies learners take control of their learning by making quality decisions about which cognitive strategies are successful, by having clear learning goals, and by planning a programme of learning which best suits them and their learning goals. For a fuller account of the nature of learning strategies with young learners see Macaro (2001a), Grenfell and Harris (1999) with intermediate, older adolescents, see Graham (1997) and with adult/advanced learners, see Oxford (1990) and O'Malley and Chamot (1990).

Cognitive strategies used in explicit vocabulary learning have to, as we have said, apply selective attention to the new word to be learnt by first noticing it (its form and its meaning) and then to processing it in working memory before committing it to long-term memory. A learner may have to have a number of selective attention 'meetings' (Nation 2001) with the new word before the sufficient number of connections are made such that long-term recall will be possible.

In the past, studies have, in the main, asked learners via questionnaires which memorization strategies they use. These have usually been part of a larger general strategy-use survey (for example Rebecca Oxford's (1990) SILL – Strategy Inventory for Language Learning). Or, vocabulary studies have measured what occurs when learners are trained to use specific strategies. Only recently have studies begun to take a more ethnographic approach to the memorization strategies that learners deploy thus revealing in greater depth the procedures that the learners themselves normally use. Moreover in these studies they were asked not only whether they used a strategy but whether they had used it *before* and *when*. One such study was by Sanaoui (1995). In her field work, ESL and FSL (French as a Second Language) participants were asked to keep a daily written record of how they learnt vocabulary over a 4-week period. These notes were then used as a starting point for interviews. Sanaoui also examined class notes, exercises in self-study guides, and the word lists they kept. She found that students tended to fall into two categories:

1. Those who used metacognitive self-awareness and action which was clearly linked to their learning goals. They had special routines and materials for ensuring vocabulary was revisited. They supplemented their in-class opportunities for vocabulary learning by self-created learning activities.
2. Those who did not use metacognitive self-awareness and who had vague learning goals (e.g. 'I want to improve my vocabulary'). They relied entirely on in-class opportunities for learning vocabulary and engaged in minimal amounts of independent study. Their range of learning activities was very restricted. One learner referred to 'passive listening of the radio while cooking' as a learning strategy.

Much of the research literature supports Sanauoi's findings. Probably some of the most robust and consistent findings in SLA literature is that learners who use strategies regularly and in combination (particularly with some metacognitive strategies) are among the most successful learners. The problem with the equation between strategy use and success being focused at the metacognitive level is that the construct of 'strategy use' becomes almost synonymous with 'motivation'. Sanaoui's description may seem to us one of learners who are highly motivated and therefore work harder! We will return to this issue in the next chapter (on motivation). For the moment let us try to list what research tells us are the strategies that learners use for memorizing vocabulary. Naturally, no one learner uses all of these. They can be grouped as follows:

Noticing something about the word
Noticing part of a word (usually written form)
Noticing the (unusual) meaning of a word
Noticing the unusual position or collocations of a word

Writing words down in some way
Repeated copying
Organised copying (e.g. by gender or by word class)
Writing down the way words sound and looking up in a dictionary later
Writing lists
Writing word cards (L1 on the back)
Writing the first l- - - - - of a w- - -
Writing and linking to a graphic image
Writing the word down with the L1 equivalent
Writing the word down as part of a sentence or a dialogue

Instant sound-link repetition (after encountering new word)
Out loud
Under breath
In silence in the head

Revision (planning future meetings with the word)
Same strategies as in 'instant repetition' but later and in a planned way (e.g.
first thing in the morning before a test)
Writing the word down on a piece of paper and placing it somewhere (e.g.
stuck to bathroom mirror)
By planning revision over a period of time (e.g. leading up to a major exam)
Recording the words on cassette and listening and repeating
Making words into a song, rhyme or rap
Using the *look, hide, say, write, check* technique

Using the lexical item
e.g. in a sentence during the day in a real communicative situation

By making associations
Contextual (connecting a word with a personal event)
Building up word-webs and word hooks (see Macaro 2001a: 204)
Linguistic associations (mnemonics and keyword technique – see below)
Imagery (connect to visual image in the mind)

Through collaborative learning
With parent or with friend to test you
Acting out with a friend (usually a short dialogue rather than single words)
Talking *about* the lexical item to someone

In my own study of memorization strategies (Macaro 2000a) a highly motivated
Italian learner of English said that he used the following strategy combinations to
ensure sound learning:

> I read and repeat all the (verbs) starting with a 'B'. After having done that about
> ten times I write them down, just as I remember them, maybe three or four
> times. After having checked them . . . if they're wrong I repeat them and rewrite
> them until there are no more mistakes. Those which are impossible to remember
> I write on a small sheet of paper which I put in my pocket and every now and
> then I read it.
> At night before going to bed I say them to someone. Early in the morning I go
> through them again for the last time . . .

Another learner said that she stuck a new word on an item of furniture in her
bedroom, at random. This meant that the new word to be learnt was not only
'frequently met' by her but that she could associate it with something familiar,
though not semantically related, and this stuck in her mind.
Lawson and Hogben (1996) used the think aloud technique on memorizing 12
new words and found that learners who recalled more words used a greater range of
strategies and more often. This is fine but clearly we cannot recommend to learners
that they use all of the above strategies for every new item of vocabulary. So what,
does the literature say, are the most effective strategies for learning vocabulary?
First of all, there have been studies that look at very general patterns in strategy
use. For example, non-causal relationships have been investigated. Gu and Johnson
(1996) correlated the *reported* memorization strategies of a very large sample (N= 850)

of Chinese L1 university students learning English with vocabulary size tests and with more general proficiency measures. They provided students with a lengthy questionnaire on strategy use. They found:

1. The majority of students used memory strategies such as *associations*, *imagery*, *visualizing the word's form* and so on. The students who limited themselves to these strategies correlated with *average* vocabulary size and proficiency levels.
2. The (small minority of) students who really excelled in vocabulary size and proficiency levels reported *additionally* using two metacognitive regulation strategy groups: *selective attention* to words (evaluating when it is worth making the effort to memorize) and *self-initiation* (making an effort to learn beyond the classroom and the exam system).

Gu and Johnson's study provides us with a broad sweep of the effects on learning of different strategy use. Again, certain combinations of cognitive strategies in conjunction with metacognitive strategies appear to lead to success.

Another broad-sweep study was carried out by Macaro (2001a). Here classes were assigned to experimental and comparison groups. The experimental groups received strategy training in memorization whilst the comparison groups did not. We found that, after four months of strategy training, the experimental group significantly outperformed the comparison group in a simple vocabulary test (i.e. the students had to provide the L2 equivalent of a written L1 word). However, this provided evidence that a range of strategies improves learning, not which ones in particular.

In order to narrow down our focus we could identify what are the essential categories of cognitive strategies that learners need to address. Nation (2001) suggests that in learning vocabulary three categories have to be respected:

Noticing: that is giving selective attention and momentarily de-contextualizing the lexical item.

Retrieval: if the new word is subsequently retrieved in some way the memory trace will be strengthened. A very consistent finding is that *spaced* meetings with the word result in more secure learning than *massed* (all at once) meetings. Furthermore, it is not simply repetition which is important but the repeated opportunity to retrieve from memory the item which is to be learned. Each retrieval of a word strengthens the path linking form and meaning and makes subsequent retrieval easier.

Generative use (creative use): Using the word in new sentences and new contexts. This builds up the connections in long-term memory. It also should help learners develop from focusing only on the similarities in the forms of words to a semantically organized lexicon.

So, if Nation is correct, a learner should be selecting strategies from these three categories. But which strategies from each of the categories? Can we narrow it down even further? One of the difficulties in providing an answer to this is that not all the above strategies have been researched and certainly not 'against one another' for their effectiveness.

Considerable research has focused on the *keyword technique* for its effectiveness. The keyword technique was first suggested by Atkinson (1975) and has been reviewed by Beaton *et al.* (1995). It involves two steps after the learner has come across a new word:

Step 1: the learner tries to think of an L1 word (the keyword) which sounds like part or all of the unknown word

Step 2: the learner thinks of a visual image, or a short series of images which will link the new word and the L1 keyword. It is additionally helpful if the images are bizarre or amusing.

The aim is to provide a link between the form of the new word (both the phonemic and graphemic 'form') and its meaning via an easily retrievable L1 word. In the case of advanced L2 learners, the keyword could be a familiar L2 word. Figure 4.3 provides an example of the keyword technique with French L2, English L1. The retrieval order is: can't remember the French word for 'to get up' – think of keyword – combined image appears – retrieval of L2 word.

How effective is the keyword technique? An early study using this technique was by Cohen and Aphek (1981) with students of Hebrew (L2). This technique was modelled for the students, showing them how making mental associations could assist in vocabulary recall. They then selected their own words from a reading text and made their own associations. The strategy appeared to lead to better performance at memorizing vocabulary.

A study by Brown and Perry (1991) investigated whether learners retained vocabulary better if they tried to make semantic associations (from example by linking words with similar categories of words in the same language) or through the keyword technique (that is, through linking words which specifically *did not* have a semantic connection). The results suggested that the semantic connections helped more than the keyword association strategy. However, the students who were asked to memorize language using both strategies, retained the vocabulary the best.

Keyword strategy

French new word:
se reveiller

English (L1) equivalent:
to wake up

Connecting image:
waking up
*because car **revving***
outside house

Figure 4.3   Keyword strategy

Avila and Sadoski (1996) investigated the keyword technique's effectiveness as a strategy in classrooms of 11-year-old Spanish students learning English as the foreign language by comparing it to simply giving learners in a control group a written equivalent in L1. Teachers were shown how to model the keyword technique with the experimental group such that these learners would be trained to use it in future. Both groups (N=63) were then tested via a cued recall test (L2-L1) and a sentence completion test (all in L2). Both groups were also interviewed to find out what strategies they had used to memorize the vocabulary. Avila and Sadoski found:

1. Students using the keyword method significantly outperformed the control group both in the cued recall test and in the sentence completion test, both immediately and after one week's delay.
2. The interviews revealed that the control group used rote learning (repetition) strategies the most (none used the keyword strategy); virtually all the experimental group reported having used the keyword strategy. They felt it was a successful strategy and found it enjoyable.

This was a well-conducted study, with randomized groups, in a real classroom situation with a reasonable sample size. The only problem regarding generalizability is related to the fact that only 10 words were memorized and tested. How effective would the keyword technique be against other strategies with much greater numbers of words? Avila and Sadoski themselves point to the fact that other researchers have found that very young children seem to have difficulty generating interactive images for themselves. There would seem to be quite a lot of effort involved in generating the connecting images for very large numbers of words. Certainly the learners in my study (Macaro 2001a) found the keyword method an effort and did not rate it highly among the strategies they used.

Van Hell and Candia Mahn (1997) also investigated the keyword technique versus rote rehearsal (i.e. repetition). They also wanted to know whether multilinguals learnt new language better than monolinguals. They investigated university students' ability to recall the L1 meaning of a very large number of new L2 words (i.e. in the receptive condition). Dutch students were asked to learn Spanish words (a new language for them) by both techniques. They found:

1. Participants using a keyword recalled fewer words and more slowly than via rote rehearsal.
2. Using both techniques, they remembered concrete words better and quicker than abstract words.
3. Concrete words benefited from being coupled with a semantically related keyword (rather than a totally unrelated keyword).

The researchers concluded that the overall pattern of their results indicated that the keyword strategy is less effective than the rote-learning strategy, at least with these experienced multilinguals. However we have to note that the students were *given* the keyword rather than generating it themselves. Since the whole aim of the keyword technique is to make links with meaning connections which have been established over many years, the keyword method is perhaps more effective when we generate our own connecting images triggered by the keywords of our choosing, a finding supported by Wang and Thomas (1995).

Further research needs to establish whether (a) the keyword technique is more effective in the receptive recall condition or in the productive recall condition; (b) whether it is as efficient for large quantities of vocabulary and on a regular basis in real classroom situations; (c) whether it is more efficient when the learner chooses his/her own keyword and connecting images.

Other comparisons of cognitive strategies have been carried out. Lotto and de Groot (1998) compared the L1 → L2 word-learning strategy with Picture → L2 word-learning strategy. Again, it was Dutch university (non-language) students who were tested on Italian vocabulary, a completely new language. The results showed:

1. Students were able to recall the Italian words *faster* if they had used the L1 → L2 word-learning strategy than if they had used the Picture → L2 word-learning strategy.
2. The L1 → L2 word-learning strategy produced *higher* recall scores than Picture → L2 learning strategy.

Interestingly, the participants generated the phonological word forms for both the pictures and the graphic word forms. This provides strong support for the role of phonology in learning vocabulary in an L2 not only when the learning material consists of auditory presented word pairs but also when presentation was graphical. However, it should be noted that this was an artificial experiment. The students were not learning Italian as a language, they were merely being tested on their ability to learn out-of-context new words.

Individual and group differences

Are some learners better vocabulary learners than others? This is a very important question which pertains to all aspects of language learning, not just vocabulary. It is important not only because it can be used to differentiate learners in tests but it is also what invites the fundamental question of strategy training. Can poor learners be trained to use strategies better thus making them better learners? Research by Gathercole and Baddeley (1989) indicates that an important factor influencing vocabulary learning is the ability of learners to hold a word in their phonological short-term memory. Their experimental research is very important because it suggests that learners need not be hindered by their working-memory limitations (message capacity and duration of message trace). They can develop meaning-associated learning strategies such as keyword association and semantic cluster association.

Milton and Meara (1998) carried out a comparative study of vocabulary knowledge between English, Greek and German 14-15-year-old learners. Behind this study were a number of assumptions and claims: that vocabulary is a good indicator of general language skills; that the British are not as good as other nations at learning languages; that the National Curriculum (England and Wales) is at least in part contributing to this deficiency. The researchers felt that there was a need to provide more substantial evidence for some of these claims. The sample (N=197) from the three countries was matched in terms of classes and the syllabuses were found, surprisingly, to match reasonably well (i.e. the topics covered were quite similar). Milton and Meara administered vocabulary tests and found:

1. The British students did worst, scoring less than 60% on average, suggesting therefore that they 'have a poor grasp of basic vocabulary'.
2. British learners spent less time learning, were set lower language goals than the Greeks and Germans.
3. In terms of vocabulary growth per hours of tuition, the learners in Britain appear to learn as fast, if not faster, than learners elsewhere (this finding would have to be qualified because it assumes that the rate of vocabulary growth is even rather than uneven – e.g. without initial vocabulary spurts).
4. After four years of language study in British schools, a quarter of the sample tested scored so low that the authors wondered whether 'they know anything at all'.

Milton and Meara conclude that the British are not necessarily bad at learning languages. Rather it was the school system that is failing them. This conclusion may be somewhat 'rushed at' for one very important reason. It may well be that 'the school system' has had to reduce its language learning goals simply because the initial motivational level of the students was low. I am not necessarily arguing this position, merely that further research is needed. It all comes back to the relationship and direction between motivation and success and this will be discussed in the next chapter. However, among adults some similar group differences have been found. In the Van Hell and Candia Mahn (1997) study described above, the Dutch multi-linguals were compared to American monolinguals (the latter were asked to learn Dutch words). The researchers found that the Dutch multilinguals did significantly better at recalling the L2 words both in terms of speed and accuracy of recall. It appears that experience in learning a FL does, as one might have hypothesized, facilitate the learning of new L2 vocabulary. The other interesting finding is that no difference was found between the keyword strategy and the rote rehearsal strategy in terms of proportion of correct words. This suggests that the keyword strategy may be more of use to inexperienced learners who are still relying heavily on their first language in order to memorize.

I have not been able to come across any studies involving vocabulary strategy training which separated groups of learners. At a general study level my own pilot study of strategy training (Macaro 1998) showed that boys benefited more than girls from training to use strategies. The fact that females have been shown to be using more strategies in the first place may be an underlying factor in this finding.

What sort of vocabulary should we learn and when?

We have already explored, at the beginning of this chapter, the most frequently occurring words. We have noted that function words are particularly prevalent in any count of high-frequency words. Nation (2001) estimates that 270 function word types account for 44% of the tokens in most texts. Function words are the 'little words' that are often overlooked or neglected in syllabuses. The other feature of this particular group of high-frequency words is that they are rarely cognates, as Table 4.2 shows from a fairly random selection of 10 high-frequency words in English and their equivalents in French, Italian, Spanish and German.

Table 4.2   High-frequency words

English	French	Italian	Spanish	German
however	cependant	comunque	no obstante	aber
near	près	vicino	cerca	nähe/in der Nähe
today	aujourd'hui	oggi	hoy	heute
am	suis	sono	soy	bin
may/can	peux	puo	puedo	darf
until	jusqu'à	fino a che	hasta	bis
another	un autre	un altro	otro	noch eins
nothing	rien	niente	nada	nichts
they	ils/elles	egli/loro	ellos/ellas	sie

The message behind this would be that firstly, these high-frequency words in general, and function words in particular, need to be learnt early on. Beginners need to have frequent meetings with these words in context and they need to ensure that they really understand their meaning in that context. Secondly, and a corollary of the first point, they should not be avoided because they are not cognates nor their salience in text minimized in favour of cognates. Cognates have a problematic function in pedagogy even if the literature tells us they are easy to learn. Let us look at a few studies involving the learnability of different kinds of word.

Lotto and de Groot's study cited earlier also looked at which words were more easily learnt both in terms of accuracy and speed of retrieval. They found that cognates were easier to learn but so were high-frequency words.

Ellis and Beaton (1993a, 1993b) confirmed that words which are acoustically and orthographically similar to L1 words are easier to understand, learn and recall than words which are dissimilar. Concrete nouns are easier to learn owing to their imageability (we can easily see the image of a 'flower', much harder to see an image of the word 'freedom'). For the same reason, and additionally because of their closer connection to syntax, verbs are harder to visualize and learn than nouns.

However, because something is easier doesn't necessarily mean that it is better for you, just as (for children only, of course!) eating chocolate is easier than eating spinach. Verbs appear to be centrally involved in linguistic development. Harley (1995) argues that an increase in the proportion of verbs relative to other word classes was positively associated with overall richness of vocabulary. It may well be that verbs, adverbs and function words lead us to greater independence of language use than nouns and adjectives.

Lastly, in a study of reading strategies (Macaro 2001a), which we will look at in later chapters in some detail, I observed that poor learners were scanning text for cognates to the detriment of making the effort to recall non-cognate words which they had definitely been exposed to. A pedagogy that over-emphasizes cognates as a pathway to learning may be creating poor vocabulary memorization and recall habits in young or beginner learners.

Conclusions

- Vocabulary is important because words contain more than the superficial meaning that might be attributed to them on type for type basis. They are at the root of the processes we use for accessing language and they are probably the most important building blocks in the production of language. With a relatively limited number of L2 words we can achieve considerable levels of foreign-language proficiency.

The variety of contexts and purposes in which and for which a foreign language is learnt makes it impossible to prescribe clear guidelines for vocabulary learning. Nevertheless in all purposes beyond that of 'survival in the target country' we need to have an in-depth knowledge of high-frequency words, particularly function words. These high-frequency words will need to be learnt and re-learnt, consolidated and reinforced. Reinforcement is best achieved through exposure to them in context. The high-frequency words do pose particular L1-L2 transfer problems for the learner and exposure to their different L2 applications is essential early in a language-learning programme. Being able to use high-frequency words in different utterances or sentences should be regarded by teachers as an important form of progression in the learner's development. In-depth word knowledge is currently undervalued, in England at least, as a criteria of progression in favour of 'topic coverage' – getting through the scheme of work or exam syllabus. The line of research which suggests that grammatical knowledge increases in line with increase in knowledge of lexical meaning is an interesting one and further research should be dedicated to this. The findings in this chapter would provide support for a syllabus that starts off with both cognates and high-frequency non-cognate words.

Vocabulary learning has been undervalued in some learning environments due to an unconfirmed and premature belief in the value of 'natural' learning, that is, uniquely from exposure to input. Linked to this is our need to re-conceptualize how the L2 learner's brain stores and retrieves lexis and how this process changes over time. We now have overwhelming evidence that, at least in the early stages of language learning, the first language plays a positive and pivotal part in increasing the lexical store. More research needs to be done in this domain before we can really begin to draw pedagogical implications for ensuring progression in lexical knowledge in tandem with linguistic skills.

In terms of rate of low-frequency vocabulary learning, research has indicated that there might exist a plateau at around the intermediate level at something like 1,000-1,300 words. Yet research also shows that large quantities of words can be learnt in a very short time. We need to investigate the teaching and learning conditions which promote constant and rapid vocabulary growth. For those students not able to visit the target country we should explore the feasibility of short intensive courses which give a boost to the vocabulary store as well as assisting progression from receptive to productive vocabulary. In England it appears to be low expectations of what vocabulary can be learnt rather than an innate national inability to learn a L2 which results in such low levels of lexical acquisition. There is no reason why any individual student, nor any groups of students, regardless of nationality or culture, cannot be trained to learn vocabulary more effectively. We need to rethink the vocabulary content of some of our syllabuses. This does not mean ditching a topic approach but by re-conceptualizing the progression within them to reflect ever more sophisticated uses of function words rather than simply acquiring an ever widening vocabulary of low-frequency words.

Vocabulary can certainly be learnt implicitly and, indeed, context appears to be essential in ensuring in-depth understanding of a word. However, consolidation and progression from receptive to productive vocabulary is clearly facilitated by selective attention being brought to bear on the new lexical item. In order for vocabulary to be learnt there has to be some selective attention to it. The human mind just does not seem to be equipped to process and store efficiently in a subconscious manner everything that comes its way. Inferring the correct meaning of a word in a given context does not necessarily mean that there is retention of the inferred meaning since the immediate communicative need will have been met. The research evidence is quite strong that inferred vocabulary is enhanced by explicit and methodical vocabulary learning. On balance, vocabulary learning is more an explicit process than an implicit one. It is probably the case that some learners get faster and faster at it and its 'explicit appearance' decreases. A threshold stage therefore seems to exist before which teachers should refrain from focusing only on developing linguistic skills but should continue to purposefully teach vocabulary.

Dictionaries and other resources such as glosses should be an integral part of a vocabulary learning programme. No 'system', such as an examination structure, should be allowed to apply a backwash effect on these essential tools of language learning. Good dictionary use is an acquired and complex set of strategies and learners need time and help with these.

We do not know as yet precisely which cognitive strategies are most effective. We do know that using cognitive strategies in combination, and (probably) with metacognitive strategies hierarchically arranged in order to evaluate them, leads to the most secure and effective vocabulary acquisition. Students with different levels of proficiency need to be given different advice about strategy use and different strategy training in order to 'push them on'.

All strategies involving vocabulary involve isolating the word from the context. The context provides the means to identify the word, not necessarily the mechanisms to learn it. On the one hand, therefore, we need to train students to use metacognitive strategies for inferring meaning. On the other, we need to discuss with students the inefficiency of single-strategy learning. They keyword associations strategy, although successful for small quantities of vocabulary, still has to prove itself for large quantities. Perhaps it is best deployed with very difficult words, those which have no immediate and obvious semantic connections. If the keyword strategy is being recommended by teachers then the students must generate their own L1-L2 word associations.

The research indicates that no strategy is of itself inefficient, be it rote learning, translation or keyword association. The crucial message to students is to generate the effort to experiment with clusters of strategies and evaluate their effectiveness. Research, however, has not focused sufficiently on which combinations of strategies are most successful. Too much interest has focused on either the distinction between implicit and explicit learning or between keyword association and rote learning rather than how all these strategies interact in the learner's brain to create networks of meaning. Connectionist theories would imply that this should be the next wave of strategy research.

Learner strategy training for vocabulary acquisition shows some of the most promising research-based findings. Interestingly it is in vocabulary memorization that learners seem able to articulate which strategies they use and when they use them. Perhaps this reflects the 'left to their own devices' nature of teaching methods with regard to vocabulary learning.

The gulf between the formidable quantities of vocabulary needed even for threshold proficiency and the limited time attributed to language learning in formal classrooms can be bridged only if learners take on the responsibility of learning more independently of teacher and materials. They need to be made aware of this and encouraged.

One 'strategy cluster' which combines implicit and explicit processes is to train learners to select consciously from the context the word or phrase that helped them infer the meaning of the new word. Thus we can ask them to identify a word they don't know; guess at the word; identify the word/phrase that helped them guess; think why it helped them guess; evaluate the strategy. This kind of information is very valuable to the teacher too in terms of identifying problems with the processes that students are going through when dealing with texts and when learning vocabulary and, worked into a normal teaching and learning sequence, it presents no more time commitment than other types of text-related exercises.

In order for learners to make rapid vocabulary gains they will need to be exposed to plenty of written texts. However, the belief that all texts should be authentic needs to be reconsidered. Reading texts are more likely to give the processing time needed for focal attention to new lexis than listening texts or participation in oral interaction. Too much focus on speaking may be detrimental to rapid vocabulary growth.

Although artificial and laboratory-based experiments of vocabulary acquisition are useful in giving insights into psycholinguistic processes, these have to be carefully balanced by the research community with studies in authentic classrooms. This is not because learners' brains are different in classrooms but because there are additional and potentially unforeseeable variables which may be interacting strongly with the processing and storage of L2 vocabulary. This contextualized research will give a deeper knowledge of the source of irregularities in the quantity and rate of vocabulary growth and the reason why it might get stuck on a plateau.

Chapter 5

Research on Attitudes and Motivation

In this chapter I will try to answer the following questions:

1. What does motivation look like?
2. How have researchers tried to research the 'construct' of motivation?
3. What does research say about general factors affecting motivation of groups of learners?
4. What does research say about individual differences among language learners?
5. What indications are there as to how we might overcome demotivation?
6. What do language teachers think?
7. What further research needs to be done?

What does motivation look like?

> Motivation provides the primary impetus to initiate learning the L2 and later the driving force to sustain the long and often tedious learning process; indeed, all other factors involved in L2 acquisition presuppose motivation to some extent. (Dörnyei 1998: 117)

In his introduction to his 1998 survey of *motivation* research Zoltán Dörnyei makes this strong claim for the central role that motivation plays in foreign- or second-language learning. Moreover, in his highly readable 2001 book of the same title he claims that motivational issues take up a surprisingly large proportion of our everyday talk: we talk about likes and dislikes; goals and expectations; we complain of being under-valued or badly led by our superiors. Given that motivational issues are so pervasive in our lives it is not surprising that, as in the case of vocabulary learning in the last chapter, motivation should figure so prominently on L2 teachers' agenda of issues that they would like research to resolve. After all, whether we have been language teachers of young children, of adolescents or of adults, we have all been faced with students who appear to lack motivation or who tell us in no uncertain terms that they have no desire to learn the foreign language. As Gary Chambers puts it with such personal feeling:

Arguably the biggest problem is posed by those pupils who are quite able but who do not want to learn a foreign language and make sure that the teacher knows it! (Chambers 1993: 13)

And therein lies the first problem with research on motivation. Motivation does not have obvious direct causes such as 'low ability'. It is quite difficult to arrive at the sources and components of motivation. It is even quite difficult to recognize it when we look for it. We will therefore spend a little more time thinking about how the 'construct' *motivation* might actually appear to us both in the classroom and as a national characteristic.

Adam might appear attentive in a German (L2) listening task but then writes virtually nothing down in response to the task. Jane may look 'motivated' by putting her hand up to answer a question in (L2) French but, when asked, her answer lacks French intonation patterns and it seems as if she doesn't care. Nicolas appears to have put enormous amounts of time into one piece of writing in (L2) English. Another piece two weeks later looks as if he has thrown down a few copied phrases from the textbook. Faridah does extremely badly at Spanish (L2) for two years and then makes enormous progress with a new subject, Italian (L3), in subsequent years.

Can we measure the different levels of motivation that Nicolas has demonstrated? Can we identify the difference between Adam's 'displayed' motivation and the cognitive effort required of the listening task? What are the factors that are leading to Faridah's higher achievement in Italian – is she 'simply more motivated' – and what does this mean? Does Jane answer without enthusiasm because she is embarrassed, anxious about getting it wrong, thinks she can't 'put on the style', is worried about being called a swot, doesn't think pronunciation is important, has not 'heard and taken up' the intonation patterns of French?

The second problem is that motivation is not something that can be easily measured in the same way that, even if imperfectly, language aptitude or proficiency can. However subjective our criteria for language proficiency are, we can nevertheless reach some sort of consensus based on standardized measurements. With motivation that's pretty difficult. We can't say that James is 10% less motivated than Maria or that Sarah is the third most motivated young woman in her class.

Motivation is a very difficult construct. It has very loose boundaries and it seems to intersect with many other variables in language learning. If motivation is so multifaceted, teacher-readers or reader-researchers will have to content themselves with some good news and some bad news. First the good news. There is plenty of very good quality research on motivation. The central importance attached to motivation by teachers is matched by the importance attached to it by researchers. This is because some researchers believe that motivation can overcome deficiencies in language aptitude or make up for a poor L2 teaching environment. Moreover, they believe that motivation is so central to human behaviour that it must hold the key to the door of success. Now the bad news. It's not a single key that opens the door but a whole bunch of keys and researchers have not yet found the one that fits the lock. In actual fact it's even more complicated than that. To extend the analogy, the door is opened by a whole series of locks each of which has more than one key and, to make life even more difficult, we probably have to work out how to use the keys *in the right order* – only then will the door open! Until we fully understand all the components of motivation and until we have grasped the essential cause-and-effect relationship between them, we will not have a single unified theory of what motivation is and, consequently, we will be held back from stating with any certainty what works in the classroom, and what will motivate our language learners.

A further way of demonstrating the difficulty of arriving at a clear understanding of motivation is to take one country's (England) L2 provision, and see very briefly how complex motivation findings are both in their multi-faceted nature and over time. In most of the studies in table 5.1, questionnaires were used with very large samples of students.

From this sketchy timeline of research and events we begin to see that motivation

Table 5.1   A brief history of foreign-language-learning attitudes in England

Author and date of survey	Some research findings related to attitudes and motivation	A selection of key events in MFL in England
Pritchard (1935)	French ranked fifth in popularity out of 11 subjects.	
	No huge variation within the age range of 12–16 Subject is genuinely liked, found to be useful, vocational. Boys find it entertaining, novel, agreeable, good fun. Those who don't favour French claim it is because they find it difficult 'it takes a long time before you can do anything with it'.	
Duckworth and Entwhistle (1974)	Second-year students: French was ranked very low for *interest* and *social benefit* and ranked very high (especially by boys) for *difficulty*. Fifth-year students: French ranked very low for interest and social benefit. Ranked in the middle for difficulty.	
Burstall (1975)	Boys are influenced by their parents into regarding languages as a female subject.	
Ormerod (1975)	French ranked fourteenth out of 17 subjects by boys and tenth by girls in terms of 'liking the subject' and 'liking their teacher'.	Development of more communicative approaches.
Harvey and Stables (1984)	Both French and German relatively unpopular, particularly among boys.	Introduction of graded tests.
Powell and Batters (1985)	Second-year students: about 37% express dislike of language learning. Boys more inclined to regard it as their least favourite subject. Boys more ethnocentric and have a poorer self-image with regard to languages. However, the idea that one sex is more likely to be better at languages is overwhelmingly rejected.	

Pritchard (1987)	76% of sample state that French 'usually interests' them. German has a more masculine image than French but perceived as less interesting, more difficult and less useful. They do not necessarily do better at German. Many in sample refuse to answer question of whether boys or girls are better at languages.	
Aplin (1991)	Students have low self-esteem because of comparatively low test marks and, possibly, low teacher aspirations.	1990 A level entries: 27,245 (Fr) 9,476 (Ger)
Stables and Stables (1996)	Data collected 1991/2. Increased European integration is having a positive effect on perceptions of the importance of languages in Year 11 but A level is considered difficult.	Introduction of National Curriculum A modern language made compulsory to 16
Chambers (1993)	Pupils acknowledge the importance of learning languages but don't claim to enjoy it (see below).	A level entries 'peak': 31,261(Fr) 11,338 (Ger)
Clarke and Trafford (1996)	Social class has a significant effect on pupil attitudes (see below).	
Williams and Burden (1999)	Year 9 and 10 pupils attribute failure to the difficulty of the subject and to being distracted by others (see below).	
Fisher and Evans (2000)	Much more favourable attitudes reported towards French people after an exchange visit (see below).	Nuffield Inquiry: MFL in England is in crisis. Some university languages departments closing.
Maubach and Morgan (2001)	Female A level students more likely than boys to attribute success to hard work rather than ability (see below).	
Jones and Jones (2001)	Most students rate languages as not enjoyable and not important, but girls have more positive attitudes than boys (see below).	
Graham (2002)	Year 12 and 13 students attribute lack of success to low ability and task difficulty (see below).	A level entries lowest after steady and uniform drop: 15,614 (Fr) 7,013 (Ger)

can be linked to a number of determinants: the usefulness of speaking another language; the influence of significant others such as parents or friends; the difficulty of the subject; its status compared to other subjects on the curriculum; world events; its 'genderedness'; one's social and cultural background; contact with the target culture. All these determinants may, in addition, interact with one another resulting in an unstable causation over a period of time. We could interpret the dramatic drop in A level entries for French and German as lack of motivation to learn a language but unless we identify the underlying factors we can do nothing to remedy the situation.

The fact that motivation is a complex issue both in its spectrum and over time does not mean that we should not make a stab at examining how far we have got with motivational research and draw some preliminary conclusions.

How have researchers tried to define motivation?

The purpose of this section is to revue a number of theories and models of motivation prior to investigating how researchers have tried to answer research questions on the construct by basing themselves on a particular theory or model.

Because of the sheer number of factors that can affect human behaviour, many researchers in L2 learning have opted for a *reductionist* approach to constructing motivational theory (Dörnyei 2001). By this I mean that they have, a priori, selected only some of the hypothesized causes of motivation and tested those, either against each other, or against achievement, or both. We can take as an example of this, what is usually considered to be a seminal work on motivation in L2 learning, Gardner and Lambert (1972). One of their foci was whether all individuals were capable of learning a second language. Their answer was a tentative 'yes' provided that the right attitudes and motivation were present. They were able to make this claim because, despite different measures of aptitude, all subjects were able to learn a L2 when in plentiful contact and with a positive attitude to the target culture. Thus, by focusing on ethnicity, ethnocentrism and nationalism, they were (at least temporarily) excluding or 'downplaying' other possible hypotheses. From these initial explorations, and further developed by Gardner (1985), sprung the notion of *orientation*. Students of second languages were classified as *integratively* or *instrumentally* orientated. They were integratively oriented if, when reporting on their reasons for wanting to learn an L2, they stressed wanting to meet and converse with speakers of that L2. They would want to interact with members of the target community for social reasons. They were instrumentally orientated if their motivation for learning an L2 was linked to its usefulness to their careers, or if it provided them with a desired qualification, or it made them better educated.

These orientations were established by factor analytic studies. Factor analysis is a statistical procedure which is able to bring together a cluster of items bound together by one common underlying factor. It is one of the principal means by which researchers have come to establish concepts and constructs. In motivational research this is usually done by questionnaire where respondents have a considerable number of attitudinal and/or behavioural questions to respond to using some kind of standardized scale.

Once constructs of motivation were arrived at, it was possible to test them against other variables such as aptitude. For example, Gardner *et al.* (1976 in Gardner 1985: 66-7) looked at correlations between achievement and intention to continue with studying French in secondary schools in Canada. Their results suggested that motivation was better than language aptitude at predicting whether students intended to continue language study.

In a similar study by Clément *et al.* (1980 in Gardner 1985: 68) involving 15-16-year-old students in Montreal (French L1, English L2), three factors were established using factor analysis which explained the covariance from the respondents. These were: integrative orientation, self confidence with English and academic achievement. The 'loading' (i.e. the factor that scored highest of the three) was on integrative orientation in terms of predicting their intention of continuing to study English. Thus these researchers were able to posit the theory that, in addition to cognitive factors (the brain's processing of the L2), and in addition to environmental factors (social class, economic status), L2 motivation contained a personality dimension. It was different from other subjects such as history or mathematics because it involved the learners in personality change, perhaps even an identity change. Learners on their way to becoming bilinguals were setting out on a journey to become different types of people.

The work of Gardner and his associates led to the Attitude/Motivation Test Battery, available in the appendix of Gardner (1985) and still recognized as a well standardized and tried and tested instrument for measuring motivation (Dörnyei 1998).

In sum, once an attempt had been made at defining motivation as a construct involving attitudes and beliefs, researchers turned their attention to finding out whether motivation or language 'ability' were likely to be better predictors of the likelihood of continuing with second-language study. The balance to date was very much tipped towards 'motivation'.

The 1990s saw a shift in the way that motivation in L2 learning had been perceived in the preceding two decades. Firstly there was a gradual movement back to incorporating cognition into theories of motivation. The main reason for this shift was propelled by attempts to define the direction of causality (the right order for trying out the keys in the locks). Does an instrumental or integrative desire to learn an L2 lead to greater cognitive effort and therefore success? Or, does greater cognitive performance (for example greater powers of vocabulary memorization and instant recall) lead to finding the subject relatively easy and therefore to being motivated to learn? We will return to this issue of direction of causality at frequent points in this chapter. We should bear in mind however that Graham (1997) found that the less successful learners in her study of 16-17-year-olds regarded a foreign language as something that can be acquired effortlessly while the more successful learners were aware of the effort required. The second shift was dedicated to expanding the construct of motivation itself, beyond the instrumental and integrative orientations. Thirdly, researchers such as Tremblay and Gardner (1995) attempted to identify what they termed a *mediator variable*. This is a variable that links and explains the relationship between two other variables. For example they proposed that *effort*, if it could be sufficiently well described, could be considered to be a mediating variable between *goal theory* (see below) and higher achievement in the L2. Fourthly, a recognition developed that the motivational construct lacked a temporal dimension. Thus, as well as trying to establish key aspects in the motivational spectrum, for example in searching for a link between *attention to a task* and *intensity of attention to task*, researchers also began to examine the *persistence of attention* over time.

Having obtained a brief insight into the broad historical developments in L2 motivational research, we will now look more specifically at theories of motivation. Perhaps it would be better to consider these as alternative models or sub-theories of motivation as they attempt to provide an explanation for the relationship between motivation and achievement whilst not excluding other explanations. In other words these different explanations can co-exist, they are not mutually exclusive.

Goal-related theory

As we have already noted this theory sees motivation comprising of a linear or perhaps a circular process. Language learners establish goals for themselves as individuals with or without the help of the teacher. The first issue, however, is what sorts of linguistic goals should learners set themselves. The theory proposes that the properties of the goal are crucial to the motivational process that will be used in achieving those goals. So, for example, linguistic goals that are set by choice (rather than imposed by the teacher) are likely to be pursued with greater motivational effort than those imposed solely by a teacher. In addition, in the generic literature on motivation, important goal properties are determined by the specificity of the goal. Locke and Kristof (1996) reviewing goal-related research conclude that goals which are specific but at the same time quite challenging are more likely to lead to higher achievement than woolly goals. It is also self-evident that specific goals which are not at all challenging are not going to lead to higher achievement. Types of goals can also vary in terms of the way they are intended to please or satisfy. The intention of the goal can be to satisfy the student alone (for example by having mastered a difficult language skill such as careful editing of written work) or they can be intended as 'performance goals' for the purposes of public recognition, in order to boost the individual ego (Dörnyei 1998: 121). Of course there is no reason why there should not be a degree of both types of intention underlying the goals set.

Goals have an effect on attitudes and motivation by:

1. focusing the learner's attention on activities and behaviour which are goal-relevant;
2. assisting the learner in evaluating the success of effort;
3. assisting the learner in gauging the intensity of effort needed;
4. encouraging persistent effort;
5. encouraging learners to draw up short-term and long-term plans in a more systematic way in order to achieve the goal.

In the late 1970s and early 1980s in England, a number of local initiatives by language teachers created a series of 'graded objectives' in modern languages, based on graded syllabuses and tests which were somewhat similar to music grades. One of the main aims of these graded objectives was to give learners short-term goals that they could achieve, providing them with clear feedback on their efforts and thereby stimulating the incentive for learning. Most experienced teachers still look back on these initiatives as highly successful in increasing motivation towards language learning, particularly among lower-achieving learners. In addition, these 'rising treads' of learning (Hope 1987) provided a strong link with *self-efficacy* (see below), the belief that individuals have with regard to what they can do. In fact a number of graded-objectives schemes developed 'can-do' sheets where learners kept a record of the areas of knowledge and skills that they had achieved.

Goal-related theory tends to be popular in secondary language learning because of its clear linear progression from goal setting to evaluation of goal achievement. It can, in a more sophisticated way, be made circular by learners reflecting back on the appropriateness of the goal at the moment of evaluation.

Expectations and values-related theory

The concept of self-efficacy, introduced above, forms part of a very influential theory (see Pintrich and Schunk 1996 for a generic overview) on the perceptions that we hold of the expectations of success and of the value of the road we have embarked upon (including the value of a specific task). Firstly, the theory proposes that we all have an innate desire to expand our knowledge and particularly an inborn curiosity to find things out (Dörnyei 1998). However, this innate desire is mediated by the likelihood (or expectation) of successful completion or achievement of a goal or task. So researchers have attempted to find out what makes learners possess these expectations of success.

The first factor contributing to an expectation of success is *attribution* as a result of past experiences. If, every time I try to read an article from the second acquisition literature, I struggle, get frustrated and have to go off and do something else, to what should I attribute this failure? Is it the writer's fault for not making his/her message clear enough? Is it my fault for not being good enough at understanding the terminology or the complex statistics? Is it the educational community's fault for suggesting that language teaching and learning should have some research evidence to back it up? Thus, that to which I attribute my failure in the past will significantly affect my future achievement behaviour. There's not much I can do (at least not very easily) about changing the way writers write applied linguistics or second-language-acquisition articles. However, I might be able to do something to improve my understanding of complex statistics. Attribution can also be in connection with success, not just failure. What do learners attribute their success in language learning to? Do they attribute it to how good the teacher is? Do they attribute it to how easy the language is? Do they claim that it is the language materials that are so exciting or is it the improved acoustics in the classroom as a result of a carpet having been laid? Is their success due to the reduced size of the class from last year? And so on. As Williams and Burden (1999) summarize attribution:

> a person's affective and cognitive reactions to success or failure on an achievement task are a function of the causal attributions that are used to explain why a particular outcome occurred. (194)

The second factor contributing to an expectation of success is *self-efficacy* – the relative measure of what learners think they can do. Educational psychologists would argue that people with a low sense of self-efficacy in a given domain perceive difficult tasks as personal threats. They will keep dwelling on their personal deficiencies rather than attacking the inherent problems in a task (Bandura 1993). These beliefs are based on cognitive processing of diverse sources, for example their peers, their teachers or their parents (Dörnyei 1998). Thus they will not attempt to do things that they don't think they can do. This may in turn reduce the level of their educational aspirations. For example, in a study by Conti (2001) university learners of Italian reported not bothering to monitor or check the accuracy of their work because they didn't feel they were good at it. When they were trained to check their written work more effectively their self-efficacy changed. They felt that they were perfectly able to do it and therefore the number of times that they checked their work vastly increased.

The third factor contributing to the expectation of success is *self-worth* and this may be related to personality. Some people's highest priority is what others think of them. Success or failure is inextricably linked to the public persona they wish to project. If I hear one of my peers saying that they spent only 15 minutes writing a 200-word composition in (L2) Spanish, whereas I spent an hour and a half, this will affect my self-efficacy. However, my public reaction may be to say: 'Yeah that's roughly how long it took me.' This is related to my self-worth. I may want to play down the amount of effort I have invested in the task in order to make my peers think I am as successful as they are. Other face-saving strategies associated with self-worth are failure with honour – striving for unattainable goals that invite failure (Dörnyei 1998); nonchalance towards an important task – I won't put much effort into it so if I fail I can publicly attribute it to my lack of effort; if I succeed despite the lack of effort, all the better in terms of my public persona.

Value attribution to success is concerned with the balance between effort and cost – the *valence*. What is the valence of learning all the irregular future tense verbs in French when (a) I can just as easily use the verb 'to go' plus the infinitive and (b) I can make myself perfectly well understood if I just pretend they're all regular? These values placed on a task are then balanced against the issue of whether I am instrumentally oriented to learn just for communication or somehow intrinsically interested in the language itself – in getting it just right.

Self-determination theory

In language learning, the concept of autonomy has now been gaining considerable ground for at least two decades. Autonomy is linked to self-determination theory because it raises the whole question of whether we learn better, or are better motivated to learn, if we have a measure of control over our learning. In a sense it is linked to the nature of the participants in the goal-setting agenda discussed earlier. The fundamental principle behind self-determination, as the term suggests, is that freedom to act as one wishes is an essential human need. Just as individual freedom in the political dimension is tempered by the need or the limitations of acting collectively, so in terms of a language-learner autonomy, individual freedom is tempered or limited by the demands and expectations both of our L1 community and of the target-language community. I might want to exercise an aspect of my autonomy by learning a kind of Americanized French, but if, as a result, French people would refuse to interact with me, there wouldn't really be much point! Nevertheless, having even a limited measure of control over my language learning would seem to be necessary in order for my endeavour to be rewarding to me. Dörnyei (1998) observes that, in the light of self-determination theory 'extrinsic motivation is no longer regarded as an antagonistic counterpart of intrinsic motivation.' (121) Rather, both behaviour as a means to an end and behaviour for its own enjoyment and self-fulfilment are perfectly compatible when seen through the lens of autonomy and self-determination.

Having explored some general theories of motivation we will now move on to consider what factors might affect motivation.

General factors affecting motivation of groups of learners

Under this section we will look at studies in attitudes and motivation under two headings:

1. Gender, social class, and the school
2. Cultural and international issues

Gender and social class and the school

A considerable amount of attention has been given to how gender acts as a variable in attitudes, motivation and achievement. As Harris (1998) records, in England, recent years have seen a plethora of articles in the media expressing concern over boys' lack of academic progress and the timeline at the beginning of this chapter reinforces this observation. She argues that the areas which need to be addressed are the need for boys to have a clear understanding of the progress they need to make; the need to create reading materials which cater more for boys' preferences; writing tasks which are at once highly structured but also relate to topics which might be of interest to boys; the need for language teachers to consider their responses to the behaviour of boys. Harris suggests that there is some evidence that boys receive more open and direct criticism of their work than do girls.

Callaghan (1998) argues that foreign-language policies in England have failed. Another glance at the timeline at the beginning of this chapter would support this view. The introduction of the National Curriculum (NC) for MFL results in no apparent improvement in attitudes towards language learning and a discernible drop in uptake. Callaghan asks what the balance is between psycholinguistic differences (cognitive processes) between boys and girls and environmental differences (social and cultural factors). She concludes that, although there is some evidence of brain lateralization – the belief that boys tend to use only one side of the brain for language processing whereas girls tend to use both – it is certainly not conclusive evidence. She also cites evidence of higher verbal fluency in girls but concludes, along with Halpern (1992), that socialization processes and out-of-school experiences are more likely causes of the distinct linguistic abilities of boys and girls. For Callaghan the following environmental differences are crucial in helping to explain boys' underachievement in languages.

1. Boys behave in such ways that, in effect, force teachers to be negative towards them.
2. On the other hand, teachers treat boys differently and, consequently, boys think teachers have different aspirations.
3. Teachers have different expectations in various subjects. They expect girls to do better.
4. Boys prefer male teachers and most MFL teachers are female. As we shall see, there is little support in more recent literature for this assertion.

Callaghan also carried out a small-scale project on the genderedness of the 16 NC topics. She concludes that six topics are girl-centred (but are the ones which are most 'revisited'); three are boy-centred; four are equally appreciated by both sexes; three are equally disliked by both sexes. He also observes that rarely in the topics is there any *in-depth* exploration of friendships, sports, music – topics which would motivate adolescents of both sexes. These adolescents are taught to speak a language 'as if they lived in a moral vacuum' (1998: 24).

There is a great deal of face value in Callaghan's assertions. However, there is at least some comparative research (in Greece and Germany) to show that, roughly speaking, these countries follow the same topic-based syllabus as the students in England (see Chapter 4) and yet students are motivated to learn the language without, apparently, any major gender differences. In my own comparative study (Macaro 2000a), I found very few significant differences between boys and girls in Italy but marked differences in England.

In the mid-1980s Bob Powell carried out a series of surveys into the relative motivation of male and female adolescents. One of the indicators of motivation that he observed was that, in schools where language students were grouped by ability, more girls were in the top sets than boys (68.6% and 31.4% respectively). If we think back to Callaghan's notion of creating social identities through teacher-student interactions and behaviours, it is not difficult to conclude that the impact of the gendered results of setting can lead to stereotyping of a subject as 'difficult for boys'. The Foreign Language Performance in Schools Report (Assessment of Performance Unit 1986) found that boys cited modern languages as a more difficult subject than girls. Does this mean that languages have therefore reached a stage where they are perceived as a 'girls' subject?

Clarke and Trafford (1996) carried out a study which sought to identify why boys had different attitudes and achievement from girls. They noted that in 1992 girls were achieving higher grades in GCSE results across the curriculum but that the difference in modern languages was particularly acute (43% girls achieving grades A-C; 26% boys achieving grades A-C). They also noted that this disparity was not uniform across the country. In some schools, boys did equally as well as girls in modern foreign languages. They therefore interviewed teachers and students in two schools in which at least one cohort of boys had outperformed national norms and matched these to two schools where boys were not achieving better results than national norms. Unfortunately the data relating to the question of 'what do some schools do better than others' is not analysed in any depth in the article. One important finding emerges, however. There was less disparity among the sexes in schools with students from a middle-class background. Clarke and Trafford found that these pupils had a clearer idea of how a foreign language could be useful to them in business and international affairs and, in addition, several pupils had regular contact with the foreign country via holidays or foreign visitors. Other findings in this study were:

1. Whether teachers were male or female was not identified as a factor in influencing attitudes. The personality of the teacher appeared to be more important.
2. Boys appeared to be more instrumentally motivated than girls.
3. Boys appear to find French more difficult than girls and relatively more difficult than other subjects.

4. There was a link between difficulty and enjoyment. One boy said: 'I think it's a (vicious) circle, if you're no good at it you're not going to enjoy it' (45).
5. No gender bias was detected in relation to the four skills. In the past there has been some suggestion that boys prefer speaking to reading and writing. The researchers found more of a link with extrovert and introvert personalities regardless of gender.
6. No gender bias was detected in expressing frustration with the repetitive nature of the learning experience.

Jones and Jones (2001) were commissioned by the Qualifications and Curriculum Authority in England to carry out a study of boys' performance in modern languages. One rationale for the study was that, nationally, pupils in languages were doing less well than in other subjects and they noted, just as Clarke and Trafford had done five years earlier, that boys were doing worse. Using questionnaires and interviews, they too compared schools operating at the national average with schools operating above the national average. Unfortunately, in this study too, the question of school effectiveness is not answered by direct reference to the data. For example the questionnaire (administered to 1,266 year-9 students) asked whether they found language learning enjoyable. The authors report that the majority did not find it enjoyable but fail to provide evidence for any significant differences between higher- and lower-achieving MFL departments in the different schools. Similarly, the majority of students reported via the questionnaire that they thought languages were not particularly important. Again, we are not provided with a cross-tabulation per higher-achieving and lower-achieving school to see if perceptions of importance were linked to school-based practice. As the questionnaire is not provided in the index to the book, we do not know whether respondents were asked whether they found the subject difficult compared to other subjects and whether this was or was not gendered. The qualitative data did suggest, however, that MFL are seen as difficult especially by boys. Although the researchers were at pains to collect data from a mixed social and economic sample, virtually no analysis is provided in relation to social class. Some findings from this study were:

1. Girls were more likely to find French enjoyable than boys. French, by and large, is the first foreign language in England. German and Spanish (usually the second, optional foreign languages) were less gendered.
2. Girls were more likely to find languages important than boys.
3. MFL, as a subject, was not particularly 'gendered'. That is, boys did not think it was particularly a girls' subject. Moreover there was no suggestion that boys were concerned as to whether a teacher was male or female.
4. Poor attitudes from some boys affected relations in class and this was resented by both girls and other boys.
5. The teacher was seen as a more central figure in the MFL classroom than in other subjects. Consequently he/she was seen as more responsible for success or failure than in other subjects (see attribution theory above).
6. Pupils wanted to know why they were doing a particular language task.

There were a number of issues and themes related to difficulty of language learning reported in the interviews:

1. demands on long-term memory;
2. requirement for continuous practice;
3. listening to the teacher speaking in the target language for long periods of time;
4. a focus on accuracy rather than content;
5. because of the cumulative nature of MFL, underachievement, once established was difficult to correct.

Jones and Jones (2001) provide the reader with a huge catalogue of quotations from the interview data. However, we are not told how the interview data was coded and consequently we do not know whether the quotations are typical, showing a majority view or examples of learner beliefs. This coupled with the other methodological concerns should lead the reader to treat the findings in the study with some caution.

Finally, a study by Maubach and Morgan (2001) asked if males and females have different learning styles and whether differences might be contributing to different achievement and performance levels. Like Callaghan (1998) Maubach and Morgan noted that the evidence for brain lateralization was weak. However, they were cognisant of the hypothesis posited by Oxford and Nyikos (1989): 'females, especially adolescents and adults, tend to be more field dependent (global) and males more field independent (analytical)'. In terms of language learning this could be interpreted as the ability to see the whole picture, perhaps understanding the gist of a difficult text, rather than focusing on complete understanding of a difficult text. They therefore wanted to test this cognitive hypothesis against the hypothesis that societal factors were more influential on the achievement and motivation of males and females. They therefore administered a questionnaire to 72 students in England (17-year-olds approximately) who were studying a foreign language to advanced level. Their findings suggest that there were no significant sex differences in the following learning styles:

1. field dependence/independence
2. deductive/inductive learning
3. tolerance of ambiguity (for example the fact that there are so many exceptions to grammatical rules)
4. visual/auditory

They did find sex differences in:

1. Self-esteem/attribution: females tended to attribute success to hard work rather than ability more than males
2. Presentation of written work: females were more keen on presentation than males
3. Reflectivity: males in this survey appeared to be less impulsive about their written work – a finding which contradicts previous literature
4. Self-confidence: males were much happier to speak in front of the class and much happier than females to ask questions of the teacher

Maubach and Morgan conclude that although some male and female tendencies may exist, in terms of learning styles more significant differences appear to relate to individual characteristics than to the gender divide.

We have noted a distinct lack of research which compares social class with foreign-language learning. Similar lack of attention has been given to the role of the school. Although a substantial body of generic research exists with regard to whether a particular school makes a difference, there is virtually none that I have found with regard to whether a school, or languages department, makes a difference to language-learning motivation (and see the above studies where this might have been possible). An initiative in England, the establishment of schools Language College status (where greater emphasis is placed on the importance of languages), is still being evaluated for its effectiveness in promoting motivation. Other initiatives in England, such as 'content teaching' (Coyle 2000), that is, teaching a subject such as history through the foreign language, lack the research evidence to suggest they improve motivation. It would be unwise, I believe, to transfer unquestioningly the success of immersion programmes in Canada to other educational contexts. Another initiative in England has involved teaching in separate classes of boys and girls. All the indications are that girls do even better under such conditions and there is even some evidence that boys do marginally better when separated from girls. Whether this kind of language-learning apartheid leads to better attitudes and motivation to continue with language learning in a post-compulsory phase, is still to be resolved. There is some research to suggests that 'setting' (dividing students into proficiency groups) causes disaffection. A small-scale qualitative study by Brown and Fletcher (2002) revealed worryingly low levels of self-efficacy and problematic self-worth in 14-year-old students of German yet these pupils were able to identify in quite profound and sensitive ways their perceptions of language learning. As one student said, 'If you get put into a low set you think "Oh well, I'm stupid . . . a lot of the attitude is I'm stupid . . . and I don't mind being stupid".' Another student pointed to the belief that 'once you get into low groups it is hard to get out . . . you don't do much work in lower groups', thus engaging in a kind of self-fulfilling prophecy. Clearly, these lines of enquiry should be pursued, but as I suggest below, it may in the long run be more fruitful to strengthen the robustness of the existing research base which suggests that early failure (due to poor approaches to learning) leads to demotivation and disaffection rather than pursuing factors such as gender, social class and school which are less susceptible to change!

Cultural and international issues

Both gender and social class were important contributing factors in a large-scale comparative study of European adolescents (Convery *et al*. 1997). These researchers were attempting to identify what were the perceptions of students from different European countries towards the developing economic, cultural and political European integration. They found that females were much more likely to see themselves as having a European identity and a very high proportion of students whose families were in social class D considered themselves to be 'not at all European' (29). However, perhaps the most intriguing differences in attitudes to European identity and European integration were found *between* the European countries surveyed. Table 5.2 gives a breakdown of responses to the question: 'Do you think of yourself as European?' We note the high percentage of English adolescents who appeared to be completely rejecting the notion of European identity, unlike the very low figure for the Dutch, Italians and Spanish. The researchers hypothesize that there is a strong correlation between the fact that the Dutch rate language learning highly (whereas language learning in England is relatively undervalued as a curriculum subject) and the feeling of European identity. However, this study is not able to establish a direction of causation: does the study of languages lead to European identity or does the identity promote the study of languages.

Table 5.2   'Do you think of yourself as European?'

	Not at all	Partly	Yes, totally
England	39.8	41.6	18.6
France	17.4	41	41.6
Germany	10.5	26.3	62.6
Italy	4.3	41	54.7
Netherlands	2.6	7	90.4
Spain	6.4	25.1	68.4

Is there, therefore, any evidence that approaches to language study lead to motivation? In a cross-national comparison of learning strategies (Macaro 2000a), I found that Italian students reported using more strategies in general than English students. Particularly, I found that they used more metacognitive strategies than English students. For example Italian students tended to do more of the following.

1. Ask the teacher to clarify when they didn't understand
2. Use the context to help them infer meaning when reading
3. Use friends to practise new language with them
4. Note down new words and have combinations of strategies for memorizing them
5. Listen to L2 cassettes out of the classroom
6. Listen to L2 songs at home
7. Use the L2 out of the classroom
8. Watch L2 videos at home

English students tended to limit their strategy use to a single strategy such as using their preferred system for memorizing vocabulary. Additionally they tended to have an over-reliance on cognates for helping them to understand and use the foreign language. Whilst it cannot be denied that the Italians were in a more favourable situation 'internationally' (in that English is an international language, and there is an anglophonic youth culture spreading via the internet), which enabled them to learn their L2 English, I did make three observations. Firstly, Italian students who were learning French also seemed to use more strategies than English students learning French. Thus the status of English could be, to *some* extent, factored out of the equation. Secondly, there was no particular reason why English students should not use at least some of the above metacognitive strategies more. Thirdly, it may well be that the methodological teaching differences were contributing to more cognitive-strategy use in Italy than in England. Particularly, Italian teachers seemed to expect higher levels of learner autonomy than English teachers. We will return to the link between learner strategies and motivation in a moment. It is useful, however, to have this international perspective in mind when considering to what extent individuals can be grouped with regard to attitudes and motivation to language learning.

The above finding receives some support in a study by Creanza (1997), in which 300 pupils from secondary schools in Rome were surveyed for their motivational orientation. Creanza found that most pupils combined instrumental and integrative orientations. The prospects of employment, cultural enrichment and overseas travel were the most cited reasons for the importance of studying a foreign language.

The importance of English as a world language has been researched by others. Dörnyei, Nyilasi and Clément (1996) surveyed 4,700 13-year-olds in Hungary to compare their motivation to learn English, German, French, Italian and Russian. From this huge sample, they found that English was by far the most popular foreign language, followed by German. The most important factor underlying the motivation to learn English was the students' strong interest in and the influence of US culture. Given historical events of the late twentieth century it is not surprising that English and German should motivate Hungarian learners more than Russian.

Fisher and Evans (2000) asked themselves whether spending time in the target country, in the form of exchange visits, helped to increase motivation. They observed that although most teachers would claim that these visits are of great benefit there is little empirically based research that establishes a connection between the experience of school exchange visits and language proficiency and attitudes. Moreover, although quite a lot of research has been done on the year abroad for university undergraduates and its relationship with motivation (Coleman 1996, 2001), there is very little for school-aged children. As research evidence showed that university students actually demonstrated a hardening of stereotypical attitudes after a year abroad, Fisher and Evans wanted to know if this was mirrored in younger learners in the compulsory phases of language learning. Using pre-visit and post-visit questionnaires and group interviews, they found that the students came back with much more favourable attitudes towards French people compared to a group of students who had not participated in the exchange.[1] Particularly positive attitudes were expressed in terms of the host country's helpfulness, good-humour, politeness, patience, tolerance and friendliness. There were also improvements in proficiency in some of the languages skills tested pre- and post-visit. The authors conclude that there must be a definite link between learning/motivation and cultural exchanges that certainly warrants the languages teacher's efforts. They recommend, however, that pupils should be helped to explore 'ways of seeing' the target culture and should receive some cultural awareness instruction before going to the target country.

Still on the subject of cultural exchanges, Taylor (2000) surveyed both teachers and pupils in schools in England. She found that boys were much less likely to take part in exchanges than girls, particularly French exchanges. The *key factor* identified by both teachers and pupils was that boys felt 'less good' at languages than girls (the self-efficacy factor). Thus the gender factor appears to be interacting with cultural issues, undermining boys' desire to visit the target country. Additional important factors were:

1. Boys were less willing to experience strange habits and food

2. Boys were more reluctant to host foreign partners
3. Boys (according to girls) were less mature

Taylor also surveyed 62 students who had decided not to go on an exchange. Apart from financial constraints, the most cited inducement to them going in future was if their friends would be going as well. These results would suggest that boys are in fact lacking in confidence both linguistically and socially. As one girl put it:

> They seem OK with their friends and everything but . . . I think they aren't so confident about going out and meeting people. (Taylor 2000: 6)

We have looked at general variables affecting motivation in L2 learning such as gender, social class, country where the language is being learnt and which language is being learnt. We note that there appears to be a remarkable lack of research evidence with regard to social class. If it is taken for granted that students from less economically privileged backgrounds will achieve lower levels of proficiency in language learning, then it would be extremely helpful to know what the reasons are. Is there something specific about language learning that leads to this state of affairs or is it common to all subjects?

Gender, social class and country where the language is being learnt only go some way towards explaining motivation. We will now go on to consider individual differences in attitudes and motivation. To do this we will need to consider the status of attitudes and motivation alongside other individual differences in learners.

What does research say about individual differences among learners?

What makes one learner different from another has been the subject of much investigation in the past decade. For those wishing to study this in greater depth Skehan (1989) is a very good starting point, offering a clear and concise overview.

We saw in the study above by Maubach and Morgan (2001) that few differences appeared to exist between males and female in terms of learning styles. It was much more likely that learning styles could be attributed to individuals. This is supported by a number of other studies particularly in the ELT literature. However it is in the very nature of ELT that cultural differences may well be masked by individual differences and vice-versa because of the very mixed nature of some ESL or EFL classrooms. Oxford and Green (1996) found that some of the stereotypes of Asian learners, as reluctant to interact and expecting a more didactic style of teaching, were not supported by their qualitative study. Particularly, some learners were able to change their learning styles to suit the situation, others' learning styles came into conflict with the teacher's teaching style and stayed that way. Sullivan (1996) provides ideas as to how to create a working environment which best suits a variety of learning styles. Perhaps one of the most important individual differences is the learner's ability to adopt a more flexible learning-style framework.

Gardner, Tremblay and Masgoret (1997) wanted to find out which variables, including motivation, most contributed to language proficiency. They surveyed via questionnaires a sample of 102 university students (English L1, French L2) in Canada who had been studying French for about 11 years. They used

1. a questionnaire which rated attitudes, motivation, anxiety, self-confidence, field dependence, learning strategies;
2. a questionnaire with self-rating scales of proficiency;
3. the students' final French grades;
4. various tests to measure proficiency.

The researchers found that five factors best accounted for the correlations among the variables in the first questionnaire:

1. self-confidence
2. language-learning strategies (both memorizing and metacognitive)
3. motivation to learn French specifically
4. language aptitude
5. combined integrative and instrumental orientations for learning L2.

When they combined the questionnaires, high levels of achievement (proficiency) strongly *correlated* with low levels of language anxiety; self confidence; 'can-do' ratings (self-efficacy). There was also some correlation between proficiency and motivation/ attitudes. However these were much less strong than the self-confidence and low-anxiety ratings. Moreover, other individual differences such as learning styles (e.g. field independence) were not particularly associated with proficiency. It seems that motivation resulted from self-confidence and self-efficacy and was the mediator variable leading to higher proficiency.

Kuhlmeier *et al.* (1996) also wanted to investigate the relationship between attitudes, motivation and achievement as well as teaching methods. However, they were keen to determine whether attitudes produce achievement or whether it was the other way round. In order to determine the direction of causality they felt that both constructs (attitudes and achievement) had to be measured at several moments in the school year. The generic research on attitudes that formed the background to their study suggested that, at the beginning of the school career and/or before new material/subjects are introduced, a student's attitudes and achievements appear to be relatively independent of each other (i.e. they are not affected by each other). As schooling progresses, and students are exposed to new learning and new content, a mutual relationship of influence arises. They therefore hypothesized that in their study of students starting a new language

1. the relationship between attitudes and achievements would be stronger at the end of the year than at the beginning;
2. if a student did well at the beginning of the year, his/her attitudes to language learning would be positive by the year's end.

The researchers selected 53 classes of 14-year-olds (Dutch) starting German (FL2). Half the classes used a communicative course (Kontakte) and half used a grammar-translation course (Kennzeichen D). The students were given *achievement tests* at the beginning and at the end of the year. An *attitude* scales questionnaire looked at enjoyment of German; perseverance in German; anxiety; integrative motivation and instrumental motivation. It also asked questions about their attitudes towards the course material and the teacher. They found, contrary to some of their expectations, that differences were significant at the point of measurement (i.e. at the beginning *and* at the end of the year) rather than changing over the course of the year. In other words,

1. at the beginning of the year positive attitudes were indeed linked to high achievement;
2. at the end of the year, positive attitudes were *still* linked to high achievement
3. initial achievements did *not* have a significant effect on their eventual attitudes at the end of the year;
4. students using a communicative course had a more positive attitude to German than those using grammar-translation course;
5. students using a communicative course achieved higher scores than those using a grammar-translation course in writing, grammar, spelling, vocabulary knowledge and listening.

There are a number of observations to be made about this study. Firstly it is unclear what is meant by 'the beginning of the year'. Was it after a week of starting learning German, or a month? In other words was it attitudes that the students were bringing with them or attitudes that they formed very early on? The fact that a similar lack of clarity obviously remains as to when the first measurements of achievement were made is also a problem. Secondly, German was these Dutch youngsters' second foreign language (after English). Had their attitudes and self-efficacy already been established towards languages in general by learning English and were they bringing these to the new subject? Thirdly, if we wish to measure the effect of success on motivation, we have to manipulate one of the variables – in this case, success. That is, we would have to bring about more successful learning among less motivated learners to see if their motivation changed over the course of time. This is what learner strategy training tries to do and we will come to this in a moment. Although this study was not able to show a causal effect over time between attitude and achievement it remains a valuable study because so little attitudinal research has attempted to measure change over time.

One researcher who did try to measure change was Hotho (1999). Why, she asked, was there so little research on change given that there is so much hard evidence that motivation can disappear, for example, by students dropping out of elective courses? She selected a sample of 14 university students on an institution-wide language programme (the students were studying other subjects as main subjects and were of different nationalities). She gave them a questionnaire every two weeks between weeks 3 and 9 of an 11-week course. Because of the small sample an analysis of variance did not reveal significant differences. Nevertheless a number of noteworthy trends manifested themselves:

1. There was very little change over time regarding the reasons for studying German. However the rank order of reasons changed: *interest in language* and *personal enhancement* overtook and displaced the importance of *job/career*.
2. As time went on they became more motivated by their main subject rather

than by their language studies. Some general motivation towards German dropped.

3. The reduction in motivation seemed to correlate with finding German more difficult than at the beginning – however they still felt they could achieve the course objectives and did not feel frustrated. And they all did well!

4. Motivation and fun did not seem to be equated (i.e. achievement and success were more important).

Hotho concludes that teachers, rather than make courses easier or more fun, should concentrate on helping students to re-focus their goals or their expectations of language learning. We also note that lack of self-efficacy (finding German more difficult) again features in motivational issues. It seems that it is a human instinct to become demotivated when the going gets a bit tough. This was clearly a finding in the research by Chambers (1993) mentioned earlier. Although he could find no conclusive aspect of language learning that students did not like, the disaffected students in his study simply found language learning hard. This may be particularly poignant for those pupils who do not find other subjects harder than do their peers.

Stables and Wikeley (1999) also reported that reasons for disliking a modern language was the respondent's perception of their ability in the subject. A modern language was seen as a difficult option compared to other subjects. Confidence in their own ability was also a major variable affecting students' motivation at post-16 as reported by Fisher (2001). Even high achievers felt insecure in their ability in foreign languages and this was the reason they gave for not continuing the subject. Moreover all those that mentioned grammar as an issue did so 'in order to comment on its difficulty' (Fisher 2001: 36), even though it was an area seen as vital for their progress and confidence. Graham (2002) also found in her study of year-12 and year-13 students that they attributed failure to low ability and to task difficulty rather than to lack of strategies for achieving tasks. She concluded that attributing unchangeable and uncontrollable factors to lack of success resulted in passivity in the face of difficulties which should cause teachers and planners some considerable concern. Early findings from my current study (Macaro in process) would suggest that even year-13s (18 year olds) about to take their final language exam, consider it more difficult than other subjects at the same level. Nearly 73% of the 96 students surveyed by questionnaire reported finding a foreign language 'much harder' or 'a bit harder' than the other subjects they were studying.

A final study on this theme of attitudes and motivation and attributions of success and failure is by Williams and Burden (1999). Arguing that these issues have for too long been examined in the positivist paradigm (questionnaires with statements that respondents are not in control of) they opted for a qualitative approach (interviews and grounded approach to data analysis) with 36 students in England from the age of 10 to 14 who were learning French. They found:

1. There was a change as the students got older (or progressed through their learning paths) in the way they were able to tell how well they were doing. The younger learners relied almost exclusively on teacher feedback. The older learners relied on teacher feedback but also on marks and test results.

2. Younger learners attributed success simply to listening and concentrating.

Older learners had a much wider range of attributions — effort + help and encouragement of others + circumstances + instrumental motivation.

3. Younger learners attributed failure to lack of concentration (i.e. their own failings, but those which they could put right with effort). The older learners included lack of concentration but added distraction by others + difficulty of work + poor teaching + lack of ability.

4. Year-9 and year-10 students viewed being distracted as a significant factor (peer pressure). Yet when asked exactly what they would have to do to improve, they revealed a limited range of learner strategies.

Williams and Burden concluded that, as the learners progress through their learning paths the attributions are socially constructed — they have been shaped by the curriculum; social interactions with significant others (teachers, peers, parents). The authors feel that students who are demotivated need to shift the attributions from external loci (teachers, peers, parents) to internal loci (their own capabilities). In order to do this they need to be taught learner strategies in order to improve aspects of their cognitive and metacognitive performance.

Poor deployment of learning strategies can be due to what some authors have called a cognitive deficit. Sparks and Ganshow (1993) posited that the source of problems with language learning was not with social factors such as attitudes and motivation but poor cognitive skills that learners were importing from their first language. They proposed what they called a Linguistic Coding Deficit Hypothesis. The hypothesis suggests that poor phonological skills are at the root of L2 learning difficulties. This would be backed up by the research on foreign-language aptitude (reviewed in Skehan 1989, 1991) which includes phonological skills as a very good predictor of eventual language performance. They argue that students who are of average or superior intelligence have a cognitive deficit that is specific to the task of reading because of its requirement of high order phonological ability. The application of this assumption to L2 learning is obvious. The authors therefore advocate

1. teaching the phonology of the L2 when the student *begins* the L2 course;
2. teaching the phonology of the L1 before L2 learning begins, preferably in early primary school;
3. L1 and L2 teachers getting together in this initiative.

In order to test their hypothesis Ganshow and Sparks (1996) selected a sample 154 females aged 14-16 in a single-sex private school — first year of a 3-year foreign language course (either French, German or Spanish). They measured their: phonology/orthography; semantics; verbal memory; foreign-language aptitude. They administered a questionnaire in order to measure their levels of anxiety using the Foreign Language Classroom Anxiety Scale (Horwitz *et al.* 1986) — as a result of which the students were divided into High-anxiety; Average-anxiety; Low-anxiety. Ganshow and Sparks found:

1. The three groups were different with biggest differences obtaining between the high-anxiety and low-anxiety groups (as was predicted).
2. There were differences in L1 performance in:

Phonology/orthography (including spelling) – great significant difference here with the high-anxiety group scoring lowest
Semantics (reading comprehension *but not* vocabulary comprehension)
Memory (verbal short-term)
L1 end of year 8 grade.
3. There were differences in L2 aptitude, with the high-anxiety group demonstrating the lowest L2 aptitude.
4. There were very significant differences in final L2 grade (the low-anxiety group scoring highest).

The implications of this study are that, as differences among the groups were best noted on tasks measuring phonological/orthographic skills, it may be that the direction of causality is poor L1 coding/decoding = language anxiety = poor L2 performance. It is possible, then, that teachers need to fix the problem at the coding/decoding end. The authors conclude that 'the findings lend support to our hypothesis that native-language skills may serve as the foundation for success in the foreign-language classroom and that students' level of anxiety (or motivation) about foreign-language learning may be associated with the strength of one's language skills' (207). Thus anxiety could be a consequence rather than a cause of some foreign-language problems.

Overcoming demotivation

One of the most hopeful areas of research indirectly aimed at overcoming demotivation is learner-strategies research. Learner strategies are the actions that learners take in order to decode, process, store and retrieve language. For example, deciding to skip an unknown word in a text and come back to it later is a learner strategy. They are also the decisions they take to make the learning process easier, faster and more enjoyable (Oxford 1990). For example, deciding to listen to a cassette of the foreign language every evening is a strategy involving decision making. Space does not allow us to provide a detailed account of what strategies there are nor what categories they fall into. A number of books provide an introduction for the interested reader (Oxford 1990; Graham 1997; Cohen 1998; Macaro 2001a). In any case, I review skill-specific strategies in Chapters 6-9 of this book. The important thing here is their inter-relationship with motivation. The optimistic scenario that researchers would want to discover is that effective strategy deployment leads to language-learning success which in turn leads to high levels of motivation to both do well in the language and to continue with it. Another optimistic scenario is that demotivation can be 'treated' with learner-strategy training. That is, demotivated learners can be helped back onto the motivation train by being taught how to use strategies more effectively thus leading to greater success in learning than before. The basis for this optimism stems, in part, from the evidence above that one of the main reasons for poor attitudes to the language is that some students find it difficult. Of course we could just make language learning easier by 'dumbing it down'. However, goal theory would suggest that 'non-challenging' goals are not very motivating even if they *are* reached by the learners. What we need to do is to provide them with challenging goals and the tools with which to reach them.

Surprisingly very few studies have traced the connection between learner-strategy training and increased motivation. One such was Nunan (1997). He selected a sample of 60 students at the point of transition from the end of high school (secondary education) and entry into university. Two classes were randomly assigned as experimental and two classes as control groups. The experimental group was given pre- and post-treatment questionnaires followed by focused interviews with a sub-group of students. The strategy training focus was on

> identifying objectives;
> selective listening;
> predicting;
> confirming/checking answers with others;
> reflecting about own learning;
> self-evaluating;
> cooperating with peers;
> memorizing;
> inductive and deductive learning;
> applying L2 outside the classroom;
> classifying information/language.

Nunan found that the training resulted in a significant improvement in motivation of the experimental group over the control group. There was also significant improvement in knowledge of strategies of the experimental group over the control group. This is not surprising but it does confirm that the students were taking note of the training – that it wasn't due to some other factor.

A number of studies have shown that females use more strategies than males (Oxford and Nyikos 1989; Kaylani 1996; Macaro 2001a). Motivation was also closely bound up with strategy use. For example Oxford and Nyikos (1989) found that motivation was the highest predictor of high strategy use among university under-graduates. That is, more motivated students used learning strategies of all kinds more often than did the less motivated students. However, these strategies were more the what one might describe as the 'go out and get' strategies, 'resourceful, independent strategies' (292) rather than highly refined, day-to-day strategies – for example, for overcoming phonological difficulties when listening. Nevertheless, the correlation between strategy use, motivation and achievement in language learning is a strong one.

Another by-product of effective strategy use is that it promotes independent learning and learner autonomy and these have been identified above as being of crucial importance to human beings in terms of self-determination. Being able to select from an increased range of strategies and evaluate them for their effectiveness leads the learner to feel more empowered, more in control of the language-learning process. Wenden (1995) argues that strategies should be linked to autonomy and to task-based learning. This is because tasks are 'problem posing activities. At the heart of a task, there is a learning problem or a communication problem or both . . . [S]trategies are cognitive and/or communicative procedures deployed to deal with the problems posed by the task' (184). Relating strategies to task-based class-room approaches also develops the learner's autonomy by encouraging him/her to relate the learning to themselves as learners. They can ask themselves three important questions:

1. What is the task's purpose and how does it relate to my needs?
2. What kind of task is it?
3. How should I do the task?

These metacognitive decisions, supported by cognitive actions, are at the heart of autonomous action which in turn leads to motivation. These actions do not terminate once the task is over. Dickinson (1995) observes that the effect on learners of tests, grades and other feedback devices generally appear to depend on how they are perceived by individual learners. If learners have a sense of self-determination, they are perceived as 'useful information for further decision making'. If learners are primarily focused on demonstrating achievement to others (thus with a reduced sense of self-determination) they will more likely perceive tests as forms of control by a significant other, the teacher. Dickinson argues, as a result, that this is one of the important links between autonomy and educational theories of motivation and which account for the acclaimed power of autonomy. The study by Creanza (1997) interestingly suggested that weaker learners, asked to account for their underachievement, reported that they were likely to avoid taking a personal responsibility for their learning whilst at the same time bemoaning the fact that they were not being 'recognized' by a significant other – the teacher.

In sum, one very important area of research evidence which provides strong links to motivation is the area of learner strategies and how this, in turn, feeds in to learner autonomy. Another area that is often, anecdotally, looked at to solve problems of demotivation is that of technology in general and computer technology in particular.

The role of technology

The role of technology in developing or maintaining motivation has been explored by a number of authors, albeit indirectly. I say indirectly because, by and large, the new technology and self-access centres have not been developed in order to promote motivation but in order to provide cheap and efficient learning modes to ever increasing numbers of learners in higher education. Moreover, the prospect of technology acting as an influential variable on motivation and acquisition is, even after some 15 years of technological advance, still clouded by a lack of research evidence and theoretical underpinnings. There is still a remarkable lack of hard evidence that technology increases motivation, improves language learning or both. One of the problems is that the results of studies in computer-based learning are difficult to interpret. Different techonological environments in which the studies have been carried out, the pedagogical approaches and the 'newness' of the hardware and software all result in an unstable research base. Thus one gets a complete range of reviews on the efficacy of technology, from the fairly positive (Basena and Jamieson 1996) (cited in Felix 2001) to the outright condemnatory such as the following:

> [S]tudy after study seems to confirm that computer-based instruction reduces performance levels. (Noble 1998: 2 cited in Felix 2001)

Despite this lack of consensus on the beneficial effects of computer-based language teaching and learning, schools and universities invest huge sums of money into keeping up to date with technological innovations.

Lamb and Fisher (1999) describe a project carried out by student teachers in an urban school which explored the potential of the World Cup and the internet to motivate reluctant learners. Although the project is described in great detail its potential for generalizability is limited as the authors themselves admit. Moreover, there is actually no evidence that the students were motivated beyond the limited time frame allocated to the project. These are, no doubt, useful ideas for teachers to experiment with but they do not add up to a coherent strategy for motivating language learners over a period of years rather than weeks.

Seeve-McKenna and McKenna (2000) surveyed teacher attitudes to the use of the internet as a source of teaching. The results were not encouraging. One teacher found it 'a costly way to expose learners to authentic texts', another reported that ICT work did not 'seem to make a real difference to the children's language learning'(9).

One of the few studies to use an experimental design was by Liou (1997) who sought to investigate the attitudes of college learners to use of the World Wide Web on learning English as a foreign language. Although the overall sample was small (N = 33) the experimental group did report positive attitudes and improved learning as a result of the use of the web in teaching.

Felix (2001) carried out a substantial investigation into the potential of the web as a teaching aid both to complement face-to-face teaching and as a stand-alone course. Questionnaires were administered and interviews conducted before and after a course of instruction involving computer technology for about 50 hours. Felix found that the greatest positive attitudes were in 'feeling comfortable' with this mode of study rather than outright enjoyment. Nevertheless, those who saw mostly advantages in web-based programmes outnumbered those who saw mostly disadvantages. Felix concludes that, especially as an add-on to face-to-face teaching, the web is undeniably a viable environment for language learning. There was a suggestion that it was more motivating for students who had voluntarily enrolled in a course which was offered in a distance-learning format. These were perhaps individuals with learning styles that matched the mode of delivery.

What we need is research that directly compares ICT-based instruction with non-technical (or less technical) approaches to language learning in order to see if, over time, learners are more motivated to learn the foreign language and actually do better.

What teachers think about motivation

A number of authors have cited teacher motivation or enthusiasm as an important element in motivating learners (Dörnyei 2001). One's immediate reaction to this is that it makes sense. However, further analysis suggests that we should treat this assertion with some caution. If, as has been suggested by the research on autonomy and self-determination, the most powerful motivational force comes from the learner focusing on himself or herself, then shifting the spotlight onto the teacher would seem to be a course of action contradicting the evidence. Thus for teachers to draw the spotlight upon themselves could be a way of shifting the attribution for success to them rather than the learner. Of course, teachers have to promote the importance of their subject by outlining to the students their own motivation for having studied it and wanting to teach it (Dörnyei 2001: 179) but it is likely that an altruistic focus on the learners' growing independence will be more fruitful than maintaining a hyped up pretence of personal enthusiasm.

I will now present a list of guidelines based both on the views of practising teachers and teacher-researchers as to what aids motivation.

Dörnyei and Csizer (1998) surveyed 200 practising teachers in order to find out what they believed were the most important teaching strategies that built up and maintained motivation. The resulting analysis produced the following 'ten commandments' for motivating language learners (215).

1. Set a personal example with your own behaviour.
2. Create a pleasant relaxed atmosphere in the classroom.
3. Present the tasks properly.
4. Develop a good relationship with the learners.
5. Increase the learners' linguistic self-confidence.
6. Make the language classes interesting.
7. Promote learner autonomy.
8. Personalise the learning process.
9. Increase the learners' goal-orientedness.
10. Familiarise the learners with the target language culture.

Williams and Burden (1997) on the other hand provide the following guidelines.

1. Recognise the complexity of motivation.
2. Be aware of both initiating and sustaining motivation.
3. Discuss with learners why they are carrying out activities.
4. Involve learners in making decisions related to learning the language.
5. Involve learners in setting language-learning goals.
6. Recognise people as individuals.
7. Build up individuals' beliefs in themselves.
8. Develop internal beliefs.
9. Help move towards a mastery-oriented style.
10. Enhance intrinsic motivation.
11. Build up a supportive learning environment.
12. Give feedback that is informational.

Teachers in the Chambers (1993) survey suggested the following as a way of motivating reluctant learners.

1. Provide immediate rewards such as 'well done stickers'.
2. Improve the teacher-pupil relationship by giving them time and support.
3. Negotiate an agreement on what is acceptable and expected.
4. Insist on small groups where behaviour is more easily managed.
5. Materials and task should be appropriate to pupils' interests and level of ability.
6. Offer a variety of tasks and materials.

All these different pieces of advice strike the reader with something they have in common: they are virtually all *generic*. There is nothing second-language specific about them. There is nothing on the issue of use of the target language or the exclusion of the L1 (see Chapter 3). There is nothing on progression with respect to the relative level of the language through which the content is being delivered and the difficulty of the content itself. There is very little mention of the relationship between the individual's cultural identity and the culture of the target country or countries. There is no mention of the dominance of English as an international language and the effects of this on both learners of English as an L2 and on English (L1) learners of languages other than English. Yet, a substantial section of the literature reviewed above suggests that L2 learning is more difficult than other subjects, and that learners are more likely to become demotivated in language learning than in other subjects. I am therefore unconvinced that the answers lie exclusively in generic recommendations for motivating learners.

Conclusions

Have we got any nearer to finding out what motivation actually is? Let us start off this conclusion with where we began, with definitions of motivation. Here are two more 'in a nutshell' definitions of motivation:

> A process whereby a certain amount of instigation force arises, initiates action, and persists as long as no other force comes into play to weaken it and thereby terminate action, or until the planned outcome has been reached. (Dörnyei 1998)

> Motivation may be construed as a state of cognitive and emotional arousal, which leads to a conscious decision to act and which gives rise to a period of sustained intellectual and/or physical effort in order to attain a previously set goal. (Williams and Burden 1997: 120)

As we can see these two definitions are not too far apart. Both allude to either an initial 'force' or 'state of arousal' and then to a period during which the force or state of arousal are maintained or otherwise. What neither of the definitions is able to ascertain is precisely what gives rise to that initial force or state. In the case of the second quotation we also do not know what gave rise to the 'previously set goal'. The authors are unable to qualify their propositions because the research is not able to pinpoint the key ingredient which gives rise to a motivational impetus.

Is it actually true that motivation provides the primary impetus for learning a second language? Given the fragmentation, does motivation as a construct actually exist? Even if it exists as an umbrella term for 'the desire and effort to learn' is it actually worth studying? If it is unlikely that we will ever get a complete handle on motivation, why bother with it? The answers to these questions may lie in the fact that, as yet, we still have to prove the fundamental question of direction of causality between success at L2 learning and the desire to learn.

What we do know is that motivation is only one of the variables in an overall model of second-language learning. It cannot easily be isolated and treated as either a dependent or independent variable in its own right. It is clear that motivation cannot overcome deficiencies in language aptitude on its own. It is highly unlikely that all but a handful of learners can summon up the sustained willpower, focused and persistent attention to succeed with the long-term goal of language learning despite being presented with constant evidence of short-term failure. Only if the learner is given the tools with which to overcome difficulties can motivational aspects 'kick in'. After all, the British had plenty of motivation to resist foreign invasion in 1940 but it is highly unlikely that they could have achieved such a magnificent feat without the help of the Spitfire.

We have seen that the issue of the difficulty of learning a language is most salient when it is associated with demotivation in adolescent males, perhaps most acutely in England. There is little evidence to suggest that boys still harbour the notion that languages are a 'girly subject', nor that they are terribly affected by most teachers being female. It appears that these attitudes at the beginning of the twenty-first century have, by and large, moved on. Other hypothesized variables such as brain lateralization and learning styles also do not seem to hold water. It is much more likely that learning styles are linked to individual differences. In the case of adolescent males as a group, a vicious circle seems to have built up which comprises of lack of self-efficacy, group dynamics (particularly linked to peer pressure), lack of knowing how to learn and lack of effort. This would appear to be the most likely causal direction as there is no evidence that absolute beginners start with the 'poor group dynamics' element. Indeed, in England in Year 7 we all often talk about starting afresh on an 'even playing field'. Whatever the causal direction, it seems to me we have to start with the self-efficacy issue. Demotivated learners have to be given the tools with which to find the subject easier and make more rapid progress. It may also be that they need to understand what is actually meant by the concept of effort which, it has to be said, as teachers we are not very good at defining. It may be possible to define effort simply as the persistent application of combinations of cognitive strategies and metacognitive strategies appropriate to a clearly defined goal.

The best goals are those which are specific, challenging but achievable and in which the learner has some measure of input into how they are set. These are more likely to produce the kind of sustained effort needed for their achievement.

To return to less parochial issues. We have looked at a number of group variables and noted that some are able to predict relative levels of motivation or attitudes to the target language, some less so. Going from the largest groups to the smallest:

1. *Gender*, at least in some educational contexts, is a good predictor of motivation, strategy use or positive attitudes to learning a language.
2. *Social class* produces relative aspirations for language learning but there is insufficient research which examines this variable specifically with second-language learning.
3. There is some evidence that *age groups* differ in the way that they perceive and attribute success or failure at learning a language.
4. Different *nationalities* differ in their motivation to learn different languages. The effect on motivation of English as an international language is undeniable, even though it may be masking a much more complex story.
5. The effect on pupils of a particular *school or languages department* is less obvious from the evidence available but the teacher, regardless of their sex, is a more important figure in language classrooms than in those of other subjects.

However, this may be a consequence of the fact that language lessons are more teacher dominated rather than an inherent aspect of language learning.

These group variables interact with each other. There do appear to be important differences in terms of motivational orientations and there is strong evidence to suggest that these are caused by both historical and political factors. It remains to be seen as to whether a shift of attitudes towards an integrated Europe will bring about more favourable attitudes in England towards language learning and whether this contributes to undermining the 'they speak English everywhere' mentality. In any case this concept only has anecdotal evidence. It rarely surfaces in the literature reviewed. On the other hand, if it is true, L1 speakers of English will need to be provided with powerful additional motives for learning. One of these is that it simply improves the brain.

It seems that there is a relationship between the age of the group of learners and the effect of the school. As the learners get older the attributions of success and failure become wider in scope and therefore are pulled further and further away from the locus of possible change and solutions – the learners themselves.

We have looked at a number of individual variables: language anxiety, language aptitude, learning styles, learning strategies, self-efficacy, success and failure attribution, self-worth, self-determination/autonomy. Unlike the group variables, these individual variables are much less transparent, much less ready to give up their secret effects on motivation and ultimate proficiency.

One area that needs more research is that of phonological encoding skills. This links to the previous point of language difficulty. If poor encoding skills lead to language anxiety, poor self-efficacy and demotivation then these skills deficiencies can actually be addressed.

We desperately need more research involving absolute beginners of language learning in order to track the relationship between attitudes, the desire to learn and achievement over time. This is where the problems start. In this respect more research which addresses causality is needed. This research will need to manipulate one of the variables in longitudinal studies.

We have looked at two possible solutions: strategy training and the new technologies. The former seems to offer a more sound theoretical position and a more planned, coherent programme of intervention than the latter. It is not that, at face value, new technologies are not motivating. There is just not enough evidence as yet that they produce higher levels of motivation and certainly there is very little evidence that they produce better learning. Learner-strategy training, on the other hand, has provided a stronger evidence base that it can compensate for poor learning behaviours. In addition, routinized strategy use can provide language learners with the desire to learn and that desire can be sustained by a sense of self-determination.

In the series of recommendations provided by authors above, we noted that very few were specifically about language learning. If, as has been posited earlier, language learning is such a different psychological experience from other subjects, why is all the advice so generic? Taking also into account research reviewed in previous chapters, I will therefore finish this chapter with five highly language-specific recommendations for teachers:

1. Find out what your learners actually think about the target language and the target culture early on and track this over time.
2. Select one area of your language teaching and your students' learning that you would like to investigate for its interaction with your students' motivation.
3. Find out what language-learning strategies they use, particularly those associated with specific language-learning tasks.
4. Help individuals to use these strategies better, in a systematic and on-going way.
5. Do not adhere to any prescriptive language-teaching methodology.

Note

1. It is unclear if this was a completely different control group or whether those who had not participated had been offered the chance but had chosen not to go. If it were the latter case, one would have to treat the evidence with caution as those who had chosen to go could have been more favourable to changing their minds in the first place.

Chapter 6

Research on Reading

Reading in a foreign or second language has received a great deal of attention from researchers over the past 20 years. This is not surprising as, once the learner has progressed beyond the beginner level, the vast majority of his or her input will be in written form. This is particularly so in the case of learners of foreign languages (rather than second-language students living in the target country) where the number of contact hours with a teacher or foreign-language assistant are often limited. The tendency for written texts to gain in importance as input will be even more pronounced in the university phase of education – in literature, area studies, or L2 for academic purposes courses – where the expectation is that learners will read extensively in the L2. Interestingly reading, as a topic for research to illuminate, was not ranked as high as the other three skills by the teachers in the survey described in Chapter 1. Why should this be? Given that all of the teachers in the survey would have been involved with teaching the National Curriculum in England, which gives equal weighting to all four skills, why should reading lag so far behind speaking in their aspiration to improve language learning and why was it mentioned by only three teachers in the open-ended questions of the questionnaire?

Perhaps the answer lies in the relative invisibility of reading as a skill, both in the classroom and out of it. What I mean by this is that both the productive skills of speaking and writing can be easily monitored, at least at the end-product stage. Writing is 'handed in' to the teacher for evaluation and comment. Although the underlying processes involved in writing are far from being comprehensively understood, nevertheless teachers by and large feel they know what 'a good piece of writing is'. Similarly, the alert and sensitive teacher can make reasonably effective judgements about an individual's progress with the spoken language. They can listen to responses in questioning sequences, monitor pair and group work and evaluate oral presentations.

It is much less likely that teachers (at least in secondary classrooms) will be able to assert that a student had produced 'a very good piece of reading'. With the current orthodoxy of finding out if a student has understood a piece of text via true/false questions, multiple choice, cloze passage or synonym search, the totality of text comprehension is likely to be impossible for the teacher to monitor. From these types of tasks we can get an inkling of successful access into the text but not an accurate account of the levels of understanding nor the intricate web of strategies that the students have deployed. Moreover, students are much less likely to complain about reading than they are about listening (see for example, Chapter 5). I will not go into detail here of the differences between the two receptive skills (see Chapter 7) but given the lack of processing time that students have available when listening it is not surprising that they should identify listening as a source of difficulty or anxiety. Yet, as we shall see, reading challenging texts can cause some students a great deal of difficulty and in some cases just as much anxiety as is caused by listening texts.

A second reason that reading may not have been ranked as high by teachers in England as the other language skills is that, historically, it has been neglected at the secondary level. This view is supported by a number of theorists working in the UK context (Grenfell 1992; Klapper 1992, 1993; McGowan and Turner 1994). Problems are unlikely to arise if the conditions in which those problems might emerge are not created. Yet, as we saw in the chapter on vocabulary acquisition, reading is inextricably linked to the language-learning process and, as I shall argue, interconnects with the other three skills to such an extent that, to ignore its development, risks slowing down the rate of progress in language proficiency in general.

Models of reading in L2

Early models of L2 reading, those of the 1950s and 1960s, were based almost entirely on L1 reading models. These were divided into two cognitive and metacognitive domains. The first is how a word on a page is decoded and processed by the brain. The second is how a whole text is accessed and the meaning of it 'understood'. More recently, L2 reading models, whilst still retaining many of the features of L1 models, have begun to develop their own particular features (for example, Rumelhart 1977).

The issue of word recognition emerged as an area for research in the early 1970s because of an interest in processing times and error rates across languages. Researchers found that processing speeds depended upon fluency (whole word recognition as opposed to phonemic decoding) as well as orthography (Bernhardt 1991). Other studies investigated whether the sound systems of the language in question led to problems with word recognition. It is not surprising therefore that a combination of graphemic and phonemic issues should lead to models of word decoding and retrieval. In particular, skilled word recognition demanded that the reader of a word should not have to resort to phonemic re-coding in order to access the meaning of a word. By 're-coding' we mean the following. When a writer writes a word, what he or she is doing is encoding a sound in his or her head as conventional but entirely arbitrary squiggles on a page. The reader, when confronted with a word has, in theory, the option of sounding out that word (re-coding it in phonological form) in his or her head before asking the brain to find a meaning representation. The more frequent past *meetings* have been with the written word, the less need there should be for the reader to pass via the phonological form which would slow down the process of word recognition. Only if retrieval of meaning directly via the written form proves to be problematic, will it be necessary to call on phonological resources.

Word recognition research by and large limited itself to the surface forms of language rather than focusing on deep meaning. For example, studies in word recognition found:

1. Bilinguals, roughly equivalent in both languages, recognized words at equivalent rates in their L1 as in their L2.
2. Certain types of words caused high levels of access difficulty for L2 readers.
3. Learners were able to transfer strategies for orthography from their L1 to L2 even though these had a very different orthography (Japanese to English).
4. Certain aspects of the orthography of words made readers not notice the morphology of the word – the way bits of words can be added to words (event+ful).

Although these models of word recognition had a part to play in developing theories of L2 reading, they did result in a tendency to conceptualize reading too much at the word and sentence level rather than looking at the bigger picture.

Models of how a whole text is accessed have also gone through various developmental stages. At one time there was a sharp division between *bottom-up* models and *top-down* models. A bottom-up model conceptualizes reading essentially as a decoding of the text by the reader, a text which the writer has previously encoded. This has two consequences. Firstly, the meaning of the text is entirely driven by the writer. There is a single and restricted meaning in the text as constructed by the writer. The reader's task is merely to access that meaning through the decoding of the text. No elaboration of meaning is possible. Secondly, decoding of the surface text entails a visual focus on the identification of letters, to noticing the combinations of letters, to recognition of words, to establishing sentences via their syntactic structures and so on. Words are then associated with their semantic representations in long-term memory and sentences with their propositional units. Bottom-up models of reading were, to some extent, spawned by the word-recognition research described above.

A top-down model conceptualizes reading in a very different way. The meaning of a text is paramount and this is accessed by the reader sampling words and strings of words, and predicting and inferring the meaning underlying them. He or she can only do this by activating prior semantic, pragmatic, syntactic and discourse knowledge. Clauses or sentences will trigger ideas about the world in the reader's head which in turn will give rise to expectations of ideas that are likely to come next. Discourse features are clues which the reader seizes upon in order to create a mental picture of the structure of the text (based on previous experience of such structures) and its implications for what is to come and how it will be presented. Grammatical features, such as tense and mood, trigger more predictions or expectations of temporal sequences and cause and effect. A top-down model conceptualizes the fluent reader as an expert in his or her sampling strategies and skilled at hypothesis testing, able to integrate meaning and resolve temporary ambiguities in the text. Goodman (1967) described this model of reading as a 'psycholinguistic guessing game'.

The battle between lower levels of reading as represented by bottom-up processes and higher levels of reading as represented by top-down processes divided the research community for some considerable time. However, as in many aspects of applied linguistics, sanity won the day and eventually these two diametrically opposed models were combined into one model. This, the *interactive model* of reading, is now widely accepted as the most powerful explanation of how we go about accessing the meaning of a written text. This model combines both top-down and bottom-up strategies for deriving meaning. Reading becomes a process which draws on various knowledge sources allowing for the fact that meaning does not reside in

the text alone but is a co-construction of the writer's text and the reader's interpretation. Here, there is a constant interaction between the surface structure of the
text and the reader's own knowledge of the topic which that text is attempting to
communicate. This model involves the reader in elaborating on the meaning of the
text, inferring meaning but also at times stopping to pause and ponder over individual words and syntactic patterns and their relationships with other words and
phrases in order to confirm hypotheses, strengthen connections and build up layers of
interpretation. Most importantly, this interaction between top-down and bottom-up
processes is the primary compensation strategy that the reader has at his or her
disposal when problems of access occur. In other words, as Stanovich (1980) has
argued, strategies at either level are available for the reader to deploy in order to
compensate for a deficit at a different level. Of course this is particularly essential for
the second language reader who may have vocabulary or syntactic deficiencies and
therefore will have to draw on his or her contextual (world) knowledge in order to
infer the meaning of the unknown word or phrase. Conversely, lack of topic
knowledge (because of a lack of experience of the L2 culture, for example) may be
compensated for by a slowing down of the reading rate and an effort to ensure that all
the possible semantic representations of words are thoroughly accessed before moving
on. It is now widely accepted in the L2 reading literature that the most successful
readers are those who can operationalize the interactive model of reading using skilful
combinations of top-down and bottom-up strategies. The problem, of course, is
arriving at an understanding of what it is to deploy 'skilful combinations of strategies' when faced with different types of texts and tasks. Increasingly, researchers have
come to question the strong top-down models of efficient reading arguing that better
readers make less use of context and certainly make good use of information at the
word level (Grabe and Stoller 2002).

So far, we have looked at models of reading which apply equally well to both L1
reading and L2 reading. So is there no difference between the two other than proficiency? The answer, increasingly, is yes. Probably the most important difference in
L2 reading is that the reader has another language at his or her disposal while reading
it – their first language. Indeed some multilinguals may have many languages at their
disposal. This is a fact that has only recently drawn the attention of researchers (Kern
1994). We will return to this issue later when examining particular studies in
reading strategies. Before we move on to examining individual studies on reading, let
us take a deeper look at top-down processes.

Schema and script

What does the reader bring to the act of reading? When we talk about activating
contextual knowledge, what do we actually mean? Where does this contextual
knowledge come from and how much of it is activated?

Contextual knowledge is a combination of all the clues surrounding the text (titles,
pictures, sub-headings, text-type formats, author's name) which trigger and augment
all the world knowledge that we can bring to the topic of the text that we are reading.
This world knowledge does not exist purely and exclusively in factual form. Of course
we know that the sun rises in the east and that apples drop from trees rather than
springing from the ground, but much of our understanding of the world comes from

the way we have interpreted it in the past. Our understanding of 1980s Soviet socialism is an interpretation, not a fact, depending on our ideological stand point. This combination of hard facts and interpretations is what cognitive psychologists call schema (plural schemata). We all have schemata which help us understand a text even though we may not know the meaning of all the individual words. For example, I have given the following sentences to 11-year-olds in 'language awareness' lessons and they had no trouble telling me the approximate meaning of the words 'sklunk', 'sploff' and 'skit-skit'.

A terrible sklunk occurred yesterday morning on the London to Brighton line.
A goods sploff collided with a passenger sploff travelling at skit-skit speed.

Our schemata fill in the gaps for us. We might call it 'well-informed common sense' that the London to Brighton line is not a clothes line and that passenger trains travel at high speeds in contrast to goods trains.

But schemata do something else too. They provide the contextual glue for words that we can recognize and understand but which may not lead us to access the whole meaning of the text. There are a number of 'brainteasers' where short texts appear incomprehensible until you are told what the 'topic' of the text is. Then, suddenly, all of it makes sense (see Cook 2001: 89). For L2 readers lack of cultural awareness of the topic can cause problems of understanding as, for example, might the rules of cricket to someone from a Southern Mediterranean country.

Schemata, for many researchers, include not only the content schemata described in the last paragraph but also aspects of linguistic knowledge or formal schemata. For example the rules of discourse, the cohesion devices, the genre and the structure of a text are all used by writers to help convey meaning and are held to be a type of schema which can be drawn upon by the reader to infer meaning when the meaning of individual lexical items or phrases is unclear. Carrell (1983) questions whether the distinction between content and formal schemata exists or at least she argues that they interact to such an extent that they should be studied in combination.

Some researchers perceive a difference between what they call *schemata* and *script*. Schemata, as we have seen, form the background knowledge used to 'fill in the gaps' or 'bring all the words together' so that they make sense. Script, on the other hand, provides an element of temporal sequencing and of cause and effect. Consider the statement: *Lucien arrived at the party and handed the wine bottle to Solange.* Implied in this statement are a series of events that (Western European) convention tells us will have happened, or will happen, but which need not be stated. Lucien very likely bought the wine prior to coming to the party. If he had stolen it, the writer would have made a point of telling us. Lucien very likely knocked on the door. Solange very likely heard the knock and went to open the door. Customary as it is to bring a bottle to a party, it is unlikely that Solange will have done anything more than acknowledge the present and thank Lucien. We do not need the writer to tell us these bits of information. They are redundant because they are part of the *script*.

Although some researchers see little or no difference between schemata and script (for example Williams and Moran 1989) it is nevertheless useful to divide up our world knowledge into these two categories. One further distinction might be that script is much more socio-culturally driven (it is a knowledge shared by certain communities) whereas schemata is more individually driven (I might have a different interpretation of a painting from another individual even in the same cultural community).

The role of background knowledge in reading

A number of researchers have attempted to determine the extent to which background knowledge of a topic affects comprehension.

Why should we be interested in this?

If it is the case that our knowledge of the topic is crucial in our understanding of the text, then to what extent should we be matching up the reader's background knowledge to the text's topic? This is an issue that Parry (1993) argues has been under-researched in the literature. In an ELT context where a number of different cultures are present in the group of learners, the issue is even more crucial. If teachers are to deal effectively with readers of various cultural backgrounds they need to know more about how the different background knowledge of the learners is facilitating or creating obstacles to learning. Even within the same cultural community, some economically disadvantaged groups may encounter difficulties in applying top-down strategies in order to help them access the meaning of texts created by those not so disadvantaged.

The research evidence

Johnson (1982) found that lack of cultural familiarity with a topic such as 'Haloween' was even more important than knowledge of vocabulary among learners of English as a second language. In other words, the bottom-up strategies (focus on surface text) were not sufficient to compensate for deficiencies in their top-down inferencing[1] strategies.

Hammadou (1991) sought to investigate whether prior knowledge of a topic enabled better inferencing and whether, in turn, this was mediated by general proficiency levels of L2. She argued that background knowledge, the schema model that the learner has built up, should be balanced by 'in-text' contextual knowledge. By this she meant the links and bridges that a reader can make between the different propositions within the text. We might call this an aspect of 'the writer's schemata' because it is an attempt to see 'how the writer's thinking' is developing. Hammadou used a sample of 89 French L2 students and 77 Italian L2 students (English L1) at beginner/intermediate and advanced proficiency levels. Each group had three different texts to read dealing with different topics. All students read all three texts and were asked to write down in L1 what they had just read, without access to the original text (this approach is called a 'free recall protocol'). Subsequently they were asked to rate the topics in order of familiarity. The researcher was then able to analyse lists of inferences made by the students and divided these into 'logical inferences' and 'illogical inferences'. Hammadou found:

1. Recall (comprehension) scores did not match the ranked order of familiarity. In other words, this sample of students did not recall familiar topics better than unfamiliar ones.
2. Less advanced learners were not able to compensate for lower language proficiency by being familiar with the topic.
3. There were no significant differences between the amount of background knowledge of the topic the students had and *the number* of inferences they made.
4. There was some evidence of a relationship between language proficiency, familiarity with topic and *logical* inferences, particularly with the advanced learners of Italian. Advanced learners were able to make more logical inferences. Less advanced learners 'clearly show the traces of their own schema' (33). In other words these less advanced students allowed their own background knowledge to override in-text evidence which obviously contradicted their hypotheses.

Bügel and Buunk (1996) wanted to investigate whether gender bias in the topic of a text led to different levels of comprehension amongst males and females. Bügel had previously discovered evidence that Dutch exams contained texts with a strong gender bias. She noted that this appeared to correlate with girls not doing as well as boys in foreign-language exams in the Netherlands. Bügel and Buunk studied a huge sample (2,980) of students with an average age of 16. The students were learning English (L2). The researchers were aware of the difficulty of accurately measuring prior knowledge in a whole class of students, let alone such a huge sample. Clearly interviews were out of the question. They therefore opted for a series of three questionnaires. The first asked about reading and TV-viewing habits. The second asked the students to self-rate their prior knowledge of the topics which related to the texts they would be reading as part of the study. The third questionnaire asked them about biographic information such as gender, educational career, academic subject choice. The researchers were also aware of the difficulty of measuring comprehension. The reader will have noted, in the Hammadou study, that a free recall protocol was used where the student reads the texts, turns it over and tries to put down in L1 what they have understood. Clearly, this type of comprehension measurement introduces an additional variable, the student's memory capacity. However, Bügel and Buunk also felt that *cloze tests* focused too much on word-level understanding. On the other hand, at the opposite end of the spectrum, *summaries* permitted a demonstration of the grasp of the macrostructure of a text but might miss out on the important detail. They therefore opted for comprehension measured by *multiple choice* because this was closest to the way reading comprehension was measured in Dutch exams, testing being an underlying theme of their research. They also chose 'neutral' texts, 'male' texts and 'female' texts. Bügel and Buunk discovered:

1. As predicted, there were strong gender differences in both topic preferences and in reading/viewing habits.
2. As predicted, sex-based differences in levels of comprehension were obtained in the gender-biased texts. That is, girls understood better the text with a female topic and boys scored better in the text with a male topic.
3. Males obtained higher comprehension scores in the neutral text.

4. There were greater sex differentials in scores on the male text than on the female texts. The researchers speculate that this was perhaps because the male texts had more specialized vocabulary than did the female texts.

Unfortunately in this study there were no overall proficiency measurements. It was thus not possible to tell whether it was sex differences resulting from topic prior knowledge which provided the strongest effect on reading comprehension scores or whether it was overall language competence.

Barry and Lazarte (1998) asked themselves how readers actually go about the process of making inferences in the text they are reading and what types of inferences there are. In addition they wondered what the balance was between the syntactic complexity of the text and prior knowledge of the topic. Like other authors they identify different levels of access to meaning.

> Level 1: the verbatim representation (the word-for-word surface structure of the text)
> Level 2: the text-based representation (making links between propositions actually evident in the text)
> Level 3: the mental model (making links between propositions in the text and the reader's prior knowledge of the topic)

They reasoned that cognitive psychology would predict that level 1 would fade the quickest from short-term components in working memory, followed by levels 2 and 3 in that order. In other words the interpretation model of the text would remain the longest because of the amount of inferencing that the reader is forced to engage in. They also reasoned that the syntactic complexity of a text leads to the difficulty of 'holding on to' alternative interpretations in working memory. This in turn would lead to diminished language comprehension because of the constraints on cognitive capacity. In other words working memory cannot cope efficiently with syntactic complexity *and* high levels of inferencing simultaneously.

For their study Barry and Lazarte chose the embedded clause in a sentence as a measure of syntactic complexity. They took as an example the Spanish sentence:

En el centro del palacio, que era la parte más protegida, se encontraban, alrededor de un patio, los alojamientos del Sapa Inca y la reina.

They designated the following levels. Level 1 complexity (no embedded clause), level 2 complexity (one embedded clause) and level 3 complexity (two embedded clauses). They argued that the two embedded clauses progressively increase the syntactic complexity because

1. they interrupt the main clause;
2. readers have to assign certain syntactic elements (e.g. the prepositional phrase) to both the main clause and the embedded clauses;
3. the relationship between the verb phrase (*se encontraban*) and the noun phrase (*los alojamientos del* ...) is made difficult by the increased distance between them.

They then speculated that there are three types of inferences.

1. Within-text inferences (ideas found in the text)
2. Elaborative inferences (ideas found in the text in combination with the reader's own ideas)
3. Incorrect inferences

Using a sample of 48 students of about 16 years of age (L1 English, L2 Spanish), they divided them up into high-prior knowledge (HK) and low-prior knowledge (LK) groups – in terms of knowledge of the topic (the Incas) and familiarity with the text type (historical narrative). They gave the students three L2 texts at different levels of complexity and counted the number and different types of inferences that they made. The results showed:

1. The HK group produced significantly more inferences than the LK group.
2. The text with the lowest syntactic complexity (Level 1) produced *fewer* inferences than the next level up (but no differences between Levels 2 and 3).
3. HK and LK both inferenced more at Level 2.
4. Level of complexity did not produce more incorrect inferences.
5. HK group produced fewer incorrect inferences.
6. The 2nd level of complexity triggered more within-text inferences.

In sum, the readers with higher prior knowledge of the Incas recalled a larger proportion of the Level 1 text and generated a much greater number of inferences with a smaller proportion of incorrect ones than the readers with lower prior knowledge. That is 'they constructed a richer and more accurate mental model' than did the LK readers.

Barry and Lazarte concluded that readers who lack familiarity with the topic are apparently not efficient at maintaining and retrieving information from prior segments of the text. Therefore their inference generation is minimal and more likely to be inaccurate. In other words, the research suggests that *prior knowledge* of the topic can be used by the learner as a *strategy* to reduce the cognitive load when *syntactic complexity* makes access to meaning difficult.

On a different though related theme, Parry (1993) argued that prior knowledge is not independent of the educational system in which L2 learning is occurring. She compared two groups of students, Japanese and Nigerians both learning English (L2). She observed that Japanese students used their prior knowledge and context perhaps less than they should whereas Nigerian students went for global meaning more than they should. She speculated that this is largely due to their educational heritage. Japanese students have a highly analytical focus on literacy because of their writing system and are therefore less likely to value the importance of context and prior knowledge. Nigerian students had little need to prioritize precision over general meaning because English was essential for communication. Hence they had never been encouraged by their teachers to concentrate on bottom-up processing strategies.

Initial implications

There is still a long way to go before we can categorically state that prior knowledge makes comprehension easier. The difficulty may lie in the kind of topic in question and/or the level of linguistic knowledge needed to make a difference. Moreover readers may have prior knowledge of a topic but they may not use it as an effective strategy. In fact as in the case of Hammadou's less proficient students they may use it with adverse results! However, effective use of prior knowledge can result in very effective *working memory management* when aspects of the text pose the reader problems.

Sex differences in background knowledge clearly exist. Males and females generally bring different content schemata to texts probably as a result of different interests. Whether these 'group differences' are more pronounced than 'individual differences' (or other group differences such as social class) is not clear. Schemata which match with text topic do have an effect on access to meaning and this should be borne in mind when creating reading tests particularly at the national level. On the other hand both sexes could be encouraged to broaden their scope by reading informative texts with opposite gender topics. Clearly it would be unhelpful for teachers to 'differentiate by gender' as this would mean restricting general knowledge development. In addition it might lead to too heavy an emphasis on top-down strategies, with students relying on their prior knowledge to access text and not focusing enough on the language itself. We have to remember that reading in most L2 classrooms is intended to develop other skills as well as reading skills themselves.

At a low level, prior knowledge of a text can be provided or in some cases activated by the teacher asking questions, eliciting ideas and asking students to make predictions about the likely inferences they will be having to make of the L2 text.

We have further evidence here that gender differences in L2 learning are nation specific. Unlike in England, Dutch boys do better at languages even when gender bias in text is factored out.

The activation of prior knowledge as a learning strategy may be suppressed or overstimulated by the teaching/learning environment or the cultural origin of the learner. Whether teachers and learners should have the same schemata in order to match the cultural background (as for example, Mason 1992 argues) is open to debate. This links to the whole notion of whether the 'local' teacher is better than the native-speaker teacher 'imported' from the target country. This issue is beyond the scope of this chapter.

Reading in L2, reading in L1 and L2 proficiency

The activation of prior knowledge, as we have seen in the above studies, did result in some facilitation of reading comprehension but it may also have resulted in some obstacles being created. The difference appears to lie in appropriate use of prior knowledge as a strategy. It may also lie in the highly contentious issue of whether reading problems result from low L2 proficiency in general or whether they are a result of the reader's inability to transfer L1 reading strategies to L2 texts.

Why should we be interested in this?

The inability to read an L2 text using the same strategies as an L1 text has been called the 'short-circuit hypothesis'. This was first introduced by Clarke (1979). The hypothesis predicts that learners with limited L2 knowledge (for example limited vocabulary and syntax development), when confronted with an L2 text fail to activate all the reading strategies that they would normally activate with an L1 text forcing them to operate a limited number of bottom-up strategies. The short-circuit hypothesis is juxtaposed with the 'reading universals' hypothesis which predicts that we use the same processes and skills for reading regardless of the language that the text is in. In other words the issue is whether problems associated with reading in L2 are reading problems or language problems. Put differently, is there some kind of *threshold* before which language is the problem and after which reading strategies are the problem?

The interest in this topic for the teacher is obvious. Should the teacher concentrate on getting the language (vocabulary and syntax) up to a high level first so that the reader can then read with greater ease? Or should the teacher teach reading strategies so that the reader can cope with difficult texts and increase the language store through reading? In practical terms the former demands easy, graded texts, the latter demands more challenging texts. The former suggests an integrated L2 curriculum, the latter proposes that a 'separate reading programme' of some kind is most effective.

The research evidence

Block (1986) was one of the first to ask if reading strategies in L2 were the same as reading strategies in L1. She studied nine students in their first year at university, six with advanced proficiency in L2 English (Chinese and Spanish L1) and three L1 English but with poor reading scores in English (hence an attempt was made at some equivalence between L1 and L2 processes). Participants read one passage in L1 and one in L2 (native English students read both passages in English). Block used think-aloud protocols to elicit their strategies. In addition she gave them a multiple choice test after each think aloud. Block found that there did not seem to be a pattern of strategy use which distinguished the L2 readers from the native speakers of English or which distinguished the native speakers of Spanish from those of Chinese. She therefore asserted that strategy use is *universal* and to all intents and purposes not affected by proficiency.

Sarig (1988) investigated the relative contribution of L1 reading strategies and L2 proficiency to L2 reading. She did this by investigating the reading comprehension strategies of ten female students aged 17 or 18 who had Hebrew L1 and English L2. They had been studying English for about eight years. Whereas they had received systematic training for reading in their L1, the subjects had not been exposed to very much academic reading in their L2. The sample consisted of low, intermediate and high L2 proficiency levels. However, these levels are not what some teachers would regard as low or intermediate given the challenging nature of the texts described in the study! In other words, these students were relatively advanced students of English. Sarig compared their performances in L1 and L2 tasks using self-report. Her main findings were:

1. The identification of the 'main idea' of a text was achieved in the same way in L2 as in L1.

2. The synthesis of the main ideas in the text was achieved in the same way in both languages.
3. The same processes were found to underlie the performance of the task in both L1 and L2 — the same strategies accounted for success or failure.
4. Differences in reading approaches were more due to individuals than to the language of the text they were accessing.

Sarig therefore concluded that, at this level at least, reading in L2 was like reading in L1.

However, both these studies are contradicted by others which demonstrate that general L2 proficiency is, at least, an equally important factor in reading in the L2 as are the approaches to reading in general. For example Carrell (1991) found that L2 language proficiency was a statistically significant predictor of L2 reading ability. Bossers' (1992) study led to the conclusion that L2 knowledge is strongly related to L2 reading comprehension, even in advanced learners, and that correlations between L1 and L2 reading comprehension in readers with low and high levels of L2 proficiency did not differ significantly. In other words, L2 reading ability = L1 reading ability + L2 language proficiency.

This equation would seem obvious at face value until we introduce two variables: the difficulty of the text (i.e. its distance from the current knowledge of the learner) and the complexity of the task that we ask the learner to perform in order to demonstrate comprehension of the text.

Taillefer (1996) in fact addressed one of these additional variables by measuring whether different cognitive levels of tasks made a difference to the above equation. In other words, if the task was more demanding, did L2 language proficiency eclipse L1 reading ability as a factor or vice versa?

First though, Taillefer observed that past research had not made clear what was meant by reading ability. Was it:

1. Scanning for specific lexical items (running down a page to locate specific graphic symbols)?
2. Skimming for gist (trying to get an overall impression)?
3. Reading for meaning (building a detailed conceptual model and/or personal representation of what the text means)?

Using various pre-tests, Taillefer constructed a sample of 52 French university students by applying the criterion that they had roughly the same (high) L1 reading ability but different (English) L2 reading ability. Hence two groups became known as HiL2 and LoL2.

She then provided them with two reading tasks on the same text, (a) a scanning task (considered easier); (b) a reading for meaning task (considered harder). For this she used a free recall protocol. The justification for this method of data elicitation was that it stopped the subjects translating word-for-word, despite the disadvantage of placing emphasis on memory. Taillefer found:

1. L1 reading strategies *and* L2 proficiency were both significant predictors of L2 reading *but to different extents* in the two tasks of varying cognitive complexity.

2. Scanning (the low cognitive task) was not affected by L2 ability. Both groups did equally well on this task.
3. Reading for meaning (the high cognitive task) was strongly affected by L2 ability. Even though both groups had the same reading abilities in L1, the HiL2 group did better on this task.

Taillefer concluded that this was further evidence of the greater importance of L2 proficiency over L1 reading strategies.

Walter's (2001) series of experiments also provided strong support for a reading threshold. For example, she sampled 22 lower-intermediate learners and 23 upper-intermediate learners of English (French L1) studying in a *collège* and *lycée* respectively. They were asked to read 16 stories (short texts of 124-150 words) which corresponded to lower-intermediate proficiency level. Each participant read all 16 stories, half in L1 and half in L2, changing languages after every second story. For each test they had to fill in five gaps in a 50-word summary of the stories. She found:

1. There was virtually no differences in their L1 reading scores.
2. The *lycée* students were significantly more successful at the L2 task.
3. The *collège* students' performance in L2 deteriorated much more than that of the *lycée* students.

For Walter this was clear evidence that the *collège* group was below threshold. They were prevented from transferring their L1 strategies because of low L2 proficiency.

Lee and Shallert (1997) also put the notion of a threshold hypothesis to the test. Using a random sample of schools and over 800 Korean students aged between 14 and 17 (years 10 and 11 in England), they provided the subjects with: an English language proficiency test; an English (L2) reading comprehension test; an L1 reading comprehension test. They found:

1. A significant relationship did exist between L2 proficiency and reading scores in L2.
2. Both L1 reading ability and L2 proficiency were significant predictors of L2 reading ability.
3. (However) L2 reading ability was likely to *depend more* on overall L2 proficiency than on L1 reading ability.
4. Subjects in the high L2 proficiency group were more likely to be able to transfer L1 reading strategies to L2 reading than students in the lower L2 proficiency group. In other words, this finding lends some support to the notion of a threshold hypothesis.

Kember and Gow (1994) came at the issue from a slightly different angle. They wanted to find out whether students using English (L2) when reading for the purpose of studying other subjects (i.e. for academic purposes) used 'deep' or 'surface approaches'. These categories were originally proposed by Marton and Säljö (1976) who observed that those students who used a deep approach tried to access the meaning of the text by analysing the author's arguments. 'They tried to distil the main points the author was trying to make: they related evidence and arguments to their own knowledge and critically examined evidence presented' (8). In other words this approach would be typical of the reading for meaning task as used by Taillefer above. By contrast, those employing a 'surface approach' did not seek the underlying meaning of the text but endeavoured to rote-learn information which they thought would be useful for a subsequent assessment. As we can see, the basic research question is the same but this time the distinction between reading tasks is presented as an autonomous decision by the student in approaches to studying.

Kember and Gow used an 'approaches to studying inventory' on 159 university (Chinese L1) students and followed this up with a sub-sample of 35 interviews. They found that students with lower L2 ability were more likely to employ the 'surface approach' to reading/studying. Students adopting this narrow orientation to study were in fact seen to use predominantly bottom-up processing strategies in their reading of text. Some students were also observed to be over-reliant on top-down only strategies. In sum, they were failing to employ the interactive reading approaches. Kember and Gow posit that their findings can be interpreted in two ways:

1. Students with limited L2 *are forced* to adopt bottom-up processes.
2. Students' approaches to studying determines their approaches to reading.

They conclude, however, that there may well be a threshold below which L2 fluency is limiting the reading approaches and therefore determining the attitudes to study. This conclusion, again, gives further support to the short-circuit hypothesis.

Initial implications

Reading ability cannot be dissociated from general L2 proficiency. Reading skills are not isolated from or independent of other aspects of L2 development such as vocabulary knowledge and awareness of patterns in the language. However, the higher the level of L2 proficiency, the more L1 reading behaviour 'kicks in'. Put another way, the more distance between current L2 knowledge and text difficulty, the less there is a transfer of appropriate reading strategies from L1. Additionally, if a reading task has low cognitive demands it presents few working-memory capacity problems and therefore is not affected by general L2 proficiency. Although students with limited L2 proficiency are channelled into adopting more bottom-up processes, this does not stop students who transfer L1 strategies badly from over-using top-down strategies and therefore making wild guesses at the meaning of text. Top-down strategies are effective in L1 reading simply because of the huge number of semantic and syntactic connections stored in long-term memory which reduce the cognitive effort as compared to L2 reading. To compare the reading of the same text in L1 and L2 is fruitless because one is not comparing like with like in terms of cognitive effort. To achieve the same cognitive effort one would have to compare reading an obscure text in L1 with a familiar text in L2.

The role of phonology in reading

A number of researchers have been interested in the way that the sounds of the language affect the ability of the L2 learner to decode a written text. As we saw earlier, this gave rise to a focus on word-level research rather than regarding the reading process as a holistic problem-solving activity. However, there has recently been a return to this line of enquiry.

Why should we be interested in this?

When examining cognitive models of language acquisition in Chapter 3 we noted that one of the components of working memory which operated as a temporary 'holding system' was the phonological loop. This loop allows the brain to hold the sound of a particular language element whilst the rest of working memory decides what to do with it. Thus phonology is an important aspect of the decoding, processing, storing and retrieving processes that underlie cognitive action.

A second reason to take an interest in the role of phonology in reading is that there has been much heated debate as to whether very young children learn to read the first language better by sounding out the phonological units of the word, rather than attempting whole-word recognition. Indeed, in England the 'phonological revival' has been one of the pillars of the primary-school literacy strategy.

A third reason is that Communicative Language Teaching, with its emphasis on interacting as soon as possible with little oral correction for fear of demotivating the learner, has overlooked the possible advantages to be gained by teaching pronunciation in a formal and explicit way. Few textbooks in England, for example, place any value on teaching pronunciation at any stage of learning and, by and large, comparisons between the spoken forms and the written forms are discouraged. The latest version of the National Curriculum however, recommends that learners should be taught the principles and inter-relationships of sounds and writing in the target language (DfEE 1999). Indeed, pupils are expected by level 2 (of 9 levels) to 'match sound to print by reading aloud single familiar words and phrases' (43). Given that familiar words and phrases are very likely to encompass virtually all of the phonological units of, say, French, the implication is that teachers should teach pronunciation at the start of an L2 course so that students will be able by level 3 to 'begin to read independently'.

A fourth reason is that some languages such as Italian and Spanish have a transparent orthography. In other words, in languages such as English and French, the difference between the written form and the spoken form is very marked and in some cases highly idiosyncratic. If research were to find an important link between phonological obstacles to reading an L2 and general development of proficiency in that language, it may help shape language policy. That is, it may help us decide which foreign languages should be offered and when.

The research evidence

We will start with a study which, although carried out in strict experimental conditions (i.e. not in classroom situations), nevertheless provides us with some useful insights into the problems with phonology in normal reading situations.

Segalowitz and Hébert (1990) asked themselves what role phonological mediation plays in skilled reading. Particularly they were interested in *phonological re-coding*, the process of turning the written word back into the sounded form. In reviewing previous research they observed:

1. Phonological re-coding is probably *not involved* in accessing lexical representations during reading by skilled readers of a language.
2. Visual activation, through automatic word recognition (i.e. the direct activation of representations in the brain via the written form) is used more, in lexical access, because it is faster than phonological re-coding.
3. Phonological re-coding may occur *after* lexical access has been achieved (perhaps as a monitoring strategy).
4. Regardless of when it occurs and whether it affects lexical access, phonological codes are useful after the word has been accessed (post-lexically) in working memory (i.e. to facilitate processing such as syntactic parsing, propositional encoding, semantic integration).

The researchers therefore studied fluent bilinguals (sometime called 'balanced bilinguals') on the basis that, despite their bilingualism, they do often read more quickly in their L1 than in their L2. This is based on the assumption of less automaticity of word recognition in L2 and slower processing of orthographic redundancy in L2. They therefore chose a sample of 9 'equal reading rate' (i.e. equal in L1 and L2) subjects and 9 'non-equal reading rate' subjects in both French and English L1 groups. They used the 'homophone effect' (bear/bare) as a symptom of phonological re-coding. They performed two experiments, one at the word level and one at the sentence level.

1. *A word-decision experiment* (whether the word was a real word or not a real word). As stimuli they used word lists with homophones and control words (non-homophones) + pseudo-words. They obtained different results for each of the two languages. In the case of the French speakers, real words showed no phonological effect. Therefore French speakers probably by-pass the phonological route altogether at the word level. English speakers were sensitive to the homophone effect. Therefore English speakers are sensitive to the phonological route. The implications of this *asymmetry* between French and English is that if beginner L1 English students try to read a French (L2) word they will try to transfer an L1 re-coding strategy to L2 and fail – unless, of course, they are given the tools in the L2 for quick re-coding.
2. *A sentence verification experiment* (where a homophone was placed in a sentence thus making the sentence meaningless (e.g. *The cupboard was bear*). They found that the 'unequal reading rate' subjects (regardless of their L1) showed greater phonological re-coding effects. In other words they took longer to sort out the problem of the homophone. In L2, 'equal reading rate' subjects behaved like native speakers. The implications of this study are that phonological re-coding occurs much more at the sentence level and the less proficient you are in the language, the more it is likely to occur. A combination of sentence level re-coding and low proficiency results in processing load on working memory. Processing load may in turn result in 'giving up' on reading or by-passing important words.

Comeau *et al.* (1999) were also interested in whether *phonological awareness* crossed over between two languages, again English and French. They defined phonological awareness as 'the sensitivity to the sound structure of words' (syllables, phonemes, phoneme deletion, redundancy). They also identified two other important processing skills in which phonology is involved:

1. lexical access – the ease with which phonological representations of written speech are accessed;
2. phonological processing in working memory – maintenance of the sounds in the auditory loop allowing opportunities to synthesize speech sounds into words or parts of words.

Because there was some evidence that bilingual children can generalize their phonological awareness to another language, they chose children enrolled in French immersion classes in Canada (grades 1, 3, 5). The immersion experiment in Canada is where (in this case) English L1 children are taught virtually all subjects in French. They gave the children a battery of tests to measure how good they were at word decoding in L2 and compared this to their levels of phonological awareness in both languages. They found:

1. Phonological awareness in both languages was strongly related to word decoding. In other words, there was evidence that cross-language transfer does occur with regard to phonological awareness.
2. Phonological awareness as a predictor of successful decoding of words remained strong even when other processing abilities were controlled for.

The researchers concluded that the general ability to manipulate sounds plays a critical role in processing auditory/phonological information. This ability is crucial in learning to read in languages that have a phonologically based writing system.

Muter and Diethelm (2001) also investigated whether phonological skills help young children read better irrespective of whether they are reading in L1 or L2. Again, the two languages investigated were French and English. One of the reasons for this choice was that the syllable is a more salient unit in French than in English but the syllable is only one way of segmenting words. However, they were trying to see if there was evidence to support the 'universality of the phonology-reading connection'. They teased out the notion of phonological awareness further. They proposed that the *segmentation* of words could be considered both implicitly and explicitly:

- Implicit segmentation: the global awareness of the sound properties of words.
- Explicit segmentation: the explicit awareness of individual sounds within words.

Using a sample of 55 bilingual children aged 5 years on average in kindergarten, they hypothesized that these youngsters might have heightened sensitivity to the phonological units within words because they must 'attend to the speech stream in order to distinguish their two languages and in order to organize their developing lexicon' (189). The sample was divided into 22 English L1 and 28 non-English L1 (the rest were mixed/roughly equal L1s). All children were being taught in English in a school in Geneva. Data was collected over two years, at two data-collection points (Time 1 and Time 2) separated by one calendar year. The children were given a number of tasks which elicited phonological awareness; rhyme detection; rhyme production; word completion; phoneme deletion. Using factor analysis, Muter and Diethelm found:

1. At Time 1, three factors were underlying the data: rhyming, implicit segmentation, explicit segmentation.
2. At Time 2, only two factors were underlying the data: rhyming and phoneme segmentation (i.e. there was no evidence of an implicit/explicit split).
3. At Time 1, English L1 children achieved higher scores on general cognition, rhyme production.
4. At Time 2, the two groups could only be distinguished by their letter knowledge and vocabulary – not by their phonological awareness (that the English L1 children would score better in vocabulary was highly predictable).
5. Segmentation measures (phonological unit awareness) were stronger predictors of reading skill than rhyming measures (syllable unit awareness).

The researchers concluded that for the L2 children, learning to read in the L2 appears to draw their attention to the phonological structure of the L2. The evidence for the researchers was confirmation that reading skills can be radically improved by teaching phonemic awareness.

Erler (2003) studied the obstacles to reading being experienced by beginner learners of French (L2) in England. Her qualitative data of 11-12-year-olds suggested that these young learners were aware of the problems they had with reading the new language. As well as lack of exposure to reading in L2 in general, they reported their inability to sound out words that they saw in written form as impediments to reading:

> 'When I'm reading, I try to pronounce it . . . but if I can't and I read it . . . it just sounds completely wrong.'
> 'There's like a kind of thing that's going on in my head trying to pronounce it but when you hear it . . . it doesn't sound like anything you're hearing.'
> 'I just look at all the words and I think, these are weird . . . 'cause they're spelt completely different to what I would usually think.'

We might infer from these quotations that linking the sounding out back to the teacher who had pronounced the word became impossible. What should have been a perfectly familiar word to them, on paper, looked alien. Erler also gave a sub-sample of her students a cued word-recognition test (using mostly words that they had not encountered before in their studies) and measured the time it took them to complete the articulation of the word; the correctness of the pronunciation; their reported difficulty of the word. Students scored very low in terms of correctness of pronunciation even though they would have encountered the words' phonemes and syllables both in sound and in graphic form during L2 lessons. Erler concluded that lack of explicit training and practice in the grapheme-phoneme system of French, in addition to a lack of exposure to written texts in French, was contributing to a kind of L2 dyslexia where perfectly good readers of L1 were unable to 'read' a word in the L2.

Initial implications

Phonology is important. Phonological awareness, if it can be taught, should be taught. Given what we know of phonology as one of the pillars of language aptitude, and that aptitude is a good predictor of general success in language learning – then helping learners to understand the relationships between the sounds of the target language and its written form is important. Teachers should teach phonemes and phonological units to beginners rather than the alphabet. Teachers should encourage beginners to use a sounding-out strategy as a means of accessing meaning and facilitating early reading of more difficult (beyond oracy) texts. In conjunction with vocabulary training, this form of instruction will release some of the burden on cognitive processes during reading and allow more effective activation of other aspects of processing – e.g. the use of schemata – because progression towards faster word recognition will occur. We will return to the issue of levels of oracy and literacy later. We will now turn our attention to reading strategies in general.

Reading strategies for accessing meaning

We have examined a number of cognitive functions which can affect reading, such as phonological awareness, and we have noted trends, such as overall L2 proficiency, as being good predictors of reading ability. The evidence presented so far has been the result of very broad research designs aimed at identifying underlying factors in reading proficiency. Reading strategies, on the other hand, are the cognitive and metacognitive actions that individuals either consciously decide to use or use auto-matically when attempting to access a written text.

Why should we be interested in this?

A considerable number of authors have researched reading strategies spurred on by the literature on general learning strategies which strongly suggests that good language learners use a variety of strategies in effective combination. The search, therefore, is on to identify which are the *reading* strategies which L2 learners and L2 users at various stages in their learning bring to the task of reading.

   As we have already noted, only at the very advanced level is it possible to transfer L1 reading strategies *wholesale* to L2 texts. On the other hand, there is no evidence to suggest that a general interactive model of top-down and bottom-up processes should not apply to L2 reading. For beginner and intermediate learners therefore it is necessary to identify what specific strategies are appropriate to *their level* of reading and to help them develop these strategies.

The research evidence

Firstly, we must bear in mind that the kinds of strategy use which will be successful will vary according to the level of text and the cognitive demands of the task. For example, in a study I carried out with 14-year-old learners (Macaro 2001a: 85), the texts were pitched a little above the normal level of difficulty that these students encountered in their everyday lessons. This, together with the fact that they were asked to tell the researcher in a think-aloud protocol what the text was about in some detail (again something that they did not normally have to do in class), challenged them to resort to as many strategies in their repertoire as possible. The more successful (and we might add *autonomous*) readers appeared to match the effective combination of top-down and bottom-up strategies model. The less successful readers did not.

For example, James, one of the less successful readers in the study, in fact used too much of a top-down approach. He made wild guesses about the text which were not substantiated by actual in-text evidence. Many of these guesses were as a result of an over-reliance on 'scanning for cognates' to the neglect of other strategies. In fact one of the more obvious strategies that James neglected was stopping and spending a little time trying to retrieve words that he actually knew – a bottom-up strategy. There was no attempt at sounding out certain words, no suggestion that he looked at the word's form and wondered if it reminded him of anything familiar. When he did appear to use phonology as a strategy (for example when deciding that the French word '*jours*' means '*jouer*') he did not combine this with strategies which would have substantiated his assertion, for example by a syntax awareness strategy (you can't have the word for 'the' in front of a verb). James gave the impression that in order to access the meaning of the text he was hopping aimlessly from word to word, and from recognizable noun phrase to noun phrase even though his processing of the text might appear to be in a recognizable linear fashion. I say this because one of the characteristics of many of the less successful readers was that they skipped all the verb phrases as if they weren't there and 'landed' only on the noun phrases.

A more successful reader, Amanda, in fact spent more time in bottom-up processes and actually made the effort to recall individual words. Perhaps she had used better strategies for storing them in the past and therefore recall was easier for her. We do not know. Nevertheless, Amanda used a number of other bottom-up strategies: looking for cognates; bringing to mind aspects of French grammar (e.g. word inversion). She combined these quite effectively with a number of context-related top-down strategies:

1. Having doubts about certain inferences and interpretations
2. Spotting the overall look of the text for writing conventions
3. Using her common sense to evaluate inferences
4. Hopping back and forth in the text but, unlike James, with a definite purpose in mind
5. Making informed decisions about which difficult phrases or clauses to skip altogether
6. Keeping in mind what she hadn't been able to solve.

Similar tolerance of uncertainty was detected in a study of reading strategies by Grenfell and Harris (1999). Here a 15-year-old learner of French, Jenny, finds ways around uncertainty by monitoring for meaning using common sense. A door to a garden does not make sense and therefore the word must mean 'gate'. She also uses grammatical knowledge and semantic mapping (the connections between words) to overcome meaning-access problems.

In sum, the successful readers' use of strategies confirms the interactive model of reading proposed at the beginning of this chapter but does so according to the *level of the text* ('Gosh this is quite a hard text, I'm going to have to work hard at trying to identify at least some of the words, rather than just guess.') and according to the *level of the task* ('I'm basically being asked to translate this text so I can't get away with just scanning for a few words here and there.'). This is a crucial point to make. I will emphasize it by restating it once more. Successful access to meaning starts (and is maintained) by an evaluative decision by the reader of the *relative balance* between top-down and bottom-up strategies that they are going to need to deploy. I expect all learners use some sort of interactive model. The trick is getting the right balance according to text and task.

We saw earlier that, in a study by Block (1986), the results suggested that L2 reading is merely an extension of L1 reading. Although these findings have been countered quite comprehensively by other studies, her clustering of strategies, observed among nine students in the first year of university, confirm and add to the knowledge base about the successful reader. She found two consistent patterns of strategy use such that an able reader profile can continue to be generated. She described them as either:

1. *the 'integrator' reader* – responded only in extensive mode; integrated information; was aware of text structure; monitored his/her understanding; read on when they did not understand, in search for clues; connected sentences together at the meaning level
2. *the 'non-integrator' reader* – relied on personal experiences to help them develop a version of the text; they made few attempts to connect information.

All integrators, she found, improved their reading scores by the time they were tested six months later; few non-integrators improved and if they did, it was only a marginal improvement.

A study by Chamot and El-dinary (1999) extended the work already carried out on learning strategies by investigating the strategies of very young children. Again this was carried out in the setting of immersion programmes in Canada. Although the authors look back on two decades of research that show fairly consistently that these programmes are highly effective in developing impressive levels of L2 proficiency, they point to the fact that little is known about what students do to reach those levels.

Chamot and El-dinary asked teachers to rate pupils as high achievers and low achievers. They then conducted think-aloud interviews on a sub-sample. Because of the relatively young age of the learners (approximately 8 years old) and the newness of the research with this group, the data was analysed using a grounded approach. That is, the researchers did not have preconceptions of what categories of strategies the students might be using but instead, allowed the categories to 'emerge' from the data. This coding then led to the quantification of strategy use – again a fairly innovative use of think-aloud data. They found:

1. There were no significant differences between high and low students in overall measures of strategy use (i.e. in terms of sheer number of strategies used).
2. Low-achieving students relied very heavily on phonetic decoding (which I take to mean sounding out words), high-achieving students used background knowledge (inference, prediction and elaboration strategies).
3. Low-achieving students relied on visual cues rather than multiple sensory cues.
4. High-achieving students frequently modified earlier predictions about the story as they got more information about the text.
5. Low-achieving students got bogged down by details rather than seeing the 'bigger picture' – the overall meaning.

Chamot and El-dinary concluded that metacognitive awareness begins at quite an early age and that similar differences between high- and low-achieving learners were to be found at this age as with older L2 learners in most contexts. This stability of findings across learning contexts adds to the robust nature of learner strategy research in general.

Hood (1996) was also concerned that we know little about early foreign-language learning. Unlike the previous study, however, his exploratory study was based in England where early language learning means 11-year-olds not 8-year-olds. Particularly, he wondered, what was the motivation of pupils to carry on and keep trying when access to a text seemed to be unattainable. He therefore took a sample of 24 beginner learners of French. For reading materials he chose two stories from the series 'Bibliobus' which are graded readers. In story 1, the learners had to read and underline any words not understood (no dictionary or glossary was provided). In story 2, the learners had to read but not underline. This time they did have a glossary at the end of the story. They were then asked to volunteer information about the story to the teacher. The students were then provided with advice and materials for thinking about reading strategies. Finally, story 1 was given them again on fresh sheets and they were asked to read and underline any words not understood. They were also asked to say if they thought they had underlined more or fewer words on the second reading and why.

Hood found:

1. The vast majority of pupils (21 of 24) underlined fewer words on the second reading of story 1.
2. The vast majority were aware that they had underlined fewer words (metacognitive awareness of progress).
3. There was a huge range in underlining on the first reading (between 7-107 words!).
4. There was still a huge range of underlining on second reading (between 2-74 words!)
5. The reasons given by the students for fewer underlinings were mostly to do with having gained vocabulary from story 2 where a glossary was available. However, there were very few words in story 2 which matched story 1. Thus, in this respect, they had not gained metacognitive awareness. They knew that they had made progress but not why.

Hood concluded that an awareness of reading strategies can bear fruit. However, the author does not give a clear explanation of the strategy training that the students received, although it would seem that this was limited to 'raising awareness' of strategies. It is perhaps for this reason that the huge range remained even after the students had been trained to think more carefully about their reading strategies.

Fraser (1999) included some strategy training in her study of the lexical processing of unknown vocabulary in texts. She was motivated by the conflicting evidence with regard to the amount of vocabulary growth via the implicit process of inferencing (see vocabulary chapter). Moreover, the research to date suggested that that L2 learners who are left on their own generally *ignore* unfamiliar words, *infer* only when there is a specific need, *consult* (dictionary or someone else) sparingly and selectively. For Fraser, ignoring words completely not only led to possible misinterpretations of the text or lack of detailed understanding, but also to insufficient growth in the vocabulary store. She hypothesized that there are two types of inferencing strategies:

1. *Word-identification strategies*. These are either phonological or orthographic – i.e. the word 'sounds like' or 'looks like' something they have previously encountered. This identification is carried out via an L1 or L2 association in the learner's mental lexicon. With French L1 and English L2, an L1 association would be '*inherit*' sounds/looks like '*héritier*'. An L2 association would be '*stalking*' sounds/looks like '*talking*'. In this strategy, the thematic context plays a minimal role. There is also little control over the association without the use of an additional evaluation strategy. As in the examples given, these strategies may result in unsuccessful inferencing.
2. *Sense-creation strategies*. These are context-centred, and the result of a deliberate and effortful process. They involve both language *and* situational clues.

Fraser used a sample of eight university students (French L1, English L2) to experiment with a programme of strategy training. Phase 1 consisted of metacognitive strategy training (developing the students' awareness of use and viability of the three strategies: *ignore, infer, consult*). Phase 2 consisted of more focused language instruction (repeated modelling how to use the inferencing strategy). The programme of strategy training lasted five months in all. She found:

1. Even before the training, participants *inferred* more frequently than they *consulted*. They *consulted* more than they *ignored*.
2. If strategies were used in combination, the inferencing strategy was used *first*, almost invariably. This *hierarchy* of strategy use was maintained over time at all measures (i.e. pre, during and post training).
3. As a result of the training, the rate of ignoring decreased steadily.
4. 78% of *consults* and 52% of *inferences* resulted in full comprehension of unknown words. It is not surprising that consulting would be more successful.
5. The L1/L2 word-association strategy was as successful as the sense-creation strategy and both were much better than L2/L2 word-association strategy.
6. Successful inferencing increased significantly as a result of the strategy training.
7. Strategy training resulted in increased use of sense-creation strategies and more successful use, although it did not reach statistically significant levels, probably due to the small size of the sample.

Fraser concluded that training students to use a range of lexical processing strategies was beneficial in terms of understanding of text. Training should guide students to use elements in the immediate sentence context first as the basis for their inference and subsequently to monitor its appropriateness, via a dictionary if necessary. She felt that the results of dictionary use in effectively determining word meaning suggest that we should re-evaluate the minimal role often accorded to dictionary use in reading tasks.

The use of a dictionary to aid comprehension can be considered a conscious strategy made by the learner in response to a difficulty in the text. However, it is a complex metacognitive strategy in that, apart from the pitfalls inherent in a dictionary search, it needs to be balanced against the time taken and time allocated for the completion of the task and the difficulty of the text.

Wingate (2002) compared bilingual dictionaries and monolingual dictionaries for the purposes of reading comprehension among a group of Chinese (L1) learners of German and French. She found that the vast majority preferred using the English – German/French bilingual dictionary, even though the translations were presented in their second language. She then carried out an experiment with a sub-sample of 12 students of German. Reading comprehension was tested by means of an immediate-recall protocol and she compared the scores of students using a bilingual dictionary with those using a monolingual dictionary. She found that, although the bilingual students scored marginally higher, this was not significantly so. However, there was some suggestion that the lower-verbal-ability students achieved a greater under-standing as a result of using the bilingual dictionary. Wingate's second investigation aimed at identifying features that make monolingual dictionaries more accessible to intermediate learners. This investigation consisted of a think-aloud study with 17 learners and an experiment with 86 Chinese learners of German. Two different *definition styles* were compared for their effectiveness in facilitating reading compre-hension. What we will call *Style 1* (unlike modern English dictionaries) follows the traditional lexicographic style that is widely regarded as unsuitable for learners. In this style the definitions have extremely condensed text and complex sentences in which a super-ordinate is further defined by several subordinate clauses. In addition, the defining vocabulary is unrestricted, and often beyond the vocabulary of inter-mediate learners. By contrast, the defining vocabulary of what we will call *Style 2*, is restricted to a 'Basic German Word List' of 2,227 lexical items. The definitions follow COBUILD's style of natural, everyday language in full-sentence explanations. Redundancies and examples are frequently built into the Style 2, and these have been shown by previous research to enhance understanding. The design of the Style 2 definitions was based on:

1. recommendations in the metalexicographic literature;
2. findings from previous research into dictionary use, including a think-aloud study by Wingate;
3. psycholinguistic research into the understanding and learning of words.

An alternative to dictionary use is for the teacher to pre-empt difficulties and provide a selection of glosses to a text. A study of the use of glosses when reading L2 texts was carried out by Jacobs *et al.* (1994). These researchers asked not only whether glosses help with immediate comprehension recall but also whether L1 glosses are better than L2 glosses. They used a sample of 85 students in an American university (English L1) who were studying Spanish. These were divided into higher and lower proficiency students. The researchers put 32 glosses in the margins of a text and then asked half the students to carry out a free recall protocol (described above), the other half receiving the text without glosses. Some received glosses in L1 (i.e. direct equivalents of the word), some in L2 (i.e. synonyms or explanations of the word). They also gave the students a questionnaire on what types of glosses they preferred. The researchers found:

1. Surprisingly, there were no significant differences overall between the text with glosses and the text without glosses in terms of the recall comprehension task. However, higher proficiency students did better when they did have access to the glosses.
2. There were no significant differences in recall comprehension between the group that had the glosses in L1 or in L2. Again, this is somewhat surprising.
3. Students all preferred to have glosses rather than to have to infer the meaning of words they did not understand. There was a general preference for L1 glosses over L2 glosses and a preference for glosses in the margins of the text rather than at the foot of the page or at the end of the text.

Jacobs *et al*. attempted some conclusions from this assortment of findings. They argued that the fact that those participants with higher than average proficiency benefited more from glosses in terms of comprehension is logical. Limited glossing (such as this) only benefits comprehension if it is just above the level of comprehension of the reader. They also warned that although students said they liked texts to be glossed, the practice may lead to laziness rather than the effort of inferencing.

This is, of course, a charge that can be levelled at dictionary use when accessing the meaning of written texts and it may be a useful compromise to put the glosses at the end of the text (see Hood 1996 above) in order to balance out the 'effort' needed between inferencing and use of glosses. Both the use of glossing and dictionary use, in any case, need to be part of a strategy-training programme which helps the student make strategic decisions about what would be best for him/her at that point in time.

The fact that L1 glosses were preferred by students in the study by Jacobs *et al*., links to a point we were considering earlier, namely, that the one major difference between reading in L1 and reading in L2 is that in the latter we have another language to help us access meaning or (some would argue) to lead us into bad learning habits – constant translation.

Kern (1994) investigated how L2 readers use the L1 as a strategy for helping them overcome cognitive overload when reading an L2 text – what he called *mental translation*. He also asked himself whether reading ability affected the amount of L1 used. He noted that both teachers and learners often regard mental translation as undesirable yet they all do it. He used a sample of 51 university students (English L1, French L2), who were assigned to high, middle and low reading proficiency groups based on a reading comprehension test. The students were also selected because the researcher knew that their classes were normally conducted exclusively in L2 and translation was not normally given as a text-related task. In order to elicit the use of L1 as a strategy, Kern carried out think-aloud protocols and student task-based self-reports (i.e. reflecting back on a reading text just completed). These were administered twice with a gap of 15 weeks (Time 1 and Time 2), which means that an enormous amount of data must have been collected. Kern found:

1. Translation decreased overall between Time 1 and Time 2. As reading proficiency improved, so mental translation decreased. This was predictable.
2. Reading proficiency differences were no longer as powerful predictors of mental translation at Time 2 as they were Time 1. In other words, it was the low reading proficiency group that translated less after 15 weeks (that had made most progress), thereby bringing about the change observed in 1.
3. Mental translation as a strategy resulted in about 50% of correct interpretations of meaning. The data was not able to provide evidence of how many correct interpretations would have resulted without the use of the mental translation strategy. No comparison group, obviously, was feasible as it would be impossible to actually stop learners from using mental translation!

Kern concluded that the fact that in the high-ability group showed only a slight decrease in frequency of translation indicates that some sort of critical threshold of language development needs to be attained before mental translation can be minimized in L2 reading. Whilst concluding that a gradual progression towards minimizing mental translation was desirable (if only to increase reading rate), Kern identified a number of functional benefits of the mental translation strategy that emerged from the data:

1. It helped with consolidation of meaning. For example one student said ' I didn't quite understand it until I converted it to L1.'
2. It operated as an *affective boost*. It helped reduce insecurity and anxiety.
3. It helped to maintain concentration. It overcame working-memory limitations by allowing the reader to 'chunk' language (hold it as idea units) in working memory which would be more difficult in L2.
4. It helped the reader to avoid losing track of the meaning of the text.
5. It helped the student store words faster, again 'clearing the space' more quickly in working memory.
6 It helped to clarify the syntactic roles of certain lexical items.
7. It helped to troubleshoot visual information from the text which conflicted with readers' hypotheses (particularly when the reader shifted to bottom-up processing as a compensation strategy).

This is an important study which helps answer a number or research questions but which, as Kern admits, raises many more. One of these is the question of reading anxiety.

One of the categories of learner strategies identified by O'Malley and Chamot (1990) was *affective* strategies. These help to lower the affective filter (Krashen 1987), the barriers that learners put up against the incoming L2. We have touched on this issue in the chapter on motivation.

Taking steps to overcome anxiety is an affective strategy that has drawn a lot of research attention. Reading anxiety was studied by Saito *et al.* (1999) with university students (English L1) learning French, Japanese and Russian. They hypothesized that two aspects may create anxiety when reading a text: unfamiliar scripts (as in Russian and Japanese) and unfamiliar cultural material. They elaborate on the latter by suggesting:

> The reader would first encounter the symbols, decode them into sounds, and associate the sounds with words and then attempt to process the meaning of a text. It is at that point when the reader realizes that the words he or she has decoded do not constitute a comprehensible or logical message entity that one would expect anxiety to set in. (203)

Saito *et al.*, in reviewing the literature, found that previous studies on anxiety had found 'remarkably consistent' levels of anxiety across different languages. Moreover, previous studies had reported reading as the least anxiety inducing of the four skills.

Using questionnaires related to anxiety, the researchers were able to show evidence that:

1. Students with higher levels of anxiety in general also tended to have higher levels of reading anxiety and vice versa. That is, reading was not different from other skills in this respect.
2. Students with higher levels of reading anxiety achieved significantly lower grades than students with lower levels of reading anxiety.
3. Whilst general anxiety did not appear to be dependent on which of the three languages the students were studying, reading anxiety, specifically, did. The readers of Japanese were the most anxious of the three. Surprisingly the readers of French were more anxious than the readers of Russian. Saito *et al.* speculate that it was the phonetic asymmetry of English and French that caused this.

It seems to me that there may be more plausible explanations in that the students who had (presumably) chosen to learn Russian were somehow different – perhaps more motivated, perhaps more prepared for what to expect, perhaps they were more able language learners in general. As the authors admit, the French classes had a much higher percentage of learners 'who were enrolled in the class simply to meet a language requirement' than the Russian classes. Saito *et al.* conclude that 'it is difficult to be sure whether anxiety is the cause or the effect of the difficulties observed'. However they come down on the side that anxiety causes reading difficulties rather than reading difficulties cause anxiety. This conclusion is in contrast to conclusions we observed in the chapter on motivation. It would seem that we may just simply have to ask the learners which way the direction of causation lies rather than just relying on quantitative research.

Graham (1997) carried out a qualitative study into the reading strategies of intermediate students in England who had been studying French and German for about six years. She found that effective students overcame anxiety at the difficulty of a text by regarding its completion as 'a challenge' (114). However, when ability was felt to be unequal to the challenge, not only anxiety but also demotivation resulted. Again we are reminded of the notion of self-efficacy (see Chapter 5) in determining a student's perception of a language task.

Another reading strategy that has received some attention is the deployment of one's awareness of text structure. Early work on text structure proposed that readers store information about a text in some kind of hierarchical branching structure which they have generated from their reading of the text. In other words, if they are able to perceive the text's structure, as the author intended it, they are more likely to retain the content by storing it in terms of overarching ideas and subsidiary ideas. Raymond (1993) investigated whether training readers to use a text structure strategy helped them to recall the content of the text better. Using a sample of 43 university students in Canada (English L1, French L2) she set up experimental and control groups for a five-hour systematic strategy-training programme which consisted of discussing a text-structure strategy in terms of what it was; why it should be used; how to use it; when to use it; and evaluation of its use. The control group spent the five hours simply reading. Hence comparable time was spent on reading. For the experimental group, what the strategy was and how to use it was related to an awareness of keywords in a text which both help discern the structure and then focus the attention of the reader on the text in the best way possible. An example is given in Table 6.1.

Table 6.1   Key words and text structure

Category	Key words in text
Description	*for example, for instance, which was one, such as*
Collection	*and, in addition, first, second (etc.), before, after, more recently, then*
Causation	*as a result, since, led to, as a consequence, therefore*
Problem-solution	*the issue – the solution; the question – the answer; the query – the response*
Comparison	*not everyone, in contrast, instead, act like, however, compared to*

The student's comprehension of the text was measured (before and after the training) using a recall-of-ideas test (free recall); a reading-time measurement; and a reader self-assessment of text difficulty. Raymond found:

1. The experimental group scored higher on the post-test than did the control group, although this was in only one text.
2. Some more proficient learners were clearly already using the text-structure strategy on the pre-test and continued to do so on the post-test, perhaps spontaneously transferring it from first-language reading. In other words these 'good language learners' probably did not benefit from the training as much as their 'less good' counterparts.
3. There was no correlation between the time the students took to read the text and their recall scores. In other words the experiment was valid.

Raymond speculates that the reason why the experimental group gained in one text only was probably because the topic of the other text was more familiar to them. When a topic is unfamiliar to you, there is more need for text structure strategies.

Initial implications

For beginner and intermediate students the teacher is in a cleft stick when it comes to reading. Encourage the students to apply too early the kinds of top-down inferencing strategies they use expertly in L1 and they will make wild guesses. Focus too much on sentence-level work and the learners will feel frustrated at the low content levels of the texts that they are being given. It looks as if learners need a variety of texts for different purposes, plus reading strategies for dealing with them.

The sheer number of reading strategies used by a learner will not result in reading success. It is the combination, hierarchical structure of strategies and their evaluation that equates with reading success. On the other hand, effective reading strategy use is beginning to look like a pretty effective predictor of reading success.

The implication of the above paragraph is that 'poor' language learners require strategy training to help them become 'good language learners'. Unfortunately the evidence that learners can be trained to use strategies is not yet conclusive. As Raymond (1993) points out, 'strategy training is never clear cut or transparent. The interaction of the strategy with text content, reader interest, and background knowledge, and reader perceptions of text difficulty, requires more research' (454).

Certain teaching strategies can encourage the development of reading strategies. If you allow glosses or dictionaries to be used you not only train students to use a valuable resource strategy but you are also able to give them more challenging and therefore interesting texts.

The authenticity of reading texts

The past 20 years have witnessed teaching materials sales publicity proudly proclaim that the texts being offered the students are *authentic*. This is ironic as obviously it takes less 'author effort' and expertise (especially in this electronic age) to collect authentic reading texts than to 'make them up'.

Why should we be interested in this?

Firstly because it is not absolutely clear what is meant by an authentic text. Secondly, because text authenticity contributes to the earlier discussion of whether reading is a language problem or a reading problem. If it is merely a reading problem then the threshold for students to be able to cope with authentic texts should be quite low (or early on in their language-learning careers). Thirdly, and this may seem obvious to most teachers, I believe that the aim should be to move gradually towards authentic texts and that therefore they are indeed a sign of 'learner progression'. The question still to be answered is how fast should they move towards authentic texts?

The research evidence

The first point, what do we mean by authentic texts, has in part been answered. Widdowson (1976) proposes the term 'genuine' rather than 'authentic'. That is a text that is perceived by the reader as written for the purposes of being read, even if in reality it has been doctored for the L2 reader. A third interpretation is that authenticity is defined by the reader's response (Williams and Moran 1989) – i.e. whether the reader finds the text appropriate for his/her purpose, as a language learner or as a language user or both. This may not correspond to the writer's intention but this does not matter – it is the reader that matters.

Unfortunately, the literature is not drenched with evidence of what learners prefer, what they think they learn best from, whether they can sniff out a 'doctored' text or even whether it would worry them if they could. It would be helpful if some research which asked the learners their preferences were to be carried out.

In a sense, we have dealt with the second reason for being interested in this topic already. The overwhelming evidence seems to be that, unless you give the reader a very low cognitive task, the short-circuit hypothesis holds true. Therefore authentic texts early on should, in general, be kept to a minimum. As Williams and Moran (1989) put it: 'A key question is whether presenting students with authentic texts is necessarily the most appropriate method of helping them achieve levels of proficiency which they need to comprehend texts!' (219). On the other hand, as Fitzgerald (1994) quite rightly points out, 'the former notion that listening and speaking proficiencies are prerequisites to learning to read and write is now viewed as a misconception . . . ' (32). This is a view supported by Turner (1998) when reviewing the English National Curriculum progression (the levels of attainment) where she notes that reading works interdependently with other skills. However, she then falls for the NC's seductive call that the early levels of language learning (levels 1-3) are concerned with the simultaneous development of oracy and literacy and that 'learners must first learn to read what they can say' (33). This, in my view, is confusing two quite distinct issues: (a) the interdependence of the skills (reading can help speaking, writing and listening and vice versa; (b) the systematic hand-in-hand progression of receptive skills with productive skills. Since it may take some learners more than a year to reach level 3 in speaking, are we really suggesting that they should only read individual words and short phrases for more than a year?

A very interesting study on the issue of how soon can learners be confronted with authentic texts, albeit it with the 'ubiquitous' university students, was carried out by Maxim (2002). He gave 27 beginner students (English L1, German L2) a German novel to read after only four weeks of the course and compared this experimental group with a comparison group that was exposed to more traditional textbook reading. The treatment lasted for 10 weeks and consisted of extensive reading of a novel in class. Most of the reading was done in whole group or in pairs. This was then followed up by classroom discussions, role-plays, writing exercises, and grammatical exemplification. Maxim found:

1. There were no significant differences at the end of the intervention period in the departmental exams (all skills) between the treatment group and the comparison group. The treatment group was not disadvantaged by spending time reading the novel.
2. There was no significant difference at post-test for reading comprehension scores between the two groups – 'the equivalent reading ability of both groups at the outset of the study was maintained' (28) – both groups improved equally.
3. Both groups made equal gains in their progress with vocabulary.
4. The treatment group showed a significant increase in its ability to process read faster. Being asked to read 1,000 words per day in class appeared to limit the developing word-for-word reading habits.

Maxim concluded that the students' limited language competence did not short-circuit their ability to read authentic texts. However, this type of intensive and challenging reading had to be done under very controlled conditions, in class, with the support of their classmates and their teacher. In other words as a social co-construction of meaning. In-class group reading allowed the students to pool their understanding and allowed them to share their prior knowledge and their reading strategies. The type of novel chosen was also an important factor. It had recurring situations, accessible characters, a culturally familiar genre and stereotypical behaviours. As a final conclusion, Maxim proposed that a course with a strong reading-based focus can be implemented sooner than previously thought.

Maxim's study showed one way of increasing the students' 'reading rate', thus allowing them to read authentic texts. As Anderson (1999) observes, to many L2 readers, reading is 'a suffocatingly slow process'. He therefore advocates the explicit teaching of rapid-reading techniques. He suggests that students can be helped to increase the reading rate by (a) textual recognition (spotting similar words later in the text); (b) chunking bits of text; (c) line-by-line training (where the learner is encouraged to avoid following the line with the finger but instead encouraged to maintain concentration by placing a pencil at the end of each line of text and moving vertically down the page as he or she reads). Anderson cites a study by Cushing and Jensen (1996) in which students were able to increase their reading rate by an average of 100 wpm from an initial average of 184 wpm. One has to question, however, whether this type of reading does in fact lead to the full integration of ideas into a developing content and linguistic schema.

Initial implications

Teachers should certainly continue to explore the possibilities offered by authentic texts. However, authenticity, in the strict sense of 'written by native speakers for native speakers', is unnecessarily rigid as a criterion, although this level of authenticity might be an ultimate goal with advanced learners. On the other hand, with the right kind of classroom-based support, genuine and even authentic texts can be introduced quite early on in a limited way. However, these have to be balanced by the introduction of specially constructed texts which do build up the learner's vocabulary knowledge and syntactic awareness.

Testing reading

Testing language development is a huge topic in its own right and I will limit myself here, in the case of reading, to a few brief observations from the research literature.

Although a concept of threshold still holds sway among researchers of reading, it is still unclear what reading tests could be given to students which would accurately measure if they had gone over that threshold and when, therefore, teachers could concentrate more on reading skills and, by implication, give students authentic texts almost exclusively. As one of the purposes of testing is to discriminate between individuals, a formative assessment of threshold, based on valid and reliable testing measures, would be very helpful to the teacher. There is some tentative evidence

(Clapham 1996) that students who score less than 60% on a grammatical test are unable to apply with any degree of success top-down reading strategies. Setting the scope and difficulty of that grammatical test, of course, is itself an issue for debate.

Testing reading is problematic because it involves the inter-relationship of text and task as well as the student's language knowledge and L1 reading ability. Moreover, even within tasks there is usually a sub-structure of test items which do not necessarily match one-to-one with the information in the text. Alderson (2000) in a review of testing reading concludes that each individual reader will react to a test item differently. Those who set the tests are not in a position to predict how individual learners will react to test items. This undermines the reliability of the reading test.

The debate about what sorts of test types to use continues. There is some evidence that learning styles (particularly field independence and field dependence) affect the learners' ability to respond to cloze tests and multiple-choice texts.

In terms of validity, questions in the L2 about the content of a text have largely been discredited in favour of questions in the L1. Indeed some would advocate that translation of a text shows some of the best validity measures for the comprehension of an L2 text. The strongest argument against L1 questions and translation is the washback effect on the amount of L2 that teachers and learners will use in the classroom.

Neather *et al.* (1995) and Powell *et al.* (1996) both found that different task rubrics had an effect on the performance in the task, although these were largely L2 responses to L2 texts. They found that if the task prompts were in L2, learners frequently wanted to have access to dictionaries for fear of not understanding the instructions.

At an advanced level of language learning there is the issue of text interpretation, particularly when inference of the author's underlying meaning is required – for example in the case of irony or bias. If accessing meaning is a social co-construction process, different readers will be constructing different meanings in the lonely environment of the examination room. One solution to this is offered by Sarig (1989) by which pre-testing of answers to questions should be done by analysing model answers to questions from samples of readers from different backgrounds and then, presumably, accepting all such answers from candidates.

Alderson and Bannerjee (2002) conclude that the general consensus is still that 'it is essential to use more than one test method when attempting to measure a construct like reading comprehension' (86).

Conclusions

As we have seen, there is a great deal of research evidence with regard to reading. Unfortunately, much of this research evidence has, once again, been produced in adult (usually university) classrooms. I hope that teachers of young children and adolescents, such as those in my survey in Chapter 1, will be able to take something from this research and apply it to their context. My feeling is that it *can* be applied to most contexts principally because reading (despite some limited research evidence we have discussed) does not raise quite the same motivational or anxiety issues which we have come to associate with speaking and listening.

Nevertheless some applicability problems remain. For example, as we have seen, research has been concerned not only with comprehending texts but also with how well learners are able to recall the meaning of a text after they have read it. This is, in part, why 'free recall protocols' have been used to measure access to meaning despite their requirement for a measure of memory prowess. My guess is that they have been used because most of the researchers are operating in the 'language use' context (reading for academic purposes) rather than in a context where reading is promoted, additionally, in order to increase proficiency overall. Students here are being evaluated on how much they have retained of the content of what they have read. This, and the washback effect of discouraging bottom-up reading strategies, is the only explanation I can offer for what appears to be a fairly unnatural way of assessing access to meaning.

The interactive model of reading has stood the test of time and has now become the dominant theory underpinning most of L2 reading research. However, only recently has there been a recognition that the major distinctiveness of L2 reading is that learners are in a position to apply their L1 whilst accessing the meaning of a text and that this needs to be built into the model. Use of the L1 is an important learner strategy for reducing the cognitive load during a complex problem-solving 'reading instant'.

The importance of the knowledge that the reader brings to the L2 text can be overstated. Nevertheless, it does play a part and this is why teachers should seriously consider compensating for lack of topic knowledge by introducing pre-reading activities which increase the learner's knowledge of the topic or stimulate predictions about the topic. Without these, the reader may become overwhelmed by the problems associated with access and frustration or anxiety will set in. The application of prior knowledge appears to be an important strategy for reducing the cognitive load.

We should be wary, as teachers, of over-emphasizing schemata or scripts in the strategies that we make our learners aware of as these can send the inexperienced reader irrevocably in the wrong direction. These strategies have to be balanced with other strategies which rein in the impulse to make wild guesses. The short-circuit hypothesis appears to be fairly unassailable at the moment. Not only does it imply that early language learners cannot easily transfer L1 reading strategies to L2 texts because of lack of L2 proficiency, but that if they do transfer them they may do so ineffectively. Strategy training can advance the stage at which transference of L1 strategies to L2 reading can occur and, as a consequence, at which stage in the curriculum more difficult text, well above the learner's productive levels, can be offered. Thus, we should give beginner learners both non-authentic and 'genuine' doctored texts and gradually move towards authentic texts. In very special circumstances and using particularly innovative teaching strategies, authentic texts can be beneficial very early on.

'Good L2 readers' integrate meaning and use a balance of top-down and bottom-up strategies as appropriate to the text. The ability to arrive at the right balance is in itself governed by a series of metacognitive strategies which evaluate text difficulty and task requirements. Strategy training in this complex cognitive operation would seem to be an essential pre-requisite, for some learners, in order to improve their reading skills. Strategy-training research so far has only given an inkling as to its effectiveness in improving the performance of poor readers. Future research needs to establish via much more longitudinal methods whether strategy training improves and maintains higher reading success.

There is an increasing conviction that phonological awareness of an L2 should be taught to beginners. Teaching the alphabet of a language such as French may be useful for the limited transactions in France requiring the spelling of words but quite unhelpful in assisting learners with accessing the meaning of written texts.

In order to improve L2 reading, to make L2 reading faster, to be able to access more difficult L2 texts earlier, we have to make the whole process of reading both in and out of the L2 classroom more *visible*. True/false, multiple choice and other similar task types are all very well for keeping the students busy but they do not get at the processes involved in their reading. Teachers can easily model combinations of strategies in reading: by getting students to underline words they don't know; by getting them to circle words that might give them a clue as to the meaning of the words they don't know; by getting students to say why they have circled those words/ phrases; by getting students to limit their dictionary 'look up' and then to evaluate how effective this strategy is. All this information can be passed on to the teacher. It is at this process level, through having a dialogue with the students about the reading process, that real progress can be made.

Note

1. There is some ambiguity in the literature about the terms 'inference' and 'inferencing'. Most authors use them to mean making informed guesses from the top-down and bottom-up evidence available. Occasionally an 'inference' is taken to represent the process of arriving at a 'the author's *hidden* meaning'. I have used it in the more common former sense.

Chapter 7

Research on Listening

There are two basic ways to access spoken language. The first is on your own in a one-way listening situation. When we listen to a tape recording or watch a video or (pretend to) listen to a lecture we are essentially listening alone and trying to understand what the speaker or speakers are saying. In order to do this we can bring to the process of accessing meaning many of the strategies discussed in the previous chapter on reading. The second way that we access spoken language is by interacting with the speaker, whereby listening becomes much more than a two-way process. We began to look at this in our chapter on theory and methods. In order to understand, by interacting with the speaker in a L2 conversation, we bring a whole host of other strategies to bear in order to access what he or she is saying. We may use some of the strategies that we use when listening alone but not the other way round. That is, we cannot use *interaction strategies* when listening alone. It is for that reason that this chapter has been placed in between reading and speaking. L2 listening, at a theoretical level, 'pivots' in between these two skills. During the course of this chapter I hope to demonstrate that listening should 'pivot' between reading and speaking at a practical classroom level too. I shall also try to demonstrate that the use of the pause button by the teacher, in recorded listening activities, is the outward manifestation of the pivotal role of listening. Mysterious? Don't worry, all will be explained during the chapter. But just think about it for a moment. When learners are listening to a tape in the classroom they are not 'alone'. So, there must be a third way in which to listen!

Listening alone

By listening alone, of course, I am not referring to sitting alone in your bedroom listening to a radio or tape recorder or watching a video, although this scenario is part of listening alone. What I am distinguishing by the notion of listening alone is that the hearer does not have the opportunity to interrupt the speaker. Chambers (1996), while discussing listening to a tape recorder in a teacher-whole-class setting, lists a whole panoply of associated activities and consequences which he believes are detrimental to developing the skill of listening. In summary these are:

1. Typical classroom activities such as a text in conjunction with an exercise. (Not the way we usually listen.)
2. Correcting of the exercise is the final stage of the activity. There is rarely a logical link to the next activity.
3. Listening becomes a test of comprehension rather than a learning experience.
4. Progression in listening usually follows the textbook which does not always include important steps, especially the 'building up' of listening strategies.
5. Activities focus directly on items of detail to the neglect of the 'global level'.
6. Listening is not integrated with other skills or to other tasks such as role-play.
7. The pause button is misused by the teacher: 'this stop start approach denies pupils the opportunity of hearing enough text to be able to put it into some sort of global context' (24).
8. Listeners are not encouraged to use inferencing from localized information and prior knowledge.
9. Lack of differentiation. Chambers cites Elston (1992), 'Every time I press the play-back button in front of a class, I am condemning the whole class to work at an identical speed.'

Chambers is referring primarily to the context of learning a foreign language in England but his observations will probably ring true with readers elsewhere in the world. We will look at some suggestions that Chambers makes for improving the situation at the end of this chapter, especially as he cites his earlier study (Chambers 1993) which I reviewed in Chapter 5 which suggested that listening is far from being students' favourite classroom activity. For now, since we are on the subject of the English context, what does the English National Curriculum say about the skill of listening?

Firstly the NC (Department of Education: 1995) attainment target[1] one (listening and responding) makes no mention of 'listening as interaction'. That is, although the word 'responding' is in the title, there is no suggestion that the response should be oral let alone that it should be 'interactive'. To be fair, however, the Programmes of Study (recommendations about the sorts of activities that should be offered to the students) state that students should be taught to 'ask about meanings and seek clarification and repetition; ask and answer question and give instructions'. Thus the basis for interaction is there. However, since there are separate attainment targets for listening and for speaking, it is not surprising that the nine levels of these (eight levels plus Exceptional Performance) should give the impression that the predominant listening activity is either a teacher monologue or an audio/video recording. It should not come as a surprise therefore that Chambers finds foreign-language classrooms in England so bereft of teaching techniques which focus on the *process* of listening. Moreover, the progression through the attainment target for 'listening and responding' manifests itself very much through increasing the length, complexity, range of topics and rate of delivery of oral texts and also moving from teacher-delivered input to recorded material. Compare, for example,

Level 2: pupils show understanding of a range of familiar statements and questions, including everyday classroom language and instructions for setting tasks. They respond to a clear model of standard language, but may need items to be repeated.

with

> *Level* 6: pupils show understanding of short narratives and extracts of spoken language, drawn from a variety of topics, which include familiar language in unfamiliar contexts. They cope with language spoken at normal speed and with some interference and hesitancy.

In other words the progression is neither centred on advanced interactive listening skills nor on developing the top-down and bottom-up processes more associated with reading that we saw in the last chapter. So is listening so different from reading?

Lund (1991) provides us with a comprehensive account of the similarities and differences between listening and reading, together with a description of a comparative study. So we will look at his work in some detail. First of all he observes

> Although listening has enjoyed a theoretically pre-eminent place in L2 teaching approaches since audio-lingualism, much more research effort has been devoted to reading. (196)

Yet there are at least six major differences between accessing an oral text and accessing a written text. In an oral text (the following features are adapted from Lund 1991 and added to by the author):

1. The complete text is not available for perusal. It is perceived *as* it is uttered.
2. Text exists in time not in space.
3. The listener cannot control the pace of the text.
4. Listeners are compelled to resort to parallel distributed processing (see Chapter 3 Theories, Grammar and Methods) by integrating information from multiple sources simultaneously.
5. The sound system of the L2 poses a significant problem (listeners have to literally grasp at words).
6. Gaps in speech (pauses) are not the same as the gaps in written form (spaces between words).
7. Cognates identical in print may sound completely different in continuous sound.
8. Spoken texts, additionally, have intonation, stress, regional accents, background noise and other variations of acoustic features.

Lund argues that in oral text, decoding (the perception and processing of acoustic information) is separate from comprehension (the construction of meaning). In other words we are much more likely when listening to have to perceive the sounds of the message, hold them in the acoustic components of working memory and then begin the process of trying to understand what they mean. When reading, the decoding process can usually be by-passed unless there is a word-recognition problem or a comprehension problem that requires the reader to slow down and hold strings of language in working memory. In general there is consensus among researchers that decoding in listening and reading is different. There is less agreement about whether we go about comprehending in the same way.

Generally, it would be safe to say that in listening we deploy more top-down strategies and more often than in reading. This is almost self-evident given the speed and lack of permanence of the spoken text. How could we attend to individual vocabulary items or syntax when the speaker will have moved on? So in listening alone we *have to bring much more of ourselves* to the task of constructing meaning. It is as if our complex system of prior-knowledge (our schemata) becomes 'personified' and begins to interact with the person we are listening to. Of course, in so doing, we are much more likely to get the wrong end of the stick. These differences in reading and listening should lead us to transfer strategies (and particularly strategy training) with great caution between the two skills (Ridgeway 2000). Many of the strategies we apply in listening are associated with visual clues, including lip reading. Indeed, Ridgeway questions whether we should focus more on intensive listening to different types of text than on the strategies used to comprehend spoken text.

Lund carried out an experiment to confirm whether reading or listening to the same text produced the same amount of comprehension. He also wanted to know if proficiency levels affected the relative comprehension in the two modalities (reading and listening). He took a sample of 60 university students of German (English L1) at different levels of proficiency and randomly allocated them to either listening or reading the same text which included features of spoken discourse. The text was listened to twice or read twice and learners were asked to recall the meaning in L1. He found:

1. Beginner and intermediate students read better than they listened in terms of recall of information (as predicted).
2. Readers recalled more propositions at every level of comprehension – whether main ideas or detail (as predicted).
3. Listeners produced the most misunderstandings.
4. Repetition of text helped the readers more than the listeners (contrary to prediction).
5. At advanced level, repetition helped both listeners and readers.
6. The greatest difference between groups in listening occurred between intermediate and advanced. We are not told if this was evidence of a listening *threshold* (as we saw in our previous chapter on reading) or just an unequally distributed proficiency level.

So, listening is very different from reading and until recently there has been a constant emphasis on the supremacy of top-down processing over bottom-up processing, a supremacy which has to some extent made the leap between research and practice. However, at least three recent studies have suggested that although, top-down processing is important, bottom-up processing is actually indispensable and, in fact, may be a better predictor of listening ability than schema-oriented listening.

In Ross (1997), 40 Japanese (L1) students of English listened to 10 recorded statements and had to match each of these with one icon from a list of 25 icons or symbols. After each item the researcher asked the participant to provide an account (in L1) of what words or phrases had been heard in the preceding item and how these were related to the picture selected, in other words the reasons behind their selection of the icon. He found that both high-proficiency and low-proficiency listeners were listening out for 'keywords' in the utterances on which to base their selections. However, for less proficient listeners the keyword was more of a 'processing constraint' (236) than a short cut to inference, because they were not able to juggle with the linguistic information in working memory and search for confirming clues.

Tsui and Fullilove (1998) investigated the performances of a huge sample of Chinese (L1) learners of English on test questions. They compared questions where the correct answer, matched the schemata that the learners were likely to have had (their prior knowledge) with items where the answer conflicted with their schemata – i.e. it did not match their world view. Candidates who were able to arrive at answers for non-matching schemata items tended to be the more skilled listeners; they hypothesized that the less skilled were able to rely on guessing for the matching items, but not for non-matching ones. Bottom-up processing seemed therefore to be more important than top-down processing in discriminating between candidates' listening performance. We would have to ask the question, however, about proficiency. Presumably they were able to do the bottom-up decoding at speed. We need to ask, therefore, what was the match with overall proficiency?

Wu, Y. (1998) also investigated the relationship between the processing of the linguistic information in spoken language and the listeners' use of their background knowledge. Chinese learners of English heard a three-minute text twice – once all the way through as they completed multiple-choice questions on content, and then in sections. After each section, they were asked to recall their route to comprehension and their strategies for dealing with problems. Wu concluded that bottom-up processing was basic to successful comprehension; failure or partial success at the linguistic level can lead listeners to allow schematic knowledge to dominate their interpretation.

Of course bottom-up processing in listening increases cognitive load and any study which purports to positively correlate listening proficiency with bottom-up decoding will have to account for *overall* proficiency, particularly command of vocabulary and syntax. In other words, depending on how quick and automatic is the recall of known items of vocabulary will influence the relationship between listening proficiency and bottom-up decoding.

Brown (1995) looked at what features affected the cognitive load of a listening text. These were:

1. How many individuals (participants in the discourse) and objects are involved; the fewer the easier.
2. How clearly distinct the individuals or objects are from one another.
3. How simple the spatial relations are in the text (for example when listening to directions).
4. Whether the chronological order of the telling matched the sequence of events in the text.
5. Whether inferencing is necessary to relate each sentence to the preceding text; the less inferencing the easier.
6. How self-consistent is the new information with itself and with the information the listener already has.

In addition to lexical and syntactic complexity, cognitive load will also be affected by such features as number of embedded clauses and speed of delivery. These features are in addition to listener characteristics such as prior knowledge, mismatch between text difficulty and learner proficiency and any possible hearing defects such as glue ear (in the young) or reduction in acuity (in the old). Of course many of these features are present in reading too, but the cognitive load (the number of balls that the learner has to keep juggling at any one time) is so much greater in listening.

Rubin (1994) carried out a comprehensive review of L2 listening comprehension research but noted the dearth of hard evidence with regard to the factors which might influence comprehension. Figure 7.1 is a diagrammatic representation of the first of Rubin's five major factors affecting comprehension: text characteristics. The others are interlocutor characteristics; task characteristics; listener characteristics; process characteristics (i.e. the types and combinations of strategies used).

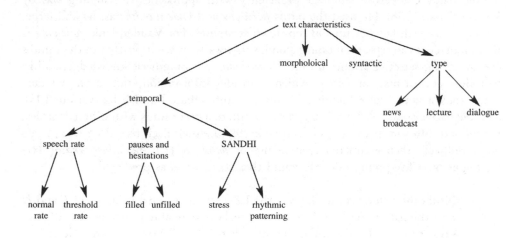

Figure 7.1 Text characteristics affecting listening comprehension. Adapted from Rubin (1994)

Rubin's review of research highlighted how some of these *text characteristics* made listening harder. All types of hesitation phenomena caused perceptual problems and comprehension in L2 learners because they get stuck in bottom-up processing during these pauses. SANDHI[2] is a term in linguistics literature for all the things that make oral text sound different from what we might call 'strings of words on a page' – for example, *contraction, liaison, elision*. SANDHI is very susceptible to proficiency levels. In other words, the lower the L2 proficiency level, the less compensation at the listener's disposal for any missing 'signal information'. In terms of *text types*, *news broadcasts* appear to be the most difficult, followed by *short lectures* (monologues with a clear intended audience) and then *dialogues*, although the difficulty appears to lie at the level of detail rather than at the level of main ideas. On the whole video appears to be beneficial in helping learners to access text. However video must be thought about carefully by the teacher as the visual support may lead to undermining the need to actually listen.

In terms of *task characteristics*, Rubin's review suggests that tasks are made more difficult if they make demands on the listener's memory or if they require the deployment of a different skill, for example note taking in L2.

As for *listener characteristics*, Rubin noted that *language-proficiency* level is a major variable in almost all the studies she reviewed. We found this also to be the case with reading, in the last chapter, when we considered the short-circuit and threshold hypotheses. Perhaps with listening it is even more acute. In other words with listening, unlike reading, there is even less time to deploy the kinds of L1 strategies that can compensate for lack of overall proficiency. Listeners' *memory capacity* and *affect* were also important variables in their ability to comprehend listening texts. Apprehension was found to relate significantly to lower performance in listening comprehension. Gender, on the other hand, did not appear to be such an important variable in listening. We shall look at one study on gender in greater detail in a moment.

One study comparing language proficiency with approaches to listening was by Vanderplank (1988). He used the terms *following* and *understanding* as, by and large, synonymous with bottom-up and top-down strategies. For Vanderplank, *following* is when a listener can repeat a message aloud, sub-vocally or see it written in the mind's eye and bring selective attention to it. *Understanding* is pragmatic knowledge, ability to follow arguments, contextual evidence, insider information, and so on. Vanderplank took a sample of 32 adults, 27 low to intermediate English L2 (various L1s), and five native speakers. They listened to 10 different recordings with different styles, genres and different 'pace' (see Vanderplank 1993 below). Each recording was played once. Subjects then estimated relative use of *following (F)* and *understanding (U)* strategies on a five-point scale. He found that there were, as predicted,

1. significant differences in the way the L2 learners listened in terms of *F* and *U* from the native speakers. The native speakers were able to operate in all three ways: $F > U$; $F < U$; $F = U$. On the other hand the L2 learners were able to operate only in: $F > U$; $F = U$. Native speakers could *bias* or *adapt* their listening towards following or understanding. Learners did not have this freedom or flexibility.
2. there were significant interactional differences (between native speakers and L2 learners) with the 10 text types. Different genres and stress patterns caused the L2 learners a number of particular *following* problems.

Vanderplank concluded that there are dangers of over-reliance on top-down processing. As listening is an active and dynamic process, teachers may need to discourage 'passive' reliance on incoming sounds. At the same time teachers may need to discourage premature reliance on native-speaker-type strategies.

Initial implications

The implications in a sense are obvious. If we do not want to induce anxiety in students we cannot expect them (all other things being equal – e.g. task expectations) to cope with the same difficulty of text as in reading. In addition, listening needs different types of strategy training from reading. The research evidence also gives us an indication of the purpose of listening to a tape twice. As Lund suggests: first exposure allows creation of context; provides opportunity to generate hypotheses; allows identification of where the gaps to focus on are. The second exposure therefore should have quite different task objectives: to use the context to infer meaning; to confirm or discard hypotheses; to fill gaps in detail that were missed the first time round. Either we train the learners to have different objectives for each exposure or we build it into the tasks themselves. A further alternative is to get them to set themselves their own objectives for each exposure to the text. Through discussion of these with the teacher, both teacher and learners could become more aware of the processes and strategies involved in listening. Vanderplank (1988) proposes a number of exercises for strategy training:

1. Stress perception and matching exercises.
2. Functional locating exercises.
3. Information and opinion-correcting exercises.
4. Self-evaluating and *shadowing* to check self-evaluation.
5. Emphasis on critical 10-15-minute 'tuning in' period.

Extensive listening and narrow listening

We will pick up on Ridgeway's point earlier about what kinds of texts to offer learners. Should the texts be difficult and authentic? If so, we would be compelled either to reduce our task's objectives or teach strategies for accessing them as best they can. Alternatively should we offer simpler, doctored texts, tailored around the topic, which contribute to learners' general language proficiency but do not develop high levels of accessing skills?

One of the dangers of taking the latter option is that learners are very rarely presented with challenging texts. They may learn the vocabulary and syntax of the doctored text but will not look upon the activity of listening as something to be accomplished in its own right. The Assessment of Performance Unit (1987) observed that, in the UK, beginner students were not being given the opportunities to hear more connected utterances, let alone more extensive texts. Of course, periods of residence abroad, even for beginners and lower intermediates, can be beneficial in developing the ability to listen. In fact Fisher and Evans (2000) report that listening, after a short period in the target country, revealed the greatest number of improved scores on a post-test – that is, it was the skill that appeared to improve the most. But residence abroad is not always possible. In most learning contexts the vast majority of the learning occurs in the classroom.

An alternative to this dichotomy between extensive listening and topic-tailored listening may be provided by what is beginning to be known as 'Narrow Listening' (Krashen 1996) where it is suggested that narrow listening can be perfectly rewarding an experience for learners in the early stages of language acquisition, whereas uncontrolled casual conversations can be too difficult. Narrow listening involves listening to very short texts on the same topic again and again until the listener feels he or she is confident with that topic or content. In a study of 255 beginner and intermediate French students in the US, Dupuy (1999) provided them with a programme of narrow listening which had the following features:

1. It was entirely student-centred (students listened to tape-recording either in class or at home).
2. Materials consisted of several brief recordings (1 to 2 minutes on each topic).
3. Topics were entirely selected by the student.
4. Students could listen as many times as they liked.

5. The recordings contained natural and informal speech with redundancies, pauses, self-corrections, false-starts, varying word rate and intonation.
6. There were no specific questions to answer. Students were encouraged simply to listen to the recordings until they felt they could understand them.
7. Students could change recordings and topics gradually, at their own pace.

Dupuy then surveyed the students for their views on the listening programme. They reported overwhelmingly that they found the programme helpful. Students self-reported that they made gains over the course of the programme in listening comprehension, fluency and vocabulary. Self-report on gains, of course, is not as reliable a measure as actual measurement of gains and with the use of comparison or control groups. Nevertheless, these tentative results may be worth taking into account, especially in a context of developing learner autonomy. Of course, these features of Narrow Listening have the early Krashen fingerprint on them in that the central assumption is that large amounts of listening practice prime the learner to acquire a second language by triggering implicit processes through which the rules of the language are internalized.

Initial implications

In the early stages we need both narrow and extensive listening with different task objectives. In other words, both the types of texts and the kinds of task we set on these different texts should have different pedagogical objectives. As in many aspects of the languages classroom, activities have a dual role: the improvement of proficiency in a discrete skill and the development of the learner's interlanguage. Some new language can be learnt from simple exposure to oral text. Some language needs repeated attention. Some language learning can be sacrificed in order to promote more efficient listening skills. Some language learning needs to have priority over skills development. These implications are quite similar, in principle, to those for reading.

Listening strategies

Unlike the reading strategies that we examined in the previous chapter, the strategies that learners use to help themselves listen or to achieve a listening task is an area that has not received a great deal of research attention. This lack of research attention may have the same origins as the reasons for which teachers should indeed be interested in listening strategy research. This is that, particularly in the teacher-whole-class situation, it is difficult to find out precisely what is going on during the process of listening, even if one's intuitions may in fact be correct. Think-aloud protocols, such as those used in reading and writing, are obviously impossible. Of course we can ask the learners what they do and introspection and retrospection techniques have been used by researchers. Some insights have been gained from these techniques as we shall see. However, interestingly, one finding from these investigations is that, compared to other skills, students have very poor perceptions and awareness of their own listening strategies (Danaher 1996).

Thus, there are two main reasons for teachers to develop an interest in listening-strategy research. Firstly, as I have intimated, we know very little about what goes on in the learners' heads when they are listening to recorded text. Walking round the classroom to see how each student is doing is not an easy undertaking and, similarly, students may not feel it appropriate to interrupt the flow of the recording to tell us about the difficulties they are having. These constraints contribute to the 'test-like' atmosphere that Chambers was describing earlier. So, empirically-based evidence of strategies used by learners would greatly benefit teachers in their approaches to listening comprehension. Secondly, as with other skills, the ultimate aim of strategy research is to go beyond description to intervention. In other words to help those individuals who do not use strategies sufficiently and in efficient combinations to experiment with new ways of listening.

The research evidence

One of the first pieces of research into listening strategies was carried out by O'Malley and his associates as part of a whole series of studies in how high school and college students in the US used strategies, both by English as a second language students and Spanish and Russian as a foreign language students. The study which most concerns us here is the one reported in O'Malley, Chamot and Küpper (1989) on listening comprehension strategies involving 11 high school students classified at the intermediate level of ESL. The data was collected via interviews with a variation on the think-aloud technique whereby the interviewer stopped the tape and asked them to relate as much as possible about what they were thinking while listening. As with other studies in this series, the researchers attempted to quantify the number of times a strategy was used. The results showed that there were significant differences between effective and ineffective listeners in the way that they self-monitored, checked for comprehension while it was taking place, related new information in the text to prior knowledge, and in their use of inferencing.

One of the problems that continues to bedevil strategy research is what exactly is the difference between a strategy, a process and a sub-skill (McDonough 1995). Rost (1990), for example, produces a very useful list of what he calls enabling and enacting skills. As we can see from my adaptation below, virtually all of these might be called strategies by other researchers.

Enabling skills

Perception

- Discriminating sounds in words
- Discriminating strong and weak forms
- Identifying use of stress and pitch

Interpretation

(at utterance level)

- Deducing the meaning of unfamiliar words
- Inferring implicit information
- Inferring links between propositions

(at inter-utterance level)

- Recognizing discourse markers
- Constructing a theme over a stretch of discourse
- Predicting content
- Identifying elements that help you to form an overall schema
- Maintaining and updating the context

(including possible speaker intentions)

- Identifying an 'interpersonal frame', speaker-to-hearer
- Monitoring changes in prosody and establishing (in)consistencies
- Noting contradictions, inadequate information, ambiguities
- Differentiating between fact and opinion

Enacting skills
An appropriate response based on the above, including:

- Selecting key points for the current task
- Transcoding information into written form (for example, notes)
- Identifying which points need clarification
- Integrating information with that from other sources
- Providing appropriate feedback to the speaker

These sub-skills or strategies in listening have an affinity with Anderson's (1985) study of listening which essentially proposes three recursive stages:

> *Stage 1*   perception. Perception is the moment when a sound begins to be noticed as being speech (rather than just a noise). At this point listeners begin to focus on the sounds of the language and store them in the phonological loop – but almost immediately begin to process these sounds for meaning
>
> *Stage 2*   parsing. At this point, listeners use words and phrases in the text to construct meaningful representations – the size of the chunk that listeners retain in working memory depends on several factors including knowledge of the language, knowledge of the topic, the quality of the signal
>
> *Stage 3*   utilization. Listeners 'probe long-term memory' to relate what they hear with what they already know – their schemata (to help them make sense of it) and scripts (in order to anticipate events) and inter-related concepts (in order to elaborate and generalize from the particular)

These stages, are not only recursive but also inter-related.

We have seen that these strategies, when lumped together as processes, do appear to vary between effective and less effective learners. Are there, therefore, any other variables in strategy use?

Bacon (1992), building on a previous, large-scale study (Bacon and Finnemann 1990) which found significant differences in strategy use between males and females, sampled 50 university students who had been judged to be motivated but not particularly highly proficient in Spanish (English L1). She got them to listen to two texts: (1) the history of mobile homes in the US (the text type was therefore narrative and culturally accessible to American students), (2) electric converters for when you go travelling. This text type was harder, descriptive, and less culturally accessible. The students had to listen to the passage and lift a finger to identify when they were 'thinking about the passage' and then self-report the strategies they used. Bacon then analysed the idea units they understood from the text and the strategies they reported using. She found:

1. The more narrative passage was more accessible and produced better comprehension and students were therefore able and willing to report a greater number of strategies.
2. Women used more metacognitive strategies than men (planning their listening, monitoring their comprehension and evaluating their strategy use) and were more likely to use metacognitive strategies when faced with the difficulties of the more technical passage.
3. Women were more consistent in their use of cognitive strategies than men, as if they had got into a routine of strategy use.
4. Women kept reminding themselves to 'think in Spanish'.
5. Men were more consistent in expressing their feelings – expressing higher levels of confidence overall.
6. Men tried to understand every word and attempted more direct translation – what Bacon calls a 'more aggressive approach'.
7. However, despite these differences in strategy use, there was no significant difference in the level of comprehension achieved by males and females.

Thus it seems that for listening, perhaps because of the different patterns of processing involved, different strategies used may be appropriate to different individuals. A number of strategies which were specific to listening (or particularly relevant to listening) were identified by Bacon's study. The metacognitive strategies were:

Prior to listening (adapted from Bacon 1992)

- Focus attention: 'Must concentrate, clear my mind, avoid distractions'
- Apply an advance organizer: 'You told me it was (about) a product so that bit must . . . '
- Go in with a plan: 'I am going to listen for words I know, for key words, for cognates'

While listening

- Self-management: 'I must get used to the speed, keep up with the speed . . . I've got to listen to this bit and still try to keep up'
- Aware of loss of attention: 'Come on . . . refocus . . . keep concentrating'

All these would appear to be useful strategies to deploy in order to get oneself ready to listen in the best possible personal conditions. Bacon's respondents also reported using a number of strategies which may or may not be effective under the extreme duress of listening:

Bottom-up processing

- Hear a word and repeat it: 'I'll hear a word and repeat it over and over'
- Use intonation and pausing to segment words and phrases: 'I listened to an entire phrase until there was a pause, then tried to understand that before it went on to the next phrase'
- Listen for all the words: 'I try to hear every word'
- Listen for each word one at a time: 'Wait for the first word I know, then another one. See if I can put them together'
- Listen to sounds rather than meaning: 'I kept hearing the "r" word, remarkable?, the accent is throwing me'

Top-down processing

- Infer; guess from context, intonation: 'it sounds like a commercial with the music'
- Visualize: 'I've got a picture in my mind as if I were really in it'
- Reference to English, translate: 'I have a dictionary in my head. When I hear a word, I leaf through my head really fast to see if I can find out what it means in English'
- Transfer; Use previous linguistic or discourse knowledge: 'I went for the topic sentence'

An area of listening strategies which has not, to my knowledge, been researched is *post-listening strategies*. Unlike reading and writing, once we have done our listening, there is no chance of listening again. But is that completely true? Is it possible that there are some *residual traces* in working memory which would allow us to monitor what we have understood (and written down, following the task requirements)? There may be some value in investigating whether efficient learners are able to draw on these *traces* as effective strategies for task completion.

Bacon observes that we must remind ourselves that we should not impose strategy use on learners but make learners aware of the range of strategies available and that a different response may be needed according to the type of passage they are listening to. Finally we should remind ourselves that strategy use needs to be evaluated for its effectiveness.

Feyten (1991) studied to what extent 'listening ability' was a good predictor of language acquisition over a period of time and of overall proficiency – in other words just how important listening is in the whole framework of L2 learning. I take 'listening ability' to mean the effective use of clusters of strategies and this is why I have included it in this section. 90 students on a summer language programme of French or Spanish (English L1) were given an initial listening test using a video. The test measured their ability to: evaluate message content; understand meaning in conversations; understand and remember information in lectures; evaluate emotional meaning in messages; follow instructions and directions. In other words, many *different* and important aspects of listening in specific contexts. At the end of their 10-week course the students were given an end of programme language-proficiency test consisting of an oral interview, a listening comprehension component, written grammar test, a reading and vocabulary component. Feyten found:

1. There were significant correlations between listening ability and overall FL acquisition. In other words those with high listening ability at the beginning made most general progress on the course by the end.
2. There were correlations between listening ability and oral proficiency skills.
3. Listening ability predicted FL proficiency better than sex, length of previous language exposure, which language (French or Spanish) they had studied on the course and the students' last contact with the language they studied on the course.

Feyten concluded that we should take listening ability more seriously. Moreover, since researchers propose that listening strategies can be developed through training, then we should be researching to what extent listening-strategy training is effective in increasing success in acquisition. Feyten's findings with regard to the importance of listening in predicting proficiency are in tune with findings in aptitude tests where an important component of aptitude is phonetic discrimination.

Graham (1997) divides listening strategies into two groups. The first group is those used by learners in order to try and improve their performance in listening in general. The second group is the strategies deployed during the process of actually trying to understand a listening text. Using retrospective interviews with 17-year-old learners of French and German in England, Graham identified a number of strategies that fell into the first group:

1. Taking part in a cultural exchange
2. Talking to friends on the telephone
3. Listening to the L2 on the radio or TV

In the second group, using (in addition) think-aloud protocols, she detected strategies such as:

1. Not focusing too much on individual words at the expense of understanding the whole text
2. Not allowing themselves to be distracted by 'false friends' or by 'redundant items'
3. Advanced preparation for a specific task (e.g. activating their schemata)
4. Selective and directed attention
5. Problem identification (identifying words that might hold the key to the meaning of the passage or part of the passage as a whole) whereas words which were 'instantly recognisable may be irrelevant to the overall meaning of the text' (51)

An interesting finding in Graham's data was that the weaker students were hampered by:

1. their slowness in identifying key items in a text;
2. frequently mishearing words or syllables and then trying to transcribe what they believed they had heard, thus becoming distracted.

For Graham, too, weaker students overcompensated for lack of lexical knowledge by overuse of top-down processing strategies. As the topic of the texts was very 'close to the students' own experiences', this reliance on schema-based knowledge to get them through the difficulties was, in fact, an impediment to comprehension.

Beeching (unpublished study) carried out a qualitative investigation of the value of video over audio for a group of post GCSE students in non-honours (majors) courses. L1 comprehension questions were used on a 10-minute commercially available film: *Quartier de rêve*. Students were asked to self-report on the strategies they used. For example, how they got the right answer; how they might have been misled by the visual aspect of the film. Beeching found that the ineffective listeners (contrary to O'Malley, Chamot and Küpper 1989 findings) did not get bogged down in 'bottom-up' strategies but relied on visual clues and cognates which, presumably, derailed them. The most effective listeners claimed that they used the grammar of the language and the sub-titles as well as coupling the visual images with the text. Interestingly these learners did not mention background or prior knowledge.

Why then does this research contradict previous conlcusions in listening-strategy research? Why is it that successive, more recent, studies have pinpointed the over-reliance of students on prior knowledge whereas the general view to date has been to avoid getting tangled up in the undergrowth? The answer surely is twofold. Firstly, the ability to listen is inextricably linked with other aspects of language proficiency. The better you 'know' a word, or chunk, or are familiar with a collocation, or a string of words, the less is the necessity to dedicate large quantities of selective attention to that particular language element. In other words, strategy deployment comparisons can only be made when other aspects of proficiency are more or less equal. Bring two learners together who have fairly similar L2 vocabulary stores, comparable confidence at recognizing syntactic clues and *then* see if they are using different strategies to comprehend oral text. Otherwise you are just not comparing like with like. Secondly, the balance between top-down strategies and bottom-up strategies is going to be decided, by the listener, on the basis of the difficulty of the text and the nature of the task related to that text. Given that 'thinking aloud', as I have already argued, is virtually impossible in a listening comprehension, any retrospective report on strategies used is going to be dependent on the task that the learner 'has envisaged' would be appropriate for the text. If he or she has not been told whether the task involves listening for detail or gist, they will make a decision for themselves. That decision may also entail their estimation of their own abilities to deal with the text as the exposure occurs. Indeed that decision, as to the balance between top-down and bottom-up strategies, may well change as the text progresses and gets harder or easier. The focus of listening-strategy instruction, therefore, should be at the deci-sion-making level, at the metacognitive level, and less at the cognitive level.

Mendelsohn (1998) argues that background knowledge is not enough in itself to compensate for problems in listening comprehension. It has to be activated in conjunction with linguistic knowledge. In order for this interaction to take place students have to be trained by committed teachers to use strategies more effectively. In addition he sees the following textbook deficiencies:

1. There is a gap between the underlying theory of listening and actual practice.
2. Textbook content is organized around topics and not strategies.
3. Little attention is devoted to the mechanics of listening.
4. Students are not taught how to listen to one type of text as opposed to another type of text.

In a very important study, Thompson and Rubin (1996) attempted to ascertain whether strategy training was effective in improving listening skills. Building on Rubin's (1994) research (see above) which identified the major characteristics that affect listening comprehension, they were determined to take into consideration in their research design aspects of strategy training which had undermined past work: limited time spent on training and lack of integration of training into the normal programme of teaching. For example a study of listening-strategy training by O'Malley (1987, cited in Thompson and Rubin) with intermediate-level high-school students over a two-week period showed some improvement but not the statistically significant improvement to warrant the time spent on the training. Similarly, Rubin, Quinn and Enos (1988, cited in Thompson and Rubin) provided English L1, Spanish L2 high school students with listening-strategy training over four days only whilst using video for comprehension. Again there was some evidence that the experimental groups outperformed the control groups but what was missing was a convincing demonstration of a positive relationship between strategy training and learner performance on listening tasks. The sample Thompson and Rubin chose was a group of third-year Russian students (English L1) at university. The strategy training was substantial and lasted two whole years and consisted of use of video both for comprehension and for strategy training. The control group looked at the same videos for comprehension but received no training. The researchers found that students who were given strategy instructions improved significantly on the video test – at least 10% improvement. Some improvement (nearing significance) was also detected on an audio test. Students learned to manage their approach to listening through the use of a series of important metacognitive strategies:

1. *Planning strategies* – deciding how many times to view a segment; whether to view with sound on or off; how to break up segment into manageable proportions.
2. *Goal-definition strategies* – deciding what to listen for, how much needs to be understood.
3. *Evaluating strategies* – assessing the effectiveness of strategies used.

This study has become influential not only because of the success consequent to the strategy training, but because of the reaffirmation of the importance of metacognitive strategies in listening and particularly strategies which relate to the task in hand. The data also revealed three successful strategies which relate directly to the genre of the viewing/listening activities:

1. *Drama genre* – general focus on the story line
2. *Interview genre* – pay particular attention to question and answer sequences
3. *News-report genre* – deploy a mental 'who, what, when, where and how' structural overview of the incoming text.

Thompson and Rubin concluded that strategy training needs to take place over long periods of time and needs to be integrated with the materials and the tasks. There is no quick fix but it is worth the time allocated to it.

Another series of studies, of an experimental nature, have looked at very different aspects of the strategies used in the 'listening alone' situation. Barcroft (2001) investigated whether changing the way learners hear a new L2 word makes them acquire it better, worse or made no difference. He also investigated if new words were retained better or worse if exposure to the words was varied acoustically. Many teachers, especially of beginners, vary the way they present new vocabulary to students by changing their voice to represent a number of moods or meanings. It would be useful therefore to know whether acoustic variation, as a self-deployed strategy, might help learners to learn new words. Barcroft carried out an experiment with 15 adults who had only a few weeks (maximum) of Spanish (mixed L1s). They were presented with three different degrees of variation on 24 words: *no variation, moderate variation* (two variations of neutral, loud and whispered) and *strong variation* (one repetition of neutral, loud, whispered, excited, childlike, nasal). The words consisted of eight animals, eight fruit and vegetables, eight classroom items – typical of beginner syllabuses in schools. They were tested immediately after the oral exposure to the words (Time 1) and 10 minutes after (Time 2). The results were very surprising:

1. No significant effects were revealed for the different acoustic variation conditions on Time 1. In other words the subjects did not learn the words any better or any worse by varying the exposure to the words.
2. No significant effects were revealed for Time 2. The subjects could not retain the words any better or worse as a result of the variation.

Barcroft argues that at a cognitive level (see the discussion on connectionism in Chapter 3 above) the only possible explanation for these results is that the two effects cancel each other out. Increasing the acoustic variation makes the connections more robust (i.e. more sturdy by virtue of establishing more different and complex sets of connections). However, this is cancelled out by weakening the strength of each connection (i.e. each individual connection would have been made stronger if the words had just been repeated without variation). In sum, it looks as if it does not matter whether you vary your teaching voice or not when presenting new vocabulary. However, we must bear in mind that these results relate to a perspective which is purely psycholinguistic, experimental and, in any case, only with motivated adults. It may be that in large, adolescent classrooms, acoustic variation helps with keeping the students' attention, and making it more fun, in which case the number of connections are both increased *and* strengthened simply because the students are actually bothering to listen to you more than if you were not varying your voice. This is why we must always be very wary of applying experiments which have not been conducted in authentic classrooms.

Scott (1994) also carried out an experiment linking sound to auditory memory and perception. She investigated whether older adult learners (people in their fifties and sixties) have reduced memory span and auditory perception than younger adults. One rationale for this investigation was that retired people are living longer, and are now learning a new foreign language in increasing numbers. Some are going abroad to contribute to voluntary aid projects and need to learn a new or develop further a second language they already have. Previous research has suggested that auditory memory span or storage capacity seems to decline slightly with age. Changes have also been detected in processing and retrieval systems and aging may affect change in attentional systems. Lastly, hearing loss, usually the perception of higher frequencies, seems to be an unfortunate feature of the aging process. So, is it very difficult for older adults to learn a foreign language? Scott compared the performance of four groups of adults: young adults who were either monolingual or bilingual; older adults who were either monolingual or bilingual. She gave them 10 tests in order to measure their:

1. Perception of speech against a noisy background
2. Recall of random digits in the same order
3. Recall of random digits in reverse order
4. Recall of L1 sentences of various lengths
5. Recall of L2 sentences of various lengths
6. Ability to detect a native accent in Spanish
7. Discrimination of Spanish phonemes out of context
8. Discrimination of Spanish phonemes in a sentence
9. Listening comprehension in L2
10. Vocabulary recognition

The good news for older learners is that Scott found:

1. Younger subjects did significantly better *only* on 9, 8, 5 and 1.
2. On the decontextualized phonemes there was no difference.
3. There was no difference in L1 auditory memory capacity.
4. Accent detection was pretty much the same for older and younger subjects.
5. Older adults had more trouble perceiving speech against a noisy background.
6. Bilinguals in general performed better than monolinguals in L1 measures of auditory memory span. Thus it may be that learning a second language influences memory capacity in some way.

Given that this evidence confirmed earlier research on deterioration of the perception of higher frequencies, Scott concluded that the lower performance of older learners on some measures appears to be more related to *perception* than memory *capacity*. 'Older adults who are healthy and mentally alert possess auditory memory capacities similar to younger adults' (1994: 276). Given that we can create teaching conditions and encourage learners to use strategies which will compensate for lower perception, this research suggests there is absolutely no reason why learning a foreign language later in life should be a major problem.

In two studies, Harley *et al.* (1995) and Harley (2000), the researchers investigated whether a listener's focus on prosodic clues (intonation, stress, volume) undermined their focus on syntax and whether this might lead to misinterpretation of meaning. In addition Harley sought to discover whether the listener's L1 and age made a difference. She noted that most previous age-related studies focused on comparing the relative success of learners who *began to learn* the L2 at different ages. In contrast, Harley's studies were concerned with learning processes *at* different ages. In her 1995 study of Cantonese learners of English, the researchers discovered that Cantonese L1 learners of ESL all focused heavily on the prosody of the L2. This study involved children in three different age groups (ranging from 2–12 years of age) and appeared to confirm previous L1 studies that the younger the learner the greater the focus on prosody at the expense of syntax (as might be expected). We are reminded of the cognitive processing model we looked at in Chapter 3 whereby competing demands on working memory result in one choice of strategy over another. Harley then replicated the Cantonese study with 35 Polish L1 students (aged between 11 and 18). She got them to listen to 30 taped sentences of which 20 were not ambiguous (prosody and syntax were in harmony) and 10 were ambiguous (prosody and syntax were in conflict). Their task was to repeat a 'special part' of the sentence. She found:

1. All students had no problem with unambiguous sentences.
2. All students had *some* problems with ambiguous sentences.
3. Polish L1 learners (just as much as Cantonese younger learners) were likely to attend to prosody rather than syntax. That is, the expected difference due to features of their respective L1s was not confirmed.
4. Listeners sometimes mentally adjusted the syntax in order to make it fit with the prosody.
5. There were no age-related differences in the Polish group (just like in the Cantonese group).

Harley concluded that, certainly in English as a foreign or second language, prosodic cues are of primary importance for listening comprehension. Whether they are as important for other second languages with less stress and intonation features (for example French) remains to be researched. In these two studies at least, it appears that the ability to override (or perhaps it would be better to say 'contain') prosodic cues and focus on syntax appears to be a sophisticated skill perhaps only available to native speakers, and older ones at that. On the other hand we might speculate that the absence of stress patterns in, for example, French causes problems for the listener whose L1 has clear stress patterns and exercises in stress differences might be of great help to students in this learning situation.

Vanderplank (1993) was also interested in the extent to which certain prosodic features, such as stress, affect comprehension. He argued that these might be of equal value in grading the difficulty of a text as the more common speech rates (words or syllables per minute). Building on previous work (Vanderplank 1985) he proposed that texts should be analysed and graded for *pacing* – the speed at which stressed words are spoken and for *spacing* – the proportion of stressed words to total number of words.

He therefore carried out a study with 30 advanced-level university students of English (L2) with various L1s, including French which has very different stress patterns from English. He asked them to listen to a recording of Margaret Thatcher (British prime minister 1979-1990) being interviewed by Kirsty Wark (Scottish TV news presenter) and gave several tasks to accomplish. One of the tasks was reading along with Thatcher. This posed them a number of difficulties and they were able to make a number of observations/discoveries: it was difficult to say one minute of her speech in the same one minute that she took; she appeared to have a slow tempo but yet spoke quickly; they found themselves sounding aggressive whereas Thatcher sounded 'calm and imperturbable'. The French (L1) students mostly had the greatest difficulty. Vanderplank's analysis showed that Thatcher had a slow tempo caused by spacing – i.e. a low proportion of stressed words to unstressed words. Unstressed words were spoken very fast. Vanderplank found that the learners had previously been unaware of the complex nature of variables in stress and rhythm. This was, in part, because the textbooks did not teach it in this way. All the students felt that such insights into stress and rhythm helped their approaches to listening. Vanderplank concluded that by using the notions of pacing and spacing it should be possible to grade passages of spoken text more accurately than simply using words or syllables per minute speech.

Initial implications

Harley's work – and that of Vanderplank – suggests that there are important implications for our selection of listening materials in the classroom. For example should teachers take note of how authentic the prosodic features of a text which has been 'doctored' are? Should some texts contain 'light prosodic features' to ensure that learners' selective attention *at least sometimes* focuses on syntactic information? On the other hand, some lower-achieving students perhaps do not take into account prosodic features as much as they should and are unaware of the clues they can sometimes give to meaning. Perhaps teachers should try to find out the processes involved when listening to texts with heavy prosodic features – for example asking the students if these features are the ones that trigger their top-down processes. Also there should be times when, in pre-listening activities, teachers draw the attention of students to prosodic features ensuring that they are not putting themselves at a disadvantage. Harley's work also has implications for the teacher's modification of input. Can a teacher's exaggerated stress and intonation lead to a lack of focus on the verbal part of the message?

The last question brings us neatly to the second form of listening. That is, what I have called 'interactive listening' but what is also sometimes referred to as two-way listening, namely, listening as part of a conversation.

Listening as interaction

Of course every individual's experience of listening is different depending on the type of work or study or lifestyle that they undertake. Nevertheless, most researchers estimate that the majority of the listening that we do is done as part of a conversation. Listening which involves interacting with others is in sharp contrast with reading, which as we have said, has contributed a great deal of the research parameters for the 'listening alone or one-way listening' situation. Whereas reading and 'listening alone' involve the slow, co-construction of meaning (via the text and what the reader/listener brings to the text) almost as an act of faith, by contrast interaction involves the *negotiation of meaning*. In the vast majority of conversations, at least where the conversations are benign and collaborative, both speakers want to arrive at a shared understanding of what each wants to say.

One problem with describing interaction is that both speakers are simultaneously also hearers. Consequently, is the person asking for clarification a speaker or a hearer? Some authors have used the term 'interlocutor' to try to solve this problem. I have found it easier, in the context of interaction as part of L2 learning, to refer to them as speaker and hearer according to the utterance in question at that particular moment. I have also used the terms L2 learner and L1 speaker, instead of the sometimes used terms native speaker and non-native speaker, because not all teachers are native speakers but may well be offering near-native input and feedback.

Negotiation of meaning for comprehending

One of the first researchers to consider the issue of meaning negotiation was Hatch. According to Pica's (1994) review of the topic, in 1978, Hatch 'made a pivotal and indelible mark on the field of SLA through her publication of two seminal papers on language learning and interaction' (Hatch 1978 in Pica 1994: 494). Hatch proposed that researchers should look towards interaction for insights into language-learning development rather than the syntax of the language. In other words she hypothesized that learners made progress as a result of real-life interaction rather than communicative competence arising out of the continuous practice of structures. One of the researchers who took up this challenge was Long (1981). From observing L2 learners interacting with L1 speakers, he concluded that what the former were doing was trying to improve the quality of the input they were getting from the L1 speaker by giving him or her some feedback – verbal or otherwise – that they had not understood. In this way, following Krashen's earlier model, the L1 speaker's input became more *finely tuned* to the immediate needs of the L2 learner-hearer allowing the latter to understand more easily. The input was made *comprehensible* as a result of this interaction. At this point in time Long called it 'modified interaction'. Long proposed that interactionally modified input comes about as a result of the following devices operated by the two parties in a conversation:

1. *Confirmation checks*. The L2 'hearer' tries to ascertain whether he or she has heard the speaker correctly, and/or whether he or she has understood the speaker ('Have I got this right?').
2. *Clarification requests*. The L2 'hearer' asks the speaker for help in understanding what the speaker has just said ('What do you mean?'; 'Do you mean X or Y?').
3. *Comprehension checks*. The speaker checks whether the 'hearer' has understood something, either verbally or by some other means ('Do you understand?').

Pica and her associates took this a stage further. They argued that it wasn't just a one-way process of feedback from L2 learner to L1 speaker but that both engaged in a process of *negotiation of meaning* in order to arrive at a satisfactory conversation. If we think about it this is obvious and it is even present in L1-L1 speaker conversations. If we don't understand the content or the language in a conversation we 'help each other out' until we do. It goes back to principles of co-operation in discourse (Grice 1975).

Pica, Young and Doughty (1987) therefore studied the interaction patterns of 16 low-intermediate learners of English (L2). They divided them into two groups and asked them to carry out a similar task of listening to 30 different *directions* in order to assemble a picture. The two groups received different 'input conditions'. Condition 1: the L1 speakers pre-modified their directions for the task (they made reductions in syntactic complexity (clauses); provided repetitions and re-phrasings). Condition 2: the directions for the task were not pre-modified but the L2 learners were encouraged to ask for clarifications – i.e. to negotiate for meaning. The researchers found:

1. The negotiation condition was significantly better at aiding direct comprehension of the directions for the task (i.e. the hearer placed the items in the correct place on the picture more often).
2. In the negotiation condition, content word repetition (nouns, verbs, adjectives) increased from a mean 0.20 per direction to a mean of 13.17 as a result of negotiation. In other words the quantity of appropriate input increased.
3. Moreover, in the negotiation condition the input was broken down or segmented into more processible units. The quality or type of input became more appropriate for the hearer.
4. Other learners who were merely 'listening into' the negotiation said they got more out of it than those 'listening into' the pre-modified input.

Pica *et al.* concluded that, when it comes to comprehension, negotiation of meaning appears to be a pretty powerful tool. As we will see in the next chapter on speaking, the concept of negotiation of meaning did not stop at comprehension but was used as a stepping stone for arguing that interaction promoted language acquisition itself.

Rost and Ross (1991) investigated the reception strategies used by Japanese (L1) learners of English at different levels of proficiency as they listened to a three-minute narrative. At key points in the story the students were encouraged to ask questions. They found:

1. There was a definite link between the range of strategies used and the general proficiency of the learners.
2. More proficient learners used *forward inferences* and *continuation signals* in order to let the speaker know that they had understood.
3. Less proficient learners used *global reprises* where the listener simply asks for complete repetition of an utterance even if only one word or one section has not been understood.
4. The choice of strategies used was limited by social constraints. Unlike in reading, where the choice of strategies is, theoretically, limitless, when interacting, listeners didn't want to appear to be rude or unhelpful by asking for too many clarifications.

A similar study was carried out by Peñate Cabrera and Bazo Martinez (2001). They used a sample of 60 Spanish (L1) primary-school children in their second year of learning English as a foreign language. The children listened to two stories under two conditions. In the first, the text had been simplified linguistically. In the second condition it had been simplified both linguistically and as a result of interactions. The children were able to follow the storyline much better under the second condition.

Building on the work of Rost and Ross (1991), Vandergrift (1997) looked more deeply into the strategies that L2 learners use in order to understand the speaker's message. He too wondered to what extent general proficiency levels affected the strategies used. He therefore used a sample of 20 high school learners of French (English L1) aged 16-17 at different levels of proficiency (i.e. they had studied French for different amounts of time). Their task was an Oral Proficiency Interview which was video-recorded. The following reception strategies were observed being used:

1. *Global reprise* (either in L1 or L2) – the listener asks for outright repetition, rephrasing or simplification.
2. *Specific reprise* (either in L1 or L2) – the listener asks a question which refers to a specific word or phrase that was not understood.
3. *Hypothesis testing* (either in L1 or L2) – the listener asks specific questions about a specific piece of information but by giving a prompt or an alternative (e.g. '*after les devoirs?*')
4. *Kinesics* – the listener indicates a need for clarification through use of his/her body language.
5. *Uptaking* – the listener uses kinesics and verbal or other non-verbal signals to indicate to the speaker to continue, that he/she understands.
6. *Faking* – the listener sends *uptaking* signals or non-committal responses in order to avoid seeking clarification and admitting to the interlocutor that he/she has not understood.

(Adapted from Vandergrift 1997)

As we can see, this list of reception strategies is a more comprehensive and refined version of the three meaning negotiation strategies proposed by Long. Vandergrift found that, as proficiency increased:

1. There was a gradual decline in the use of kinesics.
2. The learners used fewer global reprises, pinpointing more *the exact source* of the problem.
3. There was greater use of uptakes.
4. (As expected) more advanced learners were able to process chunks of words rather than single words.

The implications of these findings are that, in order to move beginners on more quickly, they can be trained to use some of the strategies of the more advanced learners – particularly specific reprise and hypothesis testing. In Macaro (2001a) I have proposed a list of L2 phrases which can be taught to students so that these receptive strategies can be used and I have also proposed materials for supporting ('scaffolding') the use of these strategies.

Initial implications

Interactive listening clearly results in better comprehension than if the L2 learner merely listens to the L1 speaker (for example a foreign-language assistant) or teacher. Engaging in interaction ensures that those parts of the input which are not intelligible are simplified. In addition, if the L1 speaker or teacher actively engages with the students in negotiating meaning (i.e. actively encourages them to use reception strategies), a more naturalistic type of interaction will ensue. One further and, although obvious, very important benefit of more interactive listening is that the listener is simply more attentive to the discourse. The imbalance between listening alone and interactive listening activities should be addressed particularly in FL classrooms where 'the outside world' does not provide scope for the latter.

Technology and listening

Earlier we examined brief evidence which suggested that video enhances listening by providing a visual context. In addition, videos expose students to a variety of authentic materials as well as clarifying some cultural content. A number of other researchers have sought to demonstrate the advantages of video over audio but particularly the use of captions or subtitles. For example Chung (1999), using a sample of 170 17-19-year-old students of English (Chinese L1), investigated whether videos used in different ways led to better listening comprehension rates. Using a Latin Square technique,[3] Chung divided the group into four proficiency levels and four conditions: (1) they were provided with advanced organizers (pre-listening activities); (2) they were provided with captions in L2; (3) they were provided with a combination of both advanced organizers and captions; (4) they were provided with neither. Multiple choice in L1 was used to test comprehension rates and an attitude questionnaire administered. The results showed:

1. The *combined condition* scored significantly higher than the other three conditions.
2. Captions were more effective than advanced organizers.
3. There were no significant differences by achievement levels.
4. 94% of students affirmed that captions helped.
5. 93% of students said they preferred L2 captions rather than Chinese subtitles.

Chung concludes that *captions* make comprehension of authentic video materials less difficult and encourage conscious language learning. Whilst the second claim could be inferred from the results, the study does not provide causal proof for this. Chung also quite rightly speculates that captions could help students bridge the gap between the development of skills in reading comprehension and aural comprehension. This is an area where strategy research might prove fruitful.

A similar study was carried out by Markham (1999). Again, this was with advanced university learners of English. 118 participants watched two education programmes (one about whales, the other about the civil rights movement). They subsequently listened to audiotapes with multiple-choice questions. Having captions on the video programmes significantly improved the students' ability to recognize words in the text of the audiotapes (when these words had previously appeared in the videotapes). Markham makes a number of practical suggestions for use of captions in video. A wealth of other suggestions, this time when watching film on video, are made by Serio and Sheikh (2002).[4]

Mediated listening

The brief incursion into technology brings us full circle back to the use of the pause button on a tape recorder as the manifestation of the pivotal role of listening between reading and speaking. We will remember that Chambers (1996) criticized the use of the pause button in listening comprehension. I want to argue that moderate use of the pause button on a tape recorder has some justification in the research literature. We will remember that I have posited that listening alone or one-way listening essentially takes its processes and learner strategies from reading but modifies them to account for the higher levels of interpretation that the listener (as opposed to the reader) has to do. The two-way type of listening involved in the negotiation of meaning is quite different. This type of listening involves processes and strategies which have an affinity with the communication strategies associated with speaking. These we will be examining in the next chapter. Do these two dimensions to listening converge in any way?

Let us try to answer that question by asking one further question: what is the teacher trying to do, when he or she uses the pause button on the tape recorder or video? I would suggest that the skilled teacher is:

1. breaking down a long text into manageable chunks thus reducing the load on the auditory component of working memory;
2. allowing the hearer the opportunity to ask for sections to be repeated which would be inappropriate if the tape was still playing;
3. allowing the hearer to stop and build up hypotheses about subsequent sections in the text rather than trying to do this while more information is arriving;
4. attempting to demonstrate the overall structure of the text through judicious use of shorter and longer repetitions of sections;
5. gathering information about the current interlanguage stage of the learners as best he or she can in the circumstances;
6. (with highly skilled use of the replay button) helping the hearer identify problems in the speech stream which, through repetition, slowly become apparent to the learner;
7. modelling a number of bottom-up strategies which, as we have seen, may be overlooked if the hearer opts to rely on prior knowledge for guessing at overall meaning;
8. buying himself/herself time in order to confirm that the hearer(s) are understanding the text and looking for signals in the hearer's body language;
9. looking for the kinds of *uptaking* signals which Vandergrift identified as being those of listeners who wanted the speech stream to continue;
10. evaluating whether the level of difficulty of text and task are appropriate for the majority of the learners in the class.

As we can see, using the pause button effectively has many of the hallmarks of *interaction* but these are superimposed on the 'listening alone' situation. The teacher's use of the pause button is his or her way of turning one-way listening into two-way listening. Furthermore it is one way of modelling strategies which are listening-specific rather than borrowed from reading. In other words this type of teacher-mediated listening is in fact a 'third way' between one-way and two-way listening. For this reason alone it should not be dismissed as bad pedagogy.

Of course, it will be desirable that learners do, at times, listen to the text all the way through in order to develop autonomy in their listening strategies and to ensure that they do deploy top-down, prior knowledge strategies. However, to expect them to do this all the time would seem to be unreasonable given the difficulties and differences we have witnessed earlier between reading and listening texts. It is of course also desirable that learners be given the opportunity to replay autonomously the recording on individual listening stations. However, it seems to me to me that teacher-whole-class listening does have justification from time to time and not just because it is more expedient in some learning contexts. The important consideration is to take Chambers' other piece of advice and not to turn every listening into a test, but rather to find out what the learners are doing.

Testing listening

If we must have testing in listening (as in other skills) then we should ensure that it is valid and reliable and that the task that we set is actually an appropriate one. As with the skill of listening, the testing of listening has received very little attention from researchers. This may well be a consequence of the difficulties associated with listening research. Research into the testing of listening presents researchers with a huge challenge. How can they discover and measure what the listener is actually hearing when exposed to different text characteristics? As Alderson and Banerjee (2002) point out, 'it is well nigh impossible to construct a pure test of listening that does not require the use of another language skill' (87). Nevertheless some useful research on validation has been carried out by Shohamy and Inbar (1991) on the effect of text and question type. They compared a *news broadcast*, a *lecturette* (an informal, partly interactive presentation) and a *consultative dialogue* (containing the assumption of a great deal of shared knowledge). All three text types contained the same topics ('the common cold' and 'drugs') and approximately the same factual content. They, not surprisingly, found that the text type the students found easiest was the most interactive one: the consultative dialogue. Given our earlier assertion that most listening is interactive, this finding undermines the current practice of testing listening in which interaction with the speaker is impossible. In terms of question types, the students were given: 'macro/global type of questions (requiring) the test taker to synthesize information, draw conclusions and focus on cause and effect relationships' (29); 'local questions' (questions of detail); and 'trivial questions' (not directly related to the main topic). The researchers found, again unsurprisingly, that the global questions were the most difficult with trivial questions varying according to the text. The researchers argue that tests must include question types of both the local and global kind and should be directly related to the purpose of the test and that 'trivial questions' did not appear to relate to any recognizable test purpose.

Alderson and Banerjee (2002), despite the lack of evidence, attempt to provide an insight into the different test types that have been scrutinized by research and I summarize these here together with my own thoughts on the topic.

Dictation has been used as a testing technique and there is evidence that text dictation procedure discriminates well between learners of different proficiency levels. There is some evidence of successful use of partial dictation (where a part of the sentence is given, the other dictated) as a test of listening comprehension. However, it only discriminates well for those languages which do not have a transparent orthography, that is, where there is not a close match between pronunciation and the written form of the language. Moreover, whilst dictation appears to be a valid test of proficiency in non-transparent languages, and is reliable (inasmuch as two markers can easily arrive at consensus about what is right and wrong), it does not have much task appropriateness unless the *text characteristics* are authentic. In other words, slow dictation, with measured repetitions, controlled by the speaker (the traditional *dictée*), is not a task likely to be found in 'the real world'. On the other hand, if it does promote acquisition, then it should not be discounted.

Transcription, on the other hand (the converting of authentic recorded text to written form by individuals with the freedom to listen and repeat as often as they wish), is a highly authentic and much under-used activity both as a learning task and as a test type. Transcription is used 'in the real world' by teachers when preparing tasks for listening materials and it has a number of business applications. Transcription would appear to have all three of the attributes of aptitude: it tests phonological decoding, it enables the learner to demonstrate analytical skills (by thinking through the separation of the morpho-syntax) and it demonstrates good memorization of correct spelling. It is also pretty difficult to reproduce a correct transcription of an idea unit without understanding the meaning of that unit! Transcription, as a learning activity, helps to memorize language chunks, thus contributing to production fluency. Indeed when I was producing authentic listening materials involving the transcription of French radio news programmes (Macaro 1985) I managed to store new vocabulary, idioms, collocations, and formulaic language in long-term memory such that I can even now remember them *and* the precise text in which I first encountered them. I have not come across any research on the validity and reliability of testing of transcription.

Summaries into L1 appear to be supported by the testing literature as being valid and reliable but only if they are preceded by a phase in which the test takers are actually taught the skills of making a good summary. In other words, the task variable has to be controlled, otherwise it would no longer be a test of listening comprehension but a test of the ability to summarize.

A similar problem lies with *recall protocols*, where test takers are asked to provide as many 'idea units' as possible in a text they have just listened to. Clearly there is the possibility that this test is, in part, measuring memory capacity. According to Alderson and Banerjee (2002), allowing test takers to make notes as they were listening had little effect either way on their test scores. If they were actively encouraged to take notes, this significantly impaired their performance, presumably because it went against a particular learning style or it was a strategy that individual students had not developed. The act of writing the notes distracted them from the act of listening.

There is also little evidence as to when is the best time to provide *questions on a text* (whether in L1 or L2) in a task. Is it best to do it well before listening to the text, just before the listening, or after the listening. It is surprising that previewing did not result in more correct answers. This would certainly seem to undermine the practice of teachers carrying out pre-listening activities in order to stimulate prediction strategies in the students. My reaction is that more research is needed on when to provide the students/candidates with the comprehension questions.

Multiple-choice questions are not without their controversies. One of the problems is the location in the text of the information that each item is asking for. There is evidence to suggest that if it is located at the beginning of the text it is more easily found by the test taker. This would make sense as, in listening, the cognitive load is very likely to increase as the text progresses. One solution to this might be that more difficult idea units should be located at the start of a listening text (i.e. as teachers we should look for such texts). There is also research evidence that *distractors* (the wrong answers in the choices) which have the same lexical items as unimportant information in the text, 'derail' the listener. This would undermine the validity of the multiple-choice test as it would be testing the ability of the candidate not to be derailed. On the other hand, the validity of multiple choice ultimately comes down to 'item analysis': whether the success rate of candidates on a particular multiple-choice item is matched by performance of the best candidates overall. Nevertheless, concerns need to be expressed regarding the backwash effect on pedagogy of multiple choice. It may be that multiple choice encourages the listener to focus on scanning for a phonological/orthographic match-up, instead of concentrating on meaning. It should also be borne in mind that some research reviewed above (e.g. Tsui and Fullilove 1998) suggests that bottom-up processing is more accurate than top-down processing in discriminating between different levels of proficiency. That is, able listeners can in fact provide greater evidence that they have understood detailed information.

Initial implications

It would appear that the best listening tests (i.e. not necessarily listening activities) are:

1. those that minimize the interference of the task on the listener's demonstration of comprehension;
2. those that have a good washback effect on learning tasks;
3. those that do not require productive skills to demonstrate comprehension.

On the other hand, the above criteria are essentially for the 'listening alone, one-way' type of listening. As I have argued earlier, the bulk of listening occurs in interaction. There are no tests that I can think of which measure listening skills during oral interaction, these being constantly brushed aside in favour of measuring productive oral skills. It would be interesting to construct a test whereby what was being measured was the listener's ability to (a) negotiate meaning and (b) to arrive at comprehension of the speaker's messages.

Additionally, some of the most interesting tests are those that combine a number of language skills in order to achieve a macro-task or project. For examples see the Institute of Linguists exams. These involve all four language skills in a problem-solving dynamic. Whether these tests can be said to have equal validity and reliability as the more simple mono-skill tests is still open to discussion as multi-skill tests generate issues regarding what it is to test underlying abilities (Skehan 1998, Bachman 1990).

Conclusions

In spite of the limited amount of research into listening, both as a skill in itself and in its contribution to second-language acquisition, this chapter has given us some initial building blocks on which further research can build. Nevertheless, the data issuing from researchers, teachers and the learners themselves is still very limited and it would be an insecure knowledge base upon which to make too many proposals and recommendations for practice. More research is needed particularly in the following:

1. Does a listening threshold exist? If it does, is it merely a composite of vocabulary and syntactical knowledge, or does it have more to do with skills in phonetic decoding?
2. Is there a point in listeners' development when they can say that they are 'tuned in' to the language and what exactly does this mean?
3. Is there such a construct as a 'fluent listener'? Is flexible chunking of language in the long-term-memory store the one variable that helps to decrease cognitive load in working memory whilst listening and to allow more capacity for selective attention to phonological or syntactical problems?
4. Are the results of experiments obtained in restricted and artificial settings comparable or even applicable to authentic classrooms with all the additional variables that these have? Certainly more high-quality classroom-based research is necessary. This would help to provide teachers with answers to simple but important everyday questions such as 'Should I play the tape loud or soft, and with how many repetitions?'

Although the knowledge base is thinner than in the other topics in this book, we do have some insights which can inform practice.

Probably the most important of these is that we should not lose sight of the fact that so much of our listening involves interaction, the chance to ask the speaker for help in the L2 learner's efforts to understand them. This crucial fact is, sadly, often overlooked in the target-language, teacher-dominated classroom. Negotiating meaning still appears to lead to better understanding than non-modified or even pre-modified input. However, without a determined effort by the teacher, particularly with younger or more timid learners, receptive strategies will not happen because of the power relationships in the discourse between teachers and students.

Extended listening is a much more demanding skill than reading, involving the activation of brain components, personal schemata, parallel processing, and instant decision making far beyond the demands made by reading. As a consequence teachers should be very sensitive to the frustrations that may arise whilst listening and the demotivation that may ensue in one-way listening. We should not be surprised, moreover, by some of the 'global misunderstandings' that some learners might make.

Use of video and video captions in L2 seem to be an excellent resource for enhancing comprehension and captions may lead learners to momentarily throw the spotlight on new language elements, make form-meaning associations and even replicate reading strategies in listening.

I have argued that the debate regarding whether to use the pause button on audio or video recordings is related to a theoretical one which probably needs further investigation. If more recent research is right, and effective learners are not those who are able to stand back and use their prior knowledge to compensate for problems in texts, but perhaps those who can quickly search in the undergrowth for confirming information, then the pause button is itself a way for the teacher to become the mediator between the text and the lonely listener. However, once again, these positive features of the pause button that I have proposed will only be activated if the teacher shares this pedagogical information with the learners. What strategies, the teacher should ask them, are we both engaging in when I press the pause button?

The evidence from strategy research suggests that, in listening even more than in the other skills, we should refrain from imposing certain strategies on individual learners. On the other hand, lack of self-awareness, perhaps induced by 'the obscurity' of the listening process, requires greater time devoted to raising awareness of the potential strategies that students could deploy and evaluate. Thus strategy training in metacognitive and affective strategies should progress through all the normal stages of training with cognitive-strategy training being the only category that could be limited to the awareness stage only.

Strategy research needs to apply itself to being more task-specific rather than text-specific. The non-task-based think aloud may not be telling us the whole story of what the listener is going through in the classroom.

Strategy training, the research suggests, requires a more long-term commitment by teachers than was previously thought. Moreover, training may not have paid enough attention to those strategies which are involved in non-verbal cognitive activity, such as prosody.

We will leave this chapter with a few, specific and additional recommendations from Chambers (1996) which, in the absence of further evidence to the contrary, seem to me like pretty sensible advice. He argues that when exposing students to oral text we should give them pre-listening activities which predict what is to come. In addition, learners should be given while-listening activities and post-listening activities. All these should focus on different aspects of the listening process. Moreover, if they do come up with the wrong answer, rather than penalizing pupils for making an error they should be congratulated for their application of a strategy and encouraged to refine it.

Notes

1. The attainment targets are statements of what students should be able to attain at various stages of their language-learning programmes.
2. Unfortunately, Rubin (1994) does not provide us with the exact meaning of SANDHI but provides a reference to Halliday, M.A.K. (1987), Spoken and written modes of meaning, in R. Horowitz and J. Samuels (eds.) *Comprehending oral and written language*, 55-82 (New York: Harcourt Brace).
3. A Latin Square technique is where you have the same number of groups for the same number of different conditions. Thus every group experiences every condition.
4. Reader please note that this article is in Italian.

Chapter 8

Research on Oral Interaction

In Chapter 3 we began considering the theoretical foundations and the research evidence related to speaking in a foreign language. This is because a fundamental, overarching question in second-language learning is whether the target language is best learnt explicitly and consciously (focusing on the forms of the language) or whether it is best learnt implicitly and subconsciously by actually using the language. Essentially, the implicit and subconscious dimension of the answer to that question is perceived as occurring through the oral medium although, as we have seen in Chapter 6, there is also a fair amount of evidence that language can be learnt by simply reading extensively. In fact, both the main models presented in Chapter 3, the Universal Grammar model and the Cognitive Processing models, have been interpreted by theoreticians and practitioners as operating essentially via listening and speaking. In Chapter 7, I tried to argue that listening, as an interactive process, was the pivotal point between reading and speaking. Thus it will not surprise the reader if, in our discussion of oral interaction, we go over ground already covered under the theme of aural comprehension. We cannot dissociate the progress learners will make with regard to their proficiency in speaking from the quality of the oral input they are exposed to and the interaction they are invited to engage in. In this chapter therefore we will be building on the ideas and evidence presented in Chapter 3, particularly when we consider the research carried out on the value of oral interaction in the L2, and building on the exploration of issues in interactive listening encountered in the last chapter. Classroom interaction in the target language is the psycholinguistic device in a teacher's pedagogic tool box which sets the teaching of languages apart from all other subjects. It is in oral interaction that the often-quoted maxim is most apparent, namely, that we teach the content of the subject by using the subject as the medium of delivery.

Before we look at the various findings and theories of interaction we will briefly take into consideration a model of speaking. In other words, how do we actually produce the sounds and articulate the ideas that form one side of the process of interaction – the speaker's contribution to the interaction?

A model of speaking which seems to have stood the test of time is Levelt's (1989) model of L1 speaking (see Figure 8.1). In this model, the Anderson's (1983) Adaptive Control of Thought model (see Chapter 3, p. 44) is incorporated by establishing a fundamental need for declarative knowledge to become proceduralized knowledge in each component of the model. If we want to speak fluently and fast we cannot rely on declarative knowledge. It simply would take us too long to examine each word in the conscious, selective attention component of working memory before being able to articulate it via the speech organs. In L1 it has been calculated that we speak at an average of 150 words per minute (de Bot 1992). Thus the only possible answer is that these processes, in fluent speech, have become procedural. You 'know how' to do them just as easily and as quickly as, if you are an advanced pianist, you 'know how' to play a half-diminished chord or a minor scale on your instrument. You simply match the requirement with its execution rather than 'thinking about it' in a conscious and explicit way. Moreover, in order to increase fluency, the processes can run in parallel and the production is incremental. As soon as part of an utterance has passed from one component of the model to another that first component can be working on another part of the utterance. Finally, speech is made fast by the levels of activation of the lexical store in long-term memory brought about by 'the topic' being discussed. Semantic clusters of words are literally 'at the ready' to be selected. Thus working memory is not forced to search the whole of the lexical store every time it wants to produce a word.

As we can see from Figure 8.1 the generation of speech first starts with an *idea* in what Levelt calls 'the conceptualizer' drawn from the encyclopaedic knowledge store.

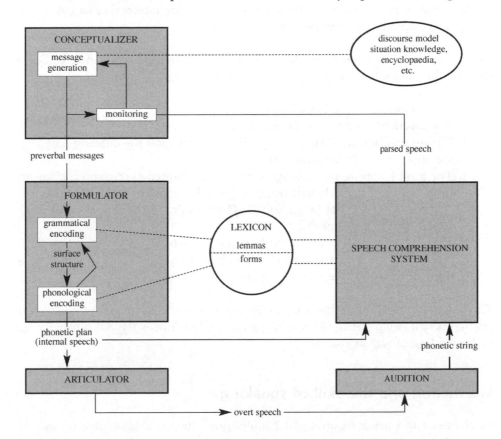

Figure 8.1   Levelt's model of speech production. Taken from de Bot 1992

The idea has a macro-planning level (an over-arching communicative goal); and a micro-planning level (elaboration of intention though selection of information). Nevertheless, in the conceptualizer, the idea is at a pre-verbal stage. It has no *form* in terms of language. The idea then passes to the formulator where it is given language form via phonological encoding and grammatical encoding – in other words, an acceptable syntax. The idea now has some language attached to it but it is still inside the speaker's head. It is still 'internal speech'. Before it can become external or overt speech it must pass through the articulator.

De Bot (1992) adapted Levelt's model in order to account for bilinguals. By bilingual here is meant anyone with a recognizable level of competence in a second or third language, not necessarily equal or 'balanced' bilinguals. The adaptation had to account for the following facts:

1. The two language systems can be used entirely separately or mixed depending on the situation, as we saw in the discussion on codeswitching in Chapter 3.
2. There are cross-linguistic differences. Languages have different 'parameters'.
3. Bilingualism does not lead to the slowing down of production, or at least only very little.
4. The adult speaker does not master, except in very rare cases, the L2 system to the same extent as the L1.
5. Speakers are able to cope with potentially unlimited numbers of languages and must represent the interactions between these.

De Bot therefore concluded, on the basis of second-language-acquisition evidence, that the formulator has *a different system* for each language. In addition:

1. The knowledge store is *not* language specific.
2. The macro-planning is *not* language specific.
3. The micro-planning *is* language specific. This activates the different language-specific sections of the formulator.
4. The lexical store is *not* language specific (see Chapter 4). However, elements from one language (L1) will be more strongly linked to each other than to elements from another language (L2). This results in the formation of *subsets* which are language specific.
5. There is only one articulator for bilinguals which has an extensive set of sounds and pitch patterns which serves both languages. This is why it is so difficult to sound like a native speaker.

The 'water-tightness' of de Bot's L2 adaptation of Levelt's L1 model of speech production is still being put to the test by researchers but it does serve as a base for our understanding of oral interaction.

Interaction and the skill of speaking

At the heart of current theories of L2 interaction, there is a basic premise that L2 input does not necessarily or automatically lead to acquisition. As we saw in Chapter 3, theories of L2 interaction sprang from a dissatisfaction with Krashen's (1985)

Comprehensible Input Hypothesis. As we saw in the previous chapter, listening comprehension can be enhanced by learners being *active* in the listening process in two ways. Firstly, by bringing their own knowledge and world experience to the language they hear, and secondly by interacting with the person who is speaking to them. It is to the latter that we will now turn in some detail.

As I have intimated above, interaction in the L2 classroom is widespread. Very few classrooms adopt a 'just listen to me and you will learn' approach although I have witnessed a few lessons where you might begin to wonder whether this wasn't in fact the teacher's central teaching technique! Listening-based methodologies such as Total Physical Response (Asher 1969) do not appear to work for the 'mass-market' of L2 learning. Moreover, few individuals can claim to have learnt a language simply by listening to a cassette, for example, in the car on the way to work. Even if they had, the interactionist theoreticians would interject, they must in some way have interacted with the cassette on their own, perhaps by *sotto-voce* repetition or by articulating responses. Thus, if comprehensible input is insufficient for acquisition, the argument goes, acquisition must come as a result of *people talking to one another*.

Negotiation of meaning and the role of output

What sort of interaction leads to acquisition? Can we define it in its entirety? Can we select the bits that best lead to acquisition? Or are there certain criteria that must be present for acquisition to take place? Can we measure the sufficient quantity needed for acquisition to occur?

Why should we continue to be interested in this?

Teachers may well ask themselves at what point in their lesson or series of lessons is new language actually acquired. Is it acquired immediately the learner has engaged with the new language element? Or is it incremental, as a result of repeated exposure, focused attention, and use? These questions go to the very heart of communicative approaches to language teaching. In order to account for acquisition resulting from oral interaction, researchers were obliged to take a stage further the concept that L2 learners or users force, request or encourage their interlocutor to help them understand. These researchers now observed the way that *both* native speakers (e.g. teachers or language assistants) and L2 speakers tried to understand each other when they hit upon a communication problem and the resulting modification in the learners' speech that resulted from this interaction. Thus the concept of the 'negotiation of meaning' in interaction was very readily taken up by researchers because they saw an additional function to it. They hypothesized that in 'the negotiation process', the L2 learner would acquire the previously unknown language item (be it a lexical, grammatical or idiomatic item). One of the reasons for this was that if they could substantiate the hypothesis that L2 structures *resulted from* interaction, rather than that practising L2 structures *led to* or *enabled* interaction, they could provide a more substantial theoretical base for communicative language teaching. In other words, learners acquire language by communicating in the classroom. This would be quite different from learners acquiring language in the classroom in non-communicative ways and then demonstrating this acquisition through communicative tasks.

To recap our deliberations in previous discussions of interaction then. The results of research by Long and also by Pica led to the following propositions:

1. Acquisition can only result from input which is comprehensible. This is obvious. You cannot learn something you cannot understand.
2. Interactionally modified input improves the quality of that input, making it more accessible for the learner to work on.
3. Interactionally modified input leads to acquisition.

The research evidence

Researchers, therefore, have investigated the *extent* to which interactionally modified input leads to acquisition. For example, Newton (1995) carried out a case study on a 21-year-old Taiwanese student of English in New Zealand who was getting low scores (compared to others in the class) for vocabulary learning. He gave the students information-gap tasks and negotiation-type tasks to perform. He found that the student made significant gains with previously (pre-test) unknown words only if those words had been used in the interaction required by the tasks, not if they had been words occurring merely in the procedural instructions from the teacher. He concluded that for unknown words to be acquired they have to be *processed deeply* and that modified interaction provided the student with the selective attention to the lexical items for them to be acquired. However, not all unknown words used in the interaction were acquired and Newton felt that there were still some questions left unanswered about how interaction assists acquisition. One question which might also be asked is 'Does interactionally modified input lead to improved oral production as well as acquisition?' In other words, does an acquired lexical item come more quickly to the mouth of an L2 speaker as a result of it being acquired through interactionally modified input?

In a whole series of studies carried out by Pica (1988) and Pica and her associates (1989, 1991), conversations were closely studied between L1 speakers (native speakers, NS) and L2 learners (non-native speakers, NNS). In the 1988 study Pica found that in 95% of the occasions when the native speakers indicated that they had not understood, it led the non-native speakers to make their contribution comprehensible. That is, they *forced* the Comprehensible Output from the learners. Pica *et al.* (1989, 1991) studied 32 low-intermediate Japanese (L1) learners of English doing four different communication tasks. They found:

1. When the native speaker signalled that they could not understand the learners, the learners reformulated their utterances.
2. When the native speaker *repeated* (with a signal of incomprehension) certain incorrect learner utterances, learners had another go at them.
3. Feedback to mis-pronunciation and to grammatical errors occurred in the native speaker's signals that they hadn't understood or had noted that the utterance was incorrect. Of these signals, 47% resulted in actual recasts.
4. Learner responses to native speaker signals contained structural modification

of their original utterance (usually segmentation – cutting up the problematic bit and saying it in a different way).

Pica *et al.* noted some structural modification as well as lexical modification by both the native speakers and by the non-native speakers. An example of structural modification by the native speaker was the moving of the problem word from being the object of an utterance to being the subject of an utterance and then describing it. Pica (1994) provides the following example where the non-comprehended object – a garage – is foreground (becomes the subject of the next utterance) through a structural modification until the learner understands:

> NS: and I have a garage on the side with three little black windows
> NNS: three black windows?
> NS: you know what a garage is?
> NNS: no
> NS: um, it's attached to the house. It's a building attached to the house in which you keep your cars and called a garage, OK, so it looks like a big house and a little house, but they're attached
> NNS: oh it's a small house
> NS: uhuh
> NNS: uhuh, and black roof?
> NS: uhuh
> NNS: yeah, oh, maybe, let's see, yeah, I understand
> (from Pica 1994: 511)

In the literature there is more evidence of acquisition of lexis as a result of modified interaction than there is of acquisition of grammatical patterns of the target language. For example, Ellis *et al.* (1994) carried out two studies involving high-school students in Japan studying English (L2) to see if interaction led to the acquisition of vocabulary. The students were divided into treatment and comparison groups. Pretests were administered to all groups. The treatment group received three kinds of input: unmodified input, pre-modified input and interactionally modified input. They found, as a result of written post-tests, that the interactionally modified input led not only to better comprehension but also to more new vocabulary being acquired and retained. We should note two things. Firstly, as with the Pica *et al.* study, we can observe that the findings are to do with the acquisition of vocabulary rather than grammatical structures. Secondly, the acquisition is measured under written test conditions. The acquisition is of *competence*. It is not a measurement of its improved oral production under the more pressurized conditions of interaction.

We should note that, in addition to having more finely tuned input, the L2 learner, through the negotiation of meaning devices, is buying time in order to better process the incoming input. This is an important point because it suggests that a new lexical element, in order for it to be acquired, has to be *noticed*. By noticing we mean that it is held in *selective attention* long enough for sufficient connections to be established in long-term memory. One way of ensuring the noticing of a new element, therefore, is if we are *forced to speak* it. Swain (1985) argued that one is more likely to notice the form of a word or the syntax of an utterance if one is likely to use it as 'output' (speech production) in the immediate future. Thus, while negotiated meaning allows the learner to 'control the agenda' (Skehan 1998: 17), forced output, it was claimed, encourages (via a washback effect) focus on the forms of the language. Swain claimed that for interlanguage development, learners need to be 'pushed' into speaking more coherently, more appropriately and ultimately more precisely. The notion of forced output has become known, we have already noted, as the Comprehensible Output Hypothesis.

The interactive model of L2 acquisition has led to the establishing and the consolidation of the Communicative Language Teaching approach world-wide although in its interpretations, as we saw in Chapter 3, this has become quite an eclectic approach. However, as a model it is not without its critics. For example Wu, B. (1998) claims that interaction is not sufficiently comprehensive to explain acquisition. Wu's criticisms are:

1. It cannot account for most verbal exchanges in classroom interactions since in practice (in many L2 classrooms) there is little negotiation of meaning! So, he asks, how do we acquire all the rest of the target language?
2. Incomprehensible input (when a learner does not understand) often results in silence rather than the learners signalling to the teacher that they haven't understood.
3. Some learners only participate in the interaction *when and if* the input is understood.
4. Acquisition exists side by side with interaction. It is parallel to it not a result of a linear process where a moment of modified interaction leads to acquisition of that specific language element.

Wu therefore proposes a much more complex dynamic model of interaction where it has ever-increasing cumulative effects both on the learner's progression of acquisition *and* on the teacher's construction and reconstruction of the learning environment. In his model, both output production and input reception involve memory and inner speech and there is 'an interplay between the external mechanism of verbal exchanges and the internal mechanism of linguistic processing' (1998: 528). There is not enough space here to examine in greater detail such a complex model and the interested reader will need to go to the original.

Pica (1994) also acknowledges the limitations of negotiation as a tool for learning:

1. (As Wu also notes) it cannot account for all the L2 learning.
2. Interaction which focuses on comprehensibility does not necessarily produce target-language-like forms.
3. Negotiation is mostly on lexis and on larger syntactic units – focus on morphology is rare.
4. Negotiation may not always be an acceptable form of interactional behaviour.

I would take this further and argue that it is not often pedagogically possible in classrooms with large numbers of students. We have only to look at the length of some of the exchanges in the Pica (1994) data to wonder what the other 29 students would be doing, especially if those students were demotivated adolescents!

As Pica (1994) concludes, overall we can safely say that negotiation provides learners with the opportunities to attend to L2 form. However, there is insufficient evidence that it directly leads to the acquisition of forms.

Initial implications

If speaking (in the form of forced output) is important for interlanguage development then it is going to be important that learners are encouraged to speak. Interaction does indeed seem to provide the glasshouse conditions for learning to grow and for interlanguage to progress quickly, even if the current model, as Wu argues, does not hold sufficient explanatory power for how they grow and progress. However, teachers cannot, as yet, put all their eggs in the interaction basket. We cannot assume that engaging the learners solely in communicative activities (meaning-oriented exchanges) will lead to the acquisition of grammatical patterns. Some of the evidence we reviewed in Chapter 3, however, may suggest that communicative interaction alone can lead to the acquisition of *some* grammatical patterns. Thus a balance between message and medium-focused interaction looks like being necessary for some complex grammatical patterns.

There is another problem. Whilst interaction may provide the theoretical conditions for learning to progress, it is difficult to get everyone to speak a lot in classrooms with many learners, and we cannot guarantee that those who are not speaking are engaging silently with the interaction of others. Quality of teacher-whole-class interaction is going to be important if the quantity (from the point of view of the students) is hard to come by. We will examine quality of interaction later. There is another way to ensure plenty of student talk in the 'numerous' L2 classroom and that is through pair and group work.

Learner-learner interaction

A number of researchers have studied learner-learner interaction, or student-centred oral work, although not necessarily with the same objectives in mind. Some have looked at the interaction from the point of view of learner autonomy, some from the point of view of task-based learning as an alternative to more traditional lesson progressions such as presentation, practice and production (PPP) (see Chapter 3).

Why should we be interested in this?

Put differently, given that learner talk appears to be of crucial importance for some aspects of acquisition and that large quantities of learner talk are not easily achieved in the teacher-whole-class interaction (not to mention the anxiety that this type of interaction might engender), why don't teachers offer more pair and group work to their learners? There are, I believe, three inter-related reasons. The first is that teachers believe that the language has to be 'put in' before it can be produced in a communicative way. As we saw in Chapter 3, objections to task-based approaches are that they are too focused on communication of meaning rather than on acquiring the next stage of the individual or group's interlanguage. Teachers prefer to be in control of the linguistic progression that the learners will make. As we saw in the discussion above, there is some evidence to support this position. Related to this is the fact that 'presenting' and then 'practising' new language is quite time consuming and teachers may feel that there is no time left in the lessons for the communicative production stage. Thus, the third P (Production) of the PPP gets squeezed out. Task-based syllabuses are, furthermore, difficult to conceptualize compared to topic-based or structural-based syllabuses. Secondly, there is the fear of students (particularly children or adolescents) going off task, off topic, off target language (i.e. speaking in L1) or all three of these. Teachers assume that pairs talking in L1 must be off task. Thirdly, teachers worry that learners are going to be exposed to their partner's incorrect models of the target language and that exposure will lead to 'fossilized use' of these erroneous forms. As we can see, all three of these objections are, in part, concerned with teacher control of learning. This is not surprising and it is not necessarily to be condemned (as some authors do). After all, teachers feel (and have!) a responsibility towards their charges. That responsibility is often governed by the demands of their local examination system.

The research evidence

One of the earliest studies of learner-learner interaction was by Varonis and Gass (1985). They were coming at the issue from the point of view of the negotiation of meaning being 'a good thing' and wondered whether this type of interaction would be as beneficial as teacher-learner interaction. Using a variety of age groups, they therefore compared native speaker-native speaker interaction (NS-NS); NS – non-native speaker (NS-NNS) interaction and NNS-NNS interaction. They found:

1. NS-NS interaction produced the least negotiated meaning. NSs preferred self-correction (for examples of 'slips') and, in any case, why correct when you have understood?
2. NS-NNS produced *some* negotiated meaning.
3. NNS-NNS produced *the most* negotiated meaning because (a) there was the greatest amount opportunity for so doing and (b) there was no embarrassment.
4. Adolescent learners worked harder at sustaining the interaction than did the younger learners.
5. Interlocutors seeking particular information were more likely to initiate negotiation than interlocutors holding the information. It was from this finding that, as we shall see, researchers and practitioners began to look at the types of tasks being offered in paired activities.

Further work by a number of researchers, in part, backs up this positive position for learner-learner interaction. In a review, Pica *et al.* (1996) found that interaction was of the same kind between learner-learner pairings and learner-L1 speaker pairings. However, L2-learner-L1-speaker pairings resulted in greater quantities of modified input. Of course the latter pairing also assures on-task behaviour and, possibly, maximum L2 use. I say possibly because in my experience some foreign-language assistants do have a tendency to resort to excessive translation modes ('How do you say X?' 'Tell me how you would say Y.').

Two studies (Brooks and Donato 1994 and Brooks, Donato and McGlone 1997) investigated the issue of whether students stayed on task and in the target language. They used information-gap tasks and recorded the interaction of the learners. In the

1994 study, they investigated the interaction of third-year high school students (English L1, Spanish L2). They found:

1. Students talked about their own talk.
2. They talked about how to do the task.
3. They used the L1 in order to help them steer their way through the task.
4. Students whispered to themselves in order to try out language or work through a problem.

Building on these findings, in their 1997 study the researchers recorded the interaction of six intermediate learners of Spanish (L2, English L1) at a US university. Thus there were three pairs of students. Five information-gap tasks were provided for the participants with a gap of a couple of days in between each one. Similar results to the adolescent students were found:

1. *Talk about talk*. Students often commented on their own speaking (e.g. 'that's a good word'). These statements served to assist the student's own participation by reflecting upon their own activity and the language resources they had available. Talk about talk decreased slightly over the five tasks.
2. *Talk about the task*. Learners externalized statements about procedures or emotional reactions to the tasks – 'es un poco difficil'. Talk about task decreased significantly over the five tasks (as they became familiar with procedures).
3. *Talking in L1*. This was used both for talk about talk and for talk about the task. L1 was significantly reduced over the five tasks. The use of English actually 'enabled them to support and sustain their interaction' (531).
4. *Whispering to the self*. They used this strategy to self-regulate, to steer their thoughts in order to accomplish the task. This type of 'externalization of inner speech', as we know, is present in many of the task-oriented activities that we perform, from memorizing a list of things to do, to working through a mathematical problem.

Similar findings were obtained in a study by Antón and DiCamilla (1998). This time the students were collaborating on a writing task. The researchers found that they used the L1, for the purpose of externalizing their inner speech, allowing them to achieve their task objectives.

Knight (1996) found that, although learners were using their first language in shared tasks, they were doing so in order to negotiate meaning and, particularly, to discuss unknown words in the second language. This may have led to learning of new words as much as if they had been negotiating meaning in L2.

Speaking, then, has a dual function. It serves not only to communicate information but also as a tool with which to think and with which to organize. Therefore our failure, as teachers and researchers, 'to capture the full array of what learners are attempting to achieve discursively, especially during a problem-solving, information-gap task' (Brooks *et al.* 1997: 525) may be due to our lack of understanding or belief that there is more to communication than simply getting a message across. Moreover, we should not judge the success of an oral pair-work task simply on the basis of whether the language used was correct or not.

Another aspect that has concerned many teachers is how to set up learner-learner activities in terms of pairing by similar proficiency or otherwise. Partly this is because of the potential for exposing learners to incorrect utterances and partly this is because of the need to stretch the more proficient learners whilst ensuring consolidation and progression among the least proficient.

Iwashita (2001) therefore wanted to find out what the different effect on the interaction was of students working in pairs of the same or different proficiency levels. Particularly, Iwashita wanted to look for evidence of restructuring of the learner's interlanguage – that is, evidence that their mental models of the syntactic patterns were *progressing* as a result of the forced output in paired activities. Taking a sample of 24 Australian university students (mostly English L1) studying Japanese, the researcher divided these into proficiency pairs: High-High; Low-Low; High-Low. The students were given two types of task: a two-way jigsaw task and a one-way information-gap task. Iwashita then coded the data for C-units (any utterance that has a communicative value, including one-word answers). Iwashita also searched and coded the data for clarification requests and confirmation checks (i.e. two of the three strategies in modified interaction). The researcher found:

1. Over both tasks High-Low pairs produced the most C-units. Learners basically talked more with a learner of different proficiency (although, not surprisingly, they produced more errors as a result).
2. None of the groups produced significantly more opportunities for modified output.
3. Generally learners produced more confirmation checks than clarification requests.
4. Proficiency level was, again, not a variable in terms of confirmation checks or clarification requests.
5. Generally, more modifications were made in the one-way task than the two-way jigsaw task.
6. Generally there were more syntactic modifications than lexical modifications resulting in modified output.
7. Low-proficiency learners modified more when working with partners at a higher level.

In sum, the difference in proficiency did not seem to adversely affect the frequency of interaction and of modified output. The lower-proficiency learners got a lot out of working with the higher-proficiency learners without the latter being disadvantaged. The learner's internal grammar was being affected equally in all types of group but possibly more in the one-way information task.

We saw in Chapter 4 how in a study by Ellis and He (1999) producing new words in learner-learner interaction enabled students to both understand more easily and also resulted in better vocabulary acquisition, both receptive and productive. These authors claim that the learner-learner (modified-output interaction) created better learning conditions than the teacher-learner modified interaction. It has to be said, however, that this descriptive account does not prove that better acquisition is *always* the case in the learner-learner interaction condition. Teacher-student interaction doesn't have to be dialogically asymmetrical (see below). However, it is an unfortunate fact that, due to practical constraints, it usually is.

Two-way information tasks can result in highly structured interaction, using a very limited range of vocabulary and few modifications. In my study of lower secondary classrooms (Macaro 1997) I investigated the beliefs and attitudes of teachers and learners towards pair-work tasks, towards the issue of L1 use and also the extent of 'structuring' that adolescent learners should be provided with. Focus groups of learners were given statements on cards to rank-order in terms of how close the statements were to their own experience. The most favoured rank ordering was as follows:

1. It (pair-work) makes you feel comfortable and confident
2. You learn a lot and remember a lot
3. It's OK but you do tend to chat in English
4. Sometimes my partner doesn't want to work with me
5. It's not good, I prefer talking to the teacher
6 It's a waste of time

In other words by far the vast majority of pupils reacted favourably to pair work and group work. The minority who had a negative attitude to it tended to be associated with a single class or teacher. Moreover, in the more open-ended part of the focus group sessions they emphasized that they remembered more language from paired activities and pointed to the fact that the teacher was able to give them more focused support as he/she went round the pairs. Much of the L1 use was, as in the studies above, connected with how to proceed with a task.

As for the teachers, the conclusion I drew from the data (questionnaire and interviews) was that they too were generally positive about learner-learner activities. However, teachers felt that the task, particularly with lower-proficiency learners, had to be highly structured. Structuring for teachers amounted to two inter-related dimensions: (1) structuring of the language – that is the teacher had to clearly define the language that the students should be using rather than encouraging exploration, meaning negotiation and risk taking; (2) structuring of the task – the learners should have very clear procedural pathways in order to complete the task. This, in turn, controls the participants' discourse structure. Both these control dimensions, I would argue, result in easier management of the collaborative part of a lesson but do not encourage some essential processes suggested by the research literature.

Nakahama *et al.* (2001) also looked at the issue of the effect on interlanguage of structured information-gap tasks as compared to more open-ended conversation tasks. This study, however, focused on L2-learner–L1-speaker interaction (for example a student working one to one with the teacher or with a foreign-language assistant). The researchers were interested in this theme because previous studies suggested:

1. Controlled task-based interactions produce more *repair negotiations* than less structured interaction (such as a 'conversation on a topic').
2. Controlled task-based interactions require precise production.
3. Uncontrolled interaction allows avoidance of topic rather than repair negotiation.

In other words, previous research suggested that highly structured tasks led to better learning and faster progression. Nakahama *et al.* were unconvinced by this. Particularly, they felt that these results might be due to the possibility that interlanguage progression was not as obvious in unstructured conversations or that it might take longer to develop, but it was nevertheless present. A previous study by Nakahama (1997) found that *trigger types* (the cues which 'trigger' negotiation of meaning) in conversation were different from those in information-gap tasks because the latter focused on low-level items such as words or morpho-syntactic items.

They also pointed out that previous research had not focused 'on how the discourse emerging from the conversational activity attains a greater overall complexity as the talk progresses' (Nakahama *et al.* 2001: 381). They therefore carried out a qualitative study of three Japanese students studying English at a US university. They gave them two tasks to perform: (1) an information-gap activity on two pictures with eight differences; (2) a conversation task with general topic guidelines. They found:

1. The information-gap activity did indeed trigger more repair negotiation than the conversation activity.
2. However, the *quality* of the repair negotiation was higher in the conversation activity. In greater detail, the conversation produced
   (a) Triggers which were more global rather than single lexical (as in the 1997 study by Nakahama).
   (b) Longer lengths of turn.
   (c) Greater complexity of utterances (measured by verb phrases).
   (d) Greater shifts between tenses, verbal aspect (the information-gap task was accomplished entirely in the present tense).

In addition:

   (e) The conversation task focused on *convergence towards* mutually shared schemata (i.e. to finding out about each other's prior knowledge). Therefore more negotiation of meaning was able to take place.
   (f) The conversation task allowed learners to take the initiative more (equal discourse control).
   (g) The conversation task contained more 'pushed output' (forcing learners to say something new to them).
   (h) There was more silence in the information-gap activity (the repair work was probably being done in the brain rather than in open negotiation).
   (i) There were more complex negotiation cycles in the conversation task (allowing divergence from topic and return to topic) – they negotiated meaning in order to achieve coherence in the entire interaction.

Nakahama *et al.* (2001), in their conclusions, supported my contention that information-gap activities control the discourse and determine the structure of the discourse. In a sense they encourage the learners to focus more on achieving the task than on developing their interlanguage.

Although evidence suggests that both teachers and learners value learner-learner interaction, not all studies have resulted in unambiguous support for student-centred learning in general. For example Garrett and Shortall (2002) used a sample of Brazilian beginner, elementary and intermediate students learning English to find out, by questionnaire, whether they preferred teacher-fronted activities or student-centred activities. In addition they asked them to rate these teaching approaches by relating them to grammar-based learning and fluency-based (presumably meaning interaction-based) learning. They found:

1. All learners preferred learning grammar in teacher-centred rather than learner-centred activities.
2. Student-centred fluency activities were more relaxing than teacher-fronted fluency activities and were more fun.
3. Different levels of learners had different preferences. For example, teacher-fronted activities were judged to be better for learning grammar-based content by beginners than by intermediate learners.

They concluded that preferences for student-centred work were not as marked as has often been claimed and that activities need to take into account different needs for different learners at different stages of their learning careers. However, it will be noted that these are very broad brush strokes about general learning styles rather than tightly focused on pair interaction. Even at an advanced level of 'academic learner' it has been found that students had little difficulty participating in small-group work or in pairs compared to having to cope with interacting in teacher-whole-group situations (Ferris 1998).

A further question that needs to be answered is whether, when and how teachers should intervene when monitoring learner-learner interaction. In my own study described earlier (Macaro 1997: 153), only 7% of secondary school teachers believed that pair work was best left unmonitored. Their responses to the issue of errors in pair work leading to fossilization would also suggest that a substantial majority felt that they should intervene by correcting when monitoring. Lynch (1997) argues against this type of intervention based on the Comprehensible Output Hypothesis. In his analysis of three learner-learner episodes, when there was evidence of a communication breakdown, he concludes that, of the following three forms of intervention, only the first two are valid pedagogically:

1. The teacher's role is to initiate the process of negotiation of meaning.
2. The teacher's role is to support by confirming that a request for clarification is appropriate.
3. The teacher's role is to change the focus or direction of the interaction thus avoiding the communication breakdown.

He argues that the third type of intervention leads to a lost opportunity for modified interaction and forced output. Presumably, simply providing the learners with the correct model would also lead to this type of lost opportunity. The problem with Lynch's three communication-breakdown episodes is that they are all about the speaker's inability to communicate a word (i.e. a vocabulary meaning problem). They are not a syntax problem. Consequently we might still be left unconvinced that a teacher's non-intervention can lead to correct forced output when the learner-learner message transmission breaks down because of a grammar problem.

Initial implications

Learner-learner interaction is still able to provide the best possible solution to the problem of large classes. In addition, it has value in itself as a pedagogical activity, creating excellent conditions for the negotiation of meaning. However, for the remaining uncertainties to be resolved requires great knowledge and skill on the part of the teacher.

Firstly, to make judgements about learners' task-related behaviour on the basis of fleeting perceptions of L1 use may not take into account the real effort being expended for the completion of the task.

Secondly, the type of task is important. If providing learner pairs with unstructured conversation-type tasks is impossible within a short learning sequence then it should definitely be an eventual longer-term aim. It would seem a not very productive use of foreign-language assistants' time for them to engage in highly structured information-gap activities with their students. Rather they should be trained and encouraged to improve the quality of the interaction using conversation-type tasks which trigger the negotiation of meaning.

Thirdly, putting together (or allowing) different proficiency levels in a pair may not be a pedagogical issue for teachers to worry about as much as they might anticipate.

Lynch provides sound advice with regard to teacher intervention in paired or group activities. He suggest that teachers should intervene as late as possible in a communication breakdown situation, thus allowing learners to make their own repair. If they cannot make their own repair, teachers should intervene by nudging the learners towards a solution rather than providing the solution. This 'ideal' pedagogy may of course not be possible with large classes. However, the advice I provide student teachers with is to go for quality of monitoring and intervention (in pair work) rather than quantity. A solution therefore is to 'sample' smaller numbers of pairs each lesson rather than trying to get round to them all. Teacher intervention or feedback to grammar-based errors when 'listening in' to learner-learner interaction would seem appropriate given that this focus on form would be happening in non-threatening situations. However, as in whole-class interaction, the teacher intervention should be such that the learners are able to effect their own self-repair by using the kinds of *negotiation of form* feedback strategies discussed in Chapter 3.

Quality of teacher-fronted interaction

We have examined a number of features of learner-learner or learner-L1 speaker interaction. It is now time to return to the interaction between the skilled teacher and the whole of the class and look for some measures of quality which we have not yet touched upon.

Why should we be interested in measures of quality?

Learner-learner interaction is not likely to be a predominant feature of the L2 classroom unless a task-based learning approach really takes root. Even then, some teacher-fronted interaction with the whole class will be inevitable. Teacher-fronted interaction is actually integral to the PPP model. Given the endurance of teacher-fronted interaction then, we should at least be working towards a set of criteria which ensures that it is of the highest quality possible. We cannot assume that any kind of interaction will lead to acquisition. It may merely have the trappings of meaning negotiation and comprehensible output. By highest quality I mean that, at any one time:

1. it should be serving the needs of the vast majority of, if not all, the students in the class;
2. it should be ensuring psycholinguistic progression – developing the learners' interlanguage – by providing cognitively challenging mental processing;
3. it should be providing the learners with sufficient time and space in which to decode, retrieve and process information;
4. it should take into account sociolinguistic factors such as the creation of positive and enabling classroom identities and discouraging peer-pressure to the contrary;
5. it should take into account the evidence that teacher feedback has a measurable impact on 1, 2, 3 and 4. Teachers may not be aware of the gap between their perception of the kinds of feedback they have given and what they actually gave (Tsui 1992:89).

I will divide the following review into psycholinguistic and sociolinguistic research, although cognisant of the fact that the two inevitably overlap. A practical guide on how to achieve high-quality interaction is also provided in Tsui (1995).

The research evidence

One of the features of quality of interaction research is that, as one would expect, it places a much greater importance on classroom discourse analysis. As Allwright and Bailey (1991) point out, transcriptions of lessons give us insights into how interaction develops as a dynamic phenomenon in ways that data that have been coded and analysed quantatively are unable to do. As a consequence of this, summarizing the research evidence in a reader friendly way in such limited space becomes quite problematic as so much of the information in the data is contextualized by the discourse itself.

Antòn (1999) looked at quality of teacher-fronted interaction from a learner-centredness perspective but with an emphasis on psycholinguistic processes. In other words she was interested in not only how social behaviour resulted from interaction but also how syntax development occurred during interaction – a gradual awareness of the rules of the language. She analysed the discourse of two teachers (one teaching French the other Italian) and their students in secondary classrooms in the US (English L1). She found that the first teacher created an interaction in which knowledge was *co-constructed* (which she termed a *dialogic* approach). The second teacher created an interaction in which knowledge was *transmitted*. There were four basic features in the co-construction approach:

1. *Focus on grammatical patterns: consciousness-raising of grammatical forms* (e.g. when introducing the auxiliary in the perfect tense). The dialogic teacher elicited problems and solutions from the learners. When they got stuck she didn't just tell them but provided more examples so that learners could reflect on the forms in context.

   In the alternative *transmission approach* the learners were the 'passive receptacle of knowledge' – they were simply told by the teacher what the rule or pattern was. The learner was not challenged with any problem to solve.

2. *Providing feedback (to error).* The 'knowledge transmission' teacher just told the learners they were wrong. The dialogic teacher achieved this through the interaction which led them to an awareness of being wrong. Through a dialogic approach the teacher managed to make learning a collaborative effort and to place responsibility for arriving at the correct model on members of the classroom community.

3. *Turn allocation.* The dialogic teacher frequently opened the floor for individual bidding. Even when turns were allocated by the teacher, she usually looked out for signals of willingness to volunteer and/or called on a student who was already vocalizing the answer or gesturing.

4. *Learning styles and strategies.* Through questioning, the dialogic teacher was able to guide the learner from a general (and unhelpful) statement such as 'I don't like this' (in England teachers may be more familiar with 'I can't do any of this!') to specifying the exact learning difficulty such that it could be solved. She also encouraged learners to identify their learning styles and to try new learning strategies.

Antòn concluded that the *dialogic* approach goes beyond the explicit-implicit dichotomy where teaching grammar is juxtaposed with 'natural acquisition' processes. The dialogic approach assists the students with independent hypothesis construction. Moreover, through skilful use of interaction the teacher transfers to the learners not only the responsibility for their own learning but also for each other's learning.

Walsh (2002) was also interested in demonstrating that it is the quality of interaction rather than the quantity that matters. He observed that there exists considerable evidence that 'teachers who constantly seek clarification, check for confirmation and who do not always accept the first contribution, maximise learning potential'. He therefore selected a sample of eight experienced teachers and asked them to make a 30-minute recording each of any part of their lesson which involved teacher-fronted interaction. This produced a total of eight hours of recordings. Walsh's analysis of the data revealed a number of features which either helped to construct learning potential or obstructed it.

Facilitative features

1. Direct error correction through an explicit recast. This was far less intrusive and time consuming than 'sensitive' correction. This finding in part contradicts Antòn (1999). Walsh (citing Seedhouse's (1997) findings), argues that error-correction is in any case preferred by learners.

2. Content feedback which manifests itself in personal (and authentic-sounding) reactions to what the student has said.
3. Checking for confirmation and encouraging clarification requests – in line with previous research already discussed.
4. A turn-taking structure in which the teacher takes a back seat.
5. Extended wait-time providing learners with enough processing time to answer a question.
6. Scaffolding – to pre-empt breakdown by feeding in missing language items. However, these scaffolding strategies should be the minimum needed to resume the student's turn. They should also not pre-empt what the student is going to say.
7. Learners self-select their turns either in response to the teacher or by 'latching on' to the previous student turn.
8. And following from 7, student-student negotiation of meaning is present even in teacher-fronted interaction.

Obstructive features

1. The teacher completes the turn for the student.
2. The teacher interrupts the student's turn in order to correct.
3. No negotiation of meaning is detectable via clarification requests, confirmation checks.
4. The teacher echoes the student response even if it is correct. As Walsh argues, teacher echo is one of the prime reasons for excessive interaction between the teacher and a single student.
5. IRF turn-taking structure as the predominant discourse pattern.

As we can see most of the facilitative discourse features echo those praised by Antòn. The issue of whether to provide immediate correction in the feedback is complex. We have looked at some research evidence to this in Chapter 3. I have argued that it probably needs to be situation specific – a judgement for a teacher to make on the spot according to a number of criteria including time available and the personality of the student s/he is correcting. We will return to this theme once again in a moment.

The teacher-echo feature is one which I have been particularly investigating although not in a formal research context. It seems to me from my observations that to echo a correct student response has three possible functions. First, it is a device which enables other students to hear what one student has said because the teacher's voice is usually louder. Second, it provides just one more instance of the correct model. Third, it is a discourse 'move' which helps the teacher hang on to the reins of the interaction – an aspect of discourse control. I would argue that all three of these functions of teacher echo have a pejorative effect on the learners:

1. They encourage learners to speak quietly ('Why should I speak loudly if s/he's going to say it after me anyway.').
2. They discourage the learners from valuing the contributions of their peers ('Why listen to Emma's version when Mr Macaro is going to give us his version anyway ... ').

3. They confirm the impression that the interaction is just a mechanical exercise not a proper conversation.
4. They automatically create an imbalance between teacher talk and student talk. As a proportion of an IRF sequence it is, after all, a minimum of two thirds of talk by the teacher.

To return briefly to Walsh (2002). He argues that 'appropriate language use is more likely to occur when teachers are sufficiently aware of their goal at a given moment in a lesson to match their teaching aim, their pedagogic purpose, to their language use' (5). In order to be able to match the goal to the interaction, he concludes, teachers should find out about the interaction they are creating in the classroom by recording themselves and analysing their transcripts. Clearly this is a very time-consuming undertaking. However, there are alternatives to this. One way is to ask student teachers to do it both for themselves and for their mentors' lessons. The other way is for teachers to get involved with interested researchers.

In a study I carried out with my colleague Trevor Mutton (Macaro and Mutton 2002), we proposed that quality interaction could be furthered by working with teachers in a 'co-researcher' model. That is, that teachers who do not have time to analyse their interaction can have it done by researchers to their mutual benefit. Two experienced teachers agreed therefore to have three year-8 (13-year-olds) lessons video-recorded over a period of six months. The researchers agreed to do the following from an analysis of the teacher-fronted interaction:

1. Provide the teachers with a transcription of each of the lessons.
2. Provide the teachers with a timed analysis of each of the lessons in terms of teacher talk and student talk.
3. Provide the teachers with a measurement of length of turns.
4. Provide the teachers with an analysis of the proportion of verbs to nouns used by teacher and students.

The two teachers agreed to do the following:

1. Watch the video-recording of each of their lessons.
2. Read through the transcription of each of their lessons.
3. Look at the timed analysis tables.
4. Look at the turn analysis tables.
5. Look at the figures for the proportion of verbs to nouns.
6. Provide a comment on all the above in a brief questionnaire.

The four of us found that the quality of the interaction did change over the three lessons. Specifically:

1. The proportion of student talk to teacher talk increased.
2. The students' turns got longer.
3. The proportion of verbs to nouns (in one of the teachers' lessons) used by the students increased.

As the detailed analysis of one lesson took at least a day, it became clear to us that teachers could not, without time off, be expected to analyse in detail the transcripts of their own lessons. However, the two teachers did become more aware of their inter-action as a result of the research and said they found the research useful. Trevor and I learnt a lot, as well as getting a journal article out of the study. This was only a small exploratory study but we feel confident in proposing this symbiotic endeavour as a model for future teacher development and systematic exploration of interaction features.

A reason for considering the proportion of nouns to verbs is that it is my belief that, in England, the language curriculum (the schemes of work) for beginners to lower intermediates is too noun based. This is easily discernible by looking not only at the schemes of work but also the textbooks used in this age group and is a feature that has been identified in other research (e.g. Metcalfe *et al.* 1998). My contention is that this is, in part, responsible for the lack of progression in speaking noted by among others, the inspectorate in England (Dobson 1998). Learners cannot develop the autonomy of language competence (Macaro 1997) needed to be able to say what they want to say without exposure to and active involvement in the use of verbs. I am certainly not arguing here for a great deal of explicit focus or systematic work on verb forms and verb endings, merely that teachers and learners should use lots of verbs and very frequently in their interaction instead of limiting themselves to substituting a noun in a formulaic phrase (see discussion in Chapter 3).

The above analysis of quality of interaction has centred almost exclusively on the psycholinguistic process. We will now look at quality of interaction in an area which has received a great deal of attention, the sociolinguistic function of classroom interaction. This research has, as its overarching theme, the hypothesis that not only is knowledge constructed through teacher-student interaction but also the social identities of the students, the way they feel about themselves.

An early study by Westgate *et al.* (1985), using a blend of discourse analysis and ethnographic procedures, suggested that the very structure of teacher-fronted inter-action in L2 lessons might be playing a contributory part to learner demotivation. One of the researchers was attached to a foreign-language department of a secondary school in England and lessons were recorded and transcribed, and interactional patterns were identified. The researchers (and the teachers) were surprised at how little interactional space was being granted to the students. Moreover, the lessons were characterized by exemplification rather than explanation. This contributed to the lack of 'content' making the talk very unnatural, teachers providing the students with the very words and indeed the very features of words with which to talk. Students, in order to cope with public exposure in teacher space, were required to have some very special social skills and survival strategies. Some of these survival strategies amounted to attempts at avoidance of being invited to speak.

Breen (2001) identifies a number of very similar features in all L2 classroom contexts with regard to teacher attitudes and feedback to students' speech. Learner reactions to corrections vary. This is probably the result of how teachers respond to learner participation. This, in turn, may superimpose a degree of risk for many learners and the possibility of threat to their self-esteem in a public situation also leads to an ambiguity of the purpose of the discourse. Some learners find navigating through these different types of discourses very difficult.

Elsewhere (Macaro 1997: 56-7) I have proposed 20 aspects of (young adolescent) L2 classroom interaction which go towards making it a peculiar and particular discourse domain, one in which, as Cicurel (1989) suggests, learners are involved in a discourse performance. The following are a few features not already alluded to in the discussion so far. It is a place where in front of an audience:

1. learners are asked to perform the role of characters they may never have encountered;
2. learning the lines has to be done without the script;
3. the learner has to articulate the language of others (textbook characters) as if it were his/her own language;
4. learners have suddenly to switch to being themselves;
5. rehearsals turn into performances and then quickly back to rehearsals;
6. learners are asked to give information about themselves, the truth of which is unimportant;
7. learners are asked to give information about themselves, the truth of which is *very* important.

Above all it is a place where:

> the topic of the discourse, the linguistic interaction, the pace of delivery, the intensity of language and action, the management of the physical environment, the establishment of social norms are all dominated by one member of the group (the teacher) speaking a language both foreign to him/her and to the pupils.

It is little wonder that some learners find that they cannot fit into this social environment, one inevitably and entirely constructed by the interaction. It should not come as a surprise to us that Stables and Wikeley (1999) allude to the 'differentials in power relationships' between teachers and learners which may contribute to demotivation and poor behaviour. As Breen (2001) argues, we cannot abstract learning from the social context in which it occurs, a view shared by other authors who decry the lack of emphasis on the sociocultural context (Roberts 1998; Tarone and Swain 1995).

Hall's (1996, 1998) studies focused on the discursive practices of one teacher and a Spanish (L2) class of 15 students in ninth grade, but particularly on the teacher's interaction over one semester with four male students codenamed: Pablo, Santo, Jaime and Raùl who had started off the semester contributing equally to the class interaction. These students had been required to take Spanish because they were placed in a high-achieving group. Using weekly audio-recordings and field notes, Hall was able to trace the pattern of turn taking of the four students. She classified teacher and student utterances as *cooperative* or *uncooperative*. Uncooperative utterances were those that appeared to be *inappropriate* at that particular moment in time and did not facilitate 'the creation of a shared perspective among interactants' (Hall 1998: 290).

Hall found:

(a) The typical structure in teacher-fronted interaction was the Initiation-Response-Feedback (IRF) sequence.

(b) In almost 43% of all the IRF exchanges in which any of the four students were involved, each turn was cooperative.

(c) In most cases it was *the teacher* who produced an uncooperative response by ignoring the student's *Initiation* as in the following:

Student: Who is she?
Teacher: *No es estudiante de español no es importante.*
(she isn't a student of Spanish, it isn't important)
Student: Oh.

A teacher's cooperative response was to take up the student's utterance and attempt to fit it into the task-at-hand:

Student (off topic): How do you say firearms?
Teacher: *Pistolas ... Santa Claus te trajo una pistola ... te trajo Santa Claus una pistola?*
Student: *Sí.*

For Hall, it is the way in which the students are treated differently that is the most significant finding:

Two distinct groups of learners are formed, a primary and a secondary group. Each group has different rights to the floor in terms of the kinds of contributions that are made, the degree of teacher attention that is received, and the role that students are allowed to play in contributing to these exchanges. (1998: 298)

Even though Jaime and Raùl contribute a lot to the talk, the teacher affirms their contributions much less than he does those of Pablo and Santo. This is the case both for Jaime and Raùl's cooperative *Responses* and for their cooperative *Initiations*. Where the students try to digress from the topic, the teacher affirms or reacts cooperatively to those of Pablo and Santo but does not do so with those of Jamie and Raùl,
   The effect on the students' participation patterns, Hall discovers, are considerable.

[Firstly] these differences in turn taking make apparent a distinction in the kinds of learner identities these students are developing ... these distinctions result in the formation of two different status groups, a primary and a secondary group, each with different participatory roles and rights to the floor. The two students in the primary group, Pablo and Santo, receive more cooperative and more cooperatively extended attention from the teacher. They are allowed to initiate more talk and even to take over each other's turns. Personal information about them is brought into the practice and shared with the other students. In some cases it is collectively built upon and thus treated as significant to the developing knowledge of the classroom culture. (1998: 298)

Secondly, whilst at the beginning of the semester the data collected from Raùl, and Jamie shows that they were generally enthusiastic about learning Spanish, by the end of the semester they felt frustrated by what they perceived as their inability to learn Spanish. Thus, Hall concludes:

while the evidence does not show direct connection between these differences (in turn taking rights) and the students' developing interactional abilities and attitudes towards Spanish, it is likely that the differences had at least some impact on them as well as on the teacher's evaluations of their individual potential as Spanish language learners. (1998: 307)

Hall's study demonstrates the power of discourse analysis to delve below the surface of teaching practices, classroom events and recognizable pedagogic activities.

Initial implications

Teacher-fronted interaction is an important topic as a subject of research. Not only does it provide us with insights into what might be the best possible features of interaction – quality interaction – but it also helps us to understand how interaction shapes the classroom atmosphere. It is likely that, given time and resources, we could determine what are the factors which contribute to some teachers being able to establish a cooperative atmosphere conducive to learning which would be based more than on superficial or holistic assessment of a teacher's personality. This has important implications for teacher training. Breaking down interaction and analysing it for its effects on social conditioning as well as its effects on acquisition could be a vital tool in assisting novice teachers reach higher levels of competence more quickly.

Fluency *and* accuracy?

The topic of what it is to be orally fluent in a language and how learners move towards fluency has received surprisingly lightweight attention in the literature.

Why should we be interested in this?

The correct balance between fluency and accuracy would seem to be at the heart of a teacher's attempts to evaluate the linguistic progress that a learner is making. Examiners' attempts to judge proficiency have almost invariably included fluency and accuracy, as for example in the grade descriptors for A-level languages in England and Wales. In the National Curriculum for Modern Foreign Languages (in England) the word 'fluent' appears only once under the level of 'Exceptional Performance'. Although some reference is made to factors which might impede fluency, such as 'hesitation', it is unclear what might be causing this hesitation and in any case hesitation is mentioned only twice under level 2, 'the delivery (may be) hesitant' and level 6 'although they may be hesitant at times, they make themselves understood with little or no difficulty'. On the other hand references to accuracy are more frequent if somewhat focused on pronunciation and, I would argue, not based on any recognizable logical progression.

> Level 1: pronunciation may be approximate.
> Level 2: pronunciation may still be approximate.
> *Level 3: accuracy not mentioned.*

Level 4: pronunciation is generally accurate; some consistency in intonation.

Level 5: there may be some mistakes.

Level 6: accuracy not mentioned.

Level 7: good pronunciation and intonation; accuracy is such that they are readily understood.

Level 8: good pronunciation and intonation; largely accurate with few mistakes.

Level 9: exceptional performance: consistently accurate pronunciation; make few errors.

Clearly, then, we need a much more comprehensive understanding of what it is to be orally fluent in a L2 and the cost that this may impose on spoken accuracy and vice versa.

The research evidence

One starting point in our search for the balance between fluency and accuracy is the proposition that an L2 learner or user will actually *want* to communicate. Macintyre *et al.* (1998) have attempted to come up with a situational model of 'Willingness to Communicate' (WTC). This is too wide-reaching and comprehensive to be discussed here but one aspect of it might be important for us to consider. They claim that their WTC construct refers to a person's WTC *at a specific time*. 'By considering why a person is willing to talk at one time and not another, we can appreciate the important factors influencing classroom communication and "real world" contact' (558). In this perspective, therefore, fluency is not a constant. It is perfectly possible for a student to be highly communicative in the classroom, exuding all the trappings of fluency but to stumble, over-monitor or clam up when he or she is in a foreign country or in an exam (and, of course, vice versa). Moreover, fluency for advanced learners in familiar topics may not correspond to fluency in an academic context. In other words the balance between fluency and accuracy is related to the willingness to communicate in different situations.

Towell *et al.* (1996) are very persuasive in their proposition that fluency is a complex construct. They point out that the reason that we might pause during an utterance can be due to different things.

1. The demands of a particular task.
2. A characteristic of the individual.
3. Difficulty in knowing what to say.
4. Difficulty in knowing how to verbalize an idea already in the brain.
5. Establishing the correct balance between length of utterance and the linguistic structure of the utterance.

Nevertheless, through their research, they attempted to provide some accurate measurement guidelines for fluency. They used a sample of 12 students of French (English L1) at a university in England selected on the basis of their 'homogeneity' in their pre-university examinations (A levels) plus a cloze test. They were tested in their second year, that is the year before going abroad (Time 1) and after they returned (Time 2). The students were asked to retell in L2 the story of a seven-minute film. The researchers used the following measurements of time variables in order to arrive at an evaluation of their fluency in the L2:

1. *Speaking rate*: total number of syllables (including pauses) divided by total time taken to retell the story.
2. *Articulation rate*: total number of syllables divided by the time taken to produce them but excluding pause time.
3. *Phonation/time ratio*: percentage of time spent speaking as a proportion of time taken to produce the speech sample (excluding pauses).
4. *Mean length of runs*: average number of syllables produced in utterances between short pauses (pauses of at least 0.28 seconds).
5. *Average length of pauses.*

In Table 8.1 I try to summarize the findings by Towell *et al.* I hope that I have done so in a manner which is faithful to their important study.

Table 8.1. Summary of findings by Towell *et al.* (1996)

Finding	Implication or conclusion by the researchers
L2 speaking rate increased between T1 and T2	Improvements observed in the overall measure of the speaking rate were mostly accounted for by changes in the Mean Length of Run. In other words, the students were communicating more quickly because they were able to produce longer utterances without pausing to process language before articulating it.
Mean length of run increased considerably at T2. The students were able to produce longer utterances without pausing	The *Mean length of runs*, therefore, is the best indicator of development in fluency. The major changes which produced this increase in the *Mean length of runs* must have happened in the 'formulator' (see Model of Speaking Figure at the beginning of this chapter). That is, proceduralization had occurred in the student's ability to convert ideas into inner speech. Proceduralization could only have occurred as a result of linguistic knowledge being converted and stored as procedural knowledge rather than changes in the ways the students had learnt to conceptualize the knowledge in the L2.
There was a significant increase in the articulation rate at T2 (though not huge)	Although there was some evidence of change in the 'articulator', the increase in the rate of sound production contributed to increase in fluency only in a minor way.
There was no increase in average length of pause	Increase in fluency does not come about by reducing the length of pauses. Rather, the same length of pauses are able to 'stack up' longer utterances.
There was no decrease in Phonation/time ratio	

The qualitative data from this study also suggests that, as well as length of units, the complexity of the units increased (as might be expected). The findings from this study provide important information which should be considered when drawing up criteria for assessing fluency and permitting both teachers and examiners to evaluate fluency more accurately and less subjectively.

Even a short time spent in a foreign country appears to produce greater fluency and to do so even with less advanced learners. We have already examined the study by Fisher and Evans (2000) in the chapter on motivation (Chapter 5) in that time spent in France resulted in more favourable attitudes among adolescent students in England. These researchers also found that speaking fluency improved in terms of more confident delivery and a wider range of vocabulary but also in terms of pronunciation and in aspects of syntax (perfect tense, reflexives, first person plural endings).

Teacher feedback on students' oral contributions can also contribute to learner fluency, however. This occurs by creating beliefs in learners, through interaction, of what aspects of language learning are important, usually represented (somewhat coarsely) by a division between a teacher's focus on fluency and focus on accuracy. Of course, experience tells us that no teacher only ever focuses on either fluency or accuracy. An interesting study on this topic was carried out by Dekeyser (1993). Noting that little empirical research had been carried out on the effects of oral error correction on subsequent oral fluency and accuracy (unlike in the domain of written language), he selected a sample of 35 Belgian students (L1 Flemish) learning French aged approximately 17. These students studied French for 3-4 hours per week and most reported never using French outside the classroom. Using a pre- and post-test design, Dekeyser introduced a *treatment* of one year in the form of two teachers. One teacher agreed never to provide explicit error correction, the other agreed to (nearly always) provide explicit error correction. The teachers were matched for personality, quality of input and interaction. A sample of ten hours of lessons were recorded and analysed. The pre- and post-tests consisted of:

1. an aptitude test (to measure how error correction interacted with previous aptitude);
2. an extrinsic motivation questionnaire (if you are *goal-oriented* in your learning does this override anti-error correction feelings?);
3. an anxiety questionnaire (does error correction produce anxiety or is it bad for students who are already anxious?);
4. a proficiency test (three oral communication tasks assessing both fluency and accuracy);
5. a grammatical achievement test.

Dekeyser found:

1. When the language tests were analysed together, there was no main effect of error correction (i.e. error correction – or the lack of it – did not affect oral proficiency nor grammatical achievement).
2. Students with higher *previous* achievements in speaking were, in fact, less likely to benefit from error correction.
3. Students with strong grammatical sensitivity, as measured by the aptitude test, did not particularly benefit from error correction (a surprising result!).

4. Students with weak extrinsic motivation benefited marginally from error correction.
5. Students with low anxiety *did* benefit from error correction but only in the written test (i.e. high-anxiety students did no worse in the oral tasks as a result of a year's error correction).

These results really do call into question some of the assumptions that we have, as teachers and researchers, about the effects of error correction. The 'coarse' patterns of interaction, as represented by the two teachers in Dekeyser's study, clearly do not produce uniform effects in large groups of learners. Further research may establish more *individual differences* in terms of reactions to error correction and its effect on oral proficiency. It is a pity that the students in this study were not (in addition) simply asked how they felt as a result of error correction and that more qualitative techniques were not used. On the other hand the researcher did go some way towards narrowing down the groups. By using a test which separated out the 'very high scoring students' from the 'very low scoring students' the following more pronounced results obtained:

1. Students with high pre-test scores did better on the grammar post-test as a result of error correction.
2. Students with high extrinsic motivation did better on oral accuracy and oral fluency without error correction (a suggestion that error correction did have an effect on 'dampening their enthusiasm' for speaking).

Whether teachers can ever be expected to know their students so well that they can consistently target individuals with different kinds of feedback is a moot point. It may be possible to do this given the continuity of contact with the learners over a number of years and with small groups. Another consideration is that this study investigated students at a relatively advanced stage of learning. Intuition would suggest that oral error correction may have positive effects (develop the interlanguage more quickly) or negative effects (induce anxiety) in learners at a much earlier stage of learning when they are beginning to move from the formulaic stage to the generative stage.

Hurman (1992) carried out a study into the effects on oral fluency and accuracy of the new General Certificate of Secondary Education (GCSE) in England. The GCSE is taken at the end of compulsory education and, since 1988, following international communicative trends, has promoted, via a washback effect, less focus on accuracy. Some authors now claim that the GCSE does not provide a sound basis for study of a foreign language at Advanced level (A level). Hurman therefore surveyed A-level examiners marking the oral exam of the first A-level cohort who had previously taken a GCSE exam. From the 50 returns he reported:

1. Two thirds of examiners claimed there was a difference in this first cohort from previous cohorts.
2. Virtually all claimed that the level of spoken accuracy had declined.
3. Most felt that students now had more fluency, had better pronunciation, less hesitation and more initiative, and could produce more relevant vocabulary and information.

4. The range of language was considered to be higher by a narrow majority of examiners.

Relationship between courses, performance and exams is very close (the washback effect). It is probably impossible to encourage increased oral fluency without some reduction in accuracy, even though a study with young children by Nikolov and Krashen (1997) might suggest that it can in some cases. My doubts in this are twofold. Firstly, in order to increase fluency, less time can be spent by the teacher on developing accuracy through the teaching of formal grammar or through focus on form in interaction. Secondly, because of working memory limitations, the students cannot maintain a high level of fluency *and* simultaneously direct selective attention to form without slowing down unless they have sufficiently proceduralized through chunking longer utterances as in the Towell study. One problem with the Hurman study is that it does not take into account another variable. It does not mention that the cohort studied had a very different type of A-level course as well, one which also privileged fluency and content over accuracy. In other words, the change in the cohort could not be attributed solely to the GCSE.

Pronunciation and intonation

Pronunciation accuracy was studied by Elliot (1995). Particularly he asked whether explicit pronunciation instruction improved pronunciation. We might reflect for a moment on why pronunciation had until recently declined in importance in the L2 classroom, by adding to Elliot's suggestions. Firstly, the ability to communicate information does not depend on minor variations in pronunciation from the 'standard' models. It has thus not been seen as an important part of communicative competence. Secondly, in the 1960s and 1970s the language lab no longer promoted the teacher as the provider of target-language pronunciation models. Pronunciation practice would be happening implicitly thanks to the tape recorder and perhaps it just 'dropped out' from the teacher's repertoire of activities. Thirdly, because as teachers we hypothesize that, the older the learner, the harder they find pronunciation, we also automatically avoid it with younger learners. Fourthly, in non-ELT circles at least, there has been a tendency to lump all languages together in teacher education and professional development. Thus if pronunciation practice is not really needed in Spanish and Italian, then it is not needed in French – which is intuitively untrue. It may be that by dropping the practice of pronunciation we have deprived the learner not only of the ability to 'sound more French' but also (see Chapter 6) the ability to access reading texts by sounding out the phonemes of unknown words.

To return to Elliot's study. He had previously carried out research which suggested that those subjects who were more concerned about their pronunciation of the L2 tended to have better mastery of TL allophones. He also found that Field Independence (FI), the ability to spot a specific element from the whole context, related significantly to pronunciation accuracy. For this reason he, in addition to his main research question, wondered whether the learner's attitude to pronunciation affected the success of the instruction and whether FI was a variable. Using a pre- and post-test design, he divided a sample of 66 undergraduates studying Spanish L2 (English L1) at a US university into experimental and control groups. The experimental group differed only in terms of the pronunciation treatment that it was provided with which lasted one semester. The control group subjects were corrected only when an utterance was unintelligible. Additionally, students were given an *Attitude* (to pronunciation) questionnaire and a Field Independence test (Group Embedded Figures). Elliot found:

1. At pre-test there were no significant differences between the pronunciation of the two groups.
2. At post-test there were significant differences between the two groups. There was a high gain in pronunciation accuracy in the experimental group.
3. At pre-test both attitude and FI significantly related to pronunciation ability.
4. At post-test attitude and FI were no longer significant predictors of pronunciation ability. In other words, the treatment was the stronger predictor of good pronunciation.
5. 92% of the students in the experimental group were positive about the intervention.

We do not know if treatment (10-15 minutes per day) detracted from other language skills but it would seem unlikely and in the light of my observation above may well have enhanced them. Elliot concludes:

> It would be interesting to determine the effects of similar training during the initial stages of the learning process. One can speculate that greater improvement would result because phonological fossilisation would not be so significant at an early stage. (1995: 539)

Levis (1999) argues that research into *intonation* should bring about a completely different way of teaching it to what is currently offered in textbooks. For Levis, intonation makes an independent contribution to the meaning of utterances shaping meaning drastically and dramatically and thus making the study of intonation by L2 learners vital. An example of how intonation can affect meaning is provided in the example from Macaro (2001a) in Table 8.2 where, with the same four words in a dialogue, a completely different meaning can be negotiated.

A further very important function of intonation is for the speaker to signal that they are about to finish a turn. Citing Crystal (1969), Levis points to the finding that, in 90% of naturally occurring utterances, there is a stress on the last content word (noun, verb, adjective, adverb). This gives a clue to the listener that the turn is about to finish. Moreover research shows that although there are variances in pitch throughout an utterance, this variance can basically be narrowed down to its *significant pitch*, the overall impression of pitch and contour that the hearer receives and/or can detect. Levis, therefore, offers a simplified form of intonation for teachers to work with consisting of two primary elements:

Nuclear stress (focus on only one word – what did YOU see?)
Final intonation (What did you *see?*)

He then proposes a series of pedagogical guidelines for teaching intonation:

1. Teach intonation in an explicit context, not in decontextualized individual

Table 8.2   Changing meaning through intonation

Student 1: Hungry	Student 1 asks student 2 if s/he is hungry.
Student 2: Again	Student 2 replies that yes, as always, s/he is.
Student 1: Empty fridge	Student 1 says: 'Well that's tough, look the fridge is empty.'
Student 2: Fish and chips	Student 2 says: 'Look, I've got enough money to buy us both fish and chips.'
Student 1: Hungry	Student 1 tells student 2 that s/he's feeling hungry.
Student 2: Again	Student 2 is exasperated because this happens all the time.
Student 1: Empty fridge	Student 1 asks if the fridge is empty.
Student 2: Fish and chips	Student 2 opens the fridge and pulls out a plate of horrible cold fish and chips

From Macaro (2001a)

sentences. The communicative content of a particular intonation changes dramatically according to the context.
2. Make learnable and generalizable statements about meaning which are derived from stress and intonation. The meaning is not generalizable from sentence to sentence. So describe meaning in general terms and use specific examples to convey specific meanings.
3. Teach intonation in the context of a communicative purpose. The primary reason to teach intonation should be to highlight its use in communication.
4. Teach intonation with realistic, authentic language. People don't speak in sentences but in elliptical utterances where missing information is supplied by context and the rest of the discourse.

I have not been able to locate any studies that demonstrate that teaching intonation improves communicative competence. However, I have proposed (in Macaro 2001a) techniques for modelling such teaching so that learners can develop strategies which encourage them to use the tools of intonation to compensate for lack of language in a given situation as well as to make meaning more accessible to the listener. It is to the subject of compensation strategies (perhaps these days more often called communication strategies) that we will now turn.

Why should we be interested in communication strategies?

Listen attentively to any piece of spoken interaction between two speakers of whom at least one is speaking in an L2, and you will be able to detect communication strategies being used. Communication strategies are, in essence, deployed to solve the problems that L2 speakers encounter in interaction when they do not have enough linguistic knowledge to communicate the intended message as easily as they would were they speaking in their first language. Some authors (for example, see a number of contributions in Kasper and Kellerman 1997) would argue that they can also be used to compensate for lack of discourse knowledge (for example, not knowing turn-taking rules) and sociolinguistic knowledge (how to behave linguistically in a particular situation). Yet, as Dörnyei and Scott (1997), in their recent review, point out, L2 courses do not generally prepare students to cope with performance problems in the spoken medium. One of the reasons for this is that courses tend to compensate for lack of linguistic knowledge not by providing learners with compensation strategies to 'tide them over' until they can construct a more appropriate verbal utterance, but by providing the learners with a grammatically correct sentence from which they will have to formulate an acceptable, context-bound, utterance some time in the future. In other words, we need to investigate how speech production over a period of time, in a learner, mirrors interlanguage development. Sentences mask this development, whereas encouraging learners to use communication strategies brings this development more effectively into the open.

The research evidence

Space does not allow anything more than a cursory treatment of the history of Communication Strategies (CS). Readers interested in pursuing their development over the last 30 years might refer to Selinker (1972), Tarone (1977), and Canale and Swain (1980) who included them in their concept of communicative competence. The following treat communication strategies in their own right: Faerch and Kasper (1983, 1986), Bialystock (1990), Kasper and Kellerman (1997), Dörnyei and Scott (1997), These last authors propose that we can classify CSs in a number of ways. Firstly we can identify the source of the problem:

1. The L2 speaker is the source of the problem. For example he or she doesn't know the word.
2. The interlocutor is the source of the problem. The hearer fails to decode the message by using the context and asks for a clarification. (See the discussion on meaning negotiation earlier.)
3. The source of the problem is lack of processing time and the pressure to get the message across quickly. The speaker may well know the language necessary for communication but retrieval is slow. (Try telling a joke in L2 at a dinner party and you will know what I mean!)

The solutions that CS provide can be reduced to two categories. We can either change the original message generated in 'the conceptualizer' by conveying less meaning or by abandoning the message altogether and saying something else. Alternatively we can enhance what resources we have available at that moment in time by shoring up the language with a number of linguistic devices. I have argued elsewhere (Macaro 2001a, 2002b) that communication strategies should be regarded as somewhat different from learning strategies inasmuch as they only indirectly affect learning of the language. This is because neither by changing the content of the message nor by keeping the content of the message and adding to the (insufficient) language do we learn new vocabulary or revise mental models of syntax. It is true that we can create the environment by which we may learn something indirectly. A native speaker may help us to tell the joke by supplying a neat little phrase we didn't know. However, we will not be increasing directly, via the communication strategy, the number of connections to a word or a syntactic pattern simply by avoiding them. In this sense my position contrasts with the second of the three classifications proposed by Dörnyei and Scott (1997), above which I would classify as learning strategies. Indeed, I would argue that an excessive and skilled user of CSs may well create the interaction circumstances whereby native-speaker interlocutors who know him/her well *no longer* provide feedback which will develop his/her interlanguage. Nevertheless, mine is probably a minority view and the following is an adaptation of a categorization system offered by Dörnyei and Scott (1997) with examples (not a definitive taxonomy) of CSs:

Table 8.3 Categories of communication strategies

Direct strategies (alternative, manageable, self-contained)	Indirect strategies (facilitate the conveyance of meaning by creating the right/better conditions)	Interactive strategies (participants carry out the trouble-shooting cooperatively
Circumlocution	Fillers	Appeals for help
Approximation	Repetitions	Comprehension check
Foreignizing	Using strategy markers	Asking/giving confirmation
Mime	Feigning understanding	Guessing

For a comprehensive taxonomy of CSs see Dörnyei and Scott (1997) who provide well over 30 strategies with clear descriptions and useful examples.

An early study in which there was an attempt to train learners to use communication strategies was reported in Faerch and Kasper (1986). Adolescent Danish learners of English (L2) were given an oral communication task which was video-recorded. Immediately on completion the learners were asked to state what difficulties they had encountered and how they had tried to solve them. The recording and the self-report provided the researchers with a list of strategies that the class had used collectively. The training then lasted three months, after which another recording was made. The researchers found:

1. Middle-proficiency-level learners made the most progress with using communication strategies.
2. The general attitude of the class towards errors and risk taking had changed. More learners accepted the need to make an attempt even if they did not know the right word.

No control or comparison group was used with this study and here the focus was more on increased use of CSs rather than on increasing fluency. By contrast Dadour and Robbins (1996) did use a control group with a sample of Egyptian university students studying English (L2). The experimental group received strategy training for three hours per week over more than a three-month period. The researchers found that the treatment group made significant improvements in their speaking over the control group, specifically in fluency, range of vocabulary used and grammatical awareness. Moreover, the effect of training seemed to permeate all types of strategy use, not only communication strategies.

Dörnyei (1995) carried out a study on speaking strategies using 109 Hungarian high-school students of English. A sub-group of these was trained for six weeks to use topic avoidance, circumlocution, and replacement strategies when they had difficulty under pressure to produce an oral utterance. In addition they were trained to 'buy time' using fillers and hesitation devices. Their performance was then compared to the control group which received no strategy training. Dörnyei found that in the post-test the treatment group showed improvement in the quantity and quality of the circumlocutions that the students deployed, largely assisted by the increased use of fillers. The students' attitudes towards the training was positive.

Cohen, Weaver and Li (1995) carried out a study of 55 intermediate-level students (French or Norwegian L2) at the university of Minnesota, using six teachers. 32 students made up the experimental group and received strategy-based training in speaking for about 10 weeks, the training being embedded into their regular classroom activities. A sub-group of 21 students provided verbal report protocols with respect to their strategy use. Three speaking tasks were designed for the pre- and post-tests consisting of a self description; story telling, a summary following the reading of a folk story; a description of their favourite city. Immediately following the completion of the tasks the students were asked to complete strategy check lists of strategies used during the tasks, particularly strategies used in advanced preparation for speaking; strategies used as self-monitoring while speaking; self-reflection strategies after speaking. Examples included:

- Deep-breathing to relax, rehearsal, visualizing oneself as 'prepared to speak', note taking, prediction of potential difficulties, self-encouragement, identifying the purpose of the task, relating the task to similar situations;
- Concentration, word coinage, substitution, asking for clarification, attention to grammatical forms, delaying speaking, not giving up, avoiding frustration, monitoring performance;
- Reflection on task performance, plans for future learning, self-rewarding, reviewing strategy check lists.

The researchers found:

1. The experimental group outperformed the comparison group on the third speaking task. The experimental group performed better not only in fluency but also in grammatical accuracy.
2. The French group (only) performed better on range of vocabulary than the comparison group.
3. An increase in reported strategy use was linked to improved task performance.

Cohen, Weaver and Li concluded that strategy-based instruction for speaking should have an important role in the L2 classroom and that strategy instruction should be closely linked to specific tasks.

A very comprehensive study of communication strategies (Nakatani 2002), and whether strategy training can improve oral production, involved 62 Japanese university students of English (L2). This study aimed to develop a strategy-training programme which extended the students' available strategies instead of subjecting students to drastic change. Nakatani developed a reliable inventory of strategies using factor analysis based on a large sample. The treatment, as customary, was sandwiched in between pre- and post-test oral communication tasks. Nakatani found:

1. Significant improvement in oral test scores at post-test for the experimental group.
2. Significant increase in strategy use of experimental over control group in most categories of strategies, both self-report and observed in the transcriptions.

Initial implications of communication strategies

The implications of the Nakatani study are still being arrived at as I write (Nakatani personal communication) but it would seem that we could conclude that communication strategies should be taught. They will certainly help with communication and indirectly improve learning by increasing interaction time. Moreover, given the often documented reluctance of some cultural groups (e.g. the Japanese) to speak without monitoring, strategy training may well be able to counter both the learning environment and cultural learning styles.

The findings in general would suggest that strategy awareness and strategy training in speaking tasks is a very valuable way of improving the performance of speaking although it may only help to develop competence in an indirect way. One of the most crucial implications of the positive findings is that teachers need to develop, or need to be trained to incorporate, strategy instruction into their interaction (as an implicit form of instruction) and into 'time-out from learning' activities in more explicit forms of strategy training.

Testing oral proficiency

We saw in the Towell *et al.* (1996) study (above) that measures of fluency have to be carefully researched before confidence can be attached to the testing of linguistic progress. Care needs to be taken, if for no other reason than because both formal testing and informal evaluation can have major repercussions for language learners. Perhaps it is in the area of speaking that validity and reliability are most threatened because of the non-permanent nature of the evidence. Even if the learner's oral production is recorded there may be paralinguistic features (body language), which are intended to aid with the transmission of the message, that are missed.

Hurman (1996) wondered how reliable were the examiners' judgements about the content and accuracy of candidates' responses in role-play tests at GCSE. He argued that it is possible to confuse lack of communication with inaccuracy and vice versa. He also proposed that variables affecting examiner reliability might include:

1. some examiners applying the context more than others in making a judgement;
2. the relative application of a previous utterance which *implies* information in the target utterance;

3. relative acceptability by the examiner of the misuse of tenses.

He therefore took 60 experienced examiners and asked them to provide scores for two candidates whose role-play test had been recorded. The examiners were then divided into two groups. One group (group A) spent a few seconds reflecting on the answer before awarding the mark (repeating the answer to themselves, twice). The other group (group B) made an instantaneous decision. Hurman found:

1. For candidate 1 there was a higher degree of agreement in group A examiners than in group B examiners (at a statistically significant level).
2. For candidate 2 there was a slight but not a significant difference between the two examiner groups.
3. There was wide variation in both groups.

Reflecting for a few seconds before awarding the mark appears to provide examiners *with some* measure of greater objectivity, but not conclusively so. In any case, pausing in the middle of a role-play renders the activity somewhat inauthentic and produces some fairly stilted discourse. Probably the only way to counteract subjectivity is to mark a recording of the role-play immediately after the test. Of course this has resource implications.

Richards and Chambers (1992) looked at the reliability of the conversation component of GCSE exams. Criteria at the Higher Level of the component included some reference to linguistic quality and complexity, but precise definition of these was lacking. They found that while teachers' impressions of features such as range of vocabulary were very accurate, there was an alarmingly low level of agreement with the researchers' objective measure of 'complexity of structures'. There was also a lack of objective measure of 'fluency' and 'use of idiom'.

Chambers and Richards (1995) then also looked at the validity and authenticity of the conversation test at GCSE and wondered to what extent native-speaker conversation matched L2 learners' test conversation bearing in mind that the exam criteria suggests that it should be a conversation which has not been rehearsed. They examined 28 taped conversations of Higher Level candidates who produced an average of 118 words and 23.9 clauses. They then carried out 25 videotaped interviews with French 15-year-olds on the same GCSE themes. These produced an average 437 words; 56.9 clauses. Apart from this lack of 'match' they found that there were problems with the authenticity of the task:

1. The native speakers appeared to regard the house/flat descriptions theme as not being a socially acceptable topic of conversation – almost as an invasion of privacy.
2. The 'daily routine' theme seemed inauthentic to the native speakers and, in any case, produced few reflexive verbs.
3. The 'town and amenities' theme and 'school life' theme were very productive.

Consequently, as the authors suggest, we may need to re-examine the validity of these conversation tests. Are they actually testing the L2 learner's ability to hold a conversation with a native speaker or are they testing the acquisition of grammar? Chambers and Richards (1995) also found:

1. The native speakers used significantly more relative clauses than the GCSE candidates (especially *qui*).
2. Native speakers used indirect object pronouns (*me, nous, vous*). The candidates did not use any.
3. The candidates used the future tense whereas the native speakers used *aller* + infinitive.
4. The native speakers used the imperfect tense significantly more.

The researchers concluded that, although not all levels of complexity, fluency, etc., should be modelled on native-speaker performance, nevertheless we should take these more into account in both our language curriculum and the examining of conversations.

Alderson and Banerjee (2002) provide a review of language-testing research with regard to speaking. I will briefly summarize some of the main conclusions that they draw:

1. It would be better to call the conversation a face-to-face interview. Even this re-conceptualization, however, throws up problems with the asymmetrical relationship between tester and the candidate which might obscure differences in the real performance potential or proficiency of the candidate.
2. Pairs of interviewers may provide greater reliability. Holistic judgements could be made by the interlocutor and an analytic score provided by the observer.
3. Computer-based tests offer the guarantee that each candidate will receive the same test (task instructions and support will be identical) but we do not yet know what the effect of this mode of test delivery will be on the candidate.
4. Whether planning time (e.g. before a role-play) is a variable on test performance depends on the proficiency level of the candidate. When presented with a cognitively challenging task, high-proficiency candidates are more likely to produce more accurate answers. Low-proficiency candidates do not appear to benefit from longer planning time. However, I would argue, based on the evidence on communication strategies, they may do so if they are trained to use the planning time wisely!
5. Examiners' perceptions of grammatical accuracy seem to have the strongest influences on how they score candidates.

Conclusions

Oral interaction in the second language offers a possible reconciliation of the two main models of language acquisition, Universal Grammar and Connectionism (see Chapter 3). It does this by demonstrating that it would be difficult to acquire all the language that we do acquire in the L2 classroom simply as a result of speaking in general, and negotiation of meaning and forced output in particular. There simply aren't that many opportunities for this to be the case. This would give credence to the parameter-setting hypothesis. On the other hand without strategies involving cognitive processing that enable 'learning problems' in the L2 to be brought into selective attention, and therefore deeper processing, we would not be able to acquire certain features of the language. Some L2 structures are learnt incrementally, by a process of learner construction, not from a single input which triggers the parameter setting. These two models, in post critical-age learners, far from being dichotomous, actually *need* to co-exist, at least in terms of models of learning which are accessible for teachers, if not for acquisition theorists.

Virtually all of the research on the beneficial effects of interaction has been on competence, that is, testing acquisition of vocabulary and grammar in non-oral-task situations. Although it may seem intuitive, we need further evidence that interaction directly improves oral proficiency.

The Comprehensible Output Hypothesis would seem to have led to an interpretation of CLT which is somewhat dominated by the promotion of oral interaction in the classroom. Whilst the evidence points to plenty of talk facilitating interlanguage development it should not contribute to the downgrading of skills involving the written form. Particularly, the Comprehensible Output Hypothesis is not robustly supported by the research evidence beyond the acquisition of vocabulary. Further classroom-based experiments need to determine the relative effects of forced output on the acquisition of syntax.

In large classes there are two ways in which the teacher can ensure that learners get the opportunity to acquire language through talk – excluding the use of future incredibly powerful computers, that is. The first is through quality teacher-fronted interaction consisting of cognitively challenging dialogue with features such as sufficient length of turn and appropriate feedback. The second is through frequent and high-quality learner-learner interaction where value is placed on the negotiation of meaning in tasks which bring to selective attention certain features of the target language. We should continue to explore learner-learner interaction which does not necessarily result from presentation and practice. We also need to view differently what appears to be off-task behaviour. At the very least we should stave off negative judgement of pair-work tasks until we have more comprehensive research on which to draw. Once we have re-affirmed our confidence in learner-learner interaction we should additionally strive towards more unstructured conversation-type tasks, especially as learners progress through a topic or theme.

As in other chapters in this book the evidence suggests that better teaching and learning will ensue if, as teachers, we shift our gaze from the product of learning and towards the processes involved in that learning. In speaking, too, we need to find out from the learners what they are doing in order to formulate speech, to interact, to add to meaning and so on. Communication strategies are certainly a part of that shift in our gaze and it is clear that good communicators use strategies wisely and in clever combination. Some recent findings look quite promising with regard to training for communication strategies in that it actually produces better learning outcomes in speaking. Whether these improved outcomes transfer from speaking to other skills too, remains to be discovered.

We should also note that the research strongly suggests that the heart as well as the brain can be affected by variables in the interaction. Roles and identities may be negatively affected by interaction in which the teacher unwittingly undermines self-efficacy or self-worth.

The issue of how we measure progression in speaking still needs further research but some current curricula (as in the English National Curriculum) demonstrate a lack of coherence, a lack of logic and a lack of understanding of the research evidence.

This undermines the teachers' confidence and skills to diagnose their learners' development. There is a body of evidence emerging on aspects of progression in speaking such as fluency, pronunciation and intonation. How these interrelate to other aspects such as accuracy and vocabulary range (as well as content of course) is hugely complex and still needs further study. To do nothing, however, and accept the status quo is, in my view, unacceptable.

As for pronunciation, we may seriously need to rethink our neglect of teaching it, especially in languages with non-transparent orthographies such as those of French and English. The theme of phonology is not absent from our discussion in this chapter of how to promote the production and the communication of meaning. But again, pronunciation and intonation are probably more valuable as indicators of processes that the learners are going through than as value measures of spoken accuracy.

The whole question of how we assess speaking, and precisely what we are trying to assess when we do, very much lacks both national and international consensus.

Chapter 9

Research on Writing

In this penultimate chapter we will explore the research evidence on second-language writing. Although it is the last of the four chapters on language skills, after listening, reading and speaking, I would hate to give the impression that it is so placed because that is where research suggests it should come in the pedagogical pecking order; that communicative approaches to language learning privilege oral communication way above written communication. Far from it. In fact, as we shall see, one of the underlying themes that the research literature explores is the place of writing in the overall language-acquisition process. Nor should its 'fourth place' suggest that learners should only attempt writing after they have gone through an extensive period of 'reception'– that is, they should listen and read before they write. Finally, its 'fourth place' should not lead us to conclude that the main function of writing is to provide us with an assessment of what language has been learnt by a student in any given topic nor what overall progress a student has made. Unfortunately, however, the spotlight of research has often fallen upon writing as the *demonstrable product of learning* and has therefore given the impression that writing's prime role is to provide evidence for assessment.

In addition to there being fewer studies in writing than in reading and speaking, the research endeavour has not been one characterized by clarity, coherence and unity of purpose. Reichelt (2001) asks a number of important unanswered questions with regard to writing. Firstly, what do we mean by writing proficiency? We have explored the issue of what we mean by overall language proficiency throughout this book. In Chapter 5 particularly we reviewed research which examined the inter-relationship of attitudes and motivation with *proficiency*, *ability* and *success* in language learning. In the case of writing, should we regard proficiency as being able to put across content (the information we wish to communicate) coherently and cohesively so that an intended reader (audience) can understand without too much extra effort? Or do we mean that the writer writes with accuracy? And if we mean writing with accuracy, is that accuracy related to some almost unreachable native-speaker ideal? Or do we mean that accuracy is relative to the expected level of accuracy at that parti-cular stage in the student's learning programme? Moreover does accuracy relate to orthography (in the case of deep orthographic languages such as English and French) or to morphology and syntax? And what is the function therefore of writing? Is it to provide practice in a staged selection of syntactic features? Is it to demonstrate an understanding of the literature or the culture of the target language?

Whilst there are many studies which directly or indirectly attempt to answer these questions, Reichelt concludes that there is no real consensus on any of these issues and that research has failed to provide us with a path which might lead us to that consensus. The reasons for this unhelpful situation are a lack of systematic collaborative research effort; many studies have been done in artificial settings rather than real classrooms; studies do not mirror the usual classroom writing task or authentic writing conditions.

Underlying the above questions and the research effort so far are the following 'sub-issues':

1. Should learners, when they write, be allowed to write what they want to write? In other words, to what extent should a writing topic be prescribed by the teacher?
2. To what extent should the actual language that a writer uses be limited by the teacher in terms of the syntax, morphology and idiom that he/she might use?
3. Do we get learners to write in the L2 in order to improve their writing, in order to consolidate their other language skills, or both? If both, which is the more important?
4. Should we teach learners how to write by showing them how we think it should be done or should we encourage learners to be active participants in the process of improving their writing through a process of exploration?

I hope to demonstrate through the research evidence that these issues are interconnected and we will return to them at the end of the chapter by way of conclusion. Because they are interconnected it is not easy to deposit research-based studies into neat compartments. However, in the interests of accessibility we will look at the following categories of research endeavour.

1. The effects of different writing task types
2. Research into the writing process and approaches to teaching
3. How writers actually get down to the business of putting pen to paper – the formulating process
4. The effects of dictionary use
5. The effect of feedback on students' writing (mainly from the teacher but also peer feedback)
6. The effect of strategy use on writing proficiency and the impact of strategy-training programmes
7. The impact of computers on writing proficiency

Before we do this, however, we have to ask ourselves briefly what researchers believe the process of writing actually is.

Interestingly, there have been few attempts at providing a theoretical model of L2 writing. Flower and Hayes (1981) provided a cognitive model of composition in general (i.e. essentially for L1 writing) by exploring the question: what guides the decisions writers make as they write? They then proposed a tripartite model based on *planning*, *translating* and *reviewing*. The *planning* was the organizational part of the process which interacted with what the task demanded and the goals that the writer was setting himself or herself. *Translating* (contrary to what the reader may think) was about 'putting ideas into visible language'. More recently writers in SLA have (understandably) come to call this process *formulating* (giving ideas a visible form). *Reviewing* incorporated all the revising and evaluating actions that writers undertake. These three thinking processes, Flower and Hayes pointed out:

1. interact recursively (they mirror the complex inner-thought processes of the writer not the three-stage linear growth of the written product);
2. have to be 'orchestrated' by writers as they write;
3. have a hierarchical and highly embedded organization (any process can interrupt and/or can be embedded in any other);
4. lead to high-level goals and sub-goals being generated. These goals may change as the three processes move the actual writing of the text along.

This model, as de Larios *et al.* (1999) point out, makes no reference to how propositions (ideas stored in LTM) 'become' sentences in text during the formulation process. One of the elements missing would appear to be the vital operations performed by working memory (see Chapter 3) which would have to evaluate, process, modify and generate the first retrieved language-encoded elements from LTM. Moreover, the model does not, I would argue, give sufficient prominence to the role that the L1 plays in this formulating process. We will return to this last problem later. For the moment let us propose a model of L2 writing that operates something like the one suggested in Figure 9.1. In this model there are two internal components (working memory and long-term memory) and three external components (the task requirements, resources such as dictionaries and textbooks, the on-going written product).

In the explanation of Figure 9.1 (see below), *monitoring* refers to the cognitive and metacognitive strategies of comparing *either* the mental models temporarily articulated in working memory *or* the written output with internalized mental models of the language. *Checking*, on the other hand, refers to comparing *either* one's mental models of the language *or* the written output with available external resources such as dictionaries, the textbook, previous writing, teacher worksheets and so forth. We also note that when evaluation takes place during the formulation stage, I am proposing that this is based on the relative effectiveness of three strategies: re-combination of unanalysed formulas; restructuring via partial analysis; generation through translation. This last process I hope will become clearer after we have looked at the strategies section of this chapter.

Note that with each new word and phrase that is written by the writer, the written product changes its effect on all the other components, both external and internal. This contributes to the recursive nature of the whole process which can be seen to be working through the six constantly recurring functions proposed in Figure 9.1:

1. the elicitation of task requirements;
2. the setting (and re-setting) of communicative goals as a result of the process of matching task requirements to current linguistic knowledge in LTM;
3. the evaluating of retrieved language by WM from LTM both as L1/L2

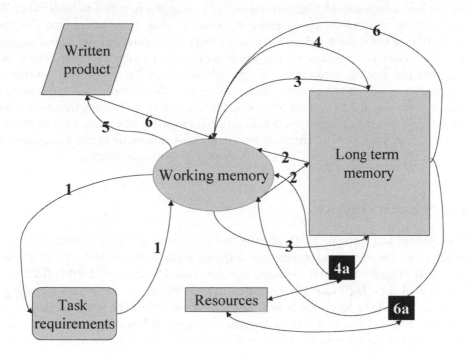

Figure 9.1   Model of L2 writing

     equivalents and as L2 formulaic language, the processing of that language, its modification and eventual sentence (or part sentence) generation;
4. the monitoring and/or checking process (4a) or the recourse to resources to assist language generation before text is written;
5. written formulations;
6. monitoring and/or checking (6a) of on-going written text.

The effects of different writing task types

A number of researchers have explored how different types of writing tasks interact with the other components proposed in Figure 9.1.

Why should we be interested in this?

One reason that we should be interested in this is because language curricula are in a constant state of flux. These have an effect on and in turn affect approaches to language testing and examining. In England at least, it is very rare that teachers are given clear and logical reasons why the FL curriculum is changing and/or why test types are changing.

    Writing tasks can be descriptive, narrative, discursive or the products of demonstrating understanding through the target language. But which is the easiest/

hardest and which should beginner learners (for example) be asked to undertake? We have seen in the chapter on listening (Chapter 7) that radio broadcasts, the least interactive of texts, were judged to be more difficult to comprehend than dialogues. Are there criteria by which we can judge writing tasks? For example, which best describes the writing performance of the individual student and which contributes best to the enhancement of other skills? Moreover, do different task types have an effect on the way the L2 learner plans what he/she writes, and which task type causes the greatest amount of anxiety? Do learners prefer to write what they want to write or what they are told to write about? If we knew answers to some of these questions we might gain an insight into what motivates and demotivates learners.

The research evidence

Way, Joiner and Seaman (2000) investigated the effects of three different task types: descriptive, narrative and expository (explanatory/argumentative). Their subjects were 330 beginner and near beginner learners from 15 classes of French (L2) in the US (English L1). Each task was presented in the context of a reply to a teenage pen pal from France. In other words each task had more or less the same requirement of content. Three different types of writing prompts (rubrics) were designed: (bare prompt) a simple explanation of the task in English; (vocabulary prompt) a simple explanation of the task in English, plus vocabulary list; (prose prompt) a simple explanation of the task in English plus a letter from the pen pal on the topic. Three writing samples were collected from each student during three consecutive months and various measurements of syntactic complexity and measurements of accuracy were carried out. The descriptive task proved to be the easiest of the three types of tasks followed by the narrative task. In terms of prompts, the prose prompt consistently produced writing samples with the best overall quality, the greatest fluency and the greatest syntactic complexity and the highest accuracy. The vocabulary prompt typically ranked second. These findings are not surprising as the prose prompt would have permitted the learners to lift chunks from the pen pal letter to use for their own writing (although the researchers argue that there is evidence that some students didn't), whereas the bare prompt would have needed the maximum amount of sentence generation. In a sense their findings would validate a curriculum with this sort of writing task progression. However, the authors do point out that these beginner learners were capable of successfully attempting simple narration tasks. If one were to add to this the most 'supportive' prompt type, we could argue that beginner learners are probably capable of more advanced writing activities than they are sometimes offered. We will return to this issue of cognitive challenge in writing activities later in this section. Additionally, the authors argue, the evidence suggests that the reading-writing connection (as in the prose prompt) should be used more in an L2 setting.

Koda (1993) also found that narrative writing may be more difficult than descriptive writing. Using a sample of 25 college students (English L1) studying Japanese, they asked them to write abut a familiar place (descriptive task) and about a happy incident they had recently experienced (narrative task). Their linguistic knowledge had been previously measured through a series of vocabulary and grammar tests. The two tasks were then analysed for their linguistic features (e.g. text length, sentence length, diversity of vocabulary); their topical structure (discourse coherence); and general quality (using a range of measures but including an overall judgement of quality). Amongst other things, Koda found:

1. Vocabulary knowledge correlated highly with quality ratings in both tasks.
2. Grammatical knowledge correlated much more with the narrative task.
3. More complex structuring and progression was a feature of the narrative task.

The implications of these findings are that, on the one hand, teachers should be aware of the difficulty of narrative tasks with beginner and lower-intermediate learners. On the other hand, a diet of descriptive writing tasks only may not be providing opportunities for learners to make progress with some essential aspects of acquisition.

Other researchers have looked at the effects of task types by requiring their learners to write dialogue journals. These are diaries regularly kept and shown to the teacher who provides a written response, usually limited to content thus encouraging the learners to continue with the dialogue. The advantage of this type of writing is that the student is much freer to write about what they want to write. The disadvantage is that they may not focus on certain (new) language structures or vocabulary and therefore not consolidate new learning. Baudrand-Aertker (1992) investigated the writing of 21 third-year high school students of French of mixed ages and mixed cultural backgrounds who wrote in journals in dialogue with the teacher. They were asked to write at least two entries per week over a nine-month period. The researcher also gave them writing proficiency tests and attitude questionnaires. Using a pre-test, post-test design the researcher found:

1. The students made significant improvement in their writing over the period of intervention.
2. Students showed a positive attitude towards writing in their dialogue journals 'both affectively and academically' (101).
3. Students felt that the journals helped them improve their overall knowledge of the TL rather than their grammar.
4. Most students did not want the teacher to correct their grammatical mistakes, or at least only the 'most obvious errors' (103).

Although the study used high levels of triangulation to provide evidence of writing improvement, there was no comparison group and therefore we do not know if writers in equivalent classes, who had not been given journals to write, would not have made the same progress. Nevertheless the results would seem encouraging.

Initial implications

We have seen that different writing-task types do pose different levels of difficulties for learners. Descriptive tasks require a greater focus on nouns and adjectives whereas narration tasks require a high verb density. Discursive tasks involve high levels of idiomatic, phrasal verb knowledge plus the ability to generate complex sentences. However, if we do not expose our learners to texts with high verb density and require them to subsequently use verbs in their writings they will not develop their language competence beyond the use of the formulaic phrase nor will they be able to transfer their knowledge to different settings.

Task-type difficulty can be mediated by the task rubrics (or prompts) in various ways. The task rubrics, however, change the processes that the task requires quite dramatically. Teachers need to establish what the purpose and linguistic objectives of a particular kind of task rubric are and ensure that these objectives fit into an overall framework of progression.

There are other ways to overcome writing-task difficulties and these are discussed below. However, task types cannot be the only variables affecting difficulty. Different topics may make tasks that appear easy in fact become quite hard. Another variable, of course, is the level of knowledge that an individual learner has of the L2 vocabulary needed for a task. The above research on task difficulty only applies when all other things are equalized.

Research into the writing process and approaches to teaching

Writing processes and approaches to teaching have been the focus of attention of practitioners and researchers alike for some years now. Process writing, as a pedagogical approach, owes much to the work of authors such as Raimes (1987), Zamel (1987), Hudelson (1988) and Leki (1990). What is process writing, then? Silva (1990) talks about establishing 'a positive, encouraging and collaborative working environment within which students with ample time and minimum interference can work through their composing processes' (15). The teacher's role is to help students develop viable strategies for getting started, drafting and revising their work. This approach differs from the notion that teachers should focus on the product, that is, what the student produces for the teacher to mark or correct. In addition, they differ from the approach which suggests that teachers should provide explicit grammar instruction, examples from written texts and then see if learners can reproduce these correctly in written form.

Why should we be interested in this?

This theme is at the very heart of why and how we ask learners to write at all, unless of course we are preparing students for some sort of specific course aim such as writing for academic purposes. Do integrated forms of language-teaching pedagogy, where skills support one another, bring about better proficiency in general and writing in particular? What is the relationship between teacher input and writing proficiency? Should we teach grammar, the grammar needed for a specific writing, explicitly? How much should teachers interfere with the way learners write in the L2? Is this the best way to make learners autonomous in their L2 writing?

The research evidence

We have already seen that Way *et al.* (2000) argue that their research findings support the notion of bringing reading and writing much closer together. Reichelt reviews three unpublished studies (Nummikoski 1991; Gallego de Bibleche 1993; Becker 1991) which I have not been able to read in the original. Nummikoski (1991) studied the effects of both reading and writing on 127 first-year Russian beginners. He divided them up into three groups: a group that undertook interactive writing with the teacher; a group that did reading only; a group that did writing only. Nummikoski found that there were no significant differences between the interactive group and the other two groups. This would appear to run contrary to the evidence being offered by Way *et al.* that writing can be improved through extensive exposure to reading materials. However, aspects of Nummikoski's research design, according to Reichelt, were somewhat weak and results should be treated with some caution. Gallego de Bibleche (1993) set up two groups of primary (elementary) level students. The first group was asked to engage in a pre-writing activity, free writing, pair work, writing a rough draft and then peer review for revision. The second group received direct grammar instruction, grammar exercises, produced draft compositions marked by the teacher. The experimental group (group 1) outperformed the control group on length and organization of composition but there was no difference in the content, the language use, the syntactic complexity and the reduction in the number of errors. Becker (1991) investigated what she called 'clustering' (brainstorming?) for five minutes before writing with an experimental group. The experimental group produced more imaginative ideas and interesting ideas than a control group. Moreover, the novice (beginners) sub-group of the sample also outperformed the control group with regard to fluency.

Two further studies would suggest that specific grammar instruction does not lead to holistic improvements in writing proficiency. We have already looked in some detail at Frantzen's (1995) study where, although students improved on a grammar test, they performed no better than a control group on the accuracy of their essay writing.

Manley and Calk (1997) gave 14 university students in an advanced French composition course, pre- and post-treatment questionnaires regarding their attitudes to explicit grammar teaching. There was no control group. The students wrote four compositions, over a period of time, after which some specific grammar teaching, resulting from error patterns detected, was provided on the following four rules (i.e. one rule after each composition): the *passé composé*; noun-adjective agreement; possessive adjectives; the definite article. A final (fifth) composition was analysed for errors and compared to the previous four. In addition 'holistic grading' was carried out on the five compositions. Manley and Calk found:

1. In the pre-treatment questionnaire students were favourably disposed to grammar but not able to provide any discernible pattern of what grammar they found easy and difficult.
2. In the post-treatment questionnaire, most students said they found the explicit grammar teaching useful but were less positive about whether it actually increased their editing processes.

3. The final composition demonstrated reduction in errors in noun-adjective agreement; possessive adjectives; definite article but not in the *passé composé*.
4. When compositions were graded 'holistically' there was no significant improvement.

The researchers concluded that this was further evidence that some structures are acquired late. We should also note that this provides further evidence of 'discrete point learning' but not of overall improvement in performance at writing.

This theme of teacher involvement in the writing process (as opposed to the practice of providing the students with correct models of the language from which to arrive at a written product) was explored by me in a study involving 14-15-year-olds (Macaro 2001a). As in Becker (1991), year-10 (lower-intermediate) students were encouraged to brainstorm for 5-10 minutes before commencing a writing activity in French (L2). This was the first part of a process aimed at ensuring that, at least in reaction to part of the task, students were retrieving from LTM elements of language (usually short formulaic phrases and vocabulary) that they actually already knew and could be matched to task requirements. As part of this teaching approach it was important that students did not attempt to use a dictionary or to try to generate sentences at this stage. This then left the students with aspects of task requirements which they were not able to retrieve directly from LTM. They were then encouraged to try out two further approaches: (a) to use a dictionary selectively in order to minimize dictionary mistakes and also not to exceed time allocation and (b) to focus on only two syntactic aspects (1) ensuring the correct number of verbs needed to formulate a tense (i.e. not the accuracy of the verb form) and (2) to look for the effect of gender and plurals on adjectives. They received no other grammatical instruction during the four-month intervention period and were taught as normal for the other skills. On the post-test the intervention group outperformed the control group who had received no treatment as described above. The conclusions from this study will be described below under the section on learning strategies. However, we note at this stage that this teaching approach had a strong focus on permitting the student to discover, apply and evaluate a process of writing which had a recognizable structure and which took into account what the writer wanted to say and *what the writer already knew* how to say. In addition, a key feature was that there was a 'very light touch' on the grammar of the L2.

Also under the current heading we will look at a study by Tsui and Ng (2000). Although this study was primarily about teacher and peer feedback (which we will be looking at in detail below), it does provide us with a clear example of what an approach to process-writing looks like when it attemps to create an enabling environment. Tsui and Ng describe the following 12 stages the students were taken through in writing cycles that lasted six weeks. (The grade 12 and 13 students were in a secondary Hong Kong school which used English as the medium of instruction.)

1. Brainstorming: pre-writing tasks (whole class)
2. Draft outline
3. Peer comments
4. Revision of outline
5. Writing of first draft
6. Peer comments on first draft

7. Revision of first draft
8. Teacher comments on second draft
9. Revision of second draft
10 Teacher comments on third draft
11. Revision of third draft
12. Final draft
   (Adapted from Tsui and Ng 2000)

In this type of classroom the teacher develops the notion of collaborative learning and enlists the help of peers (as well as his/her own help) in assisting students develop viable strategies in all stages of the composing process.

Initial implications

There appears to be little evidence that the traditional and prevailing approach to FL writing which involves learning to produce 'sentence level, error-free text within a progression of tasks and under conditions of careful guidance' (Heilenman 1991) is successful in achieving holistic competence (i.e. focus both on content and on form) with L2 writers. Learners may well find greater satisfaction, freedom of expression and ultimately motivation if they are allowed to experiment with drafting and redrafting of their own language, not necessarily at the end of a topic of work. Efficient writers do not write in a static pattern, but in a series of dynamic processes (Yonglin 1995). Another of the aims of process writing is to help learners find out more about themselves as writers. If the focus is to be, in part, on improving accuracy, then learners' attention, *at some point*, must be brought to bear on their writing errors. The question which is still unresolved is *when* and *how* should their attention to their errors be drawn and how can this too contribute to the learners' knowledge about themselves? Advocates of process writing would suggest the focus on form, including some explicit grammar teaching, should come at the end of a multidraft process.

Planning, formulating and the learner's first language

We now need to consider the ways in which learners go about the process of putting pen to paper. That is, that recognisable stage in the recursive process in which an idea in the writer's brain becomes a sentence or part of a sentence on a piece of paper or a computer screen.

Why should we be interested in this?

What is the total number of ways in which learners can plan and formulate written text? Can we, as teachers, safely assume that we know what is the best way of planning? Are we perhaps prescribing the strategies for formulating text we apply (or applied) ourselves when learning a language for other learners who may have processed and stored language differently from us? Might their metacognitive processes (organizational, evaluative) be so different from ours that they have found their own best course of action? Are there pitfalls in teaching strategies for formulating language that are common to all writers? What is the role of the writer's L1 in the process of formulation? As I have indicated in the model of L2 writing proposed at the beginning of this chapter, the formulation stage of the process is probably the most complex. The process also has close links with the discussion on development and progression that we encountered in Chapter 3.

The research evidence

Friedlander (1990) wanted to investigate whether the first language of Chinese (L1) students of English (L2) at university had an effect on their writing. He argued that previous research evidence suggested that retrieving information from LTM via the L1 and then translating it into L2 resulted in working memory overload which in turn led to mistakes being committed. On the other hand, he noted that several studies suggested that thinking in the first language actually aided writers in retrieving topic information from LTM in the first place. Thus, Friedlander wanted to test whether a topic learnt in L1 was better retrieved in L1 in an L2 writing task. He also wanted to know whether advanced writers had developed their L2 to such an extent that translation from L1 did not have a harmful effect on their writing. The students were asked to perform two written tasks. In the first task they were to plan in their L1. In the second they were to plan in the L2. Planning consisted of brainstorming ideas on the topic and organizing these ideas in preparation for the actual writing part of the task. Friedlander made the two 'topics' different by asking the students to write about a Chinese festival (thus a topic the students had definitely only experienced in their L1) and about life at the American university (thus a topic that the students had essentially experienced in the L2). This provided a matrix as in Table 9.1.

Table 9.1   Matrix

A Task planned in L1		X Task related to previous (L1) cultural experience
B Task planned in L2		Y Task related to target-country experience

Adapted from Friedlander (1990:114)

He then called **AX** and **BY** the 'matched conditions' and **AY** and **BX** the 'mismatch conditions' for planning. Friedlander found that the students demonstrated much higher quality of planning in the matched condition than in the mismatch condition. Students produced more details, richer ideas and wrote longer and better plans. Moreover, the essays themselves (which of course were in L2), resulting from the planning in the matched condition, were longer than and of superior quality to those used in the mismatch condition. Friedlander concluded that when (advanced) writers use their second language to write on a topic related to their first language, and when they plan in their second language, they are constrained in terms of the amount of material retrieved; in contrast, translation does not appear to hinder writers in their text production by causing them to take more time over their texts. (1990: 118)

A similar study was carried out by Kobayashi and Rinnert (1992) using 48 Japanese (L1) university students of English (L2). Here the comparison between translating from the L1 versus formulating directly from L2 was even simpler and starker in that (a) the nature of the topics was not compared and (b) half the group (on alternative days) was required to actually write the task in Japanese first and then translate it into English. Furthermore, these researchers were also interested in the students' perceptions of the relative effectiveness of writing directly in L2 as opposed to composing first in L1 and then translating.

Kobayashi and Rinnert found that the students were able to produce compositions with greater syntactic complexity and more sophisticated vocabulary use when they translated what they wanted to say from L1 than when the wrote directly in L2. The other variable was in the perceived level of the students. For students with less competence in writing the advantage of translating over direct composition in L2 was even more marked in that they produced, holistically, better quality pieces of writing (based on measures of specifics, developed ideas, clarity, interest). However, when translating, students (higher level ones particularly) made a greater number of errors which might interfere with communication than they did if they wrote directly. In terms of their own perceptions, the students felt that direct (L2) composition was easier although some felt that there were worthwhile advantages in translation in terms of cognitive challenge. Interestingly, when asked whether they had used their L1 *to think in* when trying to compose directly in L2, a substantial number of students, across the levels, reported using L1 to think in.

The language of thought has also been investigated by Qi (1998) in his case study of a bilingual adult (Chinese L1, English L2). His study built on investigations of the structure of bilingual lexicons (how the L1 and the L2 is stored – see Chapter 4) and the influence of the L1 on the acquisition of L2. Qi therefore wanted to know what the language of thought was during text composition and translation, and he compared this to the language of thought during the subject's mathematical problem solving. Each of these processes was studied at less and more complex levels. His case study findings seem to suggest:

1. Some L1 was used as the language of thought in all tasks.
2. In the (more complex) translation task the participant used more and longer sequences of L1 as the language of thought – particularly to help search for more appropriate lexical items and sentence structures.
3. There was a positive correlation between L1 use and the demands of the task.
4. More sequences of L1 as the language of thought were recorded in the mathematical problem-solving task.
5. The participant was able to encode an idea quickly in L1 before developing it further in either L1 or L2.
6. L1/L2 switching enabled an initiated thought to continue to develop and

helped generate content which the participant sometimes felt less competent to produce when she used L2 only.

Thus Qi concluded that the L1 may be used by advanced learners as the language of thought because of a subconscious need to encode efficiently a non-linguistic thought in order to develop a thinking episode; the need to facilitate the development of a thought; a need to verify lexical choices; a need to avoid overloading the working memory (429). We can see that this recursive process of thinking ideas, formulating them in lexical form and then evaluating them back against the idea, is a complex one that puts great pressure on the working memory limitations discussed in Chapter 3.

Finally, on this theme, a study by Woodall (2002) provides a slightly different perspective on the above results. Using think-aloud protocols he analysed the language switching (when the students used their L1) of 14 intermediate and 14 advanced students writing a letter about personal information (a relatively easy task) and a discursive/persuasive essay (harder task). Woodall's sample was particularly interesting because it contained students writing in both cognate languages (English-Spanish) and non-cognate languages (English-Japanese). He found:

1. As might have been predicted, intermediate students switched much more than advanced students. More advanced students used the L1 as an organizing tool, whereas switching among some less advanced students was 'out of control'.
2. The difference between intermediate and advanced students was much more marked in the non-cognate group.
3. The difficulty of the task made no difference with the intermediate students of the non-cognate group. Language switching followed similar patterns. Non-cognate languages seem to make ordered switching less likely.
4. Task difficulty contributed significantly to the *duration* but not the *frequency* of language switches. The L1 was used for longer periods but less often.
5. Frequency of switches was more related to L2 proficiency whereas duration of switches was more related to task difficulty.

Woodall concluded that language switching is not a uniform phenomenon and has different purposes. It can have beneficial effects. However, to use the L1 effectively as a language of thought when writing may need teacher guidance, particularly in non-cognate languages. We should note that this study does not fully address the 'threshold' issue. Were the intermediate non-cognate students 'out of control' with their switching because even the easier task was simply too difficult for their proficiency level?

Another aspect of formulating which has been researched is the use of *restructuring* (not to be confused with the term as described in Chapter 3). Restructuring, as defined in a study by de Larios, Murphy and Manchon (1999), is 'the search for an alternative syntactic plan once the writer predicts, anticipates or realises that the original plan is not going to be satisfactory for a variety of linguistic, ideational or textual reasons' (1999: 16). As we have noted above, the process of matching mental propositions (ideas in the brain) with L2 text is a very complex one. If the writer's formulating process is inflexible, De Larios *et al.* argue, it bars the possibility of alternative plans and forms of expression. They therefore decided to investigate, in a first (exploratory) study, different forms of restructuring and what kinds of knowledge writers process when they restructure their L2 written production. The participants were five Spanish (L1) learners of English (L2) at a Spanish university. The participants' restructuring strategies were recorded using think-aloud protocols during discursive and narrative tasks. The researchers found that restructuring occurred at:

1. the ideational level (e.g. is what I am saying relevant or important?);
2. the textual level (e.g. does what I am saying connect with the previous sentence?);
3. lexical level (e.g. I can't retrieve the L2 word and therefore must find an alternative);
4. morpho-syntactic level (e.g. I must avoid using a subjunctive as this is difficult for me).

They also found that there were two basic objectives for this restructuring process. The first was to *improve* what they had in mind (or had already written). The second was to *compensate* for what they could not write. The researchers then went on to do a second study in which they compared students with different proficiency levels. They found:

1. There were no significant differences in the restructuring times between intermediate and advanced groups.[1]
2. The intermediate group spent a lot longer restructuring for 'language-related' difficulties and less for 'ideas-related' difficulties and the demands of linguistic processing seem 'to inhibit the formulation of syntactic alternatives both at the ideational and textual levels' (33).
3. More advanced writers are capable of restructuring their discourse while simultaneously constructing and retaining a global representation of the text.
4. The results suggest a possible 'threshold' as a necessary condition for writing ability to be fully deployed in the L2.

In the study by Macaro (2001a) already in part described, lower-intermediate learners were asked to report on the *formulating strategies* they used via a questionnaire and to articulate these strategies during think-aloud protocols. The following are the total number of strategies reported, articulated or observed in this study:

1. *Retrieving* individual words or phrases from long-term memory (i.e. making an effort to do so rather than just *resourcing*).
2. *Resourcing*: using a dictionary, textbook, teacher materials or previous work done as a resource in order to compose.
3. *Predicting*: for example, prior to looking up a word in the dictionary, trying to make mental connections so that the item will 'look or sound right' when you find it.
4. *Recombining*: constructing a meaningful sentence from two or more (retrieved) chunks for the new context (topic), or by simply substituting a noun/ adjective.
5. *Restructuring*[2]: constructing a meaningful (but not necessarily correct) chunk

by changing a morpheme from a previous chunk through analysis of form (e.g. *'je l'ai vu'* becomes *'il l'ai vu'*). This strategy is only possible if the chunk is beginning to be 'unpacked' (see Chapter 3).

6. *Generating via translation*: using the L1 to produce a phrase or sentence.
7. *Evaluating formulation cluster* (i.e. strategies 4, 5, 6) for effectiveness.
8. *Evaluating resources*: e.g. whether a dictionary phrase is more likely to lead to correct form as opposed to a *recombined*, *reformulated* or *generated* phrase.
9. *Compensating*: restructuring an intended phrase because it is unlikely to be generated correctly.
10. *Applying an explicit rule*: reminding oneself that some verbs in past perfect tense take a particular auxiliary. This strategy is used in conjunction with *generating via translation*.

The think-alouds suggested that the interaction of recombining, restructuring and generating strategies are central to the cognitive effort involved in the formulation process. At a metacognitive level these three strategies are then evaluated for their effectiveness in communicating efficiently the topic content. Of course the students in my study (the effective ones, at least) deployed this cluster of strategies recursively with their planning strategies (discussed above) and with monitoring and checking strategies (discussed below). Interestingly, the sample of students as a whole reported no particular preferences for how they went about the formulating process although as Table 9.2 shows, only using whole L2 sentences they knew, was not a favoured strategy. This is not surprising as this would limit them too much. However these results do demonstrate that questionnaires are not very accurate at eliciting strategies as compared to think-aloud. We should also note a fairly heavy reliance on the use of teacher materials. This was borne out by the think-alouds (where teacher materials were not provided) where they were very much 'all at sea' and some resorted to very frequent dictionary use.

Table 9.2   Strategies used in the planning and formulating process (English L1, French L2)

	Percentages of 'a lot like me and quite like me' combined
I think of a sentence in English and then, if I know the French for it, I will use it	65.6%
I use bits of language from the materials *the teacher has given me* and put them together so that they make sense	63.7%
I think of bits of language *I know* (e.g. short phrases) and try to put them together so that they make sense	61.1%
I think of a sentence and then translate	53.5%
I think of all the French sentences I know and only use those	19.1%

Initial implications

It looks as if, even at an advanced level, the target language cannot be used by learners exclusively in the planning and formulating stages of composition. The L1 is used in order to generate ideas and to evaluate the different strategies in the formulating process. The L1 seems to be a natural and frequent behaviour in a bilingual mind engaging in an L2 task and the L1 plays a positive role in almost all sub-categories of the field of composing (Qi 1998). It would seem to be the teacher's role, therefore, to maximize the beneficial aspects of the learners' L1 use and minimize the problems that it causes. It is pointless trying to pretend that the L1 is not present, the trick is to harness its potential. The hierarchical structure of strategies (cognitive strategy cluster with above it the evaluation strategy) needs to be modelled by teachers and practised by learners. As they progress, and their proficiency increases, the balance between recombining, restructuring and generating will shift. The development of more sophisticated and flexible formulas (Chapter 3) as a result of internalization of the rule system will mean that recombination of unanalysed chunks will decrease. Similarly, the way that learners turn to resources will change as they become more proficient and start to use more complex sentences. An awareness of these strategies and these developments in their learners will help teachers provide more formative feedback to their students.

The effects of dictionary use in written composition

A number of studies have looked at how learners use dictionaries in the writing process. Given that dictionaries cost so much money it is surprising that they haven't been researched more. Moreover, no consensus has been established as to what sorts of dictionaries should be used. I know of a few learners who steadfastly refuse to use a bilingual dictionary because they assert that 'you can't learn anything from them' and that they will only use a monolingual dictionary. In fact I can remember being told by my French teacher at school that I should use only a monolingual dictionary (and was provided with a threadbare 20-year-old hardback from the languages cupboard) because a bilingual dictionary would 'make my mind lazy'. Some learners have a bilingual dictionary constantly on their desks. Some authors (e.g. Ard 1982) propose that both a bilingual dictionary and a monolingual dictionary should be used as cross references.

Why should we be interested in this?

Well, that short introduction above has already thrown up a number of major research questions that we might want answered. Are dictionaries worth the money we spend on them? Are bigger dictionaries better than small dictionaries? What sorts of information should a dictionary contain? Do monolingual dictionaries improve your writing better than bilingual ones? How do learners at various stages use dictionaries to (a) learn and (b) accomplish tasks? In England, dictionaries have been withdrawn altogether from public MFL examinations at 16 on the grounds that candidates were relying too much on dictionaries during tasks and taking too long.

Should the constraints of exams dictate if and how we encourage learners to use dictionaries?

The research evidence

Christianson (1997) reminds us that the most consistently cited drawback of bilingual dictionaries is that they reinforce the belief in a one to one relationship at word level between the L1 and the L2. Moreover, although one has the gut feeling that there is an appropriate way to use a dictionary, few authors are willing or able to describe exactly what appropriate or skilful use is. Christianson also observes that 'one finds descriptions of various dictionary use strategies ... but without elaboration as to the types of learners or tasks for which they might be best suited' (25). He therefore conducted a study of 51 Japanese (L1) students of English (L2) in their first year of university. He asked them to underline every time they looked words up in a dictionary during in-class writing assignments. He then conducted interviews based on going over their assignments with the students and attempting to recall why errors occurred, what the thought processes were and what the 'look up' strategy was. He then monitored how effective it was. His findings were:

1. Efficient dictionary use did not necessarily correlate with overall FL ability or grades – able writers did not necessarily come up with the right words or phrase.
2. Only a tiny fraction of words were looked up in a dictionary and yet, of those, *42% were used incorrectly*.
3. Bilingual dictionaries do not appear to 'provoke errors'. Even if some dictionaries provoke errors it appears that they did not do so, often enough, as to add significantly to the total error count.
4. Some dictionaries are better than others but the sophistication of the user is far more important than the quality of the dictionary.
5. Reading the 'example sentences' provided by the dictionary very likely helps with committing fewer mistakes.

The assertion that higher achievers and lower achievers were no different in their success rate at dictionary use is problematic. Perhaps higher-achieving students were simply writing different and much more complex stuff, they were being more adventurous in their planning. Moreover, we are not told what combinations of strategies they were using. For example they may have been trying to generate more sentences than the lower-achieving learners thus causing more dictionary-related problems. As we shall see later (and have seen in other chapters) one must not isolate strategies in research, it is in their combination that they are effective. Interestingly, Christianson provides the case study of a student who committed few dictionary errors. This student read the example sentences provided; thought about the influence of L1 on the choice of whether to use a noun or verb – in other words he indeed used a combination of strategies. Similarly a student who committed few dictionary errors (but with low overall word count) did not use the L1-L2 dictionary but rather thought of the L2 word and then proceeded to check it in the dictionary. This juxtaposition of two approaches would tend to support the suggestion that we have to look at the whole picture (i.e. match process with output) before we can begin to make assertions about effective dictionary use.

Christianson's study provides some very useful information about directions that research could take. For example he concludes that skilful dictionary use could help to avoid errors but to avoid all errors would probably take up too much time. Future research could therefore explore what the metacognitive strategies are that help a student evaluate content, length of output, task requirements and dictionary use. In the study quoted earlier (Macaro 2001a) we came to the conclusion that (at that level and against that task type) looking up one word in ten seemed to be about appropriate, whereas one word in five (or even less) seemed excessive and clearly suggested an inability to bring other formulating strategies into play. However, this was only a subjective reaction to the data and further research would be useful.

A number of other studies have recently been delving into dictionary use by learners. Many of these are in reaction to the introduction of dictionary use in England in national exams and then their withdrawal (see above). For example there is a series of articles by Bishop (1998, 2000a, 2000b). In his first study Bishop explored the uses to which bilingual dictionaries were being put because, despite the amusing anecdotes, very little thought or effort had been put into 'why learners of all ages, but particularly the young, seemed unable to make successful use of this valuable resource' (1998: 3). Using a two-group sample (English (L1), French (L2)) of distance-learning university adult students and year-12 comprehensive-school students, he administered a questionnaire to ask various questions about dictionary use. His findings suggested:

1. Year-12 students were less familiar with the conventions of a dictionary (e.g. symbols).
2. The main uses of a dictionary were for checking gender, spelling and meaning.
3. All students tended to reach for a dictionary when they didn't know an L2 equivalent rather than (a) think of a synonym or (b) think of different meanings that the word may have in different contexts (example given: 'plastered').
4. Apart from 1. there were not, surprisingly, huge differences in dictionary use between the two groups.

The strategy in point 3 above sometimes led to problems with composition, a finding echoed in Hurman (1998) who found that a large majority of exam candidates (GCSE) in using dictionaries showed widespread ignorance of parts of speech 'resulting in nonsensical transpositions of English into French'.

Next, Bishop wanted to assess university students' reactions to being allowed to use dictionaries in examinations (Bishop 2000a). Again using questionnaires Bishop surveyed the views of distance-learning French (L2) adult learners. He found:

1. Overwhelmingly the response to (bilingual?) dictionaries in exams was a positive one.
2. Students did not feel this would lead to a reduction in their memorization effort.
3. Given a free choice students would generally prefer to take in to the examination room a bilingual dictionary.

4. Over 30% used the dictionary more than five times in the writing test for the purposes of composition.
5. Only a small percentage used the grammar section in their dictionaries.

Finally, Bishop wrote an article (Bishop 2000b) in which he catalogued the advice he would give language students on the basis of his experiences and research. The training package in dictionary use would then be evaluated to see if the following aspects had benefited from the package:

1. Parts of speech
2. Enriched language
3. Specialist vocabulary
4. Understanding of grammar
5. Phonetics and pronunciation
6. Register
7. The ability to cross check for meaning
8. Accuracy

Given the quality of Bishop's previous work, we should look forward to reading the results of this intervention.

Other researchers who have looked at dictionary use are Barnes, Hunt and Powell (1999) who investigated beliefs about the use of dictionaries in GCSE examinations and found that teachers on the whole were positive about their introduction although they (the authors) argue that the issue has not been sufficiently researched. A similar study was conducted by Asher, Chambers and Hall (1999) who found that teachers had a wide range of policy and practice with regard to dictionary use, some being essentially reactive strategies to the top-down introduction of a new initiative, and that it was the exams that were providing a backwash effect on dictionary use rather than a principled belief in their value as a learning tool. Other researchers (e.g. Tall and Hurman 2000) found that there was a discrepancy between what the learners wanted and what their teachers were providing. For example 16-year-old candidates in national writing exams in England, claimed that the dictionary made them feel more confident and that they used the dictionary as a primary resource. Yet their teachers had advised them to use a dictionary only as 'a back up' and in the case of 40% of respondents had not provided training in the use of the dictionary.

The effect of feedback on students' writing

We will now turn to the very important issue of teacher beliefs, reactions and feedback strategies on receiving a piece of written work from a language student. There is extensive research on this and it is probably the area which has generated the most heated debate. We will also look briefly at peer feedback.

Why should we be interested in this?

First of all feedback is to a teacher as swimming is to a fish. We all do it and we all do it, for the most part, automatically. We have discussed feedback already in Chapter 3 and in the chapter on speaking and noted the traditional and almost indelible IRF sequence. In a sense, traditional L2 writing is an extended IRF sequence. The teacher initiates via a task, the learner provides his/her response in writing, the teacher provides feedback. But how do we know that the learner benefits from the feedback? And what sort of feedback does the learner benefit from most? To what extent is feedback a motivating factor in language learning?

The research evidence

Firstly, we should set the scene by reporting that there has been a comprehensive study (Black and Wiliam 1998) of teacher feedback in England (not in the field of language learning), which strongly suggests that giving grades to students (summative assessment) acts as a deterrent to them thinking about their progress, their weaknesses and their mistakes. Much better, these researchers claim, is the practice of giving formative feedback through a verbalized evaluation, particularly if that evaluation includes strategies for improvement. This general finding is echoed in a study by Kreizman (1984) who found that when students received their papers back their main interest was in the grades they had been given and only gave the teacher's comments a cursory glance.

An early study into the effects of teacher feedback in L2 writing was carried out by Semke (1982). She divided her sample of 141 university students of German (English L1), into four different groups:

> Group 1 received feedback on content, no feedback on errors
> Group 2 had their errors corrected
> Group 3 received feedback on content and had their errors corrected
> Group 4 had their errors marked with a code and were asked to make corrections

She found that there were no significant differences between the groups in terms of accuracy. Group 1, however, wrote significantly longer essays, an important finding given that they did not increase their inaccuracy as a result. We do not know how long the experimentation period went on for nor how many pieces of writing the analysis is based on.

A similar study was carried out by Robb, Ross and Shortreed (1986) where 134 Japanese university students of English (L2) were divided into four groups:

> Group 1 received explicit correction (i.e. the correct form)
> Group 2 received a code as to the type of error they had made
> Group 3 received indication that an error was there but no kind of explanation
> Group 4 received a tally in the margin of the number of errors in a line but no other information

All students were asked to revise their written work. Using quite a complex system of error analysis, the researchers found only negligible differences between the groups and concluded that improvement on the course was independent of type of feedback.

On this basis they argued that teacher's time might be more profitably spent in responding to other aspects of students' writing.

Cohen (1987) claims that when the written work is returned embellished by teacher corrections, the students groan, put it away and hope that somehow they will get fewer red marks next time. Cohen's survey of 217 university students (on a range of language courses) shows that the majority of teachers' comments were connected with grammar inaccuracy and that there was a very low incidence of comments expressed in whole sentences. Hence, he argues, students often do not understand the teacher's feedback or what it relates to and they more often than not make a mental note of the comments rather than acting upon them through some kind of revision or re-drafting. Most importantly, the (self-rated) 'poorer learners were also less likely to read through the paper and attend to the corrections'. This issue of the variables in response to teacher feedback will be the subject of our discussion on learner strategies below. The results of Cohen's (1990) study with Marilda Cavalcanti showed a noticeable lack of fit between what the teacher felt he/she was providing feedback on and what the learners either wanted or perceived was happening. Thus teacher feedback appeared to have a more limited impact on the learners than teachers would desire.

Kepner (1991) also researched the impact of different kinds of feedback on writing on 60 intermediate-level students of Spanish (English L1). The sample was divided into two groups, the first received *message-related feedback* (comments in L2 on regular journal entries including summarizing, reader reaction, quality of communication, suggestions for extending or improving on the topic). The second group received *error corrections* (all sentence-level errors corrected and reasons for corrections provided via a brief rule or note). The group was also divided into two by (L1) high-verbal ability and low-verbal ability. The trial lasted one semester. She analysed the higher-level proposition (ideas content) count and all incidences of errors of grammar and vocabulary. She found:

1. Students who received the message-related comments produced significantly greater number of higher-level propositions.
2. There were no significant differences in terms of number of errors produced.
3. The high-verbal-ability students produced a greater number of higher-level propositions than low-verbal-ability students.

Porte (1997) looked at the cause or causes of why some students performed badly in L2 writing. He argued that in studies which compare higher and lower achieving students 'little information tends to be provided, or thought necessary, about the language learning background, motivation, or reasons for failure of "poor" students' (62) and that the danger in this may lie in what the outcomes of such comparison may blind us to, with regard to both the nature of the poor learner's strategies and the motivation for much of these learners' behaviours. If we assume that teachers' strategies vary, the possibility exists that students' revision strategies may also be seen to be a response to teachers' strategies as perceived by the students. Porte therefore investigated 71 underachievers at writing via various writing proficiency tests and via interviews. He found:

1. The majority of participants regarded revision as important but only because it would bring about an improvement of the final grade awarded to the text (rather than, say, to their learning in general or future writing in particular).
2. They regarded revision as an activity which affects the surface aspect of text only. In other words they conceived of revision as a proofreading exercise.
3. The focus of revision was very much at the word level.
4. There was also evidence that some underachievers regarded overt signs of their revision as producing a negative effect upon the teacher and, more importantly, the grade. Yet few participants recalled any explicit instruction in revision. Rather, they sometimes adopted the above revision behaviour as a result of their interpretation of what the teacher wanted, implicitly, from the feedback they got.

Perhaps as a result of this discomfort with the meagre benefits of teacher feedback, a number of researchers have compared teacher feedback with peer feedback. We have already glanced at the study by Tsui and Ng (2000) in the context of writing-process approaches to teaching. We will now examine their findings with regard to benefit derived from peer feedback. Whilst recognizing that peer comments may have their disadvantages (peers give advice that does not necessarily facilitate learning; writers have difficulty deciding whether their peer's comments are valid), they nevertheless argue that peer feedback is pitched more at the learners' level of interest. Using questionnaires and interviews with a sample of 27 Hong Kong students of English (L2) in years 12 and 13, the practitioner/researchers found their results were very mixed with regard to the writers' revision strategies:

1. Some incorporated high percentages of both teacher and peer comments.
2. Some incorporated more teacher comments than peer comments.
3. Some incorporated low percentages of peer comments.

Of course these mixed results may be due to different attitudes to the importance placed on the teacher's role and that peers, as 'reviewers', are likely to be highly variable whereas the teacher, in theory at least, is invariable. Nevertheless Tsui and Ng conclude that peer review/comments had the following functions:

1. It enhanced a sense of audience. Students perceived the teacher and peers differently as readers.
2. Reading peers' writings raised the linguistic awareness of the 'reviewers'. The students expressed an inability to spot their own weaknesses and peer comments helped them notice the problems.
3. It encouraged collaborative learning. In peer sessions the students had the opportunity to clarify their intended meanings to the reader (a form of back-translation), and to negotiate a way of conveying the intended meaning more effectively.
4. It fostered ownership of text. Peer comments were not seen as authoritative. Students felt that they had autonomy over their own text and could make their own decisions on whether they should take the comments on board or not.

Piasecki (1998) compared the reactions of 112 third-year (year 9) students of Spanish (English L2) to both peer and teacher feedback over eight weeks. No significant gains were made by either group. However, eight weeks would seem to be a very short time to demonstrate real gains by either method and, in any case, no overall measurement of the writing quality is given in this study.

Paulus (1999) also compared the effect of peer and teacher writing, this time on 11 undergraduate students of English (L2). This researcher observed the strategies used by the students as they revised an essay on which comments had been made by fellow students. The results were similar to Tsui and Ng. The peer review did bring about revisions but not as much as via the teacher's feedback. Moreover, not all revisions resulted in improved essays.

Initial implications

It doesn't look as if teacher feedback is very effective in bringing about improvement in language accuracy. Moreover, none of the different types of feedback appear to be much more effective than any other. These results are somewhat dispiriting given the amount of effort that teachers put into providing feedback to written work. Yet the evidence does seem sufficiently strong to question the effort expended. Truscott (1996, 1999) takes a different stance. He argues that it can be positively harmful to learners. There is probably less evidence of this than there is of its ineffectiveness.

Feedback on content seems to bring about a loosening up of the writing process and peer feedback might contribute to this in a constructive way as long as it is carefully managed. We should bear in mind that feedback of any kind is clearly not enough. It has to be combined with training students in how to participate in peer response situations and peers have to be given some training in how to provide feedback. Feedback, in other words, has to be combined with strategy training on how to handle feedback.

The effect of strategy use on writing proficiency and the impact of strategy-training programmes

Although there has been considerable discussion and research on learner strategies in general, very little of it has focused on the strategies that learners use in writing. As we have seen in previous chapters, learner strategies are those actions, operating below the level of skills and processes, that learners use in order to learn a second language or to achieve a task in a second language.

Why should we be interested in this?

The fact that teacher feedback on written accuracy doesn't appear to be very effective should not deter us from exploring ways in which we can reduce written error. There are two reasons for this. Firstly, it is pie in the sky to think that, in examinations, accuracy will not continue to be one of the criteria for assessment. Secondly (at least for the foreseeable future), students will expect to have a notion of whether their writing is improving from an accuracy point of view. It would also be useful to know to what extent learners vary in the writing strategies that they use. Do higher-achieving writers use different strategies? Are there groups of people who vary from other groups of people? Can (some) learners be trained to use strategies more effectively thereby making them more responsible for their own learning? Is self-correction, after strategy training, more effective than teacher feedback in reducing error?

The research evidence

Learners' use of writing strategies varies significantly and there appears to be, as in other skills, a correlation between effective strategy use and success at writing. For example Sasaki and Hirose (1996) report that the good writers in their study paid more attention to overall organization of their writing. Graham (1997) reports that 'less effective' writers (at upper-intermediate level) worried too much about getting it right thus impeding the writing process; 'more effective' writers would leave a linguistic problem and come back to it later; more effective writers checked for spelling and grammar *after* the main ideas had been formulated; less effective writers were inconsistent in their monitoring. On the other hand, with lower-intermediate (14-15-year-old) writers Macaro (2001a) found that the more (self-rated) effective writers were those that monitored and checked their work *as they composed*. These students were much more likely to:

1. check the spelling of words;
2. check the word order;
3. check the endings of words;
4. check that it made sense (e.g. by back-translation);
5. read the writing out loud to see if it sounded right;
6. look for mistakes they made all the time.

Of course these learners were writing much shorter compositions than were their older and/or more advanced counterparts and it may well be that after a certain threshold of writing proficiency has been reached the combinations of revision strategies needs to be very different.

There have been very few intervention studies in writing strategies. They are, nevertheless, useful to consider here. Aziz (1995) compared the effect on overall writing performance and grammatical agreement (French L2) of two different sorts of writing strategy training. She divided a group of 72 university students (English L1) into two groups. The first group received strategy training only at the cognitive level. They were trained to use a number of strategies when note-taking from a dictated (spoken) source, to then reconstruct this material into a composition and to check for error. The second group received the same training as the first group but in addition received training in metacognitive strategies, that is, in self-monitoring and self-evaluation. In fact the second group were encouraged to 'pair' their cognitive and metacognitive strategies. In order to train learners to deploy self-monitoring and self-evaluations the researcher devised a number of advice and check lists which reminded the students to monitor and to evaluate their composing processes. We should remind ourselves of the definition given of metacognitive strategies:

> individuals' knowledge, constant awareness, and conscious attempts to take control of their cognitive activities; to devise ways of overcoming obstacles and to plan and evaluate their language learning. (Aziz 1995)

Aziz used pre-test and post-test. She found:

1. On average the overall writing quality on the composition did not improve as a result of the cognitive training alone.
2. The group that received cognitive-strategy training only, did improve on grammatical agreement.
3. Those students who received paired cognitive and metacognitive strategy training did significantly better on both overall writing quality and grammatical agreement.

Conti (2001) devised a one-year programme of writing-strategy training for 10 university students of Italian (L2, mixed L1s) ranging from lower to upper intermediate. Before starting the programme he took samples of their writing, did some think-aloud protocols and gave them questionnaires with respect to their strategy use. As part of the programme of strategy training he used a number of materials in order to 'scaffold' the learners' strategy use as follows:

1. A correction sheet which encouraged them to deal with mistakes that had been identified by the teacher by thinking of what might be the correct model, the possible causes for it, what action they were going to take to avoid a recurrence of the error, and by trying to provide examples of what the grammatical rule might be.
2. An error-targeting check list which encouraged them to target errors when editing the next essay and to evaluate and document the strategy that helped them to spot the mistake(s).
3. An editing strategies reminder which was a list of revision strategies that the students could use when writing.

At the end of the training programme the students made gains, when compared to another very similar group of students who had not received strategy training, in that they significantly reduced their number of errors (both lexical and grammatical) without prejudicing or reducing the quality of the content of their writing. The data showed that they did this largely by increasing the monitoring of their writing for familiar errors and that overall the number of errors that they self-corrected increased. Conti's students had been trained to handle the teacher's feedback more effectively.

In the Macaro (2001a) study, a similar set of 'scaffolding' techniques were used. The students were given:

1. a 'tenses sheet' designed to encourage them to ask themselves the question of how many verbs a particular tense carried (French L2) every time they composed a sentence;

2. a noun-adjective agreement sheet designed to trigger a *monitor* of what they had written;
3. a back-translation symbol designed to trigger a 'back-translation' of a phrase or sentence they had written in order to see if it made sense.

Again, the students in the experimental group appeared to make significant gains over the comparison group after the period of strategy training.

Similar to scaffolding sheets is strategy training via *mnemonic strategies*. A US study (Klohs 1994) involving 72 secondary students of French (English L1) aged 15-17, focused on mnemonic strategies as a means of improving writing. The students were randomly assigned to a treatment group and a control group. The treatment period lasted four and a half weeks. A mnemonic strategy requires the learner to recognize a production problem when writing; to call on a particular mnemonic device, previously taught, designed to match the writing problem; to organize the information in a process of synthesis leading to a comprehensible end-product; to assess the end product for comprehensibility and accuracy (Klohs 1994: 6). Four mnemonic strategies were taught:

1. *Gesture*. For example, students were trained to use or recall a hand gesture for the difference based on continuous/non-continuous action between the French *imparfait* and the *passé composé* (note however the criticism made of this approach in Chapter 3).
2. *Musical*. For example, putting a verb paradigm to music.
3. *Rhythm*. For example as in a rap.
4. *Acronym*. For example, *situé* which represents the only five letters with which French past participles can end.

Both the treatment group and the control groups were pre- and post-tested with a grammar test and a writing task focusing on the areas covered. Klohs found that the treatment group made significant gains over the control group both in the grammar test and the writing task. The results are encouraging but one has to ask whether the treatment group improved in more holistic terms rather than in the narrow focus of the study.

Walker (2001) carried out a study with students at the university of Sheffield (UK) into the role of learner strategies in promoting language acquisition with pairs of students learning each other's languages (tandem partnerships). Through a series of case studies she describes how learning was enhanced and partners were able 'to perform beyond their competence' (110). Strategies used ranged from mutual goal setting to error correction. In other words the partner appeared to operate successfully as a substitute teacher with respect to strategy awareness raising and training.

Finally we will look at a more unusual approach attempted by Creswell (2000). The rationale for his intervention was that in normal approaches to writing students get 'blocked' when their lack of linguistic resources leads them to abandon or simplify the ideas they would like to formulate. With teacher-initiated feedback the teacher has no means of knowing what problems the student is having nor which hypotheses about the L2 the writer is trying to test through his/her writing. He therefore developed a system of getting the students to write *marginal annotations*. In other words students wrote the teacher a message in the margins of the first draft of a composition about the problems they were experiencing with their compositions, as they evolved, and asking for feedback. The teacher responded to these annotations in writing. He found that students produced both higher-order annotations (content level; paragraph level; cohesion questions) and lower-level annotations/questions (Can I say this? Is it this or this? Do I need a 'X' here?). Students reacted favourably to the process in that it helped them extend themselves in their writing by confronting their 'formulation' problems. According to Creswell the 'training was effective in creating a context in which students were able to work responsibly'. Although this is an interesting approach to metacognitive strategy training and merits further research, the study itself was somewhat limited by the very small sample size (seven adult learners), the length of the intervention and the absence of any sort of comparison group.

Initial implications

It looks as if there is a connection between strategy use and effective writing although this connection may be a lot more complex than the above studies would suggest. Strategy training appears to be effective, particularly if the focus is on metacognitive strategies. The research field at this stage, however, is quite limited. Nevertheless, if these limited results are replicated in the future, we may be able to resolve the content versus accuracy dichotomy. In other words, by training students to think more deeply about teacher feedback on accuracy, a shift will occur in the minds of the learner from accuracy to development of an internalized rule system. They will worry less about producing a correct piece of work next time they are asked to write and concern themselves more with taking responsibility for making progress with their language learning with respect to being able to express themselves more and more in target-like forms.

The impact of computers on writing in a L2

An obvious problem with research on the effectiveness of computers as aids to language learning is that, with the rapid advances in hardware and software, it becomes so quickly out of date. For example, we could take a study like that of Herrmann (1990) in which a comparison was made of the gains in writing proficiency between a group of students who used software in order to practise language drills and a group of students who worked collaboratively to produce a newspaper. Neither group made any significant gains in their writing proficiency as a result of the contact with the electronic medium. Firstly we could object that there was no pen and paper control group to compare the results with anyway. Secondly, what relevance could these findings possibly have to practitioners in the early years of the twenty-first century with all the sophistication of graphics and sound (for drill practice) not to mention 'Publisher' and access to the Internet (for the purposes of creating a newspaper in the L2)?

So why should we be interested in this?

Well, one reason is that schools and higher-education institutions are investing an enormous amount of money into computers and it would be quite useful to say to the taxpayer that there is an educational return on his or her investment. The other reason is that language teachers and researchers would appear to have had very little say in the development of software but are, as usual, reacting to what the market is producing for them. If we knew what worked for language learners we could put pressure on L2 software writers to produce CALL (Computer aided language learning) materials that we could have confidence in. Lastly, we need to break away from the mindset that, just because learners appear to be working contentedly at the computer, they are necessarily benefiting from the endeavour in terms of their language learning.

The research evidence

Unfortunately the evidence in favour of CALL as a means of improving writing proficiency is hard to come by. McGuire's (1997) study of students using a particular interactive software[3] showed no significant gains in their writing proficiency. Leh's (1997) study of extensive e-mailing did not bring about a significant difference in writing performance. Florez-Estrada (1995) compared interactive writing (i.e. interacting with the teacher) via computer with traditional writing. The computer group outperformed the other group on appropriate use of key grammar points and on depth and breadth of content. However, the computer group did three times as much writing – perhaps as a result of being motivated – than the other group. Whilst this might be a positive result in some ways, where did the additional time come from and at the expense of what other language skills?

An interesting avenue has been explored by Truscott and Morley (2001). They were interested to see if aspects of cross-cultural learning could be enhanced via computer mediated communication (CMC) in Tandem-learning (reciprocal language learning between two different native speakers) situations. Their rationale was that they detected a need among university students to develop cross-cultural competence more effectively. They felt that 'rather than merely learning about another culture students need to develop the ability to recognise and critically evaluate difference and otherness from an informed, objective and sensitive point of view'(18). Moreover, they bemoaned the fact that attendance at face-to-face (Tandem) meetings had proved difficult (both from a social-interactive viewpoint and a timetabling viewpoint). They therefore decided to experiment with an on-line forum.

Using a virtual environment called *Extended Learning Environment Network* (ELEN) they encouraged students to talk about 'critical incidents' related to relationships between different cultural groups. They found:

1. Students began to move away from the blanket condemnation of the target culture towards an acceptance that the host (UK) culture is like any other in having both positive and negative features.
2. Students seemed to invest more of their own emotions in the on-line seminars than in the face-to-face.

3. Students' written evaluations were positive.
4. Those who were lacking confidence either generally or in the L2 were not placed at a disadvantage.
5. The interaction became more personalized (inner feelings were shared).
6. The on-line seminar was more 'democratic' – less teacher controlled – than the face-to-face.
7. It gave the students the opportunity to practise a style of discourse which was not normally open to them (i.e. more informal yet a weighty topic).

No report is given as to whether the students improved in their L2 writing proficiency. However, this was not one of the research questions.

Electronic mail had been used in an earlier investigation by Trenchs (1996) using three studies. The participants were three pupils in sixth grade in New York. She collected a number of e-mail exchanges between herself (the teacher) and the pupils. She also videotaped the pupils whilst they used the computer for e-mailing and she interviewed them after the videotaped sessions. She found that e-mail activity gave students freedom to apply personal writing styles and explore language in different ways. However, for some it was too challenging because they needed more structure. Trenchs concludes that a balance needs to be struck between initial teacher guidance and subsequent freedom.

Spelman Miller (2000) studied advanced university undergraduate writers as they wrote two different tasks at the computer by using a special piece of software which recorded their key strokes (e.g. deletions, scrolling) and their pauses. This technique was, in part, in response to the problems associated with think-aloud protocols. Spelman Miller found that although the two tasks should have produced different writing behaviours because of their different cognitive demands, in fact there was little difference. She concludes that this sort of information could be very useful in learner-tutor discussions about their writing sessions and also in learner-learner cooperative writing sessions.

Initial implications

It looks as if computer-assisted language learning has not produced conclusive evidence that it 'assists language learning'. Certainly there is little evidence that it has advantages over other forms of teaching. Very few studies suggest that it directly enhances writing skills or improves knowledge of the grammar system of the target language. But perhaps we have been asking the wrong research questions. For example, there is evidence that it acts as a motivating force in language learning, as we have seen in Chapter 5. Within the domain of writing, CMC offers a protected environment which may be conducive to furthering writing skills especially if the objectives of the activities are directly linked to communication rather than accuracy, and to resolving a shared problem rather than enhancing the mental lexicon or the internalized rule system.

Conclusions

We began this section by quoting from Melinda Reichelt's review of writing studies where she claimed there is no consensus on any of the issues and that research has failed to provide an evidence base for practice to consider. Taken as separate issues, it is true that the powerful research evidence is missing. However, this fragmented picture of research begins to come together in answering an overarching question. That question might be formulated thus:

'What classroom practices are *not* beneficial to writing in particular and language learning in general?'

The conclusive research evidence is that there are *virtually none* which are *not* beneficial. Most individual practices fit comfortably in an eclectic view of communicative writing. The issue is the overall focus and, as a consequence, the order in which practices and activities might be offered to students.

It is clear that writers should not allow the content of their writing to be dictated by the potential inaccuracy (or accuracy) of their written product. In order to do this they and their teachers have to focus on the process of their writing: their planning, formulating, monitoring and checking. However, because composing, unlike speaking, is a recursive, slow, less-interactive and embedded endeavour, the processes within it are highly complex. Both teachers and learners (and future researchers) need to focus their efforts on the writer as he/she is writing rather than the finished product. The finished product gives the false appearance of a linear process, one that does not get us to the heart of the problem. All the false starts and dead ends and deletions of text production cannot be observed from analysis of the written product alone (Spelman Miller 2000).

Feedback from the teacher, therefore, should focus on the difficulties (and successes) that learners are experiencing as they write. Evaluation (frequently) should not be about what final product they achieve but their relative success at overcoming problems. On the other hand, feedback on accuracy should not be excluded provided that (a) the learner also gets feedback on whether the message was understood and whether the content was appropriately structured, (b) the learner is actively involved in the feedback on accuracy, (c) that feedback on the level of content is linked and compared to the level of accuracy. Strategy training would appear to be crucial in involving the learners in this. Metacognition is the key. Some learners need to become much more aware of themselves as language learners, thinking about what they know, standing back and reflecting, taking control and seeking advice.

Simply providing the correct models of the language does not appear to encourage the cognitive challenge that results in the enlargement and flexibility in the mental models that learners of the L2 need to develop. Although the evidence for this, taken on its own, is inconclusive, combined with factors above and below it becomes very strong. Further research must involve a more long-term longitudinal study which compares exploratory writing versus correct model manipulation and should do so at different ages and different proficiency levels.

For the vast majority of writers, the bilingual dictionary is perceived as a useful resource. Used effectively, research seems to tell us, it contributes to success in writing. In principle, dictionaries ought to be allowed in exams. To ban them is to penalize good dictionary users. However, students are not sufficiently trained to use dictionaries effectively. Perhaps this is because we do not yet have the research evidence upon which to base that training. Further research should trace dictionary-use practices with successful writing outcomes. However, it will have to take into account certain variables including task-type, language proficiency and the concept of language threshold.

Although (all other things being equal) descriptive writing is easier than narrative and discursive writing, if it is the exclusive diet of beginners and lower intermediates, it may be holding them back in their language learning by not developing aspects of the rule system, such as verbs and tenses. Narrative writing should certainly be introduced earlier in the FL curriculum in England. Further questions for research to answer are: what learning processes do task prompts which require reading before writing activate as opposed to task-prompts that require self-generated language? Given our above overarching finding, both must contribute to progression. The question still to be answered is: what should the balance of the diet be?

Self-generated language will always involve some element of translation from L1 no matter how advanced the L2 writer. In addition, even advanced L2 writers use their first language to assist the transition from an idea to the written phrase. Teachers should therefore provide balanced advice and assistance about over-reliance on word-for-word translation and re-combining language that the writer already feels he/she 'knows' in L2. Further research is needed into valid individual differences in learners in the formulating process and into the tensions between re-combining, restructuring and L1-L2 translation at different levels of proficiency. The research evidence suggests that the part that strategy training has to play in these writing processes is increasing but we need further evidence of long-term gains as well as more holistic language-proficiency gains.

Finally, computers cannot yet replace the language teacher. The composition processes are so complex that there is still a very important role for the teacher in helping learners to express themselves in written form. However, it may be that computers have a more indirect influence and benefit on writing skills.

Notes

1. However they don't state whether the advanced learners produced better work.
2. In Macaro (2001a), I called this strategy reformulation but I now think restructuring is less confusing and more appropriate in the light of discussions in Chapter 3.
3. Mundo Hispano – see Reichelt (2001).

Chapter 10

Conclusions

In Chapters 1 and 2, I started off with a gripe. I complained that the EFL market dominated the research scene in second-language learning and that this was somehow disassociated from the learning of other foreign languages. I bemoaned the fact that the North American context appeared to be the primary research arena to the neglect of other contexts such as Europe, and particularly Britain. I complained about the fact that, at first glance, the subjects or participants of research were overwhelmingly university students or other adults rather than young beginners or adolescents. Were these complaints justified? For the most part, they were. The studies reviewed throughout the book do indeed feature English as the predominant language. If they are not studying English, research subjects are very often first-year university students in North America. It has to be said, however, that some journals, for example *The Modern Language Journal*, appear recently to have been making valiant efforts to redress the imbalance, particularly with regard to the language being studied. Moreover, it is hardly surprising that researchers are investigating first-year university students since the former are usually university teachers wanting to know how to improve the performance of the latter.

There is, nevertheless, a shameful lack of research at the young learner, adolescent, beginner or lower-intermediate levels. It is almost as if students with a second-language vocabulary in the hundreds rather than in the thousands, students still using set phrases rather than complex sentences, students who struggle with reading postcards rather than texts about engineering, are just not worth bothering with. Yet we know that attitudes to foreign-language learning are formed early and that poor attitudes to foreign-language learning go hand in hand with poor attitudes to foreigners. We urgently need a reorientation of the research focus. It is unlikely that this reorientation will come from those who teach languages to university students. Why should they? This new research impetus, it seems to me, can only come from those operating in departments of education working in collaboration with language teachers in the primary and secondary sector.

There are also problems with the research effort as a whole. Lack of overall coherence, in terms of which topics need researching, which problems need answering and which research designs might best answer those problems, is a feature of the international second-language-acquisition scene.

There is also a distinct lack of clarity of nomenclature. Processes, skills, sub-skills, strategies are all used quite often without sufficient definition in the literature. This is because the first wave of research on learner strategies has not made the necessary links with psycholinguistics, despite claims to the contrary. Concepts such as proficiency, language ability, and aptitude are also not sufficiently discrete. This lack of precision is, in part, the consequence of the different contexts authors are working in. However, I believe it is also the consequence of lack of conceptualization of what it is to learn a language over time. Thus in the literature the term 'advanced learner' can sometimes mean someone who is more proficient in the language than someone else, sometimes it can mean someone who is in a class which has studied the language longer than another class. The term 'successful learner' is not always, as I would conceptualize it, one which denotes a student who is identified as accessing or producing the L2 more effectively than other learners without having had any significant additional instruction in the language – in other words someone who achieves greater competence and performance all other things being equal. Indeed, sometimes the concept of 'experienced learner', which I take as meaning someone who may be on his/her second or even third foreign language, is used for 'high-achieving learner' or 'skilled bilingual'. This causes problems. A number of studies investigate, for example, use of a particular language-learning behaviour and attribute one particular language behaviour to students with different *proficiencies* attempting the same tasks. Clearly this cannot be a valid comparison. My behaviour as a language learner at intermediate level against a highly difficult task cannot be compared (except in a very superficial and unimportant sense) with a highly proficient learner's behaviour with the same task. I may still be a better language learner than the highly proficient student. This lack of clarity is not particularly helpful in, for example, making comparisons in relation to strategy deployment where what is clearly needed is a fairly homogeneous group of students with similar learning histories and similar proficiency levels and to see *if then* effective strategy deployment makes a difference with skills such as reading and writing.

The problems identified by teachers in the survey in Chapter 1 with regard to access to research and comprehensibility of the research have also been justified. Although journals are readily available in major university libraries they are not for the most part *accessible* for practitioners with little spare time. Most require a huge investment in terms of slowly getting to grips with the metalanguage and many rely on highly sophisticated statistical analyses way beyond the reach of most teachers because of the amount of previous study that statistics require. Whether so much emphasis on quantitative methods is justified, I'm not sure. Certainly with large samples and taking into account a range of studies, one begins to get an overall picture of trends. With some quantitative evidence we even approach a stage where we can see cause and effect in action. However, I feel that in doing so we sometimes miss the obvious. Triangulation via qualitative methods, even in those studies where cause and effect begin to emerge, does help the reader to reach into the reality of the evidence, to see ultimately we are talking about human beings. Having said this, in England there has been a distinct lack of secure, rigorous and generalizable studies of foreign-language learners and, indeed, a lack of quantitative research.

Whilst waiting for this major shift in research endeavour, those who are involved with the teaching of younger and less advanced learners will just have to make do with what there is already. They will need to connect with and adapt research with a very different focus and in very different contexts. This is what this book has tried to do. So, has it been possible to make links between research in EFL and research in MFL, between adults and adolescents, between Birmingham, England and Birmingham, Alabama? I feel that it has. Well I would say that, wouldn't I? – I have to justify the book. But if we start with the premise that learning English as a foreign language is not inherently different from learning other foreign languages, then the links are possible. If we accept that people's brains aren't that different, or at least they aren't made different by the classroom their hosts are sitting in, then the underlying themes of the research do straddle the contexts, the problems are often the same and researchers and practitioners at different age levels can begin to talk to one another. We need to peer through the swirling mists of contexts and institutions and get to the essence of learning a second language.

So, what are the overall findings of the review itself. Firstly, there is the issue of eclecticism versus highly delineated methods of teaching. The message from the evidence is that it is highly dangerous for both teachers and policy makers to impose restricted practices in the classroom. Research findings give us a vision of learners chafing against the restrictions imposed upon them by syllabuses, national policies and classroom practices based on unfounded orthodoxies. Where the consensus is less secure is in the balance between different types of teaching practices and learning behaviours. In general, however, we should be asking 'What I have I left out of my teaching which might be detrimental to my students' learning?' and not 'What must I not do because research says it is wrong?' Research says that very little is actually wrong.

Next we need to ask whether overarching theories of language acquisition have direct relevance to classroom practice. In Chapter 3 we looked at innate and universal versus cognitive models of L2 acquisition, particularly connectionism. The two models would appear irreconcilable. The only way that they can be reconciled is by the notion that the brain, in making its connections, has a high predisposition to looking for patterns and for building up an architecture of connections against which new linguistic information is sorted. This architecture is probabilistic rather than absolute. The theory is that it arises through the strength of the connections not from a genetically transmitted cerebral structure based on universal language rules. Whether this theory will continue to hold sway, in SLA research, over universal grammar remains to be seen. In a sense, it doesn't matter that much to teachers in L2 classrooms. The fact that the architecture is operating *as if* there were rules should simply remind us of the importance of the quality of the input not the quantity of it. Just talking at our learners, connectionist theory implies, will not result in rapid language acquisition. We need to talk *with* them.

What does the evidence say about the teaching of grammar? Well, just as the 'innate versus environment' dichotomy is not resolved, neither is the implicit-explicit conundrum. However, we do know that the answer does not lie at either of the two extremes. This applies to the acquisition of the rule system, vocabulary and the ability to access both written and spoken texts. It is clear from the research evidence that in virtually all classroom contexts implicit learning takes place but it is enhanced by drawing the attention of the learner, explicitly, to vocabulary and to syntax. Explicit teaching of any sort, whether it be grammar or syntax, seems to result in improvements in tasks which are directly related to that kind of teaching, but not to overall free and creative performance. There is little evidence for the efficacy of explicit grammar teaching. By this I mean taking long periods of time out from meaning-based interaction, usually at the beginning of a topic, and explaining the rules of the language through examples and paradigms. So we need a balance. But is that balance to be found in the teacher or the learners? On the one hand teachers must offer students a range of activities which incorporate and promote both implicit and explicit processes. This will ensure broad coverage of individuals within the group. At the same time individual learners need to become more aware of their learning strategies and to redress imbalances and to work to more effective combinations. The broad consensus is that language classrooms should still be, in essence, those where meaning-oriented exchanges predominate over message-oriented exchanges. It is up to the skilled teacher to ensure that occasional focus on form does not disrupt this general pattern of interaction. The evidence suggests that focus on form as part of a meaning-based discourse provides the optimum amount of spotlighting of new target-language models such that development of interlanguage can take place. Some easier rules can then be reinforced in an explicit way but even then this should be at the end of a sequence of learning not at the beginning of it, or even better, when there is evidence that an individual learner would benefit from explicit instruction.

Should there be any kind of learning about languages in general? There is a strong feeling among some authors that an awareness of language early on in an L2 curriculum could be beneficial to learners. Although I have not reviewed (nor indeed come across) any empirical evidence that a specific course in language awareness helps second-language learners to learn, the call for its introduction (for example by Eric Hawkins in numerous publications, and by Little and Singleton 1991) would find a theoretical echo in some of our earlier discussions: for example, in making discoveries about where function words diverge (see Chapter 4). Experimental research into the benefits of initial (or indeed parallel) language awareness courses is sadly lacking.

Does the research indicate whether learning problems are more to do with individual psychological differences, or is it more to do with the outside world, the environment surrounding the learner which motivates the learner to dedicate time and effort to the task? I would say the answer is inconclusive but the tendency is more towards the psychological differences. At least these offer more hope of solutions than trying to change societal norms. Some progress has been made with identifying what motivates learners to learn. What we do know is that it is inextricably linked to other factors such as self-efficacy and locus of attribution. On the one hand learners need to look for solutions in themselves rather than in the behaviour of teachers, peers or the subject itself. On the other hand they need to feel that there are solutions available to their problems. That research suggests that demotivation results from deficiencies in the way individuals learn rather than some deep-seated lack of desire to learn should be seen as a positive and hopeful situation, one which can be remedied by teacher-learner partnerships. In order to achieve the sustained intellectual and physical effort needed to learn a second language, students need to feel that they have within themselves the capacity to put things right.

Does the research give us insights into how learners progress and develop? Certainly, the concept of interlanguage, of learners exploring the target language systematically, still has much to offer the teacher. The concept of a threshold as a stage in the development process is also acquiring a certain stability. Threshold appears to be present in all language skills. However, this needs further definition through research. For example, in reading and listening it is not clear where the threshold lies nor whether the threshold beyond which a reader can deploy L1 strategies is related only to his/her language competence or whether it is a combination of competence *and* text difficulty. Give a very difficult text to even a very advanced language learner and some compensatory strategies based on text decoding will take place. Is this the same process as happens to an L1 reader confronted with a very difficult and unfamiliar text? If so, this would suggest merely a continuum where incremental advances in competence can be matched by incremental increases in text difficulty. Threshold, by contrast, would suggest an *actual step* in vocabulary and grammar knowledge before which an L2 reader can *never* deploy L1 strategies no matter how simplified a text he/she is confronted with. At the moment the literature posits such a step but without having, to my knowledge, examined 'pre-threshold learners' with simplified texts. If a threshold is there, the implications are that we need to bring learners as quickly as possible over the threshold so that they can start operating with a more balanced combination of strategies. This would argue for early and intensive language programmes incorporating both easy texts for access to meaning and difficult texts for the building up of strategic knowledge.

What does the research say about *where* we should look for evidence in our students that they are working hard and making progress? The theme of process versus product runs like an unbroken thread throughout all the chapters. Research has rightly targeted the way that learners go about their language learning and compared this with what they are able to produce. This approach has a lot to offer teachers in the classroom. Let us worry less about beautiful pieces of writing or excellently performed role-plays and let us concentrate more on the behaviours and the stages the learners go through when confronted with the tasks we set them. This shift in the 'what, when and how' of the process of looking at learners' language acquisition also requires a shift in how we assess and feedback on their progress. Learners have become accustomed to having evaluative feedback on their products. However, formative feedback, coupled with ideas for how they might take on themselves the responsibility for improving is going to be more in tune with this shift than summative feedback and we may need some creative ways of providing this feeding back in order to reconcile these inherent tensions.

Teachers in the survey wanted to know more about speaking. Perhaps this was because, despite the highly preferential status given to it in most CLT classrooms, the results of that effort, in England at least, are low. Oral interaction between teacher and learners will continue to be one of the prime vehicles of language pedagogy. We have seen oral interaction raise itself as an issue in the chapter on theory and methods, in the chapter on listening when we discussed interactive listening and in the chapter on speaking itself. If oral interaction is so important, we need to arrive at principles and criteria for what constitutes quality interaction. The research suggests that these criteria are possible and we have begun to look at concepts such as cognitive challenge, negotiation of meaning, and providing students with greater control of the topic and direction of the talk. We have also noted that the research evidence is still very positive about pair and group work but that this should be subjected to similar quality criteria scrutiny as teacher-whole-class interaction. On the other hand an enormous amount of research effort has focused directly on meaning negotiation because of the hypothesis that this is where acquisition takes place. We have seen that the evidence provided is that negotiation is very vocabulary based with little meaning negotiation resulting from grammatical misunderstandings. The evidence therefore cannot be, in my view, as conclusive of its impact on the learner's interlanguage as might be supposed from the attention directed to it.

What does the research say about the use of the first language in the classroom? This book has examined the positive and negative influence of the learner's L1 on second-language learning. We can conclude that its negative effects have in the past been grossly over-stated. Especially in near cognate languages there is a whole host of strategies that the learner can deploy which use the L1 in a positive way, particularly with regard to reducing the learning burden. This does not mean that we should return to a methodology which relies entirely on the analysis of the contrasts in the two languages and frequent translation between them. Rather it implies an increasingly sophisticated pedagogy where the teaching strategies are in tune with the learning strategies of the students, where the teacher facilitates optimum use of the L1 in the students' learning but also helps to steer them away from the dangers of over-reliance on the L1 for all activities.

What does research suggest about the importance of phonological awareness? This theme too has found its way into most of the chapters. We have noted that phonological awareness is an important component of language aptitude. It is likely therefore that its neglect in recent years has not been justified. The evidence points to clear advantages in helping learners to make links between the sounds of the target language and the way that it is written. These advantages are not only in the obvious skill of reading, but also in listening and speaking where language can be sounded out, albeit at great speed and under considerable pressures.

What does the research evidence say about learning to learn? Strategy-training research is not as advanced as strategy-elicitation and strategy-identification research. We know with much greater certainty what a good language learner looks like but we are less sure we know how to make the less good language learner improve. Certainly, strategy instruction seems to imply a much longer-term commitment than was previously envisaged in short introductory programmes of learner training. Scaffolded training, running alongside the language programme, appears to offer the best opportunities for students to maximize their learning.

Despite my earlier grumbling about the current state of SLA research, some progress has been made. A number of themes, theories and beliefs have been sustained by this review of the evidence, even though they have had to be modified and refined. This is a good thing. Continuity with modification is more likely to appeal to teachers than major pendulum swings. However, in order to make even greater strides with respect to which approaches deliver the best learning we need a strengthening of the partnership between teachers and researchers. Teachers should be actively involved in shaping the direction of research. The researchers' contribution should be in ensuring that the research effort becomes unfettered, systematic, coherent and rigorous.

References

Aitchison, J. (1994) *Words in the Mind*. Oxford: Blackwell.

Alderson, J. C. (2000) *Assessing Reading*. Cambridge: Cambridge University Press.

Alderson, J. C. and Banerjee, J. (2002) Language testing and assessment (Part 2). *Language Teaching*, 35, 79–113.

Allwright, D. and Bailey, K. (1991) *Focus on the Language Classroom*. Cambridge: Cambridge University Press.

Anderson, J. R. (1983) *The Architecture of Cognition*. Cambridge, MA: Harvard University Press.

Anderson, J. R. (1985) *Cognitive Psychology and its Implications*. New York: Freeman.

Anderson, N. (1999) *Exploring Second Language Reading: Issues and Strategies*. London: Heinle and Heinle.

Antòn, M. (1999) The discourse of a learner-centred classroom: sociocultural perspectives on teacher-learner interaction in the second-language classroom. *The Modern Language Journal*, 83, 3, 303–18.

Antòn, M. and DiCamilla, F. (1998) Socio-cognitive functions of L1 collaborative interactions in the L2 classroom. *Canadian Modern Language Review*, 54, 3, 314–2.

Aplin, R. (1991) The ones who got away: the views of those who opt out of languages. *Language Learning Journal*, 4, 2–4.

Ard, J. (1982) The use of bilingual dictionaries by ESL students while writing. *ITL Review of Applied Linguistics*, 58, 1–27.

Asher, C. (1969) The total physical response approach to second language learning. *The Modern Language Journal*, 50, 3–17.

Asher, C., Chambers, G. and Hall, K. (1999) Dictionary use in MFL examinations in the GCSE: how schools are meeting the challenge. *Language Learning Journal*, 19, 28–32.

Assessment Performance Unit (APU) (1986) *Foreign Language Performance in Schools*. Department of Education and Science: HMSO.

Assessment Performance Unit (1987) *Foreign Languages: Listening and Reading*. Windsor: NFER-Nelson.

Atkinson, R. C. (1975) Mnemotechnics in second-language learning. *American Psychologist*, 30, 821–8.

Avila, E. and Sadoski, M. (1996) Exploring new applications of the keyword method to acquire English vocabulary. *Language Learning*, 46, 3, 379–95.

Ayoun, D. (2001) The role of negative and positive feedback in the second language acquisition of the *passé composé* and *imparfait*. *Modern Language Journal*, 85, 2, 226–43.

Aziz, L. (1995) A model of paired cognitive and metacognitive strategies: its effect on second language grammar and writing performance. Unpublished doctoral dissertation, University of San Francisco.

Bachman, L. (1990) *Fundamental Considerations in Language Testing.* Oxford: Oxford University Press.

Bacon, S. M. (1992) The relationship between gender, comprehension, processing strategies and cognitive and affective response in foreign language listening. *The Modern Language Journal*, 76, 2, 160–76.

Bacon, S. M. and Finnemann, M. (1990) A study of the attitudes, motives, and strategies of university foreign-language students in relation to authentic oral and written output. *Modern Language Journal*, 74, 459–72.

Baddeley, A. D. and Hitch, G. J. (1974) Working memory. In G. H. Bower (ed.) *The Psychology of Learning and Motivation: Advances in Research and Theory.* New York: Academic Press.

Baddeley, A. D. and Logie, R. H. (1999) Working memory: the multiple component model. In A. Miyake and P. Shah (eds) *Models of Working Memory: Mechanisms of Active Maintenance and Executive Control.* Cambridge: Cambridge University Press.

Bailey, N., Madden, C. and Krashen, S. (1974) Is there a 'natural sequence' in adult second language learning? *Language Learning*, 21, 235–43.

Bandura, A. (1993) Perceived self-efficacy in cognitive development and functioning. *Educational Psychologist*, 28, 117–48.

Barcroft, J. (2001) Acoustic variation and lexical acquisition. *Language Learning*, 51, 4, 563–90.

Barnes, A., Hunt, M. and Powell, B. (1999) Dictionary use in the teaching and examining of MFLs at GCSE. *Language Learning Journal*, 19, 19–27.

Barry, S. and Lazarte, A. A. (1998) Evidence for mental models: how do prior knowledge, syntactic complexity, and reading topic affect inference generation in a recall task for nonnative readers of Spanish? *Modern Language Journal*, 82, 2, 176–93.

Basena, D. and Jamieson, J (1996) CALL research in second language learning: 1990-1994. *CAELL* 7, 1, 14–22.

Baudrand-Aertker L. (1992) Dialogue journal writing in a foreign language classroom: assessing communicative competence and proficiency. Unpublished doctoral dissertation. Louisiana State University.

Bautier-Castaing, E. (1977) Acquisition comparée de la syntaxe du Français par des enfants francophones et non francophones. *Etudes de linguistique appliquée*, 27, 19–41.

Beaton, A., Gruneberg, M. and Ellis, N. (1995) Retention of foreign language vocabulary learned using the keyword method: a ten year follow up. *Second Language Research*, 11, 2, 112–20.

Becker, C. (1991) Quantity and quality of writing German in early acquisition: a case for associative activities in foreign language courses. Unpublished doctoral dissertation. University of Southern California. Cited in Reichelt (2001).

Beeching, K. (unpublished study) Understanding spontaneous spoken French: the teachability of listening strategies. University of the West of England.

Benati, A. (2001) A comparative study of the effects of processing instruction and output-based instruction on the acquisition of the Italian future tense. *Language Teaching Research*, 5, 2, 95–127.

Bensoussan, M. and Laufer, B. (1984) Lexical guessing in context in EFL reading comprehension. *Journal of Research in Reading*, 7, 15–32.

Bernhardt, E. B. (1991) *Reading Development in a Second Language: Theoretical, Empirical, and Classroom Perspectives.* Norwood, NJ: Ablex Publishing Corporation.

Bialystock, E. (1990) *Communication Strategies.* Oxford: Blackwell.

Bishop, G. (1998) Research into the use being made of bilingual dictionaries by language learners. *Language Learning Journal*, 18, 3–8.

Bishop, G. (2000a) Dictionaries, examinations and stress. *Language Learning Journal*, 21, 57–65.

Bishop, G. (2000b) Developing learner strategies in the use of dictionaries as a productive language learning tool. *Language Learning Journal*, 22, 58–62.

Black. P. and Wiliam, D. (1998) *Inside the Black Box*. London: King's College School of Education.

Block, E. (1986) The comprehension strategies of second language readers. *TESOL Quarterly*, 20, 3, 463–93.

Bloomfield, L. (1933) *Language*. New York: Holt.

Blyth, C. (1997) A constructivist approach to grammar: teaching teachers to teach aspect. *Modern Language Journal*, 81, 1, 50–66.

Bossers, B. (1992) *Reading in Two Languages: a Study of Reading Comprehension in Dutch as a Second Language and Turkish as a First Language*. Rotterdam, The Netherlands: Drukkerij Van Driel. Cited in Taillefer (1996).

Breen, M. P. (2001) Overt participation and covert acquisition in the languages classroom. In M. P. Breen (ed.) *Learner Contributions to Language Learning: New Directions in Research*. Harlow: Pearson Education Limited.

Brooks, F. B. and Donato, R. (1994) Vygotskian approaches to understanding foreign language learner discourse during communicative tasks. *Hispania*, 77, 262–74.

Brooks, F. B., Donato, R. and McGlone, J. V. (1997) When are they going to say 'it' right? Understanding learner talk during pair-work activity. *Foreign Language Annals*, 30, 4, 524–41.

Brown, G. (1995) Dimensions of difficulty in listening comprehension. In D. J. Mendelsohn and J. Rubin (eds) *A guide for the Teaching of Second Language Listening*. CA, USA: Dominie Press.

Brown, K. and Fletcher, A. (2002) Disaffection or disruptive engagement? A collaborative inquiry into pupils' behaviour and their perceptions of their learning modern languages lessons. *Pedagogy, Culture and Society*, 10, 2, 169–92.

Brown, T. S. and Perry, F. L. (1991) A comparison of three learning strategies for ESL vocabulary acquisition. *TESOL Quarterly*, 25, 655–70.

Bügel, K. and Buunk, B. P. (1996) Sex differences in foreign language text comprehension: the role of interests and prior knowledge. *Modern Language Journal*, 80, 1, 15–31.

Burstall, C. (1975) Factors affecting foreign language learning: a consideration of some recent research findings. *Language Teaching and Linguistics Abstracts*, 8, 5–125.

Byrnes, H. (2000) Shaping the discourse of practice: the role of linguistics and psychology in language teaching and learning. *Modern Language Journal*, 84, 4, 472–94.

Callaghan, M. (1998) An investigation into the causes of boys' underachievement in French. *Language Learning Journal*, 17, 2–7.

Calvé, P. (1992) Corriger ou ne pas corriger, là n'est pas la question. *The Canadian Modern Language Review*, 48, 3, 458–71.

Canale, M. and Swain, M. (1980) Theoretical bases of communicative approaches to second language teaching and testing. *Applied Linguistics* 1, 1–47.

Carrell, P. L. (1983) Some issues in studying the role of schemata, or background knowledge, in second language comprehension. *Reading in a Foreign Language*, 1, 81–92.

Carrell, P. L. (1991) Second language reading: reading ability or language proficiency? *Applied Linguistics*, 12, 159–79.

Castellotti, V. (1998). Langue étrangère et français en milieu scolaire: didactiser l'alternance? Paris: *Etudes de Linguistique Appliquée, 108*, 401–10.

Chambers, F. and Richards, B. (1995) The 'free conversation' and the assessment of oral proficiency. *Language Learning Journal*, 11, 6–10.

Chambers, G. (1993) Taking the 'de' out of demotivation. *Language Learning Journal*, 7, 13–16.

Chambers, G. (1996) Listening, Why? How? *Language Learning Journal*, 14, 23–7.

Chamot, A. U. and El-Dinary, P. B. (1999) Children's learning strategies in language immersion classrooms. *The Modern Language Journal*, 83, 3, 319–38.

Chamot, A. U., Küpper, L. and Impink-Hernandez, M. V. (1988) *A Study of Learning Strategies in Foreign Language Instruction: Findings of the Longitudinal Study.* McLean, VA: Interstate Research Associates. Cited at length in O'Malley and Chamot (1990).

Chomsky, N. (1965). *Aspects of the Theory of Syntax.* Cambridge, MA: MIT Press.

Chomsky, N. (1980). *Rules and Representations.* New York: Columbia University Press.

Christianson, K. (1997) Dictionary use by EFL writers: what really happens? *Journal of Second Language Writing*, 6, 1, 23–43.

Chung, J.-M. (1999) The effects of using video texts supported with advance organizers and captions on Chinese college students' listening comprehension: an empirical study. *Foreign Language Annals*, 32, 3, 295–308.

Cicurel, F. (1989) La mise en scène du discours didactique dans l'enseignement des langues étrangères. *Bulletin CILA* 49, 7–20.

Clapham, C. (1996) The development of IELTS: a study of the effect of background knowledge on reading comprehension. *Studies in Language Testing Series, Vol. 4.* Cambridge: Cambridge University Press. Cited in Alderson and Bannerjee (2002).

Clarke, A. and Trafford, J. (1996) Return to gender: boys' and girls' attitudes and achievements. *Language Learning Journal*, 14, 40–9.

Clarke, M. A. (1979) Reading in Spanish and English: evidence from adult ESL students. *Language Learning*, 29, 121–50.

Clément, R., Gardner R. C. and Smythe, P. C. (1980) Social and individual factors in second language acquisition. *Canadian Journal of Behavioural Science*, 12, 293–302.

Cohen, A. (1998) *Strategies in Learning and Using a Second Language.* London: Longman.

Cohen, A. D. (1987) Student processing of feedback on their compositions. In A. L. Wenden and J. Rubin (eds) *Learner Strategies in Language Learning*, 57–69. Englewood Cliffs, NJ: Prentice-Hall.

Cohen, A. D. and Aphek, E. (1981) Easifying second language learning. *Studies in Second Language Acquisition*, 3, 2, 221–35.

Cohen, A. D. and Cavalcanti, M. C. (1990) Feedback on compositions: teacher and student verbal reports. In B. Kroll (ed.) (1990).

Cohen, A. D., Weaver, S. J. and Li, T.-Y. (1995) *The Impact of Strategies-Based Instruction on Speaking a Foreign Language.* Research Report. Center for Advanced Research on Language Acquisition, University of Minnesota, Minneapolis, MN. Cited at length in Cohen (1998).

Coleman, J. (1996) *Studying Languages: a Survey of British and European Students. The Proficiency, Background, Attitudes and Motivation of Students of Foreign Languages in the United Kingdom and Europe.* London: CILT.

Coleman, J. (2001) *Lessons for the Future: Evaluating FDTL Languages.* In J. A. Coleman *et al.* (eds) (2001).

Coleman, J. A., Ferney, D., Head, D. and Rix, R. (eds) (2001) *Language Learning Futures: Issues and Strategies for Modern Languages Provision in Higher Education.* London: CILT.

Comeau, L., Cormier, P., Grandmaison, E. and Lacroix, D. (1999) A longitudinal study of phonological processing skills in children learning to read in a second language. *Journal of Educational Psychology*, 91, 1, 29–43.

Conti, G. (2001) E possibile migliorare l'efficacia della correzione attraverso l'istruzione strategica? *Tuttitalia*, 23, 4–14.

Convery A., Evans M., Green S., Macaro E., Mellor J. (1997) *Pupils' Perceptions of Europe*. London: Cassell.

Cook, V. (1999) Going beyond the native speaker in language teaching. *TESOL Quarterly*, 33, 2, 185–209.

Cook, V. (2001) *Second Language Learning and Language Teaching*. London: Arnold.

Coste, D. (1998). Alternances didactiques. Paris: *Etudes de Linguistique Appliquée*, 108, 393–400.

Coyle, D. (2000) Raising the profile and prestige of Modern Foreign Languages in the whole school curriculum. In K. Field (ed.) *Issues in Modern Language Teaching*. London: Routledge, 255–68.

Creanza, M. A. (1997) La motivazione all'apprendimento della lingua inglese nella scuola superiore. *Rassegna Italiana di Linguistica Applicata*, 29, 3, 97–114.

Creswell, A. (2000). Self-monitoring in student writing: developing learner responsibility. *ELT Journal*, 54, 3, 235–44.

Crystal, D. (1969) *Prosodic Systems and Intonation in English*. Cambridge: Cambridge University Press.

Cummins, J. (1976) The influence of bilingualism on cognitive growth: a synthesis of research findings and an explanatory hypothesis. *Working Papers on Bilingualism*. Ontario Institute for Studies in Education, 1–43.

Cushing, W. S. and Jensen, L. (1996) Reading rate improvement in university ESL classes. *The CATESOL Journal*, 9, 55–71. Cited in Anderson (1999).

Dadour, S. and Robbins, J. (1996) University-level studies using strategy instruction to improve speaking ability in Egypt and Japan. In R. Oxford (ed.) *Language Learning Strategies around the World: Cross Cultural Perspectives* (Technical Report 13), Second Language Teaching and Curriculum Center, University of Hawaii, Honolulu, 157–66.

Daniels, J. (2000) Intensive language work as a catalyst for classroom learning and an antidote to 'vocabulary dormancy'. *Language Learning Journal*, 21, 13–18.

de Bot, K. (1992) A bilingual production model: Levelt's 'speaking' model adapted. *Applied Linguistics*, 13, 1, 1–24.

De Groot, A. M. B. and Hoeks, J. C. J. (1995) The development of bilingual memory: evidence from word translation by trilinguals. *Language Learning*, 45, 683–724.

de Larios, J. C., Murphy, L. and Manchon, R. (1999) The use of restructuring strategies in EFL writing: a study of Spanish learners of English as a foreign language. *Journal of Second Language Writing*, 8, 1, 13–44.

Dekeyser, R. M. (1993) The effect of error correction on L2 grammar knowledge and oral proficiency. *Modern Language Journal*, 77, 4, 501–14.

Department for Education and Employment (DfEE) (1999) *Modern Foreign Languages: the National Curriculum for England*. London: HMSO.

Department of Education (1995) *Modern Foreign Languages in the National Curriculum*. London: HMSO.

di Pietro, R. J. (1987) *Strategic Interaction*. Cambridge: Cambridge University Press.

Dickinson, L. (1995) Autonomy and motivation. *System*, 23, 2, 165–74.

Dobson, A. (1998) *Reflections on Inspection findings 1996/97*. London: CILT.

Dörnyei, Z. (1995) On the teachability of communication strategies. *TESOL Quarterly*, 29, 1, 55–85.

Dörnyei, Z. (1998) Motivation in second and foreign language learning. *Language Teaching* 31, 117–35.

Dörnyei, Z. (2001) *Teaching and Researching Motivation*. London: Longman.

Dörnyei, Z. and Csizér, K. (1998) Ten commandments for motivating language learners: results of an empirical study. *Language Teaching Research*, 2, 203–29.

Dörnyei, Z. and Scott, M. L. (1997) Communication strategies in a second language: definitions and taxonomies. *Language Learning*, 47, 1, 173–210.

Dörnyei, Z., Nyilasi, F. and Clément, R. (1996) Hungarian school children's motivation to learn foreign languages: a comparison of five target languages. *Novelty*, 3, 6–16. Cited in Dörnyei (2001).

Doughty, C. (1994) Finetuning of feedback by competent speakers to language learners. In J. Atlantis (ed.) Georgetown University Roundtable (GURT) 1993. 96–108, Washington, DC: Georgetown University Press. Cited in Lyster (1998).

Doughty, C. and Varela, E. (1998) Communicative focus on form. In C. Doughty and J. Williams (eds) *Focus on Form in Classroom Second Language Acquisition*, 114–138. Cambridge: Cambridge University Press.

Duckworth, P. and Entwhistle, N. J. (1974) Attitudes to school subjects: a repertory grid technique. *British Journal of Educational Psychology*, 44, 76–83.

Dulay, H. and Burt, M. (1974) Natural sequences in child second language acquisition. *Language Learning*, 24, 253–78.

Dupuy, B. C. (1999) Narrow listening: an alternative way to develop and enhance listening comprehension in students of French as a foreign language. *System*, 27, 351–61.

Elliot, R. A. (1995) Foreign language phonology: field independence, attitude, and the success of formal instruction in Spanish pronunciation. *Modern Language Journal*, 79, 4, 530–42.

Ellis, N. (1995) *Vocabulary Acquisition: Psychological Perspectives*. Vocabulary Acquisition Research Group: University of Wales, Swansea, Virtual Library, htth://www.swan.ac.uk/cals/vlibrary/ne95a.html.

Ellis, N. (2001) Memory for Language. In P. Robinson (ed.) *Cognition and Second Language Instruction*. Cambridge: Cambridge University Press.

Ellis, N. and Beaton A. (1993a) Psycholinguistic determinants of foreign language vocabulary learning. *Language Learning*, 43, 559–617.

Ellis, N. and Beaton A. (1993b) Factors affecting the learning of foreign language vocabulary: imagery, keyword mediators and phonological short term memory. *Quarterly Journal of Experimental Psychology*.

Ellis, R. (1994) *The Study of Second Language Acquisition*. Oxford: Oxford University Press.

Ellis, R. (1995) Modified input and the acquisition of word meanings. *Applied Linguistics*, 16, 409–41.

Ellis, R. and He, X. (1999) The roles of modified input and output in the incidental acquisition of word meanings. *Studies in Second Language Acquisition*, 21, 285–301.

Ellis, R. and Heimbach, R. (1997) Bugs and birds: children's acquisition of second language vocabulary through interaction. *System*, 25, 247–59.

Ellis, R., Tanaka Y. and Yamazaki, N. (1994) Classroom interaction, comprehension and the acquisition of L2 word meanings. *Language Learning*, 44, 449–91.

Ellis, R., Basturkmen, H. and Loewen, S. (2001) Learner uptake in communicative ESL lessons. *Language Learning*, 51, 2, 281–318.

Elston, T. (1992) 'In one ear....' *Times Educational Supplement*, 3 April, 77.

Erler, L. (2003) Year 7's Experiences of Reading French as a Foreign Language. Unpublished doctoral thesis, University of Oxford, Department of Educational Studies.

Faerch, G. and Kasper, G. (1983) *Strategies In Interlanguage Communication*. Harlow: Longman.

Faerch, G. and Kasper, G. (1986) Strategic competence in foreign language teaching. In G. Kasper (ed.) *Learning, Teaching and Communication in the Foreign Language Classroom*. Aarhus University: Aarhus University Press, 179–94.

Felix, U. (2001) The web's potential for language learning: the student's perspective. *ReCALL*, 13, 1, 47–58.

Ferris, D. (1998) Students' views of academic aural/oral skills: a comparative needs analysis. *TESOL Quarterly*, 32, 2, 298–318.

Feyten, C. M. (1991) The power of listening ability: an overlooked dimension in language acquisition. *Modern Language Journal*, 75, 2, 173–80.

Fisher, L. (2001) Modern foreign languages recruitment post-16: the pupils' perspective. *Language Learning Journal*, 23, 33–40.

Fisher, L. and Evans, M. (2000) The school exchange visit: effects on attitudes and proficiency in language learning. *Language Learning Journal*, 22, 11–16.

Fitzgerald, J. (1994) How literacy emerges: foreign language implications. *Language Learning Journal*, 9, 32–5.

Florez-Estrada, N. (1995) Some effects of native-nonnative communication via computer e-mail interaction on the development of foreign language proficiency. Unpublished doctoral dissertation, University of Pittsburgh. Cited in Reichelt (2001).

Flower, L. and Hayes, J. R. (1981) A cognitive process theory of writing. *College Composition and Communication*, 32, 365–87.

Forth, I. and Naismith, J. (1995) The good the bad and the ugly: some problems with grammar rules. *Language Learning Journal*, 11, 78–81.

Frantzen, D. (1995) The effects of grammar supplementation on written accuracy in an intermediate Spanish content course. *Modern Language Journal*, 79, 3, 329–55.

Fraser, C. A. (1999) Lexical processing strategy use and vocabulary learning through reading. *Studies in Second Language Acquisition*, 21, 225–41.

Friedlander, A. (1990) Composing in English: effects of first language on writing in English as a second language. In Kroll (ed.) (1990), 109–125.

Fröhlich, M., Spada, N. and Allen, P. (1985) Differences in the communicative orientation of L2 classrooms. *TESOL Quarterly*, 19, 1, 27–58.

Fukkink, R. G. and de Glopper, K. (1998) Effects of instruction in deriving word meaning from context: a meta-analysis. *Review of Educational Research*, 68, 4, 450–69.

Gallego de Bibleche, O. (1993) A comparative study of the process versus product approach to the instruction of writing in Spanish as a foreign language. Unpublished doctoral dissertation, The Pennsylvania State University, University Park. Cited in Reichelt (2001).

Ganshow, L. and Sparks, R. (1996) Anxiety about foreign language learning among high school women. *Modern Language Journal*, 80, 2, 199–212.

Garabédian, M. and Lerasle, M. (1998). L'alternance codique, la double contrainte. *Etudes de Linguistique Appliquée*, 108, 433–43.

Gardner, R. C. (1985) *Social Psychology and Second Language Learning: the Role of Attitudes and Motivation.* London: Edward Arnold.

Gardner, R. C. and Lambert, W. E. (1972) *Attitudes and Motivation in Second Language Learning.* Rowley, MA: Newbury House.

Gardner, R. C., Smythe, P. C., Clément, R. and Gliksman, L. (1976) Second language acquisition: a social psychological perspective. *Canadian Modern Language Review*, 32, 198–213.

Gardner, R. C., Tremblay, P. F. and Masgoret, A.-M., (1997) Towards a full model of second language learning: an empirical investigation. *Modern Language Journal*, 81, 3, 344–62.

Garrett, P. and Shortall, T. (2002) Learners' evaluations of teacher-fronted and student-centred classroom activities. *Language Teaching Research*, 6, 1, 25–58.

Gathercole, S. E. and Baddeley, A. D. (1989) Evaluation of the role of phonological short term memory in the development of vocabulary in children: a longitudinal study. *Journal of Memory and Language*, 28, 200–13.

Goodman, K. S. (1976) Reading: a psycholinguistic guessing game. In H. Seliger and R.B.Ruddell (eds) Theoretical Models and Processes of Reading (2nd Edition), 497–508, Newark, D.E. International Reading Association.

Grabe, W. and Stoller, F. L. (2002) *Teaching and Researching Reading.* London: Longman.

Graham, S. (1997) *Effective Language Learning*. Clevedon: Multilingual Matters.

Graham, S. (2002) Experiences of learning French: a snapshot at years 11, 12 and 13. *Language Learning Journal*, 25, 15–20.

Green, P. and Hecht, K. (1992) Implicit and explicit grammar: an empirical study. *Applied Linguistics*, 13, 168–84.

Grenfell. M. (1992) Process reading in the communicative classroom. *Language Learning Journal*, 6, 48–52.

Grenfell, M. and Harris, V. (1999) *Modern Languages and Learning Strategies: in Theory and Practice*. London: Routledge.

Grice, J. E. (1975) Logic and conversation. In P. Cole and J. Morgan (eds) *Syntax and Semantics 3: Speech Acts*. New York: Academy Press.

Gu, Y. and Johnson, R. K. (1996) Vocabulary learning strategies and language learning outcomes. *Language Learning*, 46, 4, 643–79.

Hall, J. K. (1996) The discursive formation of a Spanish as foreign language classroom community. Paper presented at AILA 1996, 11th World Congress of Applied Linguistics (August), Jyvaskyla, Finland.

Hall, J. K. (1998) Differential teacher attention to student utterances: the construction of different opportunities for learning in the IRF. *Linguistics and Education*, 9, 3, 287–311.

Halpern, D. F. (1992) *Sex Differences in Cognitive Abilities*, Hillsdale, NJ: Lawrence Erlbaum. Cited in Callaghan (1998).

Hammadou, J. (1991) Interrelationships among prior knowledge, inference and language proficiency in foreign language reading. *Modern Language Journal*, 75, 1, 27–38.

Harley, B. (1989) Functional grammar in French immersion: a classroom experiment. *Applied Linguistics*, 10, 331–59.

Harley, B. (1995) The lexicon in second language research. In B. Harley (ed.) *Lexical Issues in Language Learning*. Amsterdam: Research Club in Language Learning, Ann Arbor, 1–28.

Harley, B. (2000) Listening strategies in ESL: do age and L1 make a difference? *TESOL Quarterly*, 34, 4, 769–77.

Harley, B. and Swain, M. (1984) The interlanguage of immersion students and its implications for second language teaching. In A. Davies, C. Criper and A. Howatt (eds) *Interlanguage*. Edinburgh: Edinburgh University Press.

Harley, B., Howard, J. and Hart, D. (1995) Second language processing at different ages: do younger learners pay more attention to prosodic cues to sentence structure? *Language Learning*, 45, 43–71.

Harris, V. (1988) Making boys make progress. *Language Learning Journal*, 18, 56–62.

Harvey, T. J. and Stables, A. (1984) Gender differences in subject preference and perceptions of subject importance among third year secondary school pupils in single-sex and mixed comprehensive schools. *Educational Studies*, 10, 3, 243–53.

Hatch, E. (1978) Acquisition of syntax in a second language. In J. C. Richards (ed.) *Understanding Second and Foreign Language Learning: Issues and Approaches*. Rowley, MA: Newbury House. Cited in Pica (1994), 34–69.

Havranek, G. (1999) The effectiveness of corrective feedback: preliminary results of an empirical study. *Acquisition et Interaction en Langue Etrangère. Actes du 8ème Colloque EUROSLA*, Paris 1998. Volume 2, 189–206.

Heilenman, L. (1991) Writing in foreign language classrooms: process and reality. In J. E. Alatis (ed.) *Georgetown University Round Table on Languages and Linguistics*. Washington DC: Georgetown University Press. 273–88. Cited in Reichelt (2001).

Hermans, D., Bongaerts, T., de Bot, K. and Schreuder, R. (1998) Producing words in a foreign language: Can speakers prevent interference from their first language? *Bilingualism: Language and Cognition*, 1, 3, 213–29.

Herrmann, F. (1990) Instrumental and agentive uses of the computer: their role in learning French as a foreign language. Unpublished doctoral dissertation, Stanford University, Sanford, CA. Cited in Reichelt (2001).

Hood, P. (1996) Early foreign language reading competence: some issues and evidence. *Language Learning Journal*, 13, 16–18.

Hope, M. (1987) GCSE: Back to the future in a school department. In D. Phillips, *Languages in Schools: From Complacency to Conviction*. London: CILT.

Horwitz, E., Horwitz, M. and Cope J. (1986) Foreign language classroom anxiety. *Modern Language Journal*, 70, 125–32.

Hotho, S. (1999) Motivation in an ab initio German classroom. *Language Learning Journal*, 20, 37–44.

Hudelson, S. (1988) Writing in a second language. *Annual Review of Applied Linguistics*, 9, 210–22.

Hurman, J. (1992) Performance in the A level speaking test by candidates with GCSE training: oral examiners' views. *Language Learning Journal*, 5, 8–10.

Hurman, J. (1996) Marking GCSE role play. *Language Learning Journal*, 13, 19–21.

Hurman, J. (1998) (unpublished) The use of dictionaries in GCSE modern foreign languages written examinations. University of Birmingham. Cited in Bishop (2000a).

Iwashita, N. (2001) The effect of learner proficiency on interactional moves and modified output in nonnative-nonnative interaction in Japanese as a foreign language. *System*, 29, 267–87.

Jacobs, G. M., Dufon, P. and Fong, C. H. (1994) L1 and L2 vocabulary glosses in L2 reading passages: their effectiveness for increasing comprehension and vocabulary knowledge. *Journal of Research in Reading*, 17, 19–28.

Johnson, P. (1982) Effects of reading comprehension on building background knowledge. *TESOL Quarterly*, 16, 503–16.

Jones, B. and Jones, G. (2001) *Boys' Performance in Modern Foreign Languages: Listening to Learners*. London: CILT.

Kasper, G. and Kellerman, E. (eds) (1997) *Communication Strategies: Psycholinguistic and Sociolinguistic Perspectives*. London: Longman, 216–37.

Kaylani, C. (1996) The influence of gender and motivation on EFL learning strategy use in Jordan. In R. Oxford (ed.) *Language Learning Strategies around the World: Cross Cultural Perspectives*. (Technical Report 13) (Second Language Teaching and Curriculum Center, 75–88. University of Hawaii, Honolulu.

Kember, D. and Gow, L. (1994) An examination of the interactive model of ESL reading from the perspective approaches to studying. *RELC Journal*, 25, 1, 1–25.

Kepner, C. (1991) An experiment in the relationship of types of written feedback to the development of second language writing skills. *Modern Language Journal*, 75, 3, 305–13.

Kern, R. G. (1994) The role of mental translation in second language reading. *Studies in Second Language Acquisition*. 16, 4, 441–61.

Klapper, J. (1992) Reading in a foreign language: theoretical issues. *Language Learning Journal*, 5, 27–30.

Klapper, J. (1993) Practicable skills and practical constraints in FL reading. *Language Learning Journal*, 7, 50–4.

Klapper, J. (1997) Language learning at school and university: the great grammar debate continues (1). *Language Learning Journal*, 16, 22–7.

Klohs, L. (1994) Use of mnemonic strategies to facilitate written production of a second language by high school French students. Unpublished doctoral dissertation, University of Minnesota, Minneapolis St. Paul.

Knight, S. (1994) Dictionary use while reading: the effects on comprehension and vocabulary acquisition for students of different verbal abilities. *Modern Language Journal*, 78, 3, 285–99.

Knight, T. (1996) Learning vocabulary through shared tasks. *Language Teacher*, 20, 24–9.

Kobayashi, H. and Rinnert, C. (1992) Effects of first language on second language writing: translation versus direct composition. *Language Learning*, 42, 2, 183–215.

Koda, K. (1993) Task induced variability in FL composition: language specific perspective. *Foreign Language Annals*, 26, 332–46.

Krashen, S. D. (1977) Some issues relating to the monitor model. In H. Brown, C. Yorio and R. Crymes (eds) *On TESOL '77*. Washington, DC: TESOL.

Krashen, S. D. (1981) *Second Language Acquisition and Second Language Learning*. Oxford: Pergamon.

Krashen, S. D. (1985) *The Input Hypothesis: Issues and Implications*. London: Longman.

Krashen, S. D. (1987) *Principles and Practice in Second Language Acquisition*. Hemel Hempstead: Prentice Hall.

Krashen, S. D. (1996) The case for narrow listening. *System*, 24, 97–100.

Krashen, S. D. and Terrell, T. (1988) *The Natural Approach: Language Acquisition in the Classroom*. London: Prentice Hall.

Kreizman, R. (1984) Student feedback regarding teacher comments on Hebrew native language compositions. Seminar paper, School of Education, Hebrew University (in Hebrew) cited in Cohen 1987.

Kroll, B. (1990) (ed.) *Second Language Writing: Research Insights for the Classroom*. Cambridge: Cambridge University Press.

Kuhlemeier, H., Van den Bergh, H. and Melse, L. (1996) Attitudes and achievements in first year of German language instruction in Dutch secondary education. *Modern Language Journal*, 80, 4, 494–508.

Lamb, T. and Fisher, J. (1999) Making connections: football, the internet and reluctant language learners. *Language Learning Journal*, 20, 32–6.

Larsen-Freeman, D. (1976) An explanation for the morpheme order of second language learners. *Language Learning*, 26, 125–34.

Laufer, B. (1989) What percentage of text lexis is essential for comprehension? In C. Lauren and M. Nordman (eds) *Special Language: From Humans Thinking to Thinking Machines*. Clevedon: Multilingual Matters. Cited in Nation (2001).

Laufer, B. (1998) The development of passive and active vocabulary in a second language: same or different? *Applied Linguistics*, 19, 2, 255–71.

Lawson, M. J. and Hogben, D. (1996) The vocabulary learning strategies of foreign language students. *Language Learning*, 46, 101–35.

Lee, J.-W. and Shallert, D. L. (1997) The relative contribution of L2 language proficiency and L1 reading ability to L2 reading performance: a test of the threshold hypothesis in an EFL context. *TESOL Quarterly*, 31, 4, 713–39.

Leh, S. (1997) Electronic mail in foreign language learning. Unpublished doctoral dissertation. Arizona State University, Tempe. Cited in Reichelt (2001).

Leki, I. (1990) Coaching from the margins: issues in written response. In Kroll (ed.) (1990).

Levelt, W. J. M. (1989) *Speaking: From Intention to Articulation*. Cambridge, MA.: The MIT Press. Cited in de Bot (1992).

Levis, J. M. (1999) Intonation in theory and practice, revisited. *TESOL Quarterly*, 33, 1, 37–64.

Libben, G. (2000) Representation and processing in the second language lexicon: the homogeneity hypothesis. In J. Archibald (ed.) *Second Language Acquisition and Theory*. Oxford: Blackwells, 229–48.

Liou, H.-C. (1997) The impact of World Wide Web texts on EFL learning. *Computer Assisted Language Learning*, 10, 5, 455–78.

Little, D. and Singleton, D. (1991) Authentic texts, pedagogical grammar and language awareness in foreign language learning. In C. James and P. Garrett (eds) *Language Awareness in the Classroom*. London: Longman.

Lochtman, K. (2000) The role of negative feedback in experiential vs. analytic foreign language learning. *Paper presented at the Conference on Instructed Second Language Learning, Brussels, Belgium*. Cited in Nicholas *et al*. (2001).

Locke, E. A. and Kristof, A. L. (1996) Volitional choices in the goal achievement process. In P. M. Gollwitzer aand J. A. Bargh (eds) *The Psychology of Action: Linking Cognition and Motivation to Behaviour*. New York: Guilford Press. Cited in Dörnyei (1998).

Long, M. (1981) Input, interaction and foreign langauge acquisition. In H. Winitz (ed.) *Native Language and Foreign Language Acquisition*. Annals of the New York Academy of Sciences 379, 259–78.

Lotto, L. and de Groot, M. B. (1998) Effects of learning method and word type on acquiring vocabulary in an unfamiliar language. *Language Learning*, 48, 1, 31–69.

Lund, R. J. (1991) A comparison of second language listening and reading comprehension. *Modern Language Journal*, 75, 2, 196–204.

Lynch, T. (1997) Nudge, nudge: teacher interventions in task-based learner talk. *ELT Journal*, 51, 4, 317–25.

Lynch, T. and Mendelsohn, D. (2002) Listening. In N. Schmitt (ed.) *An Introduction to Applied Linguistics*. London: Arnold, 193–210.

Lyster, R. (1998a) Recasts, repetition and ambiguity in L2 classroom discourse. *Studies in Second Language Acquisition*, 20, 51–80.

Lyster, R. (1998b) Negotiation of form, recasts, and explicit correction in relation to error types and learner repair in immersion classrooms. *Language Learning*, 48, 2, 183–218.

Lyster, R. and Ranta, L. (1997) Corrective feedback and learner uptake: negotiation of form in communicative classrooms. *Studies in Second Language Acquisition*, 19, 37–66.

Macaro, E. (1985) *Radio France*. London: Longman.

Macaro E. (1997) *Target Language, Collaborative Learning and Autonomy*. Clevedon: Multilingual Matters.

Macaro, E. (1998) Learner strategies: piloting awareness and training. *Tuttitalia*, 18, 10–16.

Macaro, E. (2000a) Learner strategies in foreign language learning: cross national factors. *Tuttitalia*, 22, 9–18.

Macaro, E. (2000b) Issues in target language teaching. In K. Field (ed.) *Issues in Modern Language Teaching*. London: Routledge, 171–189.

Macaro, E. (2001a) *Learner Strategies in Second and Foreign Language Classrooms*. London: Continuum.

Macaro, E. (2001b) Analysing student teachers' codeswitching in foreign language classrooms: theories and decision making. *Modern Language Journal*, 85, 4, 531–48; 82, 4, 545–62.

Macaro, E. (2002a) Pedagogia interattiva (part 2): problems with giving explanations of 'aspect' in Italian as a foreign language with English as L1. *Tuttitalia*, 25, 23–6.

Macaro, E. (2002b) Codeswitching in the L2 classroom as communication and learning strategies. Paper presented at the 35th BAAL Annual Meeting, September, Cardiff, UK.

Macaro, E. (in process) Perceptions of foreign-language difficulty of year-13 students.

Macaro, E. and Mutton, T. (2002) developing language teachers through a co-researcher model. *Language Learning Journal*, 25, 27–39.

Macintyre, P. D., Dörnyei, Z., Clément, R. and Kimberly, A. N. (1998) Conceptualizing willingness to communicate in a L2: a situational model of L2 confidence and affiliation. *Modern Language Journal*, 82, 4, 545–62.

Mackey, A. and Philp, J. (1998) Conversational interaction and second language development: recasts, responses and red-herrings? *Modern Language Journal*, 82, 283–324.

Mackey, A., Gass, S., and McDonough K. (2000) How do learners perceive implicit negative feedback? *Studies in Second Language Acquisition*, 22, 471–97.

MacWhinney, B. (1987a) The competition model. In B. MacWhinney (ed.) *Mechanisms of Language Acquisition*. Hillsdale, NJ: Erlbaum. 249–308.

MacWhinney, B. (1987b) Applying the competition model to bilingualism. *Applied Psycholinguistics*, 8, 315–27.

MacWhinney, B. (1997) Implicit and explicit processes. *Studies in Second Language Acquisition*, 19, 277–81.

MacWhinney, B. (2001) The competition model: the input, the context, and the brain. In P. Robinson (ed.) *Cognition and Second Language Instruction*. Cambridge: Cambridge University Press.

Manley, J. and Calk L. (1997) Grammar instruction for writing skills: do students perceive grammar as useful? *Foreign Language Annals*, 39, 73–83.

Markham, P. (1999) Captioned videotapes and second-language listening word recognition. *Foreign Language Annals*, 32, 3, 321–28.

Marton, F. and Säljö, R. (1976) On qualitative differences in learning, outcome and process (I). *British Journal of Educational Psychology*, 46, 4–11.

Mason, D. (1992) The role of schemata and scripts in language learning. *System*, 21, 1, 45–50.

Maubach A.-M. and Morgan, C. (2001)The relationship between gender and learning styles amongst A level modern languages students. *Language Learning Journal*, 23, 41–7.

Maxim, H. H. (2002) A study into the feasibility and effects of reading extended authentic discourse in the beginning German language classroom. *Modern Language Journal*, 86, 1, 20–35.

McClelland, J. L. and Rumelhart, D. E. (1986) (eds) *Parallel Distributed Processing: Explorations in the Microstructure of Cognition*. Cambridge, MA: MIT Press.

McDonough, S. (1995) *Strategy and Skill in Learning a Foreign Language*. London: Edward Arnold.

McGowan, P. and Turner, M. (1994) Raising reading attainment in modern languages. In A. Swarbrick (ed.) *Teaching Modern Languages*. London: Routledge, 125–40.

McGuire, P. (1997) The effects of interactive computer assignments on the writing skills and attitudes of fourth semester college students of Spanish. Unpublished doctoral dissertation, University of South Carolina, Columbia. Cited in Reichelt (2001).

McLaughlin, B. (1987) *Theories of Second Language Learning*. London: Edward Arnold.

McLaughlin, B. (1990) Restructuring. *Applied Linguistics*, 11, 2, 113–28.

Meara, P. and Buxton, B. (1987) An alternative to multiple choice vocabulary tests. *Language Testing*, 4, 142–54.

Medgyes, P. (1999) *The Non-Native Teacher*. Ismaning: Hueber.

Mendelsohn, D. J. (1998) Teaching listening. *Annual Review of Applied Linguistics*, 18, 81–101.

Metcalfe, P., Laurillard, D. and Mason, R. (1998) 'It's just a word': pupils' perceptions of verb form and function. *Language Learning Journal*, 17, 14–20.

Milton, J. and Meara, P. (1998) Are the British really bad at learning languages? *Language Learning Journal*, 18, 68–76.

Mitchell, R. (2000) Applied linguistics and evidence-based classroom practice: the case of foreign language grammar pedagogy. *Applied Linguistics*, 21, 3, 281–303.

Miyake, A. and Shah, P. (1999) (eds) *Models of Working Memory: Mechanisms of Active Maintenance and Executive Control*. Cambridge: Cambridge University Press.

Muter, V. and Diethelm, K. (2001) The contribution of phonological skills and letter knowledge to early reading development in a multilingual population. *Language Learning*, 51, 2, 187–219.

Myles, F., Hooper, J. and Mitchell, R. (1998) Rote or rule? Exploring the role of formulaic language in classroom foreign language learning. *Language Learning*, 48, 3, 323–63.

Myles, F., Mitchell, R. and Hooper, J. (1999) Interrogative chunks in French L2: A basis for creative construction? *Studies in Second Language Acquisition*, 21, 1, 49–80.

Myong, H. K. (1995) Glossing in incidental and intentional learning of foreign language vocabulary and reading. *University of Hawaii Working Papers in ESL*, 13, 49–94. Cited in Nation (2001).

Nagy, N. E., Herman, P. A. and Anderson, R. C. (1985) Learning words from context. *Reading Research Quarterly*, 20, 233–53. Cited in Fukkink and de Glopper (1998).

Nakahama, Y. (1997) Variations of negations in NS/NNS conversations involving different communicative goals. Unpublished manuscript, Georgetown University, Washington, DC. Cited in Nakahama *et al.* (2001).

Nakahama, Y., Tyler, A. and Van Lier, L. (2001) Negotiation of meaning in conversational and information gap activities: a comparative discourse analysis. *TESOL Quarterly*, 35, 3, 377–406.

Nakatani, Y. (2002) Improving oral proficiency through strategy training. Unpublished doctoral dissertation. University of Birmingham, UK.

Nation, I. S. P. (1990) *Teaching and Learning Vocabulary*. Massachusetts: Newbury House.

Nation, I. S. P. (2001) *Learning Vocabulary in Another Language*. Cambridge: Cambridge University Press.

Neather, T., Woods, C., Rodriguez, I., Davis, M. and Dunne, E. (1995) *Target Language Testing in Modern Foreign Languages*. Report of a project commissioned by the School Curriculum and Assessment Authority. London: SCAA.

Newton, J. (1995) Task-based interaction and incidental vocabulary learning: a case study. *Second Language Research*, 11, 2, 159–77.

Ney, J. W. and Pearson, B. A. (1990) Connectionism as a model of language learning: parallels in foreign language teaching. *Modern Language Journal*, 74, 4, 474–82.

Nicholas, H., Lightbown, P. and Spada, N. (2001) Recasts as feedback to language learners. *Language Learning*, 51, 4, 719–58.

Nikolov, M. and Krashen, S. (1997) Need we sacrifice accuracy for fluency? *System*, 25, 2, 197–201.

Noble, D. F. (1998) Digital Diploma Mills, Part 3, the bloom is off the rose. http://communication.uscd.edu/dl/ddm3.html. Cited in Felix (2001).

Nummikoski, E. (1991) The effects of interactive writing assignments on the written language proficiency of first year students of Russian. Unpublished doctoral dissertation, the University of Texas at Austin. Cited in Reichelt (2001).

Nunan, D. (1997) Strategy training in the language classroom: an empirical investigation. *RELC Journal*, 28, 2, 56–81.

O'Malley, J. M. (1987) The effects of training in the use of learning strategies on learning English as a second language. In A. Wenden and J. Rubin (eds) *Learner Strategies in Language Learning*. Englewood Cliffs, NJ: Prentice Hall International.

O'Malley, M. J. and Chamot, A. U. (1990). *Learning Strategies in Second Language Acquisition*. Cambridge: Cambridge University Press.

O'Malley, M. J., Chamot, A. U. and Küpper, L. (1989) Listening comprehension strategies in second language acquisition. *Applied Linguistics*, 10, 4, 418–37.

O'Malley, M. J., Chamot, A. U., Stewner-Manzanares, Küpper, L. and Russo, R. (1985) Learning strategies used by beginning and intermediate ESL students. *Language Learning*, 35, 21–46.

Ormerod, M. B. (1975) Subject preference and choice in co-educational and single-sex secondary schools. *British Journal of Educational Psychology*, 45, 257–67.

Oxford, R. L. (1990) *Language Learning Strategies: What every Teacher should Know*. Boston, MA: Heinle and Heinle.

Oxford, R. L. (1996) (ed.) Language Learning Strategies Around the World: Cross Cultural Perspectives, Honolulu (Technical Report 13) Second Language Teaching and Curriculum Center, University of Hawaii.

Oxford, R. and Crookall, D. (1990) Vocabulary learning: a critical analysis of techniques. *TESL Canada Journal*, 7, 9–30.

Oxford, R. L. and Green, J. M. (1996) Language learning histories: learners and teachers helping each other understand learning styles and strategies. *TESOL Journal*, 6, 1, 20–8.

Oxford, R. and Nyikos, M. (1989) Variables affecting choice of language learning strategies by university students. *Modern Language Journal*, 73, 3, 291–300.

Paribakht, T. S. and Wesche, M. B. (1993) Reading comprehension and second language development in a comprehension-based ESL programme. *TESL Canada Journal*, 11, 9–27.

Paribakht, T. S. and Wesche, M. B. (1996) Enhancing vocabulary acquisition though reading: a hierarchy of text-related exercise types. *Canadian Modern Language Review*, 52, 155–78.

Parry, K. (1993) The social construction of reading strategies: new directions for research. *Journal of Research in Reading*, 16, 2, 148–58.

Paulston, C. (1970) Structural pattern drills: a classification. *Foreign Language Annals*, 4, 187–93.

Paulus, T. (1999) The effect of peer and teacher feedback on student writing. *Journal of Second Language Writing*, 8, 3, 265–90.

Peñate Cabrera, M. and Bazo Martinez, P. (2001) The effects of repetition, comprehension checks and gestures on primary school children in an EFL situation. *ELT Journal*, 55, 3, 281–8.

Phillipson, R. (1992). *Linguistic Imperialism*. Oxford: Oxford University Press.

Piasecki, S. (1998) A study of the effects of peer editing on the quality of composition of third year Spanish students. Unpublished master's thesis, State University of New York, Oswego. Cited in Reichelt (2001).

Pica, T. (1988) Interlanguage adjustments as an outcome of NS-NNS negotiated interaction. *Language Learning*, 38,1, 45–73.

Pica, T. (1994) Research on negotiation: what does it reveal about second-language learning conditions, processes and outcomes? *Language Learning*, 44, 3, 493–527.

Pica, T., Young. R. and Doughty. C. (1987) The impact of interaction on comprehension. *TESOL Quarterly*, 21, 737–58.

Pica, T., Lincoln-Porter, D., Paninos D. and Linnell, J. (1996) Language learners' interaction: how does it address the input, output and feedback needs of L2 learners? *TESOL Quarterly*, 30,1, 59–84.

Pica, T., Holliday, L., Lewis, N. and Morgenthaler, L. (1989) Comprehensible output as an outcome of linguistic demands on the learner. *Studies in Second Language Acquisition*, 11, 63–90.

Pica,T., Holliday, L., Lewis, N., Berducci, D. and Newman, J. (1991) Language learning through interaction: what role does gender play? *Studies in Second Language Acquisition*, 13, 343–76.

Pienemann, M. (1984) Psychological constraints on the teachability of languages. *Studies in Second Language Acquisition*, 6, 186–214.

Pinker, S. and Prince, A. (1988) On language and connectionism: analysis of a parallel distributed model of language acquisition. *Cognition*, 29, 73–193.

Pintrich, P. L. and Schunk, D. H. (1996) *Motivation in education: theory, research, and applications*. Englewood Cliffs, NJ: Prentice Hall.

Porte, G. K. (1997) The etiology of poor second language writing: the influence of perceived teacher preferences on second language revision strategies. *Journal of Second Language Writing,* 6, 1, 61–78.

Powell, B., Barnes, A. and Graham, S. (1996) *Using the Target Language to Test Modern Foreign Language Skills.* Warwick: The Language Centre, University of Warwick.

Powell, R. C. and Batters, J. D (1985) Pupils' perceptions of foreign language learning at 12+: some gender differences. *Educational Studies,* 11, 1, 11–23.

Prabhu, N. S. (1987) *Second Language Pedagogy.* Oxford: Oxford University Press.

Prince, P. (1996) Second language vocabulary learning: the role of context versus translations as a function of proficiency. *Modern Language Journal,* 80, 4, 478–93.

Pritchard, R. A. (1935) The relative popularity of secondary school subjects at various ages. *British Journal of Educational Psychology,* 5, 157–79.

Pritchard, R. M. O. (1987) Boys' and Girls' attitudes towards French and German. *Educational Research,* 29, 1, 65–72.

Qi, D. S. (1998) An inquiry into language-switching in second language composing processes. *Canadian Modern Language Review,* 54, 3, 413–35.

Raimes, A. (1987) Why write? From purpose to pedagogy. *English Teaching Forum,* 25, 4, 36–41.

Raymond, P. M. (1993) The effects of structure strategy training on the recall of expository prose for a university student's reading French as a second language. *Modern Language Journal,* 77, 4, 445–58.

Reichelt, M. (2001) A critical review of foreign language writing research on pedagogical practices. *Modern Language Journal,* 578–98.

Richards, B. J. (1990a) *Language Development and Individual Differences: A Study of Auxiliary Verb Learning.* Cambridge: Cambridge University Press.

Richards, B. J. (1990b) Predictors of auxiliary and verb copula growth. Paper presented at the Fifth International Congress for the Study of Child Language, Budapest, Hungary.

Richards, B. J. and Chambers, F. (1992) Criteria for Oral Assessment. *Language Learning Journal,* 6, 5–9.

Richards, B. J. and Malvern, D. D. (1997) *Quantifying Lexical Diversity in the Study of Language Development.* The New Bulmershe Papers. Reading: University of Reading, Faculty of Education and Community Studies.

Ridgeway, T. (2000) Listening strategies: I beg your pardon? *ELT Journal,* 54,2, 179–85.

Rivers, W. M. (1983) *Communicating Naturally in a Second Language: Theory and practice in language teaching.* Cambridge: Cambridge University Press.

Robb, T., Ross, S. and Shortreed, I. (1986) Salience of feedback on error and its effect on EFL writing quality. *TESOL Quarterly,* 20, 1, 122–9.

Ross, S. (1997) An introspective analysis of listener inferencing on a second language listening task. In G. Kasper and E. Kellerman (eds) *Communication Strategies: Psycholinguistic and Sociolinguistic Perspectives.* London: Longman, 216–37.

Rost, M. (1990) *Listening in Language Learning.* London: Longman.

Rost, M. and Ross, S. (1991) Learner use of strategies in interaction: typology and teachability. *Language Learning,* 41, 235–73.

Rubin, J. (1994) A review of second language listening comprehension research. *Modern Language Journal,* 78, 2, 199–221.

Rubin, J., Quinn, J. and Enos, J. (1988) Improving foreign language listening comprehension. Report prepared for the US Department of Education, International Research and Studies Program. Washington DC. Project No. 017AH70028. Cited in Thompson and Rubin (1996).

Rumelhart, D. E. (1977) Toward an interactive model of reading. In S. Dornic (ed.) *Attention and Performance VI,* Hillsdale, NJ: Erlbaum Associates.

Saito, Y., Horwitz, E. K. and Garza, T. J. (1999) Foreign language reading anxiety. *Modern Language Journal*, 83, 2, 202–18.

Sanaoui, R. (1995) Adult learners' approaches to learning vocabulary in second languages. *Modern Language Journal*, 79, 1, 15–28.

Sarig, G. (1988) High-level reading in the first and in the foreign language: some comparative process data. In J. Devine, P. Carrell and D. Eskey (eds.) *Interactive Approaches to Second Language Reading*. Cambridge: Cambridege University Press. 107–20.

Sarig, G. (1989) Testing meaning construction: can we do it fairly? *Language Testing*, 6, 1, 77–94. Cited in Alderson and Bannerjee (2002).

Sasaki, M. and Hirose, K. (1996) Explanatory variables for EFL students' expository writing. *Language Learning*, 46, 137–74.

Schmidt, R. (1990) The role of consciousness in second language learning. *Applied Linguistics*, 11, 129–58.

Schmitt, N. (1998) Tracking the incremental acquisition of second language vocabulary: a longitudinal study. *Language Learning*, 48, 2, 281–317.

Schmitt, N. and Meara, P. (1997) Researching vocabulary through a word knowledge framework: word associations and verbal suffixes. *Studies in Second Language Acquisition*, 19, 17–36.

Scott, M. L. (1994) Auditory memory and perception in younger and older adult second language learners. *Studies in Second Language Acquisition*, 16, 263–81.

Seedhouse, P. (1997) The case of the missing 'no': the relationship between pedagogy and interaction. *Language Learning*, 47, 3, 547–83.

Seeve-McKenna, N. and McKenna, P. (2000) Perception and reality: bridging the internet gap. *Language Learning Journal*, 21, 8–12.

Segalowitz, N. and Hébert, M. (1990) Phonological recoding in the first and second language reading of skilled bilinguals. *Language Learning*, 40, 4, 503–38.

Selinker, L. (1972) Interlanguage. *International Review of Applied Linguistics*, 10, 3, 209–31.

Semke, H. (1982) *Correcting students' freewriting – help or hindrance?* Paper presented at the Annual Meeting of the American Council on the Teaching of Foreign Languages, New York, NY. (ERIC Document Reproduction Service No. 228850.)

Serio, A. and Sheikh, A.-M. (2002) Metodi alternativi per l'insegnamento dell'italiano: il cinema. *Tuttitalia*, 25, 14–16.

Shohamy, E. and Inbar, Y. (1991) Validation of listening comprehension tests: the effect of text and question type. *Language Testing*, 8, 1, 23–40.

Silva, T. (1990) Second language composition instruction: developments, issues, and directions in ESL. In Kroll (1990), 11–23.

Simon, D.-L. (1998). Alternance codique en classe de langue: Rupture du contrat ou survie? *Etudes de Linguistique Appliquée*, 108, 445–55.

Skehan, P. (1989) *Individual Differences in Second-Language Learning*. London: Arnold.

Skehan, P. (1991) Individual differences in second language learning. *Studies in Second Language Acquisition*, 13, 275–98.

Skehan, P. (1998) *A Cognitive Approach to Language Learning*. Oxford: Oxford University Press.

Skinner, B. (1957) *Verbal Behaviour*. New York: Appleton-Century-Crofts.

Skutnabb-Kangas, T. and Phillipson, R. (1995) *Linguistic Human Rights*. Berlin: Mouton de Gruyter.

Spada, N. (1997) Form-focussed instruction and second language acquisition: a review of classroom and laboratory research. *Language Teaching*, 30, 73–87.

Spada, N. and Lightbown, P. M. (1999) Instruction, first language influence, and developmental readiness in second language acquisition. *Modern Language Journal*, 83, 1, 1–22.

Sparks, R. and Ganshow, L. (1993) Searching for the cognitive locus of foreign language learning difficulties: linking first and second language learning. *Modern Language Journal*, 77, 3, 289–302.

Spelman Miller, K. (2000) Academic writers on-line: investigating pausing in the production of text. *Language Teaching Research,* 4/2, 123–48.

Stables, A. and Stables, S. (1996) Modern languages at A Level: the danger of curricular discontinuity. *Language Learning Journal*, 14, 50–2.

Stables, A. and Wikeley, F. (1999) From bad to worse? Pupils' attitudes to modern foreign languages at ages 14 and 15. *Language Learning Journal*, 20, 27–31.

Stanovich, K. E. (1980) Toward an interactive-compensatory model of individual differences in the development of reading fluency. *Reading Research Quarterly,* 16, 1, 32–65.

Sternberg, R. (1987) Most vocabulary is learned from context. In M. G. McKeown and M. E. Curtis. *The Nature of Vocabulary Acquisition*. Hillsdale, NJ: Lawrence Erlbaum Associates, 89–105. Cited in Knight (1994).

Sullivan, P. N. (1996) Sociocultural influences on classroom interactional style. *TESOL Journal*, 6, 1, 32–4.

Swain, M. (1985) Communicative competence: some roles of comprehensible input and comprehensible output in its development. In S. Gass and C. Madden (eds) *Input and Second Language Acquisition*. Rowley, MA: Newbury House.

Taillefer, G. F. (1996) L2 reading ability: further insight into the short-circuit hypothesis. *Modern Language Journal*, 80, 4, 461–77.

Tall, G. and Hurman, J. (2000) Using a dictionary in a written French examination: the students' experience. *Language Learning Journal*, 21, 50–6.

Tarone, E. (1977) Conscious communication strategies in interlanguage: a progress report. In H. Brown, C. Yorio and R. Crymes (eds) *On TESOL '77*. Washington, DC: TESOL, 194–203.

Tarone, E. and Swain, M. (1995) A sociolinguistic perspective on second language use in immersion classrooms. *Modern Language Journal*, 79, 2, 166–78.

Taylor, A. (2000) Boy-free zone? *Language Learning Journal*, 21, 3–7.

Terrel, T. D. (1991) The role of grammar instruction in a communicative approach. *Modern Language Journal*, 75, 1, 52–63.

Thompson, I. and Rubin, J. (1996) Can strategy instruction improve listening comprehension? *Foreign Language Annals*, 29, 3, 331–42.

Towell, R., Hawkins, R. and Bazergui, N. (1996) The development of fluency in advanced learners of French. *Applied Linguistics*, 17, 1, 84–119.

Tremblay, P. F. and Gardner, R. C. (1995) Expanding the motivations construct in language learning. *Modern Language Journal*, 79,4, 505–20.

Trenchs, M. (1996) Writing strategies in a second language: three case studies of learners using electronic mail. *Canadian Modern Language Review*, 52, 3, 464–97.

Truscott, J. (1996) The case against grammar correction in L2 writing classes. *Language Learning,* 46, 2, 327–69.

Truscott, J. (1998) Noticing in second language acquisition: a critical review. *Second Language Research*, 14, 2, 103–35.

Truscott, J. (1999) The case for 'the case against grammar correction in L2 writing classes': a response to Ferris. *Journal of Second Language Writing*, 8, 2, 111–22.

Truscott, S. and Morley, J. (2001) Cross cultural learning through computer-mediated communication. *Language Learning Journal*, 24, 17–23.

Tsui, A. B. M. (1992) Classroom discourse analysis in ESL teacher education. *Institute of Language in Education Journal*, 9, 81–96.

Tsui, A. B. M. (1995) *Introducing Classroom Interaction*. London: Penguin.

Tsui, A.B.M and Fullilove, J. (1998) Bottom-up or top-down processing as a discriminator of L2 listening performance. *Applied Linguistics*, 19, 432–51.

Tsui, A. B. M. and Ng, M. (2000) Do secondary L2 writers benefit from peer comments? *Journal of Second Language Writing*, 9, 2, 147–70.

Turner, K. (1998) Reading: meeting the demands of the National Curriculum. *Language Learning Journal*, 17, 8–13.

Upton, L. K (1969) *Talk French*. London: Mary Glasgow Publications.

Van Hell, J. G. and Candia Mahn, A. (1997) Keyword mnemonics versus rote rehearsal: learning concrete and abstract foreign words by experienced and inexperienced learners. *Language Learning*, 47, 3, 507–46.

Van Lier, L. (1988) *The Classroom and the Language Learner*. London: Longman.

Vandergrift, L. (1997) The Cinderella of communication strategies: receptive strategies in interactive listening. *Modern Language Journal*, 81, 4, 494–505.

Vanderplank, R. (1985) Isochrony and intelligibility. In J. Tommola and K. Battarbee (eds), CDEF 84 Papers from the Conference of Departments of English in Finland. Turku, Finland: Publications of the Department of English. Cited in Vanderplank (1993).

Vanderplank, R. (1988) Implications of differences in native and non-native-speaker approaches to listening. *British Journal of Language Teaching*, 26, 1, 32–41.

Vanderplank, R. (1993) 'Pacing' and 'spacing' as predictors of difficulty in speaking and understanding English. *ELT Journal*, 47, 2, 117–25.

VanPatten, B. (1996) *Input Processing and Grammar Instruction*. NJ: Ablex.

VanPatten, B. and Cadierno, T. (1993) Explicit instruction and input processing. *Studies in Second Language Acquisition*, 15, 225–43.

Varonis, E. and Gass, S. (1985) Non-native/non-native conversations for negotiation of meaning. *Applied Linguistics*, 6, 1, 71–90.

Walker, L. (2001) Collaboration and the role of learner strategies in promoting second language acquisition in tandem learning partnerships. In J. A. Coleman *et al.* (eds) (2001).

Walsh, S. (2002) Construction and obstruction: talk and learner involvement in the EFL classroom. *Language Teaching Research*, 6, 1, 3–24.

Walter, C. (2001) The L2 reading comprehension threshold and working memory. Paper given at Oxford University Language Centre, March 2001. Contact: cwalter@place-farm.demon.co.uk.

Wang, A. Y. and Thomas, M. H. (1995) Effect of keywords on long-term retention: help or hindrance? *Journal of Educational Psychology*, 87, 468–75. Cited in Nation (2001).

Watanabe, Y. (1997) Input, intake and retention: effects of increased processing on incidental learning of foreign language vocabulary. *Studies in Second Language Acquisition*, 19, 287–307.

Way, D., Joiner, E. G. and Seaman, M. A. (2000) Writing in the secondary foreign language classroom: the effects of prompts and tasks on novice learners of French. *The Modern Language Journal*, 84, 2, 171–84.

Weinert, R. (1995) The role of formulaic language in second language acquisition: a review. *Applied Linguistics*, 16, 2, 180–205.

Wenden, A. (1995) Learner training in context: a knowledge-based approach. *System*, 23, 2, 183–94.

West, M. (1953) *A General Service List of English Words*. London: Longman.

Westgate, D., Batey, J., Brownlee, J. and Butler, M. (1985) Some characteristics of interaction in foreign language classrooms. *British Educational Research Journal*, 11, 3, 271–81.

Widdowson, H. G. (1976) The authenticity of language data. In J. H. Fanslow and R. H. Crymes (eds) *On TESOL '76*. Washington: TESOL.

Williams, E. and Moran, C. (1989) Reading in a foreign language at intermediate and advanced levels with particular reference to English. *Language Teaching* (October), 217–28.

Williams, M. and Burden, R. (1997) *Psychology for Language Teachers*. Cambridge: Cambridge University Press.

Williams, M. and Burden, R. (1999) Students' developing conceptions of themselves as language learners. *The Modern Language Journal*, 83, 2, 193–201.

Wingate, U. (2002) *The Effectiveness of Different Learner Dictionaries*. Tübingen: Niemeyer.

Woodall, B. R. (2002) Language-switching: using the first language whilst writing in a second language. *Journal of Second Language Writing*, 11, 7–28.

Wright, M. (1999) Grammar in the languages classroom: findings from research. *Language Learning Journal*, 19, 33–9.

Wu, B. (1998) Towards an understanding of the dynamic process of L2 classroom interaction. *System*, 26, 525–40.

Wu, Y. (1998) What do tests of listening comprehension test? A retrospective study of EFL test-takers performing a multiple-choice task. *Language Testing*, 15, 21–44.

Yonglin, Y. (1995) Trends in the teaching of writing. *Language Learning Journal*, 12, 71–4.

Zamel, V. (1987) Recent Research on Writing Pedagogy. *TESOL Quarterly*, 21, 4, 697–715.

Zobl, H. (1985) Grammars in search of input and intake. In S.Gass and C. Madden (eds) *Input and Second Language Acquisition*. Rowley, MA: Newbury House, 329–44.

Author Index

Subject Index